C0-ATI-105

A GOOD MATCH

ALA RESEARCH SERIES

A GOOD MATCH

Library Career Opportunities for Graduates of Liberal Arts Colleges

Rebecca A. Watson-Boone

American Library Association
Chicago 2007

While extensive effort has gone into ensuring the reliability of information appearing in this book, the publisher makes no warranty, express or implied, on the accuracy or reliability of the information, and does not assume and hereby disclaims any liability to any person for any loss or damage caused by errors or omissions in this publication.

The paper used in this publication meets the minimum requirements of American National Standard for Information Sciences—Permanence of Paper for Printed Library Materials, ANSI Z39.48-1992.

Library of Congress Cataloging-in-Publication Data
Watson-Boone, Rebecca.
A good match : library career opportunities for graduates of liberal arts colleges / Rebecca A. Watson-Boone.
p. cm. — (ALA research series)
Includes bibliographical references and index.
ISBN 978-0-8389-0941-6 (alk. paper)
1. Librarians—Education—United States. 2. Library science—Vocational guidance—United States. 3. College graduates—Employment—United States. 4. Education, Humanistic—United States. 5. Librarians—Job satisfaction—United States. I. Title.
Z682.2.U5W38 2007
020.2373—dc22 2007002023

ISBN-10: 0-8389-0941-8
ISBN-13: 978-0-8389-0941-6

Printed in the United States of America

11 10 09 08 07 5 4 3 2 1

To Evan I. Farber, my inspiration, and Peter G. Watson-Boone, my beloved, for their interest in this project and their support

CONTENTS

TABLES

ACKNOWLEDGMENTS

For the past several years, I have been curious about the values that liberal arts college students might feel they gained from their college experience, in why individuals choose library and information science (LIS) as a career, and in how liberal arts college alumni who became LIS professionals might compare with a national profile of information professionals—most specifically with librarians. Evan Ira Farber, Earlham College Librarian Emeritus, suggested that I expand on a study that he and an Earlham colleague had conducted in 1991. In 2003, as I began this study, Evan made helpful suggestions, opened doors, and served as a senior colleague. I am indebted to Evan for his continued interest and assistance.

No mere "thank you" could ever convey my deep gratitude to this study's participants for their help—and my admiration for the seriousness and effort they gave to the questionnaire. A significant number of the respondents opened their hearts to express their interests, concerns, and views about their undergraduate college and about their field. Completing a 12 page, primarily open-ended questionnaire from an unknown researcher took commitment. Several remarks were similar to that of an Earlham Alum who said, "this is the longest questionnaire I believe I have ever been asked to do!" However, complete it they did—with many not just answering all of the questions but going beyond that to fill the margins or use additional paper. Their comments indicated they responded because they believe in the importance of liberal arts colleges and the education gained there or because they love the LIS work that they do and want to support study of the field. I am most grateful to all of those who responded to my invitation to participate.

My sincere appreciation to Dr. Mary Jane Scherdin, who gave so willingly of her time and expertise regarding the Myers-Briggs Type Inventory, and to the senior academic administrators and heads of the libraries at the eight colleges included in the study. They gave generously and graciously of their time to meet with me as I sought to gain a fuller understanding of their college:

Carleton: Scott Bierman, Associate Dean of the Faculty; Samuel Demas, College Librarian and Senior Lecturer
Denison: Keith Boone, Associate Provost; Scottie Cochrane, Library Director
Earlham: Len Clark, Provost; Tom Kirk, Library Director

Grinnell: James Swartz, Vice-President for Academic Affairs and Dean of the College; Christopher McKee, Librarian of the College
Kalamazoo: Anne Dueweke, Assistant Provost; Lisa Palchick, Dean of Libraries and Information Services
Lawrence: Kathleen Murray, Dean of the Faculty; Susan Richards, Director and University Librarian
Macalester: Daniel Hornbach, Provost and Dean of the Faculty; Terri Fishel, Director of the Library
Swarthmore: Robert Gross, Dean of the College; Peggy Seiden, Librarian

And finally, a most cordial thank you to the following: Dr. Denise Davis, Director of the American Library Association Office for Research and Statistics for advice and counsel; Dr. Judith Jablonski for authoring the index; and the staffs of the Oconto (WI) Public Library, and of the libraries of the University of Wisconsin-Milwaukee and the University of Wisconsin-Green Bay, without whose help materials crucial to this book would have eluded me.

INTRODUCTION

In 1992 Earlham College library director Evan Ira Farber reported that, between 1963 and 1991, over 100 Earlham alumni had gone on to do graduate work in library and information science (LIS). That figure represented 1.7 percent of all 1963-91 Earlham graduates; nationally, for that time period, the percentage of U.S. graduates entering LIS programs from all types of higher education institutions was 0.3 percent (Farber 1992; Sineath 1991). As of the year 2000, the total number of Earlham alumni from the classes of 1962-2000 who had attended LIS graduate programs stood at 179; an average of five each year of that 39-year period. Library directors at other liberal arts institutions have similarly claimed that they also sent large numbers of alumni to LIS graduate programs during that time period (e.g., Lawrence University reports 102; Kalamazoo College 186). Informally, directors of liberal arts college libraries assert that although universities, because of their larger enrollments, may annually send a greater total *number* of alumni into LIS graduate programs, liberal arts colleges continue to send a larger *percentage* of their graduates into the LIS field.

The investigation which forms the subject of *A Good Match* was a follow-up to the Earlham study (Farber and Bingham 1992). The College Alumni Librarians Study (CALS) was undertaken in 2002-03 and involved 431 library practitioners (see appendix A). The librarians whose voices are heard throughout this book are alumni ("CALS Alums") of the classes of 1962 through 2000 from eight American liberal arts colleges: Carleton, Denison, Earlham, Grinnell, Kalamazoo, Lawrence, Macalester, and Swarthmore. The Alums speak on a range of issues:

- The values they gained from their undergraduate experience
- What influenced them to choose LIS as a career
- Their views of librarians and of the LIS field, before and after they undertook graduate work
- Their satisfactions and dissatisfactions with their work and career life

A Good Match follows the progress of these librarians from their undergraduate experiences through to their choice, and later their assessment, of a career in library and information science. *Service* is a unifying theme; it has been a part of their lives during and since college. An orientation toward helping others is a fundamental characteristic both of the colleges the practitioners attended and of the career they chose. Along the way, we learn something about their families, their hobbies and civic interests, the role religion has for them, and their involvement with mentoring—both as newcomers to the field and later in their own support of new practitioners.

To some extent, these particular librarians also represent other LIS professionals. Although their original commonality was that they came from a specific set of liberal arts colleges located across a broad, middle section of the United States, a sample group of them that undertook the Myers-Briggs Type Inventory was found to have profiles very similar to the MBTI® profiles of a national study of 1,600 LIS practitioners (see Scherdin 1994b). In essence, although the CALS Alums attended a private undergraduate college, they are akin to other LIS practitioners who were in the undergraduate classes of 1962-2000 at, for example, state universities. Because of this similarity, observations made about the Alums may also describe the larger population of LIS practitioners.

I. Overview

After a brief survey of the relevant aspects of the history of American higher education in general, chapter 1 profiles the eight liberal arts colleges that the Alums attended. These colleges share with the rest of American higher education a history of adapting their curricula to support both local interests and national needs, of admitting a growing diversity of students, and of according permanent importance to a core of disciplines defined as liberal arts. The colleges provide a distinctive education for the Alums in several respects. They maintain small enrollments and emphasize teaching excellence over faculty research projects. They encourage disciplinary exploration over specialization and provide an education containing an overt, service-oriented dimension. They have few if any graduate-level programs.

Chapter 2 considers the effect that attending their chosen college had on the CALS respondents. Again, the Alums are typical of many American students in that the majority chose an institution of higher education that was either within their state of residence or near to it. They, along with their university peers, encountered disciplinary majors, minors (or perhaps concentrations), and an abundance of extracurricular opportunities. The eight colleges, however, have traditionally encouraged students to involve themselves with community service, and the college administrators report that 40 percent or more of their students regularly engage in service-learning or volunteerism within the larger communities surrounding their campus. The eight colleges appear to be successful in this effort, for when ranking their college's strengths, the CALS Alums agreed strongly that their college did well at "developing within students knowledge of, and an interest in, community and world problems."

Alums across the eight colleges and the 1962-2000 class years included in the study also felt their college was particularly strong in developing within students critical faculties and an appreciation for ideas. Chapter 2 concludes with a comparison between the respondents and the colleges' administrators of the institutional, personal, and professional values that each group believes are gained from the undergraduate experience. The Alums and the administrators agree that moral character, diversity of opinion and of background, tolerance, intellectual rigor, and lifelong learning are important values. In addition, for the Alums, the values of intellectual rigor and a world view are strongly shared regardless of whether the respondents were undergraduates during the 1960s, 1970s, 1980s, or 1990s.

Chapter 3 follows the career options that the CALS Alums considered and experienced, as well as the role of families in career choice. Although these career activities are common to all young people newly graduated from a college or university, the Alums were found to be unlike a number of their peers in several respects. In 1991, Dey et al. published a study of 25 years of trends (classes of 1966-1990) among American college and university freshmen. Their study was used for comparative purposes in this book for two reasons. First, these 25 years fall within our 39 years of coverage. Second, women comprise 78 percent of the CALS respondents and the Dey et al. respondents were distinguished by gender; thus a closer comparison could be made between the two groups. The CALS respondents are different from the typical college and university freshman in that the Alums' parents had more education and higher incomes, and a greater percentage were involved in some form of K-16 education. In comparison with over 3,500 students in graduate library and information science programs (Heim and Moen 1989), the Alums' parents were also found to have higher educational levels. The CALS Alums and the Heim and Moen LIS students were similar, however, in having an awareness of the intellectual and service orientations of the LIS field, and in believing that there were opportunities for employment.

The most prevalent occupations held by both the CALS Alums and their family members were K-12 education, business, the arts, and the health professions. Beginning in their childhood and continuing through adulthood, K-12 education has been modeled by family members and remained a career interest of the CALS members. A majority of the Alums were 20-30 years old when they first considered LIS as a career, and the factors that were significant in leading them to the field were found to be shared with current LIS graduate students (Kniffel 2004b): a love of reading, a good career fit, attraction of the intellectual aspects of the work, positive library experiences during childhood, and previous or current work experience within libraries. When asked what actually made them attend an LIS graduate program, responses indicated that such a career was seen as meeting one or more of these needs:

- It fit better than alternatives they had considered or experienced
- There were opportunities for jobs
- Its intellectual aspects were appealing

Chapter 4 looks at graduate school and the profession of library and information science through the lens of "image." As CALS participants moved toward LIS as a career, they already carried a certain image of both the field and its practitioners. As undergraduates, 59 percent had a positive impression of the field; after finishing their master's program, 63 percent expressed a positive impression. While Alums with a neutral (or no) image of the field as undergraduates gained clarity in a positive direction, those with a negative image actually increased from 13 to 23 percent by the conclusion of their graduate work. The CALS study found that more than two-thirds of the negative image was related to LIS education programs and faculty, rather than to libraries and librarians. The Alums make suggestions for how such negative images could be made more positive.

When the participants left their undergraduate college, 57 percent had a positive image of librarians—just slightly lower than the percentage with a positive impression of the field. At the end of their graduate LIS education, those with a positive view of librarians had risen to 70 percent. Also showing an increase, however, was the number who had a mixed image of librarians; that percentage had risen from 6 to 15 percent. These respondents had moved away from the positive or neutral or negative impressions they had formed while in college. Their comments suggest that as they began to see themselves as workplace-located librarians, they also began to be more critical of their new peers.

Chapter 5 centers on the library as a workplace and describes types of libraries and kinds of library work. The Alums are found in all four traditional forms of libraries: 34 percent in public, 33 percent in academic, 23 percent in special, and 11 percent in school library media centers. Fifty-three percent of the Alums have spent two to ten years in their current positions. There is a core set of responsibilities across library types that, according to the CALS participants, are both the most common and the most time-consuming: reference, collection development, administration or management, and group activities such as curriculum development and library instruction. CALS respondents in the cohorts of 1962-75 have moved into managerial positions. The younger cohorts show increased involvement with reference and group activities. Collection development and management were found to be remarkably stable, from the classes of 1962-65 through those in the 1996-2000 cohort.

The chapter includes discussion of job attributes, including salary and position title. These serve to identify distinctions among library type in job responsibility, salary range, and position title. Of particular note is the comparative breadth of the responsibilities of school library media specialists and special librarians. Based on the information provided by this study's respondents, both academic and public librarians have greater opportunities to specialize within their positions. And the findings suggest that those whose chief desire is to administer a library will reach that goal most quickly if they seek school library media specialist or special librarian positions.

Respondents illustrated the greatest commonality when they were asked to indicate levels of satisfaction with workplace factors that affected their specific jobs. Between 75 and 100 percent of the CALS participants indicated they felt *OK* or were *Satisfied* to *Very Satisfied* with those aspects which impinged most closely on their personal daily activities: their working hours, specific job responsibilities, opportunities to use their skills and abilities, job autonomy, and colleagues with whom they worked the closest. The satisfaction factors that drew concern focused mainly on advancement and salary. A comparison between the CALS Alums and a national study of over 2,000 Special Library Association and ALA academic, public, and school members (Scherdin 1994a) showed that, with the exception of feelings about co-workers, these Alums are clearly more satisfied with their own specific jobs.

Chapter 6 expands on the theme of job satisfaction by considering how the participants viewed not just LIS work in general, but also their career in the field. Across colleges and cohorts, those indicating they were very dissatisfied with their LIS career ranged from 0 to 9 percent. Only 11 percent indicated they felt it was very unlikely that they would continue as an LIS professional; many of those were in the 1962-65 cohort and contemplating retirement.

Eighty-eight percent of the CALS members would encourage today's students to enter the LIS field.

When asked what they liked "best" about LIS work, the Alums gave responses that coalesced around library functions, activities, and the workplace environment. Collection development, reference, work with children through young adults, and management or administration of a library and its staff were highly valued functions. Comments related to library activities focused on the enjoyment of helping others and of seeking or finding information through doing research. Elements of the work environment that were most valued were variety, autonomy, and intellectual challenges, along with a great boss, users, or colleagues. The involvements that respondents liked least were, most frequently, job-related activities and working conditions. The study found that CALS respondents who reported disliking aspects of their job also attached negative associations to LIS as a career: lack of respect from others, lack of understanding about the field by those outside LIS, paperwork or busywork, and lack of variety in LIS work.

Most Alums report that their career and work involvements have provided them with numerous opportunities for initiative and achievement, and they are proudest of

- The use they have made of their LIS skills and the quality of their work
- The recognition they have received from others
- Helping users
- Having made a difference in their library or community
- Their library itself

In discussing their liberal arts college and their LIS career, several Alums focused on the "liberal arts ideals of knowing a bit about everything and being able to communicate well" as being a good match with LIS work (a Lawrence '91 academic librarian). They noted the traits of inquisitiveness, of being open-minded and nonjudgmental, and of service to others as values in both the liberal arts college and in LIS.

Chapter 7 addresses two questions: Are the Alums like other LIS professionals, and do they express a service-orientation in ways other than just through their LIS work? The first question is answered by using comparison of the Myers-Briggs Type Indicator® predispositions of a sample of CALS respondents and 1,697 librarians who were ALA (i.e., academic, public, and school librarians) and SLA participants in a 1992 ACRL national study. The second question is addressed by considering how the Alums answered three service-related survey questions about their participation in civic, religious, and mentoring activities.

Review of the MBTI® comparative data found that the ALA, SLA, and CALS participants were alike except that those in the CALS sample had an even greater tendency toward introversion and orderliness than those librarians in the ACRL study ("orderliness" is within the "Judging" type of the MBTI®). Thus, the comparison established that, although the CALS respondents had a particular undergraduate experience, as librarians they are comparable to a national profile of librarians. Second, it revealed that the largest number of Alums (45 percent) are inwardly directed, favor reflection and concentration, like to pursue things in depth, and value deep friendships. They think things through before acting on them. They tend to be systematic in their approach to problems and to activities, and they are comfortable with structure inside and outside of work. Less than 10 percent demonstrated behavioral preferences that are strongly oriented toward a real concern "for what others think or want, and try[ing] to handle things with due regard for the other person's feelings . . . Sociable, popular, sympathetic" (Scherdin 1994b, 130). Thus, within the Myers-Briggs framework, the Alums are like librarians outside of this study, and the majority of CALS Alums cannot be said to demonstrate behaviors that would easily lead to an extension of service toward others outside of their workplace.

The second question covered in this chapter explored whether the Alums have, indeed, demonstrated a service orientation beyond that inherent in LIS. This question was addressed by inquiring about civic, religious, and mentoring involvements. The CALS respondents are not heavily involved in civic affairs. Fewer than 50 percent of them identified any areas of civic participation, and as the age of the Alums increased, their active engagement decreased. Cultural, religious, and fraternal organizations were the only agencies in which Alums across all colleges and cohorts held membership.

In sharp contrast to the 39 percent who responded to the question on civic engagement, over 90 percent responded to two questions specifically about religion. More of the Alums associated themselves with specific religious affiliations as undergraduates than when they were participating in the CALS survey. However, if respondents had been religious in college, they most likely still have the same religion and give it the same sense of personal importance. During their undergraduate years, those who did follow a religious practice approached it from one of several perspectives, described in the chapter as cultural, grounding, intellectual, or spiritual. While there is a connection for most Alums between themselves and religious practices, this study did not find that the CALS respondents necessarily imbued it with a strong service component.

The Alums' involvement in mentoring was the last activity analyzed for indications of a service-orientation. Mentoring is a very common form of service through which new professionals are socialized into both the field and a specific work setting. Close to two-thirds of the CALS participants have received mentoring, 46 percent have mentored others, and all of those who now mentor have been recipients of mentoring. At least some Alums from each college and each cohort have been mentored and have mentored others. Here there is strong and abundant evidence of CALS members demonstrating a desire to serve others from within the parameters of their normal work responsibilities. Mentoring was seen variously as part of one's job, as a way to give back to or recruit for the field, or as a means to support a newcomer who had "potential," or as an altruistic action. Alums who have mentored described their contributions in terms of providing counsel, moral support, and direction; helping to enhance the newcomer's skills and intellectual development; and using their influence and contacts to facilitate the newcomer's entry and possible advancement within his or her position or the LIS field. In terms of the topics covered in this chapter, it seems the CALS respondents see value in contributing to the service focus of, and within, their career field more than they do in at least the civic and religious areas of their lives.

The last chapter in *A Good Match* focuses on the concept of service. Beginning with discussion of service professions, it reviews the attraction that service work has for the CALS Alums. When the participants' self-perception of what they were good at, what they wanted, or what they value found parallels in LIS or some of its practitioners, the Alums then began the socialization process to become members of that specific profession. As the CALS participants moved from the stages of anticipatory (pregraduate work) through transitional (graduate school) to professional socialization (professional position), they "learned to be" their occupation. As Jarvis (1999, 57) points out about such a process, "It provide[s] them with an identity."

An orientation toward helping others is part of that identity. Such an orientation is a value of the field and for most of those who work in service professions. Rubin (1998, 379) says that librarianship is a social service that values people over profit, a model that "historically reaches back to an age in which professions were meant to improve the society." But not all of the Alums are passionate about improving society or about service; nor would most of them consider their LIS work a "calling." The majority, however, would describe their sense of serving others as being either a form of cooperation, or of helping, or of altruism. CALS Alums choosing "cooperation" would see their work as acting with another (a colleague or perhaps a user) toward a goal that is beneficial to both, and where both are more or less equal partners in the endeavor. Alums describing their work as "helping" would focus on the recipient of the assistance, rather than on the LIS practitioner providing it. The chapter describes the difficulty of a definition for "altruism," but those Alums who feel altruistic would agree that they expect nothing in return from the colleague or library user with whom they have interacted in some way.

A final section sums up the connection between the field, the CALS Alums as service professionals, and the value of attending a liberal arts college, as well as of choosing library and information science as one's career.

II. Consistency across College, Cohort, and Profession

Descriptive analysis can at most suggest similarities and differences between groups. However, there appears to be little substantive difference between Alums when viewed by cohort, and somewhat more difference—depending upon the question—when the Alums are viewed by college. It should be noted that there is also more commonality than difference between the Alums and the national profile of LIS professionals, as drawn from these studies:

- Morrison's (1969) study of 707 academic librarians
- White and Macklin's (1970) study of 3,516 LIS master's students' views on their education, careers, and the profession
- Heim and Moen's (1989) study of 3,484 LIS master's students' attitudes, demographics, and aspirations
- The ACRL (1992) study of 1,697 American Library Association and Special Library Association members, including the MBTI® component (see Scherdin 1994a, 1994b)

A Note on Format

The questionnaire used in the CALS study was comprised of six sections containing 74 main questions. A majority of the questions were open-ended and contained secondary questions. The questionnaire was 12 pages in length (see appendix B). Rather than repeat the questions in the text, the reader is directed to them by a parenthetical reference. An example would be "(appendix B: Q.I-7)," which refers to the Questionnaire, Section I, Question 7. Because of the amount of quantitative detail generated by the questionnaire, two data sets have been included (appendixes C-D). Where tables within the text are incomplete, or additional detail may be useful, the reader is given a Data Set reference. For instance, if the data were from the college data set, "appendix C: Q.I-7" would indicate that individual college responses to that particular question are given—along with overall averages representing all responses to that question. The Cohort Data Set is similarly arranged for those questions that received cohort analysis, and referenced as appendix D.

Although the present author has some grounding in statistical analysis and appreciates the additional dimensions such analysis can bring, it has not been undertaken in the present work, the aim of which leaned more toward the qualitative. The majority of the numerical results are therefore conveyed in percentages.

Audience

This book is intended to have value for

- Students and career counselors wishing to know more about the LIS field and its practitioners
- Library personnel managers and administrators
- Graduate LIS programs seeking to recruit students from liberal arts colleges
- Liberal arts institutions interested in assessing the effect of their educational programs on the subsequent work lives and interests of alumni
- Scholars and researchers who study professions

Because of the breadth of the intended audience, those within the LIS field are asked to excuse explanations of topics with which they are already familiar while those outside the field will, hopefully, not encounter an undue amount of professional jargon.

CHAPTER 1

American Higher Education and the Liberal Arts College

This chapter presents the history and setting of American higher education and of the liberal arts college. It focuses on the attributes of the "liberal arts" in higher education and of the liberal arts college in particular. The chapter also describes the development of the eight colleges that the alumni-librarians (the CALS Alums) attended, including identifying institutional histories and characteristics that define the particular ethos of Carleton, Denison, Earlham, Grinnell, Kalamazoo, Lawrence, Macalester, and Swarthmore.

I. The Evolution of American Higher Education

In 1636 Harvard College was established to fulfill an English Puritan belief that to serve God and one's fellow man to the fullest meant "to advance learning and perpetuate it to posterity; dreading to leave an illiterate ministry to the churches, when our present ministers shall lie in the dust" (Morison 1935, 539). However, in a sense, Harvard was also the country's first liberal arts college—for "the Puritans did not distinguish sharply between secular and theological learning; and they believed that the collegiate education proper for a minister should be the same as for an educated layman. They expected that the early colleges would produce not only ministers but Christian gentlemen who would be civic leaders" (Hofstadter and Smith 1961, 2). The College of William and Mary followed in 1693, but the colonies had small populations and many needs more pressing than higher education; only nine other colleges were established prior to 1776 (Breneman 1993; Clark 1987). Until 1745, Latin and Greek were the only subjects required for admission to a colonial college. Discourse was held in Latin (Rudolph 1962). The first year staples were Latin, Greek, logic, Hebrew, and rhetoric. In their second, third, and fourth years, students added moral philosophy and natural philosophy (which later came to be known as physics). In 1745, Yale made arithmetic an entrance requirement, and by 1766 mathematics had become a part of its freshman through junior curriculum. Students were males, generally 13-16 years of age, from the colonial elite families. They were instructed in the curriculum by tutors, who—having just received their own baccalaureate degrees—were presumed to be fully able to teach all the subjects in the curriculum.

Later, the hallmarks of the immediate post-revolutionary period were the broadening of the idea of higher education to include the preparation of young men for "responsible citizenship," and a desire by a rising middle class to take on the attributes of established society. Throughout this period, the country's view of higher education waxed and waned but was never strongly positive. Colleges were conceived of as social investment; yet unless the student was preparing for the clergy, medicine, or law, there was still not much value accorded the educational effort. Many colleges attempted to "modernize" the curriculum in an effort to educate men who subsequently would be able to "create cities out of the wilderness, explore the unknown regions of the West, and cope with the raw necessities which the exploitation of a vast and immensely rich continent demanded" (Rudolph 1962, 112). Most colleges held to the classical program while giving legitimacy to some study in modern languages (especially French and German; occasionally English), mathematics, and natural science.

Some colleges experimented with offering an occupationally oriented parallel course of study that omitted the classics. For example, although Amherst College was only founded in 1822, by 1826 its president proposed offering the following parallel program:

- French, Spanish, German, and Italian
- English literature
- Agricultural chemistry, engineering, architecture, experimental and practical physics
- American political and religious history, with an emphasis on the Puritan age
- The American constitution
- New fields of scientific knowledge

Latin and Greek were to be completely omitted, but moral and intellectual philosophy, rhetoric, and oratory would be retained (Rudolph 1962). A student in a parallel program most often received a certificate of proficiency, rather than a Bachelor of Arts degree.

Most institutions, however, accepted the basic precepts espoused in the Yale Report of 1828 in which the faculty rejected the idea "that our colleges must be 'new-modelled.'" They reaffirmed that the traditional curriculum was necessary in order to lay the foundation for character building. They believed that a classical education would elevate the newly wealthy and powerful merchants, manufacturers, and agriculturalists to be "men of superior education, of large and liberal views, of those solid and elegant attainments, which will raise them to a higher distinction, than the mere possession of property" (*Report*, quoted in Levine 1978, 545, 553).

Largely because of the Yale Report, the classical tradition held sway until after the American Civil War. However, natural science had slowly been infiltrating both the classical and parallel curricula. By the mid-nineteenth century, the so-called "new subjects"—mathematics, natural philosophy, botany, chemistry, zoology, geology, and mineralogy—had been added to the course of study in most colleges. They were afterthoughts, however, since they did not replace the classical curriculum. Here and there a professor trained in a science was added to a college faculty. In 1847 Yale established a School of Applied Chemistry within its newly authorized Department of Philosophy and the Arts; in 1852 instruction in civil engineering began (Rudolph 1962, 222).

While change seemed slow to come in the curriculum, the pace of college establishment, often followed by disestablishment, was far more rapid. It was not easy being a college. By 1860 perhaps as many as seven hundred had been both created and laid down (Pfnister 1985, 35). By 1899, among the colleges that persisted were 212 small liberal arts colleges (Bonvillian and Murphy 1996)—including the eight that the participants of this study attended.

By 1868, "the college ceased to be a cloister and became a workshop" (Stoddard 1890, 78, quoted in Veysey 1965, 61). In the later half of the 1800s, a series of changes occurred that shaped today's college and established the American university. Among them:

- The balance between the classical curriculum and the one which included "new" subjects tipped in the latter's favor.
- Trustees of many of the existing institutions shifted their concerns from a religious to a more nonsectarian base and selected presidents of the latter persuasion.
- Yale granted the first Ph.D. in 1861. By 1888 more than 100 doctorates were being awarded annually by American universities.
- Knowledge based on experimentation and the resulting scientific facts, rather than on "right thinking," became more accepted in and outside of higher education.
- The notion that knowledge can be advanced and transmitted served to strengthen the relationship between the institutions and American society.
- The 1862 Morrill Land Grant Act resulted in the establishment of a public, state-supported college in each state.
- By 1870 American colleges had grown to the point that they supported 5,553 faculty; their enrollments equaled 1.7 percent of the 18-to-21-year-old population (Clark 1987, 12; Levine 1978, 506).
- Postgraduate study in Germany by American faculty led to the establishment in 1876 of Johns Hopkins University. As the first American research institution, it emphasized graduate education.

One way to summarize the changes that occurred in the higher education landscape roughly before and after the American Civil War of 1861-65 is to note that before that time the liberal arts college

> more or less defined higher education in America. . . . [All colleges] were of roughly similar size and ambition. Some were more secular and some more innovative than others . . . [After the Civil War,] suddenly universities were everywhere, with a variety of faculties, graduate and professional as well as

undergraduate, and all with a new sense of mission and a new confidence about their relation to the country's future. (Gerety 1995, 2B)

Two developments made a significant difference to colleges and to American higher education overall. First, the 1862 Morrill Act provided land revenues to support state colleges that taught agriculture and the mechanical arts. The act made higher education practical for more Americans. Its 1890 extension provided annual federal government appropriations and stimulated state legislatures to do the same (Hofstadter and Smith 1961). Whereas before colleges were essentially private operations, the Morrill Act created the idea of the public university and put in place the beginning of what would seem like enormously large campuses, faculties, and student bodies. Second, the adoption of the post-graduate model of specialized education and research spurred colleges such as Harvard, Yale, and Princeton to become universities—institutions that established graduate fields of study alongside the undergraduate curriculum, and thus needed to foster graduate students' specialized knowledge while still educating undergraduates to be knowledgeable citizens.

By the 1950s, both the college and the university were mainstays across the country, with the doctorate becoming a virtual requirement for anyone wishing to teach in an American university. (According to Clark 1987, in 1950, 6,420 doctorates were awarded; in 1980, 32,615.) Enactment of the *Servicemen's Readjustment Act of 1944* (the GI Bill) and the *Civil Rights Act of 1964* opened up higher education to an extraordinary diversity of student gender, ethnicity, religion, age, racial identification, and physical ability.[1] In 1941, undergraduate student enrollments equaled 18 percent of American 18-21-year-olds; in 1964 the figure was 40 percent (Levine 1978). Later, the federal *Education Amendments of 1972* legislation established the basis for federal student aid: incentive grants, guaranteed student loans, and work-study funding (Breneman 1993).[2] Again, one result was a significant increase in the numbers and the diversity of students such that by 1980 undergraduate and graduate students together numbered 12,097,000. By then, there were also 686,000 faculty on campus (U.S. Census Bureau 2003). The 2000 edition of the widely used Carnegie Foundation for the Advancement of Teaching's *Carnegie Classification of Institutions of Higher Education* (hereafter *Carnegie Classification*) lists 3,941 degree-granting institutions of higher learning of various kinds in the United States.

Adoption of a curriculum that included both traditional and "modern" subjects, the emergence of the land-grant universities, and the rise of graduate education and research profoundly altered the landscape of American higher education. One outgrowth was increasing differentiation among the institutions. Whereas prior to the Civil War there was simply the liberal arts college, today there are Doctoral/Research Universities, Master's Colleges and Universities, Baccalaureate Colleges, Associate's Colleges, Specialized Institutions, and Tribal Colleges and Universities (*Carnegie Classification 2000*). Within each category there are distinctions based, fundamentally, on the number, percentage, or type of degrees granted annually. The 2000 edition of the *Carnegie Classification* (pages 1-2) includes the following descriptions:

---

[1]Public Law 78-346; Public Law 88-352.

[2]Public Law 92-318.

Doctoral/Research Universities "typically offer a wide range of baccalaureate programs, and they are committed to graduate education through the doctorate." *Extensive Institutions*: Awarded 50 or more doctoral degrees per year across at least 15 disciplines. *Intensive Institutions*: Awarded at least ten doctoral degrees per year across three or more disciplines, or at least 20 doctoral degrees per year overall.

Master's Colleges and Universities "typically offer a wide range of baccalaureate programs, and they are committed to graduate education through the master's degree." *Level I*: Awarded 40 or more master's degrees per year across three or more disciplines. *Level II*: Awarded 20 or more master's degrees per year.

Baccalaureate Colleges are "primarily undergraduate colleges with major emphasis on baccalaureate programs [or] where the majority of conferrals are below the baccalaureate level (associate's degrees and certificates)." *Liberal Arts Colleges*: Awarded at least half of their baccalaureate degrees in liberal arts fields. *General*: Awarded less than half of their baccalaureate degrees in liberal arts fields. *Baccalaureate/Associate's Colleges*: Bachelor's degrees accounted for at least 10 percent of undergraduate awards.

Associate's Colleges "offer associate's degree and certificate programs but, with few exceptions, award no baccalaureate degrees. This group includes institutions where . . . bachelor's degrees represented less than 10 percent of all undergraduate awards." This group includes community, junior, and technical colleges.

Specialized Institutions "offer degrees ranging from the bachelor's to the doctorate, and typically award a majority of degrees in a single field." Specialized institutions include theological seminaries and other specialized faith-related institutions, medical schools and medical centers; other separate health profession schools (such as chiropractic, nursing, pharmacy, or podiatry); schools of engineering and technology, of business and management, of law, and of art, music, and design; teachers colleges; and other specialized institutions (such as graduate centers, maritime academies, military institutes, and institutions that do not fit any other classification category).

Tribal Colleges and Universities, which are, "with few exceptions, tribally controlled and located on reservations. They are all members of the American Indian Higher Education Consortium."

II. The "Liberal Arts" and the "Liberal Arts College"

Liberal arts colleges have evolved from being institutions of high learning for 13-16-year-old boys, who were expected to become well-rounded American leaders, to generally private undergraduate colleges for both sexes that award at least half of their degrees in liberal arts fields. Over the course of the 1700s and 1800s, the fields considered the "liberal arts" also changed. Initially the focus was on classical languages and literatures, philosophy, religion, and mathematics. Later much of the "parallel" curriculum was absorbed, and the liberal arts expanded to include modern languages and literatures, English, and history. The laboratory sciences were added at the end of the eighteenth century. The social sciences came next: economics, government, sociology; then the behavioral sciences, such as psychology. Along the way the fine arts became standard. Most recently, various academic "studies" have taken their place in the curriculum; some are topical, such as Peace Studies, while others are ethnic (such as Polish Studies), racial (Black Studies, Asian Studies, Hispanic Studies), or gender-based (Gay Studies). Since the mid-1950s, there have been questions about the addition of vocational fields, such as accounting and nursing. In 1958, McGrath and Russell authored a monograph entitled *Are Liberal Arts Colleges Becoming Professional Schools?* Thirteen years later, Keeton declared: "The number of those who view this curricular evolution with alarm are *[sic]* declining" (1971, 9). Between 1972 and 1988, baccalaureate degrees in professional fields conferred by all private liberal arts colleges rose from 33 to 54 percent of the whole. Even for the most admissions-selective of these colleges, professional degrees rose from 11 to 24 percent (Breneman 1993). In 1994 Breneman, using a combination of the 1987 *Carnegie Classification* of institutions and an economic model of revenue and cost structures, excluded from his study of liberal arts colleges more than 400 that he determined were "essentially small professional colleges with few liberal arts majors but usually with a liberal arts core and tradition" (13). Within the context of his study, Breneman (1994, 12) defined a liberal arts college this way:

> Liberal arts colleges award the bachelor of arts degree, are residential, primarily enroll full-time students between 18 and 24 years of age, and limit the number of majors to roughly twenty to twenty-four fields in the arts, humanities, languages, social sciences, and physical sciences. They rarely enroll more than 2,500 students, and most enroll between 800 and 1,800 students. The education they provide might be described as preprofessional, for many students enroll in graduate or professional programs upon graduation, but the liberal arts college itself offers virtually no undergraduate professional education.

He goes on to say, "My definition of a liberal arts college stems directly from the earlier discussion of their role as institutions that educate rather than train. At some point, admittedly arbitrary, a college that is awarding most of its degrees in business administration, nursing, education, engineering, health professions, and communications is simply no longer a true liberal arts college" (Breneman 1994, 13).

Clearly, over time, what was accepted as a "liberal art" or at least accepted enough to make a college a liberal arts college—changed. Another way to trace this is to compare the definitions of *liberal arts* and *liberal arts college* in the *Carnegie Classification* reports. The first report (1973) did not define the liberal arts in a curricular sense. Its Doctoral Universities received federal financial support and awarded the Ph.D. Its Comprehensive Universities and Colleges I and II included institutions that offered a liberal arts program as well as one or more professional programs (e.g., teacher training or nursing), but not doctoral programs. However, the Comprehensives I and II were subject to enrollment criteria: "[Those] private institutions with fewer than 1,500 students and public institutions with fewer than 1,000 students are . . . not regarded as comprehensive with such small enrollments. Such institutions are classified as liberal arts colleges" (*Carnegie Classification 1973*, 2-3). Liberal Arts Colleges were subdivided into two groups and the report's author, Clark Kerr, struggled for a suitable definition:

> *Liberal Arts Colleges I*: The distinction between a liberal arts college and a comprehensive college is not clear-cut. Some of the institutions in this group have modest occupational programs but a strong liberal arts tradition. A good example is Oberlin, which awarded 91 Mus.B. degrees out of a total of 564 bachelor's degrees in 1967, as well as 31 M.A.T. degrees out of a total of 41 master's degrees. Its enrollment in 1970 was 2,670. Or, consider two Pennsylvania institutions, Lafayette and Swarthmore. Lafayette awarded 113 B.S. degrees in engineering in 1967 out of a total of 349 bachelor's degrees and has been classified in our Comprehensive Colleges II group. Its enrollment in 1970 was 2,161. Swarthmore has an engineering program leading to a B.S. degree, but it awarded only 11 B.S. degrees out of a total of 250 bachelor's degrees in 1967 and had a 1970 enrollment of 1,164. Swarthmore has a strong liberal arts tradition and did not meet our minimum enrollment criterion for a private college to be classified as a Comprehensive College II, but our decisions in the cases of Oberlin and Lafayette had to be at least partly judgmental.
>
> *Liberal Arts Colleges II:* These institutions include all the liberal arts colleges that did not meet our criteria for inclusion in the first group of liberal arts colleges. Again, the distinction between "liberal arts" and "comprehensive" is not clear-cut for some of the larger colleges in this group and is necessarily partly a matter of judgment. In addition, many liberal arts colleges are extensively involved in teacher training, but future teachers tend to receive their degrees in arts and sciences fields, rather than in education. (*Carnegie Classification 1973*, 3-4)

Within a category called "Professional Schools and Other Specialized Institutions," the 1973 report specified that programs were included if they were "limited exclusively or almost exclusively" to granting degrees in the specialty. Thus, schools of art, music, and design were professional, but those where art majors received a background in the arts and sciences were more likely to be categorized as liberal arts colleges or comprehensives. The 1973 report included two public and 144 private Liberal Arts I colleges. The eight colleges of the present study were found within the Liberal Arts Colleges I group.

The 1976 edition of the *Carnegie Classification* noted a decrease in the number of liberal arts colleges, due to broadening of programs and to enrollment increases sufficient to qualify several for inclusion as comprehensives. To describe Liberal Arts Colleges I and II, the 1973 text was carried forward almost in its entirety. No public, but 123 private, liberal arts colleges were included. The third edition (1987) grouped institutions primarily by the level of degrees awarded and the comprehensiveness of degree programs. It noted that while more Liberal Arts II colleges had become Comprehensives I and II, those classed as Liberal Arts I—"highly selective institutions that offer over half of their degrees in arts and science fields"—had increased both in number and in overall size of enrollment. Commenting on this in the report's preface, Ernest Boyer said "this suggests that colleges with a strong liberal arts tradition and with great pulling power have not made major curriculum adjustments in response to market place demands." Regarding those that moved from the Liberal Arts to the Comprehensive categories, he noted:

> This change reflects, in some measure, an imaginative strategy to meet the vocational needs of students. Still, a balance must be struck. There is, within the tradition of the liberal arts, a commitment to the intellectual quest, the use of reason, and respect for values unrelated to market demands. These "internal imperatives" that greatly enrich the career interests of students must also be sustained and strengthened. (*Carnegie Classification 1987*, 2)

The category of Research Universities I and II appeared for the first time in the 1987 report, setting such institutions apart from Doctorate-Granting Universities. But for our discussion, the 1987 report is significant in two other ways. First, "Liberal Arts Colleges I" were redefined: "These highly selective institutions are primarily undergraduate colleges that award more than half of their baccalaureate degrees in arts and science fields" (p. 8). Second, the "liberal arts and occupational/preprofessional" disciplines associated with Liberal Arts Colleges I were explicitly enumerated:

> The *Liberal Arts* disciplines include area studies, biological science, the fine arts, foreign languages, letters, mathematics, physical sciences, psychology, the social sciences, and interdisciplinary studies. *Occupational/pre-professional* disciplines include agriculture, the natural sciences, architecture and environmental design, business and management, communications, computer and information science, education, engineering, the health professions, home economics, law, library science, public affairs, and theology. (*Carnegie Classification 1987*, 8)

The 1994 *Carnegie Classification* continued the efforts of earlier editions to seek a common underlying basis for overall classification of American higher education institutions. Boyer noted that "the most consequential change we've made is to classify all institutions, for the first time, according to the highest level of degree conferred. . . . This means that the 'Liberal Arts' category—which is now called 'Baccalaureate'—includes all colleges where the baccalaureate is the highest degree awarded" (foreword). Thus "Comprehensives I and II" became "Master's (Comprehensive)." The Liberal Arts Colleges were defined as

> primarily undergraduate colleges with major emphasis on baccalaureate degree programs. They award 40 percent or more of their baccalaureate degrees in liberal arts fields and are restrictive in admissions. (*Carnegie Classification 1994*, xix)

The *Carnegie Classification*'s definition of the liberal arts disciplines was still expanding. By 1994, the disciplines encompassed "English language and literature, foreign languages, letters, liberal and general studies, life sciences, mathematics, philosophy and religion, physical sciences, psychology, social sciences, the visual and performing arts, area and ethnic studies, and multi- and interdisciplinary studies." The occupational/preprofessional heading was restated as "occupational and technical disciplines" and now included agriculture, allied health, architecture, business and management, communications, conservation and natural resources, education, engineering, health sciences, home economics, law and legal studies, library and archival sciences, marketing and distribution, military sciences, protective services, public administration and services, and theology (*Carnegie Classification 1994*, xx-xxi). Both liberal arts disciplines and occupational/preprofessional disciplines continued to be connected to Liberal Arts Colleges.

The latest edition (2000) of the *Classification* bases placement on the highest level of degree awarded by each institution. The Baccalaureate Colleges category is comprised of Baccalaureate Colleges—Liberal Arts; Baccalaureate Colleges—General; and Baccalaureate/ Associate's Colleges. The Liberal Arts Colleges are "primarily undergraduate colleges with major emphasis on baccalaureate programs [that award] at least half of their baccalaureate degrees in liberal arts fields" (*Carnegie Classification* 2000, Category Definitions). The Baccalaureate Colleges—General award less than half of their degrees in liberal arts fields, and the description of Baccalaureate/Associate's Colleges makes no reference to the liberal arts. The definition of liberal arts disciplines is now derived from the National Center for Education Statistics' *Classification of Instructional Programs* (CIP):[3]

> English language and literature/letters; foreign languages and literatures; biological sciences/life sciences; mathematics; philosophy and religion; physical science; psychology; social sciences and history; visual and performing arts; area, ethnic, and cultural studies; liberal arts and sciences, general studies, and humanities; and multi/interdisciplinary studies. (*Carnegie Classification 2000*, 3)

---

[3]"The National Center for Education Statistics (NCES) is located within the U.S. Department of Education and the Institute for Education Sciences, and is the primary federal entity for collecting and analyzing data related to education" (www.nces.ed.gov). CIP is a taxonomic coding scheme containing titles and descriptions of primarily postsecondary instructional programs.

Thus the current edition's list of liberal arts disciplines represents a blending of the classical liberal arts fields, the "modern" twentieth century additions, and the current twenty-first-century recognition of fields (studies) that have emerged from within or across the liberal arts and sciences disciplines.

Liberal Arts Colleges

As noted previously, the liberal arts college is the oldest of American higher education institutions and, as Breneman (1994, 4) points out, "these colleges are single-purpose institutions, with no rationale for existence beyond their capacity to educate undergraduate students." They are small by present standards with, at any particular time, an average enrollment of 1,200-1,500 undergraduates, which is positively interpreted by the institutions, students, and parents to mean low teacher-student ratios, greater student-faculty contact, and a sense of a single, integrated community. Nearly all are private rather than state-supported or controlled; being private is one of the most common characteristics of American liberal arts colleges. Most were either founded or at least strongly influenced by a religious denomination, that "with much sweat and sacrifice had initiated and sustained a place of and for their own" (Clark 1970, 3). Initially they overtly based their mission statements and rules of student conduct on religious principles. From the early 1900s forward, however, a significant number of Protestant-controlled colleges moved to being church-affiliated or church "independent." For this last type of institution, chapel or convocation attendance became optional or ceased all together (Hawkins 1999). Significant differences arose among the now wider range of liberal arts colleges in the amount of individual decision making that was offered to students in collegiate curricular, social, and intellectual arenas. Yet overall, the variety of colleges believed they provided young adults with values, norms, and knowledge that would make them contributing citizens, rather than just well-educated or well-trained workers.

For most Americans, the ideals behind the broad liberal education found in these colleges were "ambiguous, . . . nearly always difficult to define, and . . . expressed in a time-worn rhetoric that muddles the mind" (Clark 1970, 5) . Yet, common expectation within and outside the liberal arts colleges was that the colleges devoted themselves to the liberal arts, to general education, and to the surrounding of a specialized field of study with a broader understanding of and appreciation for diversity of thought and of respect for individuals. In addition to shifting from the classical curriculum to the current set of disciplines, the independent liberal arts colleges moved seriously away from a religious orientation in course content and offerings. In addition, by the 1950s, liberal arts colleges were regularly augmenting their curriculum with honors programs, international study and study abroad opportunities, student and faculty research activities, and some kind of senior project, thesis, or comprehensive examination. A number of the colleges also pushed for increased intellectual discourse in all areas of the curriculum. Indeed, many prided themselves on the rigor of their educational program.

Until at least the mid-1950s, the majority of liberal arts colleges drew their students from white, middle-to-upper class, college-educated families. Most students were male. If a college was sectarian, it preferred students from its own religious orientation; it discouraged or denied enrollment of students with other religious (or no) preference. Liberal arts colleges, generally, provided a home for (and produced) an "intellectual elite" (Hawkins 1999). Beginning in the early 1970s, the colleges were able to tap into federal student financial aid opportunities to help significantly offset the higher costs of a private college education. This in turn enabled them to broaden their student body in terms of attracting less well-off entrants. And many of the colleges also sought to broaden their student body through conscious decisions to improve campus diversity in terms of the racial, ethnic, religious, and sexual backgrounds of students. In addition to their devotion to the liberal arts, the colleges believe that they serve as communities. Contributing to this is the fact that most of them are fully residential. If students live "off campus," it is likely to be in houses owned by the college and bordering its campus.

The curriculum may have changed over time and the range of students may have expanded, but there continues to be overwhelming belief that "faculty and students work closely together, learning is collaborative rather than competitive, students are involved in their own education, there is much discussion of values, and there is a sense of family" (Pope 1996, 1). Indeed, although the liberal arts colleges identified over the years in the *Carnegie Classification* reports vary widely in their approaches to students and to education, Pope (1996, 3) finds that many share two "essential elements: a familial sense of communal enterprise that gets students heavily involved in cooperative rather than competitive learning, and a faculty of scholars devoted to helping young people develop their powers." Concomitantly, students are expected to teach and learn from each other in both curricular and informal social interactions. An explicit, intense, and positive relationship between the individual student and the college is a core value of liberal arts colleges.

In their discussion of small liberal arts colleges, Bonvillian and Murphy (1996, 7-8) invoke the following points from the Council of Independent Colleges "as an argument for both the success and long-term survival of small schools. Perhaps, more importantly, [the statement] also provides us with a clearer understanding of the character of these unique organizations and reasons why we should seek to assure their existence:

- They each possess a distinctive institutional purpose. Intangible as it may be, these colleges are permeated with a special sense of purpose made up of an intrinsic mixture of historic ideals, moral and spiritual values, devotion to quality, and a clear and direct vision of the future—all with the individual student as the centerpiece.
- They emphasize teaching excellence. Professors teach students in personal settings—and not always in the formal classroom. Faculty research and publications are adjuncts to the teaching process.
- They provide education with a moral and spiritual dimension. Most small colleges were started by religious bodies. This religious heritage, while seldom proselytized, permeates the values of these colleges. They educate the whole person. The small size and residential nature of the colleges enable intimate personal contact among students, faculty, and administrators. Small colleges foster emotional, social, moral, and spiritual development of students—as well as intellectual growth. They emphasize the liberal arts and sciences.

- Because small colleges adhere to the values of a liberal education, students find it impossible to overspecialize or to merely immerse themselves in vocational subjects. They are free and flexible. Beholden to no one but their own boards of trustees, small colleges march to the tune of their own drummer, not to the beat of a state planning bureau or a federal granting agency.
- They serve their region. Small colleges are sources of great local and regional pride. These colleges exist, in most cases, to serve the citizens of a particular region, even though they are privately supported and attract students from across the country. They are successful. In many cases for more than 200 years and in some cases for less than 20 years, small colleges have produced graduates who have succeeded, pioneered new programs, been the first, the best, the only in a field of endeavor."

Bonvillian and Murphy (1996, 8) conclude that "among their other unique characteristics, small schools were, and perhaps still are today, the bastions of liberal arts."

These collective images of liberal arts colleges reflect both the research literature and a kind of romanticism. So from the abstract, let us focus more specifically on the eight colleges that underlie this College Alumni Librarians Study (CALS): Carleton, Denison, Earlham, Grinnell, Kalamazoo, Lawrence, Macalester, and Swarthmore.

III. The Eight CALS Colleges

All eight of the colleges are private, coeducational, residential, liberal arts, undergraduate institutions.[4] They were founded between 1831 and 1874 (see appendix E)—a time in American history when individuals or communities strongly believed that additional education was necessary for local or societal development. Their founders had religious associations and convictions. Several of the college websites and publications note that, while now independent from such roots, the colleges have the highest respect for their religious origins. Denison (1831) was established by the Ohio Baptist Education Society and was originally known as the Granville Literary and Theological Institution. It took its current name in 1854 to honor William S. Denison, a generous benefactor. Kalamazoo (1833) was founded by visionary Baptists as The Michigan and Huron Institute. In 1837 the name changed to The Kalamazoo Literary Institute to reflect the town in which it is located. At one point the college was considered a branch of the University of Michigan, but in 1855 independence was reasserted and it became Kalamazoo College.

After the founding of Kalamazoo, a gap of 13 years occurred before Grinnell was established in 1846, "when a group of transplanted New Englanders with strong Congregational and social-reformer backgrounds organized as the Trustees of Iowa College" (Grinnell website, see Bibliography). Subsequently, the college moved from Davenport to Grinnell, Iowa, and

---

[4]College descriptions come from published materials and college websites (see Bibliography).

unofficially adopted the name of its major benefactor, the abolitionist minister, Josiah Bushnell Grinnell. (In 1909 the name Grinnell College was formally adopted.) The very next year (1847) was auspicious for both Earlham and Lawrence. Earlham began as a boarding school "for the guarded religious education of the children of [the Religious Society of] Friends" (quoted in Hamm 1997, 54). In 1859, a collegiate department was added and the school was named Earlham College, in honor of "Earlham Hall"—the home of the eminent English Quaker minister Joseph John Gurney, who had been an early supporter. Earlham was the second Quaker college in the world and the first coeducational one.[5] Lawrence was named after Boston merchant Amos A. Lawrence, who in 1847 sent two Methodist ministers to Wisconsin because he wished to establish a frontier college to afford "gratuitous advantage to Germans and Indians of both sexes"; classes began in 1849 (Lawrence website quoting Amos Lawrence, see Bibliography).

Swarthmore was founded by Quakers in 1864. It was named after Swarthmoor Hall, the home in England of George Fox (the founder of the Religious Society of Friends) and his wife Margaret Fell. At its founding, Swarthmore decided that enrollment would not be "confined entirely" to Quakers, and its board of trustees would be made up equally of men and women. Two years later in 1866, Carleton was founded by the Minnesota Conference of Congregational Churches, under the name of Northfield College; the first class was conducted in 1870. The name of the college was changed in 1871 in honor of benefactor William Carleton of Charlestown, Massachusetts. Macalester (1874) joined the colleges eight years after Carleton's founding with its first formal class held in 1885. Its founder, the Rev. Edward Duffield Neill, believed that "only a private college could offer both the academic quality and the values needed to prepare for leadership. He planned a college which would be equal in academic strength to the best colleges in the East. It would be Presbyterian-affiliated but nonsectarian, making it inclusive by the standards of his day" (Macalester website, see Bibliography). The college was named after Charles Macalester, a prominent Philadelphia businessman and philanthropist, who provided the college's first building (Kagin 1957). Thus, within the space of 44 years, the eight colleges were established by members of five different Christian Protestant denominations: Baptists (Denison, Kalamazoo), Congregationalists (Carleton, Grinnell), Methodists (Lawrence), Presbyterians (Macalester), and Quakers (Earlham, Swarthmore). Five were named after founders or benefactors: Carleton, Denison, Grinnell, Lawrence, and Macalester. Three reflect place names: Earlham, Kalamazoo, and Swarthmore.

The majority of the colleges were coeducational from their beginning. Denison began in 1831 as a male academy and became coeducational in 1900 when it and nearby Shepardson College for Women merged. Grinnell accepted women in 1855, nine years after its founding, although they were not officially admitted as degree students until after the Civil War (Grinnell website, see Bibliography).

While all eight institutions have historically been liberal arts colleges, Denison and Lawrence began as universities. In 1854, when the Granville Literary and Theological Institution took the name of Denison, it intended to offer courses of study that entitled it to university status. Indeed, by 1887 it had master's programs. However, in the late 1920s it decided to restrict

---

[5] Haverford College in Pennsylvania had been established in 1833.

its curriculum solely to undergraduate courses and programs although the name Denison University was retained (Denison website, see Bibliography). Lawrence likewise offered graduate level courses. But in 1913, it adopted the name Lawrence College to underscore its commitment to liberal education. As articulated by Lawrence President Plantz (1859-94) and refined by President Wriston (1925-37) "a liberal education consists in the acquisition and the refinement of standards of values—all sorts of values—physical, intellectual, emotional, aesthetic, and spiritual," and a liberal arts college should cause students to discover the world anew (Breunig 1994, 143, quoting Wriston). In 1964, Milwaukee-Downer College, which had been suffering from enrollment decreases and financial deficits, proposed a merger with Lawrence College—which resulted in reestablishment of the name Lawrence University. In both cases, Denison and Lawrence maintain strong liberal arts college foundations and consider themselves today to be colleges. As the latter's website says, Lawrence University "is what it has been for more than a century: a liberal arts college with a conservatory of music."

The colleges have commonalities in curricular, facility, enrollment, and intellectual expansion and growth over the course of their histories. During the 1861-65 American Civil War, enrollment declined, funding dissolved, and several colleges wondered if they would survive. Nollen (1953, 61) cites Grinnell historical sources: "In 1861 there was a freshman class of twelve. But then the war came. Soon all but two were in the field." He goes on to say that "it was the women students who kept the College going during the four years of the Civil War" (62). One positive result of the war was that it "cemented the East and the great Middle West into a formidable alliance of resources—natural, human, industrial, financial" (Rudolph 1962, 242). This challenged the colleges, which gradually responded by expanding their curricula and increasing facilities, enrollments, and faculty members. At Lawrence, for example, elective courses were introduced in the 1880s to support students in the classical course of study who wished to be exposed to mathematics and the sciences, and those students in the science course of study who wished to take advanced courses in French, German, English literature, or history (Breunig 1994). Grinnell's expansion included modern languages and initiation of one of the first political science courses in the country (Grinnell website, see Bibliography). Swarthmore, founded during the Civil War, decided that its curriculum would be similar to that of other colleges of the time, but there would be a greater emphasis on teaching and on science.

From the late 1800s into the first quarter of the twentieth century, the colleges' curricular interests widened. At Kalamazoo, this included limiting the bachelor's degree to the B.A.; moving to two semesters rather than three terms; substituting class work for chapel; developing majors, minors, and electives along with general and special honors; and instituting a faculty-student advisor system. Swarthmore took steps to intensify its focus on academic excellence while also developing well-rounded students. In 1921 President Aydelotte established "an Honors Program for the superior students and the traditional program for the average students" (Walton 1986, 34). Today, the Honors Program still includes seminars and independent study with final examinations given by faculty from outside Swarthmore. Students in the program graduate with honors from the college, not just from their department. Earlham moved slowly away from direct control by local Friends' meetings while trying to expand its curriculum and strengthen its academic program, increase enrollment through ever larger numbers of students from across the United States, and yet still "make a distinct contribution not only to the Quaker way of life but to the cause of liberal arts education" (Hamm 1997, 178, quoting Morris). As midcentury approached, Denison's President Shaw reflected common concerns that there was a need to align ideals with practicality when he asserted that "we have lost the universal in the particular" (Chessman and Southgate 1981, 113). At Denison, this led

> to a new program of required studies, designed to acquaint the student with the chief areas and methods of human knowledge and expression. It led to an enlarged system of guidance and counseling, intended to assist young men and women in their adjustment to college life and their preparation for future careers. It led to a renewed stress upon the college's religious program, in an effort to foster moral and spiritual values. It even led to an expansion of campus government, aimed to encourage the students' sense of responsibility. Wherever one turned in this quarter century after 1925, one found aspects of this general endeavor to realize Denison's old aim to "educate the whole man" as well as to be "a useful institution."

Bonvillian and Murray (1996, 26-27) attribute the growth within both colleges and universities during the first half of the twentieth century to three factors: (1) a public commitment, supported financially, to expand access to higher education; (2) a belief that the nation's welfare [is] dependent on an educated populace; and (3) an increase in the utilization of colleges and universities to advance the agricultural, industrial, and cultural needs of society.

Today, all eight of the colleges have nationally ranked academic programs, either overall or with reference to specific areas of study. Any number of rankings can be cited but these provide examples: A 2004 *U.S. News & World Report* article examined such factors as retention and graduation rate, percent of classes under 20 students, SAT and ACT scores, acceptance rate, and alumni-giving rate. That article ranked five of the colleges in their list of top colleges: Swarthmore (2nd), Carleton (5th), Grinnell (12th), Macalester (27th), and Lawrence (51st) ("Best Liberal Arts Colleges—Bachelor's (Nationally)" 2004). In a 2003 report on baccalaureate colleges with high numbers of students involved in study abroad, Kalamazoo is ranked 4th and Earlham 6th (Bollag 2003). Denison programs such as biology, psychology, and economics are nationally ranked in a number of sources, including HEDS (1971-2000) and Pope (1996).[6] Yet as important as such rankings may be, the colleges also firmly believe their value still lies in the liberal arts. Two cases in point are Grinnell and Swarthmore.

In its 1946 catalog, Grinnell celebrated the end of its first century and stressed that the college

> defines a liberally educated person as one who has the ability to read, write, and speak his own language well and has an appreciation of its literature; who can read at least one foreign language and has first-hand acquaintance with the literature and culture of the country in which it is spoken; who is thoroughly

---

[6]HEDS findings are based on the Baccalaureate Origins data for 1991-2000 made available by the Higher Education Data Sharing Consortium.

> grounded in the history of the modern world and in the Christian tradition, and has a sympathetic understanding of the social problems of his time; who has subjected himself to the discipline of science and learned to understand the principles and methods of the natural sciences and the part which they play in modern society; who has acquired the ability to perceive the values of the arts and to derive enjoyment from them; and who has learned to care for his own bodily health and to take an intelligent interest in the health of the community in which he lives. (Nollen 1953, 130, quoting the 1946 catalog)

This view characterized the college into the 1970s, when the curriculum changed from having a common core to one that required a major field of study and a set minimum number of graduation credits but did not have explicit general education requirements or minors. The only required course was, and still is, a first semester tutorial that is taught by faculty members from across the college to small groups of students on a topic of interest to faculty and students. Each faculty member stays with and mentors his or her group of students until the latter declare majors (Grinnell website, see Bibliography). Also in the 1970s, Grinnell undertook initiatives to gradually invest students with increasing amounts of responsibility for their own learning and their own self-governance. Grinnell's core values now reflect both its historical involvement in social issues and its belief in personal responsibility.

From its beginning in 1864, Swarthmore sought to weave together three threads: the quest for intellectual excellence, a concern for Quaker tradition, and constant self-examination. In 1978, President Friend wrote about the relationship between intellect and character:

> For if a liberal arts college does not foster that relationship, I believe that such a college does not deserve to exist. A well-educated person should be able to clear the mind of cant, to flush out doublethink, and to formulate the true and the valid as simply and clearly as possible. Such a disciplined mind should enable one to appreciate the authentic, to detect what is not genuine, and to despise rot. It should move one to make distinctions that imply value, to shape plans that combine value with purpose, to follow through on plans with determination and awareness of possibilities for improvement. It should enable one to lead a life of value, purpose, and achievement. (Walton 1986, 45)

Such perspectives reflect part of the ethos (i.e., "habit" *Greek*) of these two colleges, which Kuh (1993, 22) defines in the context of higher education as

> a belief system widely shared by faculty, students, administrators, and others. It is shaped by a core of educational values, . . . provides clues about the institution's moral character and imposes a coherence on collective experience by reconciling individual and group roles with the institution's aspirations and public image . . . [It is] an institution-specific pattern of values and principles that invokes a sense of belonging and helps people distinguish between appropriate and inappropriate behavior . . . The ethos carries messages about the relative importance of various

> educational functions—teaching, research, preparation for a career and citizenship, the cultivation of practical competencies and political sensibilities, and so on . . . Colleges with a salient ethos imprint on their students a distinctive pattern of attitudes and values.

A college's ethos, however, is not easy to identify since much of it is embedded in the daily activities of the campus community of faculty, students, administrators, and staff. Yet, it is possible to discern elements of the ethos of the eight colleges by considering their mission, purpose, or vision statements, something that most college and university catalogs and websites provide. Stuart and Moran (1998) characterize a mission statement as "a self-imposed duty," as in "this is the way we have chosen to be; this is who or what we *are*." The role of a mission statement is to articulate those concepts or principles that guide the college in establishing goals and developing itself to achieve those goals. A purpose statement adds clarity and expands on the college's raison d'être. A vision statement projects into the future and seeks to convey how the college would like to see itself. Statements may be succinct or expansive but they serve to guide and direct a college in what it must do in order to be "who we are."

Understanding Institutional Ethos through Mission and Purpose Statements

Each CALS college website includes one or more statements describing the mission of the college; several reference the colleges' academic catalogs while others are taken from strategic planning documents.[7] The statements suggest how the college must act either in order to ensure that students develop in a certain way, or in order to help students help themselves. Stripped of explanatory details, here are the core statements:

> *Carleton*: To provide a liberal education of the highest quality. The goal of such an education is to liberate individuals from the constraints imposed by ignorance or complacency and prepare them broadly to lead rewarding, creative, and useful lives.
>
> *Denison*: To inspire and educate our students to become autonomous thinkers, discerning moral agents and active citizens of a democratic society.
>
> *Earlham*: To provide the highest quality undergraduate education in the liberal arts, including the sciences, shaped by the distinctive perspectives of the Religious Society of Friends (Quakers).
>
> *Grinnell*: To educate [our] students "for the different professions and for the honorable discharge of the duties of life." [the incorporated quote is from the college's 1846 charter]

---

[7] See Bibliography: III. Websites for each college's URL.

> *Kalamazoo*: To prepare [our] graduates to better understand, live successfully within, and provide enlightened leadership to, a richly diverse and increasingly complex world.
>
> *Lawrence*: To educate men and women in the liberal arts and sciences.
>
> *Macalester*: To be a preeminent liberal arts college with an educational program known for its high standards for scholarship and its special emphasis on internationalism, multiculturalism, and service to society.
>
> *Swarthmore*: To make [our] students more valuable human beings and more useful members of society.

The additional comments each college attaches to its mission statement reveal the college's greater hopes and concerns. These expansions can also be seen as standards against which a college can measure its progress toward actualizing its mission statement. They set the tone and provide background that reveals something of the distinctive characteristics of each college—its ethos. They illustrate the place each college sets for itself at the liberal arts table. Let us now expand upon the foregoing brief statements:

Carleton: To provide a liberal education of the highest quality. The goal of such an education is to liberate individuals from the constraints imposed by ignorance or complacency and prepare them broadly to lead rewarding, creative, and useful lives.

In its "Purpose of the College" statement, Carleton focuses on education as underpinning its expectations of students:

> At its simplest, a liberal education teaches the basic skills upon which higher achievements rest: to read perceptively, to write and speak clearly, and to think analytically. Carleton draws upon these skills to foster a critical appreciation of our intellectual, aesthetic, and moral heritage and to encourage original thought. A Carleton student not only masters certain information and techniques, but also acquires a sense of curiosity and intellectual adventure, an awareness of method and purpose in a variety of fields, and an affinity for quality and integrity wherever they may be found. Nurtured by dedicated teachers in an environment that rewards growth and questioning, these values prepare students, as former Carleton trustee Martin Trow has written, to "accomplish large and important things in the world, make important discoveries, lead great institutions, influence their nation's laws and government, and add substantially to knowledge." But above all, they prepare one to lead a fully realized life in a diverse and changing world.
>
> To this end, Carleton's curriculum balances a traditional emphasis upon classic fields of study, or disciplines, with a complementary offering of

> distribution courses, electives, and interdisciplinary programs. The disciplines provide rigor and depth of training, an opportunity to test oneself against a body of knowledge and a repertory of skills that educated women and men have built, over time, into major structures of intellectual inquiry. Interdisciplinary programs not only encourage the application of these skills to questions too complex and subtle to be approached through any one discipline, but also reflect the open textured, dynamic character of the disciplines themselves.
>
> In addition, the College requires that all students, to prepare themselves for lifelong growth and continuing education, must distribute their courses among four divisions of knowledge, take at least one course centrally concerned with the recognition and affirmation of difference, and demonstrate proficiency in English composition and in a second language. For those seeking a still more varied experience, it offers a wide range of opportunities for off-campus study, many of these in foreign countries. Faculty and students alike participate actively in the creative and performing arts and athletics, both of which are integral parts of a Carleton education.
>
> Education, although a profoundly individual experience, prepares one to live fruitfully in society and contribute to its work. The liberal arts at Carleton aim to liberate as fully as possible the whole potential of each student and open the way toward a generous and interesting life. (Carleton website, see Bibliography)

Denison: To inspire and educate our students to become autonomous thinkers, discerning moral agents and active citizens of a democratic society.

The mission statement its board of trustees adopted in 1999 presents Denison as "a coeducational community of intellectual excellence and moral ideals" (Denison website, see Bibliography), adding that "through an emphasis on active learning, we engage students in the liberal arts, which fosters self-determination and demonstrates the transformative power of education. We envision our students' lives as based upon rational choice, a firm belief in human dignity and compassion unlimited by cultural, racial, sexual, religious or economic barriers, and directed toward an engagement with the central issues of our time."

The statement then delineates what is expected of faculty, students, and the institution as a whole:

> Our faculty is committed to undergraduate education. As teacher-scholar-advisers, their principal responsibility is effective teaching informed by the best scholarship. Faculty members place a priority on close interaction with students, interactive learning, and partnerships with students in original research. Our low student/faculty ratio allows for close supervision of independent research and collaborative work in small groups and classes.

> We seek to ensure an ever-broader range of racial, ethnic, international and economic backgrounds in a student body of about 2,000 students. We offer different kinds of financial aid to meet the different needs of our students.
>
> The focus of student life at Denison is a concern for the whole person. The University provides a living-learning environment sensitive to individual needs yet grounded in a concern for community, in which the principles of human dignity and ethical integrity are paramount. Students engage in a wide range of co-curricular activities that address the multidimensional character of their intellectual and personal journey.
>
> Denison is a community in which individuals respect one another and their environment. Each member of the community possesses a full range of rights and responsibilities. Foremost among these is a commitment to treat each other and our environment with mutual respect, tolerance and civility. (Denison website, see Bibliography)

The website also notes that "from its beginning, the College has been committed to serving society's need for education. It has endeavored to be, in the words of its first trustees, 'a useful Institution suited to the wants, and calculated to promote the welfare, of a rapidly growing and free country.' "

Earlham: To provide the highest quality undergraduate education in the liberal arts, including the sciences, shaped by the distinctive perspectives of the Religious Society of Friends (Quakers).

The Earlham website text explains that "a basic faith of Friends is that all truth is God's truth; thus Earlham emphasizes: pursuit of truth, wherever that pursuit leads; lack of coercion, letting the evidence lead that search; respect for the consciences of others; openness to new truth and therefore the willingness to search; veracity, rigorous integrity in dealing with the facts; application of what is known to improving our world."

Earlham sees itself as being

> among the nation's academically strongest liberal arts colleges, [and it] develops in students broad and deep competencies in both traditional and emerging disciplinary and interdisciplinary fields; moreover, Earlham educates students to work effectively together with others, to understand better the ways human organizations work, and to make complex decisions in compassionate and visionary ways. To provide education of the highest quality with these emphases, Earlham's mission requires selection of an outstanding and caring faculty committed to creating an open, cooperative, learning environment. The College provides for the continuous support and development of this faculty. The teaching-learning process at Earlham is shaped by a view of education as a process of awakening the "teacher within," so that our students will become lifelong learners. Students at Earlham are encouraged to be active, involved

> learners. The College provides extensive opportunities for students and faculty to interact with each other as persons, to learn from each other in a cooperative community, an important aspect of which is collaborative student/faculty research. (Earlham website, see Bibliography)

The statement concludes by incorporating the last part of the mission statement: "At Earlham College this education is carried on with a concern for the world in which we live and for improving human society. The College strives to educate morally sensitive leaders for future generations. Therefore Earlham stresses global education, peaceful resolution of conflict, equality of persons, and high moral standards of personal conduct."

Grinnell: To educate [our] students "for the different professions and for the honorable discharge of the duties of life."

This part of Grinnell's 2002 mission statement includes a quote from its charter in the Iowa Territory of the United States in 1846. The 2002 statement continues:

> The College pursues that mission by educating young men and women in the liberal arts through free inquiry and the open exchange of ideas. As a teaching and learning community, the College holds that knowledge is a good to be pursued both for its own sake and for the intellectual, moral, and physical well-being of individuals and of society at large. The College exists to provide a lively academic community of students and teachers of high scholarly qualifications from diverse social and cultural circumstances. The College aims to graduate women and men who can think clearly, who can speak and write persuasively and even eloquently, who can evaluate critically both their own and others' ideas, who can acquire new knowledge, and who are prepared in life and work to use their knowledge and their abilities to serve the common good. (Grinnell website, see Bibliography)

The website presents Grinnell's core values as reflecting its historical involvement in social issues and its belief in personal responsibility.

Kalamazoo: To prepare [our] graduates to better understand, live successfully within, and provide enlightened leadership to, a richly diverse and increasingly complex world.

In another section of its website, Kalamazoo says that, "As a means of carrying out this mission, members of the Kalamazoo College community provide through the curricular and co-curricular programs of the K-Plan an education of broad liberal learning deepened and enriched by experiential, international, and multicultural dimensions. The K-Plan combines rigorous liberal arts academics, career development programs, meaningful study abroad, a senior individualized project, and a residential living experience that offers a wide variety of co-curricular opportunities" (Kalamazoo website, see Bibliography).

The introduction to the college's current strategic plan further explains its distinctive "K-Plan":

> Throughout its history, Kalamazoo College has broken new ground in liberal arts education through our nationally recognized study abroad programs, our innovations in Experiential Education, and the excellence of our First-Year Experience program. Through the K-Plan, students are provided an array of opportunities to develop the knowledge, skills, and attitudes that underlie the five dimensions of a Kalamazoo College education: lifelong learning, intercultural understanding, social responsibility, career readiness, and leadership. During the next five years, we will develop key connections that undergird the K-Plan: connections among students, faculty, administration, and staff; connections with our global partners and the global community; connections within a diverse and civil campus community; and connections with our communities beyond the campus. Strengthening these connections will sustain our momentum through the end of the first decade of the 21st century, and will renew our commitments to the highest ethical standards, respect for all persons, and leadership with integrity. (Kalamazoo website, see Bibliography)

Lawrence: To educate men and women in the liberal arts and sciences.

Lawrence University's statement goes on to say that, "committed to the development of intellect and talent, the acquisition of knowledge and understanding, and the cultivation of judgment and values, Lawrence prepares students for lives of service, achievement, leadership, and personal fulfillment" (Lawrence website, see Bibliography). This is followed by a "Purpose" statement that effectively delineates a set of goals covering all aspects of the institution:

> To enroll intellectually curious students who demonstrate an abiding desire to learn and the will to join a community of scholars and artists in the vigorous pursuit of knowledge.
>
> To attract, support, and sustain a faculty of active scholars and artists devoted to the intellectual life and to the teaching of undergraduates.
>
> To attract and retain administrative and support personnel who will effectively promote the educational purposes and values of the university.
>
> To seek diversity within the university community as a means to enrich teaching and learning and to promote tolerance and understanding.
>
> To maintain an intellectual environment that: encourages excellence in teaching and scholarship; encourages dialogue and close collaboration between students and faculty; encourages an active search for knowledge and understanding; fosters the critical examination of values, ideas, and actions; supports open and free inquiry; develops aesthetic appreciation; encourages responsible commitment; challenges individuals to surpass their previous achievements, to seek new opportunities, and to explore new areas; promotes an

enduring enthusiasm for learning; develops a sense of responsibilities inherent in intellectual endeavors and social relationships; and informs and inspires student residential life.

To provide a curriculum leading to the Bachelor of Arts degree that: comprises recognized disciplines of the arts and sciences; examines the heritage of great civilizations; encompasses the current state of knowledge in the disciplines; exposes students to a wide range of subjects and intellectual approaches; engages each student actively in one or more disciplines at an advanced level; fosters opportunities for independent intellectual activity; develops students' abilities to think critically, write clearly, and speak effectively; and allows opportunities for choice and the pursuit of an individual's special interests while preserving a coherent course of study.

To provide a curriculum leading to the Bachelor of Music degree that combines professional education in music, accredited by the National Association of Schools of Music, with study in the liberal arts.

To provide a program leading to certification as public school teachers in the state of Wisconsin.

To provide opportunities for students to create and participate in extracurricular activities that are consistent with the educational goals and values of the university.

To nurture a social environment that promotes mature and responsible behavior and good citizenship.

To cultivate a safe and healthful campus environment.

To contribute to the vitality of the surrounding community and to make available programs of cultural enrichment and to draw on the knowledge and experience of members of that community in the exploration of significant issues.

To provide opportunities for alumni to maintain a lifelong connection with the institution and with each other and to encourage their continuing interest in learning.

To provide the physical and financial resources needed to support the educational purposes and to ensure the future well-being of the university. (Lawrence website, see Bibliography)

Macalester: To be a preeminent liberal arts college with an educational program known for its high standards for scholarship and its special emphasis on internationalism, multiculturalism, and service to society.

Macalester believes it emphasizes "academic excellence in the context of internationalism, diversity, and a commitment to service. Since its founding in 1874, Macalester has maintained standards for scholarship equivalent to those of the finest colleges in the country in a context of high ethical standards and social concerns."

Its website includes this "Statement of Purpose and Belief":

At Macalester College we believe that education is a fundamentally transforming experience. As a community of learners, the possibilities for this personal, social, and intellectual transformation extend to us all. We affirm the importance of the intellectual growth of the students, staff and faculty through individual and collaborative endeavor. We believe that this can best be achieved through an environment that values the diverse cultures of our world and recognizes our responsibility to provide a supportive and respectful environment for students, staff and faculty of all cultures and backgrounds.

We expect students to develop a broad understanding of the liberal arts while they are at Macalester. Students should follow a primary course of study in order to acquire an understanding of disciplinary theory and methodology; they should be able to apply their understanding of theories to address problems in the larger community. Students should develop the ability to use information and communication resources effectively, be adept at critical, analytical and logical thinking, and express themselves well in both oral and written forms. Finally, students should be prepared to take responsibility for their personal, social and intellectual choices.

We believe that the benefit of the educational experience at Macalester is the development of individuals who make informed judgments and interpretations of the broader world around them and choose actions or beliefs for which they are willing to be held accountable. We expect them to develop the ability to seek and use knowledge and experience in contexts that challenge and inform their suppositions about the world. We are committed to helping students grow intellectually and personally within an environment that models and promotes academic excellence and ethical behavior. The education a student begins at Macalester provides the basis for continuous transformation through learning and service. (Macalester website, see Bibliography)

Swarthmore: To make [our] students more valuable human beings and more useful members of society.

The Swarthmore website explains that

in accordance with the College's Quaker tradition, ... Swarthmore seeks to help its students realize their fullest intellectual and personal potential combined with a deep sense of ethical and social concern. This philosophy is expanded upon in the [following] Mission Statement of the College, [as] published in the 1989-90 president's report:

"First and foremost, the College seeks the fullest intellectual development of its students, fostering independent thinking and personal responsibility for critical judgment and creation of knowledge. Such independence builds upon but goes beyond a general education and intensive study in a given discipline. Although the locus of responsibility is in the individual, the process is often most effectively collaborative, as evident in seminars, the interaction of campus life, and research with faculty members ... The College [also] seeks to instill a sense of

> responsibility for putting one's talents to work for the betterment of others. Students at Swarthmore are particularly privileged, by both their ability and the resources available for their education. The College recognizes that its graduates can contribute to the world in many different ways, that some will engage in a life of service and sacrifice while others will succeed in activities that offer more tangible reward, but the College will have succeeded only if all its graduates seek out opportunities to share generously with others the benefits of their fully developed talents." (Swarthmore website, see Bibliography)

Through their mission statements the eight colleges present themselves as communities of learning with strong academics grounded in the liberal arts, where students develop attributes that make them morally good people who will be active contributors to the betterment of society. In 1977 Bowen wrote that "the basic educational task of colleges and universities is to help students achieve cognitive learning, emotional and moral development, and practical competence" (267). Their mission statements and expanded commentaries suggest that the eight colleges would agree that his sentiment pertains to all of them. Bowen (1977, 267) continues:

> Though most institutions have a strong tradition of freedom of thought for students as well as faculty and of aversion to overt indoctrination, in practice they are far from neutral in their influence on students. In most institutions, there is a prevailing conception of what the educated man or woman should be like. Most established curricula and degree requirements control the content of courses and the methods of instruction. And most institutions exert great influence on extracurricular life. Also, most academic communities engage in the consideration and analysis of values. They are involved in social and artistic criticism. They construct philosophical systems and ideologies and they appraise existing social policies and recommend new ones. Through all these processes, the academic community creates an ethos. This ethos is usually not promulgated officially; it is not necessarily shared by all members of the academic community; it often differs from views prevailing among the general public; and it changes over time. Yet one can say that, in a given period, the weight of academic influence is directed toward a particular cluster of values and toward a particular world outlook.

Summary

Although each college has a distinctive character and ethos, they share common characteristics of American liberal arts institutions: devotion to the liberal arts, respect for individuals, and the surrounding of a specialized field of study with a broader understanding of, an appreciation for, diversity of thought. Founded between 1831 and 1874, in the midst of significant higher education expansion in the United States, the eight colleges of the Alums also exemplify the institutions described by the Council of Independent Colleges, described earlier in this chapter, by emphasizing teaching excellence; providing education with a moral, and perhaps spiritual, dimension; encouraging exploration over specialization; and serving their region even as they attract students from across the country and around the world.

CHAPTER 2

The Alums as Undergraduates

This chapter addresses the effect that attending their chosen college had on the CALS participants. Factors behind the initial choice of a college are considered, followed by substantive discussion of intellectual, social, and psychological changes occasioned by the structure and expectations of the colleges, and of the personal and professional values the Alums believed they gained from their undergraduate experiences there. Because 78 percent of the respondents to this survey were female, if a choice could be made regarding the use of statistics from other sources, the statistics for females were chosen as being the closest for comparative purposes.

I. Geography and the Choice of a College

In their study of trends among American college and university freshmen, Dey et al. (1991, 70-71) found that, from 1969-90, the percentages of first-year women students who attended a college not more than 50 miles from their home ranged from 44.5 to 55.8 percent.[8] Between 13.2 and 17.9 percent went to an institution 51-100 miles away, 23.8 to 29.6 percent traveled 101 to 500 miles away, and only the remaining 6.7 to 10.4 percent selected a college over 500 miles from home. The eight colleges represented in this study are located in Indiana,

---

[8]Dey et al. are members of the Higher Education Research Institute (HERI) at the University of California, Los Angeles. HERI is responsible for conducting and analyzing the Cooperative Institutional Research Program (CIRP) data on college freshmen. The Dey et al. source is used in this section as it covers 1966-90—a 25-year span encompassing 63 percent of the CALS Alums (classes of 1965-90).

Iowa, Michigan, Minnesota, Ohio, Pennsylvania, and Wisconsin, and while the colleges' websites indicate that, collectively, students come from all 50 U.S. states plus many other countries, the college administrators indicate that it is common for 50 percent or more of their students to be from within the state where the college is located.

As undergraduates, the CALS respondents were similar to Dey et al.'s (1991) first-year women: 96 percent of the Alums lived in only one state as 6-12-year-old children, and 87 percent lived in that same state when they were 13-17 (see appendix B: IV-14). The Alums lived in 43 U.S. states and 16 other countries when they were 6-12 years old, and 37 states and 14 other countries when they were 13-17 years old. Two groups of states are of particular interest, as they are where a majority of the CALS study respondents lived when they were between the ages of six and seventeen.

The first group of states is comprised of Illinois, New York, Indiana, Michigan, Minnesota, Ohio, Pennsylvania, and Wisconsin. During the age period of 6-12, these eight states were home to 66 percent of the Alums when they were ages 6-12 and to 69 percent of the Alums when they were ages 13 to 17. CALS respondents who lived in Illinois when they were 13-17 favored attending Carleton, Kalamazoo, and Lawrence. Those from New York generally preferred Swarthmore and Kalamazoo. Indiana, Michigan, Minnesota, Ohio, Pennsylvania, and Wisconsin were home to between 48 and 53 percent of the Alums when the latter were ages 6-12 and 13-17, respectively. At the time of college enrollment, a majority of these Alums chose to attend Earlham, Kalamazoo, Carleton, Macalester, Denison, Swarthmore, or Lawrence.

The second group of states encompasses California, Connecticut, Iowa, Kansas, Massachusetts, Missouri, and New Jersey. Nineteen percent of the CALS respondents were resident in these seven states when they were 6-12 years old. Twenty percent of the Alums lived in those states when they were 13-17 years old. Respondents from Connecticut were most apt to attend Swarthmore, while those from California and Massachusetts generally favored Carleton, Earlham, or Swarthmore. The Alums from Iowa enrolled at Carleton, Earlham, and Macalester. Those who came from Kansas and Missouri favored Carleton and Earlham, while the Alums from New Jersey were more likely to attend Earlham and Kalamazoo. Grinnell respondents were not residents of Iowa where the college is located, but were from Connecticut, Indiana, Kansas, Nebraska, New Hampshire, South Dakota, and Wisconsin.

In terms of the size of their communities, when the Alums were aged 6-12, 17 percent lived in rural areas or small towns (less than 2,500), 53 percent lived in small to medium-sized cities (2,500-99,999), and 36 percent lived in large cities or metropolitan areas (100,000 and over) (appendix B: Q.IV-14). During the ages of 13-17, there was a small percentage movement of the Alums' families away from rural and small towns toward cities and metropolitan areas. The percentage of those living in small- to medium-sized cities dropped from 53 percent to 49 percent, and those living in rural or small towns dropped from 17 percent to 14 percent. The percentage living in large cities or metropolitan areas thus increased—from 30 percent to 36 percent.

These findings regarding home states and size of community hold stable by CALS college and class over the 39 years represented by this study.

II. Changes in Students during College

Being in college was a significant experience for the Alums—as it is for most students. Two publications provide meta-analyses of the literature on the effect of college and illustrate areas of change. They also cover an extensive portion of the 1962-2000 span of the present study. In *The Impact of College on Students* Feldman and Newcomb (1970) discuss the findings of more than 1,500 studies, and in *How College Affects Students* Pascarella and Terenzini (1991) cover the results of more than 2,600 studies. In the latter work, the chapter titles reflect areas of student engagement and change:

- Development of Verbal, Quantitative, and Subject Matter Competence
- Cognitive Skills and Intellectual Growth
- Psychosocial Changes: Identity, Self-Concept, and Self-Esteem
- Psychosocial Changes: Relating to Others and the External World
- Attitudes and Values
- Moral Development
- Educational Attainment
- Career Choice and Development
- Economic Benefits of College
- Quality of Life after College

Magdol (2003, 95-96) provides a succinct summary of the basic conclusions of both meta-analyses:

> Feldman and Newcomb [1970] reviewed studies on the effects of post-secondary education from the 1920s through the 1960s. Their general conclusion was that college seniors were more liberal than freshmen during those early decades. . . . Pascarella and Terenzini (1991) followed up . . . with a review of studies conducted in the 1970s and 1980s. In general, they concluded that college students became more liberal, tolerant of diversity, favorable to individual rights, and egalitarian about gender roles in the course of their university training.[9]

The changes may be small or large depending, certainly, on the particular student, but overall the shifts are seen as significantly large. Of particular importance for colleges, Pascarella and Terenzini (1991, 557) observe that "the research portrays the college student as changing in an integrated way, with change in any one area appearing to be part of a mutually reinforcing network or pattern of change in other areas." In the area of learning and cognitive change, students mature over the course of their undergraduate years; that is, they become better at learning how to learn. Seniors are more intellectually disciplined, better able to reason, and more

---

[9]Magdol draws upon Bowen et al. (1977) when she defines "liberal" as having an attitude that is "flexible and accepting of new ideas"; similarly she employs "conservative" to mean an attitude that is "bound by fixed ideas and by tradition" (Magdol 2003, 95).

effective speakers than freshmen. They are better able to solve problems of various types, better able to critique issues and situations, and better able to address and access both sides of a problem. That is, students "not only make statistically significant gains in factual knowledge and in a range of general cognitive and intellectual skills; they also change on a broad array of value, attitudinal, psychosocial, and moral dimensions" (Pascarella and Terenzini 1991, 557).

On the subject of student attitudes and values, Feldman and Newcomb (1970) and Pascarella and Terenzini (1991) assert that over the 1920-80 period there are consistent changes in the areas of sociopolitical, religious, and gender role attitudes and values. Pascarella and Terenzini (1991, 559) note that "it would appear that there are unmistakable and sometimes substantial freshman-to-senior shifts toward openness and a tolerance for diversity, a stronger 'other-person orientation,' and concern for individual rights and human welfare." They also find that seniors attach "a greater importance to the value of a liberal education and less importance to the value of a college education for vocational preparation" (560). This is not to say that seniors do not display concern for—or worry over—career choice, but rather that they acknowledge that intellectual challenges and the knowledge and experiences gained from their undergraduate education are, and will be, valuable assets in both their personal and professional lives.

Psychosocial changes relate to developing not just a sense of self, but also the awareness of one's self in relation to the world. In terms of the sense of self, Pascarella and Terenzini's 1991 review of the literature finds that "students appear to move toward greater self-understanding, self-definition, and personal commitment" (p. 562). They seem to leave college with a renewed sense of self-esteem. In the larger world arena, as they become independent learners, they move away from close reliance on family and friends for help with decisions. They show a general, positive disposition toward diversity in the world at large, and they are

- More tolerant of other people and their views
- More open to new ideas
- More comfortable thinking in non-stereotypic ways about those who are different from them

They also "make statistically significant gains during college in the use of principled reasoning to judge moral issues" (Pascarella and Terenzini 1991, 562). Study of these gains indicates that by the time students are seniors they are more apt to think through an issue and make an independent judgment, than to rely on previously accepted precepts associated with particular social philosophies, orientations, or religious approaches.

One conclusion from this portion of the literature is that as students move from freshmen to seniors, they do indeed learn how to think more critically. This leads them to question more, to absorb experiences inside and outside the classroom, to reorder their views on issues, to begin the process of creating their "selves" in such a manner as to reflect beliefs that they now hold. They mature—or at least are more aware that they are somewhat (and somehow) different from who they were when they entered college. Finally, Pascarella and Terenzini (1991, 579) discuss the long-term effects of college, and conclude that

> for college students as a group, the intellectual, aesthetic, social, political, religious, educational, and occupational attitudes and values one holds as a graduating senior appear to be an important determinant of the attitudes and values one holds through the adult years.

But is there a specific "liberal arts college" effect? Throughout their study, Pascarella and Terenzini (1991) find almost no distinction in the effect of different types of higher education institutions on students. Overall, they say, "institutional categorizations such as the Carnegie classification appear to tell us little about difference in between-college impacts" (597). It should be noted, however, that in 1991 the number of students attending public colleges and universities is almost four times that of the number of students enrolled in private colleges—and that Pascarella and Terenzini (1991) are reviewing over 2,600 studies; thus any particular effect of the liberal arts college may simply not be large enough to be discernible.[10] In concert, however, with their counterparts in other college and university settings, as students the CALS Alums did encounter both the curriculum and the extracurriculum of the academy.

III. Elements of a College Education

Majors

The first use of the terms *major* and *minor* appears to be in the Johns Hopkins University catalog of 1877-78 (Levine 1978), which divided student academic work into two years for a major and one year for a minor field of study. Today, the number, the kind, and the structuring of academic majors rest with each college and, more specifically, with its departments and academic programs. As seen in appendix E, the number of majors available within the CALS colleges ranges from the twenties into the forties. They include those comprising the liberal arts, as well as preprofessional fields such as business, engineering, and education, and newly emerging interdisciplinary areas. In some cases, students are drawn to majors that represent specific foci of a college. For example, at Lawrence, students find music performance, music, and music education very appealing–as befits a nationally recognized undergraduate college with its own conservatory of music (Q.I-2). At Earlham, interdisciplinary studies programs are a part of the mix: "Peace and global studies enrolls the second largest number of majors in the college. Human development and social relations is one of the largest majors of the college—and [it] combines sociology, psychology, philosophy, biology, and anthropology" (Len Clark, Provost, interview).[11]

---

[10]U.S. Bureau of the Census 2003, 147.

[11]Except where otherwise noted, all quotes from the college deans and provosts are from personal interviews (see Bibliography: Interviews).

Table 1: Alums' Academic "Majors" by Disciplinary Area

Disciplines	Majors as Named by the Alums
Fine/Performing Arts	Fine Arts; Music
Languages/Literatures	Classics; English; Foreign Language; French; German; Greek; Humanities; Latin; Liberal Arts; Linguistics; Literature; Medieval Studies; Russian; Spanish
Sciences/Mathematics	Agriculture; Biology; Chemistry; Computer Science; Geology; Mathematics; Physics
Social/Behavioral Sciences	Anthropology; Asian Studies; Communication; Education; Geography; Government; History (including Art History); Human Relations; International Relations; International Studies; Latin American Studies; Peace Studies; Philosophy; Political Science; Psychology; Religion; Social Studies; Sociology; Soviet Studies; Urban Studies; Women's Studies

Macalester's Dean Hornbach noted that the top two majors are economics and political science. "English, biology, history, and psychology are the next group. Probably over the course of the years, the biggest increases have been in psychology and economics, [and] political science and biology have remained pretty constant over the past 30 years" (Hornbach interview, see Bibliography). Swarthmore's Dean Robert Gross indicated that, in addition to established majors, there are three other ways to construct one:

> Well-greased paths like biological-anthropology, which combine two departments in a fairly structured way. Second, a student putting two departments together for themselves, and you would usually represent 5 courses from each dept. And then a third would be an intellectually, problem-centered [one] that would pull from a couple of different places.

At Grinnell, even with popular majors such as biology, history, English, political science, and economics, there are currently over 60 students pursuing double majors and another 80 students pursuing interdisciplinary concentrations (website, see Bibliography). The Lawrence website also points out fundamental requirements of student-designed majors: "Like all majors, those that are student-designed should meet the following objectives: greater knowledge of the field under study; increased methodological sophistication; and the integration of sometimes disparate, but related, areas of study."

The Alums identify 48 fields as their "majors," including a few double and triple majors (table 1). The fields most frequently chosen are English (20 percent) and History (18 percent). These are followed by eight fields that each capture either four or 5 percent of the Alums: Religion, Anthropology, Biology, French, German, Music, Psychology, and Sociology (appendix C: Q.1-2). When the majors, as named by the Alums, are grouped into very broad disciplinary areas, those within the Social/Behavioral Sciences were most frequently chosen (50 percent of all majors) with Languages and Literatures second (32 percent). The Sciences (including Mathematics) and the Fine and Performing Arts (excluding Art History) were a distant third (6 percent each).

As undergraduates, 14 to 30 percent of the Alums from all eight colleges chose English, and 10 to 38 percent selected History. Carleton, Earlham, and Macalester Alums selected the widest range of majors. Over 50 percent of Denison and of Kalamazoo Alums chose either English or History for their undergraduate field. Lawrence Alums were strongly attracted to Music and Anthropology while Art History was popular among Swarthmore Alums. The top three choices of Grinnell Alums were spread evenly among English, History, and Russian.

There is strong similarity between these findings on majors and those of other studies of LIS professionals. For example, White and Macklin's (1970) study of 3,516 LIS master's students finds 41 percent majored in a Social/Behavioral Sciences field, 38 percent in Languages and Literature, and 7 percent in the Sciences with the remaining 14 percent in a diverse set of fields. And a 1989 study by Heim and Moen of 3,484 LIS master's students finds 43 percent majored in the Social/Behavioral Sciences, 39 percent in Languages and Literature and the Fine and Performing Arts, and 7 percent in Sciences with 11 percent in other fields. English and History were particularly popular with White and Macklin's (1970) respondents: 28 percent and 17 percent respectively. The same is true for those in the Heim and Moen (1989) study: 19 percent chose English and 11 percent selected History for their undergraduate major. The 1992 ACRL study of over 2,000 American Library Association and Special Library Association members found that Language/Literature, History, and Education were the most common undergraduate majors (Scherdin 1994a).

Minors and Concentrations

Within American higher education, whereas the major is required for graduation, declared minor areas of study and course work may or may not be. "Minors" typically require fewer courses than majors, and their requirements are generally set by the departments offering them. Through the major-minor combination, students may explore a discipline in depth or bring together two or more related disciplinary fields. In many cases, the courses required in a minor are a subset of those in the same major. In other cases, minors are offered where there are not enough existent courses or faculty to develop a major (e.g., instead of a Latino studies major there may be a Latino studies minor).

"Concentrations" may be just as structured with prescribed courses as majors or minors. Or, they may represent a student-driven desire to focus on an issue, a theme, or perhaps an intellectual area that is not otherwise provided for by the college's curriculum. They may be taken along with a major, or they may take the place of a major, or they may subsequently develop into a major. As Grinnell's Dean of the College James Swartz says, "Students need to do a major and they can do a concentration in addition to a major," while at Macalester, students

> can do what is called an IDIM: Individually designed interdisciplinary major. So a student can sit down with an advisor and put together a program of study tailored to them. It has to be approved by a faculty committee that looks at those. And

> they're tough. You have to really put together a rationale on why you can't accomplish what you want to accomplish in a regular major here. (Hornbach)

Dean Hornbach goes on to note what can happen as a result: "What we have found, interestingly, is that over the years students have done these IDIMs and from those have developed interdisciplinary majors."

The Kalamazoo website stresses that

> minors and concentrations enable students to supplement a major with directed study of another realm of interest and, in the process, lend more coherence to course selections satisfying Areas of Study and other general education requirements. All but two disciplines offering a major also offer a minor, and seven concentrations are offered: African Studies, American Studies, Biochemistry-Molecular Biology, Classical Studies, Environmental Studies, Public Policy and Urban Affairs, and Women's Studies.

Carleton and Grinnell do not have minors, but each offers interdisciplinary concentrations. For example, one of Carleton's is "a concentration in cross-cultural studies that brings together international students and American students who have cross-cultural experience. They explore global issues and problems in a comparative, collaborative framework" (website, see Bibliography). At Grinnell there are concentrations in Global Development Studies, Gender and Women's Studies, and Technology Studies. Grinnell also has area study concentrations focusing on Latin America, East Asia, Western Europe, and East Europe and Russia (Swartz interview). At Denison, which has both minors and concentrations, the latter are offered in Geophysics, Latin American and Caribbean Studies, Neuroscience, and Queer Studies (website, see Bibliography).

Earlham, Kalamazoo, Lawrence, and Swarthmore, which did not have minors during most of the 39-year period covered by the 1962-2000 Alums, have gradually developed them. Assistant Provost Anne Dueweke (Kalamazoo) says that "when I was here in the '80s [as an undergraduate] there were concentrations. The students began to demand minors. Faculty thought that if we do minors, maybe [students] won't double major so much. And the students are obsessed with credentials. They make their lives harder than they need to be. And even students say 'I'm a double major in this with a minor or concentration in . . . ,' and I just want to go 'don't do that.' The minors were introduced in the early '90s."[12]

Swarthmore's Dean Gross concurs, explaining that

> we used to have what were called "concentrations"; now they're called "interdisciplinary minors." We did have interdisciplinary concentrations for many years: black studies, Latin American studies, women's studies, interpretation

---

[12]Several administrators noted a recent increase in the frequency of double majors. At Grinnell, for example, "it's gone from a relatively rare thing to 60-70 students a year—that's about 20 percent of our graduating class" (Swartz).

> theory, [and] three or four others. There was a big push by students for something called minors. They liked the security of that. So the faculty compromised with them and said, "OK, you can have minors but you can only do 1 major and 2 minors or 2 majors and no minors." The faculty was worried that students were just trying to polish their resume by doing too many different things and not having enough time to do a major in breadth.

Provost Clark of Earlham elaborates on why students pushed for minors over concentrations:

> Students and parents wanted the college to set minors—easier to explain to others (employers, peers, etc.). Students wanted certification for their work. [They] are looking for an institutional certification of their gifts and interests . . . Having it on your record is saying something about your person—at least that is the way [students] look at it. And that is why I stopped fighting students and their parents about this. *They* typically think it is way more important than any of *us* do . . . But they are relating it to a sense of self, a sense of competence, a sense of confidence that what they are interested in and what they are learning to do is important—at least important enough to be named.

When the Alums were asked to indicate their undergraduate minor, a majority from each of the colleges and cohorts pointed out that during their undergraduate years these liberal arts institutions uniformly had concentrations rather than minors (Q.I-3). Several of the colleges shifted from concentrations to minors in the mid- to late-1980s or in the 1990s, and many have always allowed students to take both a major and a concentration.

In answering the question on minors, many of the Alums who had concentrations listed them, adding "I took enough courses in . . . for a minor." Responses regarding the minor or concentration produced these findings: Overall, 37 single field minors or concentrations were noted by the Alums. The greatest number were in English (11 percent) followed by Education, French, and History (each at 9 percent), and then German (8 percent). If the fields are grouped into the same broad disciplinary areas as are used to describe their undergraduate majors, then minors or concentrations exhibit the same rank-order as the majors: Social/Behavioral Sciences (46 percent), followed by Languages and Literatures (38 percent), and then the Fine and Performing Arts (8 percent) and the Sciences (8 percent). The largest shift between choice of major and of minor is that languages were more frequently chosen as a minor than a major field of study. Also of interest: Education, which garners only 1`percent as a choice for the major, was selected by 9 percent of the Alums for their minor or concentration.

Thirty Alums alluded to the broad nature of concentrations by noting on the questionnaire that they could only indicate the multiple fields their concentrations involved. Most covered two fields, such as Art/French and English/Political Science; two particularly disparate ones are Russian/Mathematics (Macalester '62; school) and Physics/Sociology

(Swarthmore '81; academic).[13] There were also two three-field concentrations, both from Carleton: Education/Geography/Russian Studies ('71; school), and Science/Technology/Public Policy ('76; school). More than 60 percent of the concentrations combined fields from the Social/Behavioral Sciences and Languages and Literatures. Of the two (or three) field concentrations, 46 percent include a language.

Community Service and Service-Learning

Surely some wise person must have said, "Students cannot live by academics alone"! The colleges have a wide array of activities that are either quasi-connected with their academic programs or totally separate from those programs. Most of the colleges indicate they have between 50 and 100 student organizations that fall under the extracurricular description. Common quasi-academic, but nonclassroom, activities include service-learning projects and independent projects that are begun as part of course work but which continue after completion of the course. Typical nonacademic organizations include student government, religious groups, athletics, lecture series, a broad array of arts (e.g., theater, music, exhibitions, each to attend or participate in), social action clubs, student literary magazines, and college radio stations. There are also organizations that have a special place on some of the campuses; on its "Fast Facts" web page, Carleton includes the statistic that students own 1.9 Frisbees per capita, and on another page points out that in 2003-04 the women's Ultimate Frisbee team finished second in the nation.

According to Altbach (1993), students use such organizations and activities to develop their own peer cultures. In so doing, they have opportunities to adopt the colleges' values and expectations or to contrast them with values and expectations of their own. In other words, students learn by being involved (Astin 1985). Although Pascarella and Terenzini (1991, 624) find no consistent evidence "that extracurricular accomplishment has an independent influence on job status, career mobility, or earnings," it does seem to have a positive influence on leadership. From their data, it can also be inferred that involvement in such activities today would be beneficial in team-based work environments.

Using the Farber and Bingham 1991 study's list of extracurricular activities, the Alums were asked to checkmark those in which they had been involved as undergraduates, and then to further describe the activities (Q.I-4). Table 2 indicates, by college, the Alums' experiences. *Social Services* includes social work and activities such as work with the ill or disabled, tutoring, and helping the underprivileged. *Other* includes a myriad of activities from one-time events (e.g., May Day celebrations) to organizational activities (e.g., campus newspaper, campus and national groups, religious organizations, fraternities and sororities,) to paid work and work study. Some Alums also consider study abroad extracurricular. Campus organizations include student clubs and committees, and Alums across all the colleges indicated an involvement in them. National organizations include those such as the Sierra Club and national political party

---

[13]Throughout this study, Alums who are being quoted are identified by their college, then by cohort beginning year, then by type of library with which they are associated: academic, public, school, or special.

Table 2: Extracurricular Activities While at College (by College)

Extracurricular Activity	Avg. (%)	College (%)							
		C	D	E	G	K	L	M	S
Artistic (music, drama, etc.)	27	28	24	30	29	26	33	20	27
Athletics	15	23	14	13	5	13	9	15	19
Politics (student govt., etc.)	10	10	6	9	14	6	6	16	14
Radio/Film, etc.	8	8	6	8	5	11	7	10	5
Social Services	15	14	22	11	24	15	13	17	14
"Other"	19	13	26	18	24	21	26	19	16
No activities	6	5	2	11	0	8	6	3	4

membership. Alums from all eight colleges noted "paid work" as an extracurricular activity for them.

If the choices are ranked by percentage of CALS participants involved, then those from seven of the eight colleges choose *Artistic* for the category of greatest engagement. Denison Alums' top ranking of *Other* is due primarily to the existence for a time of campus fraternities. *Artistic (music, drama, etc.)* includes either attendance at such events or some form of active participation in the events. For all the Alums, after *Artistic* and *Other* come *Athletics* (as attendee or as participant), *Social Services* and *Politics*, then *Radio/Film* and *No Activities*. Only 6 percent of Alums did not engage in any extracurricular activities while in college.

If the choices are analyzed by cohort instead of by college, the most popular activity is *Artistic* across all eight cohorts (Q.I-4; table 3).[14] After that, the cohorts differ: The 1962-70, 1976-90, and 1996-2000 cohorts were those most involved in activities associated with the *Other* category—notably, organizations of various kinds, paid work, and study abroad; the 1971-75 and 1991-96 cohorts placed greater emphasis on *Social Services*. Next, a large number of Alums from the 1962-65, 1971-75, and 1981-95 cohorts were active in *Athletics*, although the 1962-65 cohort also favored *Politics* and a large number of the 1986-90 cohort cited *Social Services*.

The colleges also differ in terms of the kind of *Other* activity in which the Alums engaged. The greatest number of Carleton and Denison Alums who marked this category described individual activities (defined as one-on-one involvements, such as being a buddy to a nursing home resident), and fairly heavily involvement in religious and church-related activities. Grinnell Alums singled out strong connections with K-12 schools. Earlham Alums focused on several one-time events, the major one being the annual May Day celebration. The Greek system engaged Alums from some of the classes at Denison, Lawrence, and Kalamazoo. Alums from

---

[14]Recall that due to 1962 being the initial class included in this study, the first cohort (1962-65) contains four years; the rest contain five years.

Table 3: Extracurricular Activities While at College (by Cohort)

Extracurricular Activity	Avg. (%)	Cohort (%) 62-	66-	71-	76-	81-	86-	91-	96-
Artistic (music, drama, etc.)	27	31	22	27	30	28	31	26	37
Athletics	15	12	14	16	15	16	13	18	21
Politics (student govt., etc.)	10	12	14	10	6	9	5	10	0
Radio/Film, etc.	8	3	7	8	9	13	12	7	5
Social Services	15	11	15	17	17	6	13	22	11
"Other"	19	20	21	14	20	24	21	16	21
None	6	10	9	7	4	4	5	1	5

five of the eight colleges invested heavily enough in paid work to make it their third most frequent *Other* activity.

There are some differences by cohort. The 1962-70 Alums were directly affected by the Vietnam War, and several of them listed "anti-war demonstrations" as extracurricular activities within *Social Services* or *Other*. There is some indication that tutoring was more popular in the 1991-2000 period than for earlier cohorts. However, general volunteer work in the larger community around the college is found consistently across all colleges and class years.

Service

In interviews with the college administrators, sentiment toward service to and within one's broader community is a constant refrain. One way in which it is exhibited is through a large and consistent involvement in the *Social Services* and *Other* categories by respondents from all eight colleges and classes. These two categories included opportunities for Alums to work with others, either on an individual, one-to-one basis or as part of a group. Going deeper into their responses, it is clear that the majority of activity-clusters included some form of community service or, among the 1990-2000 classes, service-learning. Rhoads (1998, 279) and others point out that "over recent years there has been an incredible growth in attention paid to community service and service learning." For these Alums, it appears that such "attention" has existed to some degree at their colleges since at least 1962.

While community service is "understood as a student-initiated, extracurricular activity" (Battistoni 1998, vii), it is different from service-learning. In the seventeenth and eighteenth centuries, "community service" meant service to one's church and the civic community. In the nineteenth century, "connections between campus, community, and service remain central in American higher education, symbolized particularly in the founding of Phillips Brooks House at Harvard in 1894 (the nation's oldest student community service organization) and in the links between the University of Chicago and the settlement house movement (specifically, Hull House)" (Battistoni 1998, vii). Over the 1962-2000 period covered by this study, some forms of student community service were consistently present as an extracurricular activity, such as tutoring off-campus in K-12 schools or in after-school settings. Others, such as literacy projects, reflect more recent areas of student interest.

According to Putnam (2000), whereas nationally nearly half of all Americans participated in community endeavors in the 1960s, by the 1990s the number had dropped to less than one-quarter. Putnam (2000, 132) finds that "while individualized acts of benevolence, such as reading to a shut-in, have resisted the nationwide decline in civic involvement, community projects that require collective effort, such as refurbishing a neighborhood park, have not." From the 1960s to the end of the twentieth century, there was a national trend toward "materialism, individualism, and competitiveness" (Astin 1993, 4, quoted in Speck 2001; Grusec et al. 2002; Taylor 1991). For liberal arts colleges, student service involvement varied during this period but was always present. In contrast to the substantiated and consistent interest these liberal arts college graduates demonstrated in various forms of service, a mid-1960s survey of seniors at Berkeley and Stanford reports that only 8-10 percent indicated they were "frequently" involved in off-campus service activities such as working with the unemployed or with minority groups (Sanford 1966, 26). In a 1984 study, the Carnegie Foundation finds that "even with athletics and all of the student-sponsored projects, almost two out of five of today's undergraduates still say they do *not* feel a sense of community at their institution" (Boyer 1987; emphasis in original). Again, in contrast, at liberal arts colleges four out of five felt that they were part of a community. Later in his commentary, Boyer (1987, 218) goes on to "recommend that every student complete a service project." Increasingly, the tool used for accomplishing this is "service-learning" (Rhoads 1998).

Service-Learning

Service-learning, which is different from volunteer community service, is now part of the curriculum in many middle schools, high schools, colleges and universities.[15] A component within the structure of an academic course, it includes off-campus projects or work based in a nonacademic community; it seeks to enhance classroom learning with on-site learning (Olsen 1997; Battistoni 1998; Speck 2001). This combination of community work with classroom instruction helps "prepare students to participate in public life, thus integrating theory and practice . . . The main intention of service-learning [is] to ensure that academic study is integrated with the larger public life" (Speck 2001, 4). Although elements of it existed previously within the parameters of community service, service-learning as a formal part of the curriculum of many colleges "has become the pedagogy of the 1990s" (Hironimus-Wendt and Lovell-Troy 1999, 360). An ERIC search on the term "service-learning" (all material formats) for 1990-2000 finds a low of three matches in 1991 and a high of 119 in 1998. Hironimus-Wendt and Lovell-Troy (1999, 361) state that three basic components of a service-learning program are

---

[15]A report on Minnesota's 1997-99 high school classes finds that "virtually all students participated in at least one work- or service-based learning experience" (*The Minnesota High School Follow-Up Survey*, 2000).

> (1) Students are either required or offered the opportunity to participate in supplemental or "co-curricular" service-related activities; (2) the instructors deliberately choose participating sites so as to maximize the likelihood that students will encounter community members actively immersed in issues related directly to the course content; and (3) students must intentionally "reflect on" or analyze their service-related observations and experiences.

Whether as special projects, internships, or other formats, in its explicit connection of service-in-the-community to academics, service-learning uses "a community or public service experience to enhance the meaning and impact of traditional course content" (Astin 1997, 9).

Not all of the eight colleges have strong service-learning programs, but all have very strong volunteer programs. The combination can run deep. Dean Hornbach notes that about 80 percent of Macalester's students do volunteer work, and that

> something like 70 percent of [graduates] have had a class that has had a service learning component or has had an internship component with it. Our American Studies program, for example, has a required civic engagement component. Our environmental studies program has a required internship component. We have a fairly large internship office that is for both academic and co-curricular internships. So all kinds of things. It's just a part of the way students live their lives here, both in terms of volunteerism and service learning. And we're doing more with the faculty with the service learning component, and in terms of internships. The president this year at the opening faculty meeting challenged every department to once again sit back and "evaluate what you're doing in your department and what you can do to utilize our urban environment to a better extent." (Hornbach interview, see Bibliography)

Kalamazoo Assistant Provost Dueweke comments that

> our students love the service-learning courses. In addition to service-learning we have a lot of students volunteering in the community. The students are initiating projects in the community, and we're seeing that [those are] being sustained by successive generations of students. We have a very close partnership with the K-6 elementary school just a couple of blocks north. It's a relatively poor district, high percentage of minority students, and we have literally hundreds of students working over at the Woodward school at any given time—either as volunteers, [or] they can do their work study there, [or] through service learning courses. So the part about serving in your community and also learning from that has really grown. A group of faculty started it informally in the late 1990s, and one of our trustees made a gift to endow a full-time director position and faculty stipends to develop service learning courses, and student stipends for service learning projects. Since then, it's really taken off. (Dueweke interview, see Bibliography)

At Swarthmore, the Eugene M. Lang Center for Civic and Social Responsibility "offers workshops and special programs to prepare students for work in communities as well as to provide opportunities for reflection on those experiences, especially in relation to their academic programs and to their plans for civic engagement after graduation. Center staff also work with members of the faculty who wish to include community-based learning in their courses and seminars" (Swarthmore website, see Bibliography). There is also an annual scholarship for a first-year student that includes a summer internship and funds a service project. In considering service-learning, Swarthmore Dean Gross adds that "our primary focus is not just serving sandwiches to the homeless but understanding the dynamics of homelessness and how the society is structured to permit that. That is where the service-learning piece comes in: we want students to be literate about social structures and dynamics so that they can change some of the causes" (interview).

In addition to service-learning courses, there is a significant number of community-volunteer examples. The Lawrence website provides the following data:

> Forty percent of Lawrence students engage in voluntary service and have been honored for their efforts on behalf of regional and community groups. In recent years, Lawrence students have established a Habitat for Humanity chapter, implemented an annual Relay for Life in support of cancer research, and designed a mentoring program with Big Brothers/Big Sisters and the Boys & Girls Club of the Fox Valley.[16]
>
> Each year Lawrence athletes, who represent 13 men's and ten women's sports, volunteer their time to organize and facilitate sports training camps for local youth.
>
> Through Summer Volunteer Opportunity Grants, Lawrence students are able to devote their energies and talents to worthy volunteer activities. Recent grantees have spent their summers assisting the Mead House for Troubled Youth and Joshua House, a receiving home for abused and neglected children.
>
> One of Lawrence's longest-standing volunteer programs, LARY (Lawrence Assistance Reaching Youth), encourages students to serve as mentors for at-risk elementary and middle school students in the Appleton area. (See Bibliography)

The Macalester website states that "about 50 percent of students each semester volunteer with shelters, tutoring programs, Habitat for Humanity, human-service, environmental and arts organizations" (see Bibliography). At Earlham, during the 2002-03 academic year, "students contributed 34,500 hours of community service" (Earlham website, see Bibliography).

On the subject of student community service, Associate Provost Boone at Denison remarks that

---

[16]Refers to the Fox River, along which Appleton and neighboring towns are located.

> a really big value that we really push hard is service. Our mission statement starts off by saying "Our purpose is to inspire and educate our students to become autonomous thinkers, discerning moral agents, and active citizens of a democratic society." . . . Service [is] understood as being service to the community, belonging to the community, and having some responsibility toward them. And this is preparation for students when they graduate, to continue that activity—not to cut it off after they've left Denison but to continue it in the form of community activities and civic engagement . . . The biggest organization on campus by far is the Denison Community Association (DCA). There are more students who put in more hours on that than any other single organization . . . [DCA] becomes an expectation when students come here. There are tens of thousands of hours put into this. It's right at the forefront at what we do, and it's a whole office with vans and cars and things that ferry out students back and forth to do service mainly in this county, and in some of the poorer parts of this county as well. So the whole notion of community responsibility is a huge value. (Boone interview, see Bibliography)

Both Dean Murray (Lawrence) and Dean Hornbach (Macalester) noted that their colleges participate in "Into the Streets." A part of freshman orientation week, it engages incoming students in a range of activities that take place in the community surrounding the college. Lawrence "faculty, staff and students go out and do various volunteer projects in town for a specific afternoon," and at Macalester "a couple of first year classes did voter registration" (interviews; see Bibliography). At Grinnell, Dean Swartz emphasized that service to the community

> is valued among [students], it's valued by the institution. We also have traditionally had, and have put more emphasis on in the past number of years, service opportunities post-graduation. So Grinnell is one of the leading institutions in placing individuals in the Peace Corps. We've been very active with Teach for America. We have a number of programs that we fund internally that are similar to that kind of activity internationally—where we pay a couple of students to go teach English at a middle school in China, to teach in Nepal, to teach in South Africa. So there is an array of things that we do to try to assist with students' [service interests]. (Swartz interview; see Bibliography)

In *Bowling Alone: The Collapse and Revival of American Community*, Putnam (2000, 133) concludes a chapter on "Altruism, Volunteering, and Philanthropy" by saying that there is an increasing amount of evidence that "suggests that young Americans in the 1990s displayed a commitment to volunteerism without parallel among their immediate predecessors." For both the CALS Alums and their colleges, volunteerism and other kinds of service were consistent elements in their sense of collegiate engagement.

Table 4: Most Important Reasons for Getting an Undergraduate Education

Reasons (Ranked)	CALS Alums	Morrison
Develop one's critical faculties/appreciation of ideas	1	1
Develop one's knowledge of, and interest in, community and world problems	2	2
Develop one's ability to get along with different kinds of people	3	6
Develop special competence in a particular academic discipline	4	3
Help develop one's moral capacities, ethical standards and values	5	5
Provide vocational or preprofessional training	6	4
Other	7	7

IV. The Value of an Undergraduate Education

In his 1958-59 study of 707 academic librarians, Morrison (1969) presented his participants with a list of quality-based statements on the value of an undergraduate education. Seven of his eight questions were used in the present study in order to compare the Alums with his respondents, who were from both liberal arts colleges and public universities (Q.I-6). Morrison's characterizations of the reasons for obtaining an undergraduate education are as follows:

- To provide vocational or preprofessional training
- To develop skills and techniques directly applicable to one's future career
- To develop one's ability to get along with different kinds of people
- To develop one's critical faculties and appreciation for ideas
- To develop special competence in a particular academic discipline
- To develop one's knowledge of, and interest in, community and world problems
- To help develop one's moral capacities, ethical standards and values
- Preparation for marriage and family [not used in this study]
- Other (specify)

Whereas Morrison's participants were asked to select only two of the statements to represent what they thought should be the most important reasons for obtaining an undergraduate education, respondents in the present study could mark as many of the statements as they felt were appropriate, and they typically selected three or four. The Alums were also asked to indicate those areas in which their undergraduate college was "Particularly Strong," and those in which they felt their college was "Deficient." Table 4 gives the Alums' preferences in the "Most Important" category, along with the ranking of Morrison's respondents.

Table 5: Reasons for Obtaining an Undergraduate Education (by College)

Reasons (Ranked)	Avg (%)	Colleges (%)							
		C	D	E	G	K	L	M	S
1 - Develop one's critical faculties/appreciation of ideas	26	27	27	25	28	27	28	26	26
2 - Develop one's knowledge of, and interest in, community/world problems	19	17	17	19	24	18	17	23	21
3 - Develop one's ability to get along with different kinds of people	15	16	14	15	24	15	14	15	15
4 - Develop special competence in a particular academic discipline	15	15	18	15	10	14	18	13	15
5 - Help develop one's moral capacities, ethical standards and values	15	16	13	17	3	14	13	14	15
6 - Provide vocational or preprofessional training	7	4	7	6	0	9	9	8	4
7 - Other	3	5	4	2	10	3	8	2	4

Both the CALS Alums and Morrison's respondents agree that knowledge development is the most important reason for an undergraduate education. *Developing one's critical faculties* and *Developing one's knowledge of, and interest in, community and world problems* were chosen by the greatest number of respondents in both studies. As can be seen in tables 5 and 6, this finding is consistent across all eight CALS colleges and cohorts. It is clear that knowledge has been highly sought after by those who went into the LIS field from the 1950s through 2000. The item of greatest difference between Morrison's respondents and those in this study is *Developing one's ability to get along with different kinds of people.* Where the CALS Alums rank this third in importance, Morrison's librarians place it sixth of the seven items.

The perceived importance of an undergraduate education is one of the few questions asked in this study where distinctions can be seen between viewing responses by college and by cohort (Q.I-6A). Table 5 shows that, by college, Swarthmore Alums most closely mirror the overall percentage ordering of the seven statements. Denison and Lawrence Alums placed *Developing special competence in an academic discipline* second, followed by the "community/world problems" choice. The remaining six colleges placed *Developing one's knowledge of, and interest in, community and world problems* second. Grinnell Alums felt as strongly about the importance of *Developing one's ability to get along with different kinds of people* as they did about *One's knowledge of, and interest in, community and world problems.*

Across both college and cohort, the greatest number of Alums chose *Developing one's critical faculties and appreciation for ideas* as the most important reason for an undergraduate education (tables 5 and 6). Respondents from six of the eight colleges, and from all the cohorts,

Table 6: Reasons for Obtaining an Undergraduate Education (by Cohort)

Reasons (Ranked)	Avg (%)	Cohort (%) 62-	66-	71-	76-	81-	86-	91-	96-
1 - Develop one's critical faculties/appreciation of ideas	26	26	25	27	27	29	28	27	21
2 - Develop one's knowledge of, and interest in, community/world problems	19	20	19	20	17	18	21	16	18
3 - Develop one's ability to get along with different kinds of people	15	16	15	14	17	16	14	16	16
4 - Develop special competence in a particular academic discipline	15	15	16	16	15	16	12	14	16
5 - Help develop one's moral capacities, ethical standards and values	15	15	15	15	15	14	14	13	16
6 - Provide vocational or preprofessional training	7	5	7	5	8	4	5	10	11
7 - Other	3	3	3	3	2	3	5	5	3

placed *Developing one's knowledge of, and interest in, community and world problems* second on their list.

The 1976-80 and 1991-96 cohorts considered *Developing one's ability to get along with different kinds of people* as important as having an interest in community and world problems. And only the 1991-2000 cohorts gave *Providing vocational or preprofessional training* double-digit support, as opposed to the other six cohorts and all eight of the colleges. The importance the two most recent cohorts give to vocational or preprofessional training may suggest that they hold a stronger sense of connection than the other cohorts do, to their undergraduate institution as a vehicle for learning skills that they now find are needed in the workplace.

The Colleges' Strengths

When asked to select from these important reasons the ones in which their college displayed particular strength, the Alums generally marked three of the seven statements (Q.I-6B). All eight colleges were ranked by the Alums as strongest in *Developing one's critical faculties* . . . , and in general, they all see their particular college as placing more emphasis on academic competence than on the social concern issues. Table 7 shows how the Alums differently rank their college's strengths. On the question of "vocational or preprofessional training," only Earlham Alums felt the college placed particular importance on this area, with comments stressing the preprofessional rather than the vocational aspect. Alums from the other college indicated that they did not expect their college to provide such training and, therefore, did not see it as relevant when identifying strengths. In contrast to the Alums from the other

Table 7: Alums' Ranking of College "Strengths" (Rank)

Reasons	Avg.	Colleges							
		C	D	E	G	K	L	M	S
Develop one's critical faculties/appreciation of ideas	1	1	1	1	1	1	1	1	1
Develop one's knowledge of, and interest in, community/world problems	2	3	3	2	2	2	4	2	2
Help develop one's moral capacities, ethical standards and values	3	2	4	3	6	5	3	4	3
Develop special competence in a particular academic discipline	3	2	2	5	4	4	2	5	3
Develop one's ability to get along with different kinds of people	5	4	5	4	3	3	5	3	4
Provide vocational or preprofessional training	6	6	6	3	7	6	6	6	6
Other	7	5	7	6	5	7	7	7	5

colleges, those from Lawrence did not see the college as being particularly strong in *Developing one's knowledge of, and interest in, community and world problems.* They see Lawrence's strength, instead, as lying in *Developing student competence in an academic discipline.*

The Colleges' Deficiencies

Only a few Alums indicated that their college might be deficient in one or more of the seven areas (Q.I-6C). The statement garnering the largest choice across college and cohort was *Providing vocational or preprofessional training*—noted by 65 percent of the Alums who responded to this question. Many indicated that they do not expect their college to have this as a goal, and that ipso facto that *might* mean it could be considered a deficiency. Grinnell and Earlham Alums expressed the least dissatisfaction with their colleges. A few Lawrence and Macalester Alums felt their colleges could do more in every area. However, in general, being deficient was just not something the Alums associated with their undergraduate institutions.

Other Reasons for Getting an Undergraduate Education

The seventh choice within each topic was *Other*, and a small number of Alums made comments here. The focus was on the individual, and these comments illustrate the Alums' points:

- Maturity: "Learn life skills, how to be independent, handle yourself as an adult" (Earlham '86; special librarian); "Mature in a structured environment" (Kalamazoo '91; special)
- Self: "Help develop a sense of self as a free agent" (Swarthmore '91; public); "Develop social ties and friendship" (Grinnell '66; school)

Values: Institutional, Personal, and Professional

In their interviews, the college administrators were asked what they believe are the values that their college holds—and the values that their incoming and their graduating students hold. For some administrators, this provided an opportunity to muse on what he or she saw as "the big values"; for others, values were described in terms of the everyday life at the college or as part of their college's heritage.

Dean Swartz, for instance, drew upon collegiate history. He believes that Grinnell values

> a strong sense of community, of interactions between students and faculty members, respect, and there has been since the founding of the college a strong sense of commitment to social justice. The college was founded in the 1840s by a band of abolitionists and Grinnell was a very important place in the Social Gospel movement, and I think a sense of social activism and social justice has been with the college for a long period of time. In that way there are a lot of parallels with Earlham, out of a different tradition, but a fair number of parallels. And I think that kind of thing isn't unusual among Midwestern liberal arts colleges founded in the mid-1800s. There are a bunch of us; we all have our distinctive identities but fairly similar kinds of value sets. (Swartz interview, see Bibliography)

Some of that similarity of value sets has already been seen through our perusal of the colleges' mission statements. Two deans spoke directly to mission in reflecting on institutional and student values. Dean Hornbach talked about the Macalester mission statement as a thread that runs throughout the college and that reflects its values

> Macalester has a pretty tight mission statement in our college catalog and then a longer statement of purpose and beliefs. And they actually are lived out here. They aren't just sitting in the catalog. I think you could ask just about anyone on campus—faculty, staff, students—what the values of Macalester are, and they would pretty much recite the mission statement about "academic excellence with a special emphasis on internationalism, multiculturalism, and service to society" . . . It's lived out in our curriculum, in our co-curricular activities and programs, and really guides just about everything we do. (Hornbach interview, see Bibliography)

He noted that in an alumni survey done around 2000, between 90 and 98 percent of respondents found excellence, internationalism, multiculturalism, and service to society either "somewhat" or "very" important to both the past and the future of the college. "Everybody knew the mission of the institution, and this was a survey of all alumni. And there was very little difference among the decades in their understanding of Macalester's mission."

Dean Gross (Swarthmore), also reflected his college's mission statement when he said:

> I think the two primary values of Swarthmore are intellectual excellence and social responsibility. And I would say that in looking for prospective students one of the things we look for is a LOL: love of learning. A passion for inquiry that transcends grades. How do we find that? Probably from what students write [in] essays and what their teachers write in their recommendations but it doesn't appear in their transcript or test scores. But there really is a marked difference in satisfaction between students who come with that and students who don't. The social responsibility piece I think is also part of our image. Maybe a piece of the Quaker heritage—obviously less intense than Earlham, but nevertheless part of our history. And many—not all—are attracted by that. I think many of the [students] leave here with either an active or an implicit acceptance of [social responsibility]. (Gross interview, see Bibliography)

Indeed, Len Clark, Earlham College Provost, spoke from the point of the college's Quaker perspective in describing the values of both the college and its students:

> I think Earlham values can be summarized from George Fox's saying, "Friends should walk cheerfully over the earth, answering that of God in everyone." I don't think the fundamental concept there is unique to Quakers . . . so I ask myself "if you were creating a college and trying to make it help people do that—'walk cheerfully over the earth, answering that of God in everyone'—what would be the main features of the distinctive education that a college would provide?" One of them is that education would have to be cooperative. It would have to be learning from and with other people. Because the notion of answering that of God means that fundamental to your experience should be engagement, listening, listening enough to know what is coming from the other person, and then answering it . . . Earlham has been a deeply cooperative place for as long as I've known it . . . A second feature would be a profoundly international education. It's "over the earth" in answering that of God in everyone and Quakers have long had that kind of world mission outlook. Not to go and convert people, but to know and engage with them, to minister to them, to listen, to try to understand—and Earlham has a remarkable array of programs. A third thing I think you would do in building a college like that is to make it service-oriented. I think that if you emphasize "answering" in George Fox's phrase you get a sense of that. Quakers are—if you think about diversity—not just going to be tolerant, and they're not just going to celebrate diversity—they're going to engage with it, they're going to answer. (Clark interview, see Bibliography)

Earlham is a strongly academic, faith-based community of learners (Clark interview; Kuh 1993; Pope 1996). As Provost Clark indicated in Pope (1996, 161): "From the first day their [i.e., the students'] responsibility to learn from and with other students is stressed. That is a Quaker tenet and part of the mission of the college. It takes new students by surprise but then liberates them." Thus, for students, "listening and answering" starts

> with the first year, where you get intense small class experience with students engaging with a text trying to discern the voice of the author. Also trying to listen hard at how other people are coming at that text and learning from that. And then evaluating one another's work and helping one another understand how to make it better. Students don't automatically come here equipped with those kinds of values. They may like the idea of cooperation but they don't know how to do it, most of them—and in fact America does not reinforce cooperative education in that sense. It emphasizes competition. I think that this learning from and with others is fundamental to [Earlham]. And it comes from its Quaker values. (Clark interview, see Bibliography)

Keith Boone, Associate Provost at Denison, holds the same view as Clark that students come in with a certain set of values: "We think they do, but we think there is a lot of room for shaping." One of the fundamental values he identifies for Denison is diversity:

> There is intellectual diversity because we think that real learning takes place when your assumptions are challenged. And then there is the diversity component of being able to work with others—to understand others. We think that those two are symbiotic with each other—they go hand in hand . . . And it all comes from our mission statement that "we have a firm belief in human dignity and compassion unlimited by cultural, racial, sexual, religious, or economic barriers." So I would say that is one of the big values that we think we try our darnedest through our courses and all the other value arenas [to accomplish]—we try and we think we bring students a long way. Because I think these are formative years. Most of our students, because they are self-selected from a prospective pool, come here with some sense of that. But I think we hammer it home, again on the intellectual front, the critical analysis front, the extrinsic educational value of being exposed to a diversity perspective, and on the front of the way we treat other human beings . . . I would say that diversity is a cardinal value in terms of what we want to accomplish . . . Another huge value is honesty and integrity. We are really strong on that; we're strict. We teach it to our students formally in the first class that they have . . . I think the other really big value that we really push hard is service. Our mission statement starts off by saying "Our purpose is to inspire and educate our students to become autonomous thinkers, discerning moral agents, and active citizens of a democratic society." In terms of service, through our student organizations, we have service understood as being service to

> the community, belonging to the community, and having some responsibility toward them. (Boone interview, see Bibliography)

Boone believes that by the end of their undergraduate years, Denison students have made "big strides" in areas like critical thinking, community service responsibility, and diversity. He feels those strides have come from both formal programs and informally—"in living and emphasizing everyday the relationships between students and faculty and through the informal channels of projecting what your values are."

Carleton's Associate Dean of the College Bierman also points to integrity as a value. Incoming students, he believes, should value curiosity, a strong work ethic, engagement, and integrity. Upon graduation

> we certainly expect them to be curious, have a work ethic, be engaged, have integrity, [and also] . . . an appreciation of complexity, of difference, of aesthetics, and of leadership . . . Engagement is something students have put a ton of energy into . . . And some of that "something" should be intellectually based, but it may also very well have a strong service component to it. . . . Integrity [refers to] how you go about being engaged in what you are doing—is there integrity to what you're doing?— and a recognition of your place in the world. Appreciation of complexity [refers to] the way that you approach issues and problems . . . Difference means a lot of things [but basically] if you appreciate that difference provides insights then you must appreciate that seeking out difference helps you in life's work . . . Leadership means an expectation that you will help frame questions, that you will help frame strategies for solving those questions, and [for] setting an agenda for the set of organizations that you are a part of. (Bierman interview, see Bibliography)

Kalamazoo Assistant Provost Dueweke points out that

> the college values rigorous academics. That's the most important thing here. The college values, like any liberal arts college, a close relationship between faculty and students, fellowship in learning (which was language used by a president here in the '20s and '30s), a community of learners, engagement in a common endeavor, that kind of thing . . . It's interesting that your study starts in 1962 because 1962 is when we implemented the "K Plan." And the college highly values the K Plan that combines rigorous liberal arts academics with the experiential components with a career development experience, study abroad experience, and senior abroad project . . . The outcomes of the K Plan [are] lifelong learning, career readiness, intercultural understanding, leadership, and social responsibility.

At Lawrence, Dean Murray reflected on the fact that the university attracts prospective students who initially say, " 'Hmm, can't go there, it's just way too liberal' and we have other students who look at Lawrence and say, 'it's way too conservative.' " Yet, after they become students, they find that they and the university have similar values: "The breadth of the liberal arts, and then the depth of study within a major . . . They value the small class-size and the one-on-one experiences that they have by being in a small place." She adds that, "We tend to hear from alums somewhere down the road, saying, 'I didn't realize while I was there what was happening, and how important certain experiences were.' Sometimes they're in a classroom; more often it's in the residence hall or an outside-of-class experience for them." Lawrence seeks to broaden students' values, while at the same time respecting those initial differences.

For these college representatives, institutional and student values meld together. Values they believe the college rests on are to be encouraged and developed in their students. Values commonly identified and emphasized across the colleges focus on rigor in intellectual activity, diversity (both intellectual and respect for others), and social responsibility through service. Each college presses more on one perhaps than on the others. These academic administrators believe students are attracted to their colleges in part because they already are developing an appreciation for such values, and they believe their graduates embody those values.

From this consideration of the colleges, interviews with college administrators, and review of some of the literature about the colleges, at least parts of each one's ethos have become clearer. Carleton is a place that embodies "curiosity and intellectual adventure, an awareness of method and purpose in a variety of fields, and an affinity for quality and integrity wherever they may be found" (*Purpose of the College*). Denison emphasizes active learning through involvement with and service to others. Earlham's ethos includes the Quaker tenets of listening and learning from others, and being part of a community of learners as guides for living. At Grinnell, student self-governance and self-development within a learning community are key, with the college serving as guide. Kalamazoo is defined by the K Plan's integration of individual involvement in a global community, and Lawrence by its emphasis on liberal learning. Macalester embodies social activism set within an international arena, as illustrated by the ritual of having flown the UN flag since that organization was founded (Hornbach interview). And, Swarthmore's ethos shows three threads: the quest for intellectual excellence, a concern for Quaker tradition, and constant self-examination with the life of the mind as the center post (Walton 1986).

The deans and provosts were asked if the view of the value of undergraduate education held by their college has changed over time, especially over the 1960-2000 period. All of them believe there has been very little change in their college's essential educational philosophy, values, and ethos. Some mentioned specific things that illustrate overall constancy or isolated change. As Kalamazoo Assistant Provost Dueweke points out that

> within the components of the education there have been shifts. Study abroad when it started was to improve your language skills, get more cultured. And now study abroad would not be seen that way. It would be to immerse yourself in another culture, learn about another way of life, another way of looking at things. Many now go to third world countries rather than to Europe. But the basic outcome – even though we may use different language—is to be liberally

> educated and to serve your society well and to live a meaningful life. (Dueweke interview, see Bibliography)

Associate Provost Boone notes that at Denison "even back in the mid-'80s we were strongly interested in diversity and we were either the first or one of the first in the country to have a curricular requirement in diversity." The overall commonality and distinctiveness of the eight colleges is well depicted in Dean Hornbach's comments:

> As curricula changed around the country in the '60s, '70s, and to the present, Macalester recognized it could go in one of two paths. It could recommit itself to a basic liberal arts education conceived in the new way of producing citizen leaders by producing liberally educated individuals, or it could have the path of saying, "We're going to make our commitment to more of a vocational way of training people for civic service." Both admirable and wonderful things to do. And the college would have done well to choose either path. The path that the college chose was to reinforce its commitment to the liberal arts in producing well-educated, liberally trained students who could then be the leaders in society in the future. I think that's what we have committed ourselves to. We've worked really hard to provide a very high quality academic experience for our students—one that competes well with the top liberal arts colleges in the country, but one that has these very focused components related to thinking globally with our international perspective, understanding that you can't be a liberally educated person if you are not engaged in looking at issues from all kinds of cultural perspectives—not just a nod to other cultural perspectives, but you have to live those other cultural perspectives in order to actually understand what's going on—and with real service to society. And so a deep commitment to understanding that liberal education is probably the best for preparing students for life in a complex world, but really emphasizing those special components of our mission. (interview, see Bibliography)

Educated Alumni

As part of their interview for this study, the eight college administrators were asked to describe qualities typical of educated alumni of their institutions. Using their responses, let us now imagine that they are meeting together in the same room and are discussing this topic. Their interview comments indicate that educated alumni demonstrate two attributes. One attribute that the administrators quickly describe is specific skills. The other attribute they speak of in more deliberative and thought-provoking terms is beliefs. Both attributes rest upon a foundation composed of the values their college expresses. Here is some of what the eight administrators say in describing educated Alums:[17]

---

[17]Direct quotes are not used, as verb tenses and sentence sequences have been changed to create this "conversation."

Deans Murray (Lawrence) and Swartz (Grinnell): Educated Alums have developed the kinds of skills that we value in a liberal education: communication skills, and critical thinking, and the like. They read and think critically; write very well; speak well—things that serve them no matter what they study down the road, or what field they go into . . . They have a skill-set that they carry with them no matter what they do.

Associate Dean Bierman (Carleton): I would add that educated Alums also

- Critically evaluate evidence (text, numbers, other non-text pieces of evidence)
- Pose clear and important questions
- See, appreciate, and articulate the qualities of beauty and aesthetics
- Develop and implement a strategy when seeking to bring evidence to bear on important questions. That is, they engage the right people to help provide that evidence because they appreciate "difference": they know the situation benefits by engaging others as they develop strategies or bring evidence to bear on problems and issues.

Dean Gross (Swarthmore): We did some focus groups with seniors a couple of months ago. And they did say that they have learned the skills: they can write better than their peers, they can understand stuff, and so on. But they demonstrate more than that. I think they have a stronger sense of social responsibility. They have more curiosity about the world. For many there is a kind of passion for the world, for their careers, for ideas. Our educated Alums are more engaged citizens and people.

Dean Hornbach (Macalester): Our alumni are about as diverse as you can imagine. Certainly we have the students who go out and start businesses or work for large corporations and do a fabulous job and make a lot of money. But these educated Alums also tend to, even in those circumstances, think about what that means and how they can use whatever it is that they've done to enhance society, or to connect back to Macalester and their experience there. So we have a lot of students who go on to work in non-profits and NGOs, as well as graduates who go on to work in business—but both kinds then find ways to give back to society, to others.

Dean Swartz (Grinnell): Educated Alums have a strong sense of community and respect for others. They have a broad, strong sense of social justice; that is, providing the opportunities and encouragement for all to be the best that they can be, to have the opportunity of education, of enough food to eat, of a sort of free and productive and rewarding life.

Dean Murray (Lawrence): Yes, many have come to value community service in both member and leadership roles.

Associate Dean Bierman (Carleton): I also see an inclination to engage issues with courage and integrity—in terms of their workplace, their home life, and their broader political community. And they demonstrate an honesty in conducting these endeavors.

Dean Gross (Swarthmore): It seems that educated alumni use the skills and beliefs that they have fostered during their undergraduate experience to become engaged with the world.

Provost Clark (Earlham): Part of that engagement is demonstrated by Alums who have international understanding (diplomats, scholars, facilitators and leaders of various kinds). And there are those who take a liberal education and run with it—that is, those who directly apply it. There are the peacemakers, and the educators who stress cooperative education—learning from each other. And we nurture a lot of people who go on to do those kinds of things. I am especially proud of those who excel at those things.

Assistant Provost Dueweke (Kalamazoo): I agree that educated Alums have the skills and characteristics to think critically, to learn independently and have a sense of social responsibility. I also see many who demonstrate a passion for lifelong learning. And they have a sense of intercultural understanding and a knowledge of other cultures—not being ethnocentric themselves, but seeing themselves as part of a culture—how they are part of the U.S. culture, and the complexities of working across cultures. Many have gained from the experience of studying in another country or at least away from campus.

Associate Provost Boone (Denison): And I agree that our Alums engage themselves not just in their tasks at hand, but in lifelong education of some kind or another. This helps many of them show accomplishment in their field of work. But I think we would also agree that, from surveys and our own observations, they do not seem to rest on their laurels.

Would You Attend Again?

According to Burton Clark (1970, 251-252):

> No matter how radical their political and religious beliefs, the alumni of a college are likely to be deeply conservative about changing its character. Of all the major groups who must believe in the special nature of a college if it is to become distinctive, the alumni are the best located to hold beliefs enduringly pure, the students come next, then the faculty, then the administration . . . The alumni are, of course, much further removed [from the specific strains encountered in a changing environment]. For them the idea of the college, the warm legend, can be everything.

The CALS Alums were asked, "Would you go to [your undergraduate] college today if you were graduating from high school?" (Q.I-5). Overall, 78 percent said they would indeed attend their same undergraduate college again if they were just now graduating from high school. The lowest percentage was 64 percent at both Denison and Swarthmore; the highest was 88 percent at Earlham, Grinnell, and Macalester. Lawrence, Kalamazoo, and Carleton Alums weighed in at 70-78 percent. Overall, 14 percent said "no" and 8 percent were not sure if they would enroll again. In six of the class cohorts, the range of "yes" responses varies from 70 to 78 percent; 83 percent of the 1981-85 classes said they would re-enroll and a striking 91 percent of the 1991-95 Alums also responded "yes." Looking at this by cohort within college, Alums who said "no" or who were not certain are distributed throughout the 39 years covered by the study. The only exception is the Lawrence classes of 1962-75, a period that accounts for 55 percent of all Lawrence respondents. While 58 percent of these particular Alums say they would attend again, a high of 35 percent say "No," with 8 percent uncertain.

The survey question asked those who said No, "What has changed about the college—or about you?" The areas of commonality from those who commented were

- It is too geographically isolated.
- It is too expensive.
- It has changed too much.
- It was just not a good fit for me.

Alums from six of the eight colleges indicated that their school is isolated. Kalamazoo and Lawrence Alums seemed most concerned about this.[18] However, most Alums associated the isolation not with the college being in an unappealing locale, but with their own individual needs to be in larger cities or further away from home. A few Kalamazoo Alums also were concerned that the college had changed significantly with all the reasons given summed up by one alum, who remarked that it had "lost its uniqueness re: foreign study, career-service, quarter system, [and] religious roots" (Kalamazoo '66; school). Several Lawrence and Kalamazoo Alums indicated that this time around they would at least spend more time comparing the college with other institutions before finally deciding.

There were respondents from all eight colleges who indicated that cost is a major reason they would not attend again. This is frequently explained by comments similar to this one:

> I would *want* to go to Denison just as much, but I think current *costs* would prevent it! Too expensive today! Family *not* wealthy, but not qualifying for aid, either. (Denison '66; public; emphasis in original)

---

[18]On Lawrence's website (see Bibliography), two current students note changes: "Now, with the Performing Arts Center and a new storefront space for the Appleton Art Center, students have more reason to wander down the Avenue instead of staying on campus for their cultural fix" (Class of '03). "The renovations are essential not only to Appleton but also to Lawrence. Kids going off to college are simply not as interested in a school if they feel there isn't anything much offered off campus" (Class of '04).

While Alums from five of the eight schools indicated that "fit" is a problem, those from Denison, Earlham, and Swarthmore felt this most strongly, with comments centering around a lack of connection between the students' personal interests and the atmosphere, structure, or programs of the college. A 1971 Swarthmore graduate exemplifies the kinds of concerns this group of Alums has:

> I was not happy there then. Campus life seems better developed, studio arts are credit courses, community service [is] common—maybe social cliques don't dominate. I have more confidence in my style of thinking and my interests. I was not especially good S'more material. The climate promoted analytic thinking and arrogance. We were the generation that challenged that narrowness. (Swarthmore '71; public)

Only 2 percent of the "no/not sure" respondents said they feel the college was too hard academically. This small group comes from Carleton, Earlham, and Swarthmore and generally expresses reactions like this one from a different Swarthmore alum: "If I had to do it over again, I might not go to such a selective, demanding college. . . . except that I do feel good that I am a Swarthmore graduate (who got good grades there). And it was a good school" ('71; public). This comment reflects overall the feelings of Alums who question attending their undergraduate college again: they value the college, are proud of having a connection with it, but are aware there are other places where they might have been happier or might have done just as well.

The Alums' Values: Personal and Professional

The Alums were also asked "What personal or professional values do you believe your undergraduate college helped you develop?" (Q.I-7). Over 80 percent of the Alums answered the question. Those who did not, generally commented that they developed their core values before college—most notably from their parents. Those who answered the question provided comments that shed light not just on themselves as individuals, but also on their colleges, their profession, and the times.

Most of the responding Alums provided two or three comments to express what they felt were the personal or professional values their college years helped them to develop. The result was over a thousand words, phrases, and sentences. Initially, 22 values were derived from analyzing the comments. These values coalesce around four broad concepts: Self, Others, Education, and Work.

Self encapsulates values that are directed toward the individual Alum, such as: "I value being honest and fair," and "I value having an open mind, taking personal responsibility, thinking critically, studying something." The reader might think that the last two phrases refer to the topic of Education, but they are more a part of Self because Alums discuss them not as a concept "out there" but as "something I do."

Others signifies that the Alum has taken a step outside herself or himself and is placing the focus on other people. Here the values are about respect, service to or care of others, tolerance toward others, and acknowledging the diversity of people. In the concept of Others there is a sense that the Alum sees himself or herself as part of a larger community—that there is a connection between Self and Others.

Education refers to learning-related areas that the respondents value, specifically arts and culture; intellectual rigor, analysis, critical discourse, and research; and learning in the broad conceptual sense that includes lifelong learning.

Work values focus on "my work": being creative or innovative; one's work ethic; engaging in hard work; doing the best work that one can; engaging in teamwork and being collegial; and work skills such as problem-solving.

Table 8 reflects the values identified most frequently in the comments of Alums of each college. *Diversity* garners the greatest mention across the colleges. This value is broad for it includes differences of opinions or views as well as racial, ethnic, and cultural differences. It encompasses appreciating and being interested in the variety and heterogeneity of people, as well as their approaches to life and learning; their thoughts as well as their character. Some Alums pointed out that valuing diversity does not mean agreeing with specific views, but that such diversity of thought is a good aspect of American society. It is "an appreciation of difference" (Carleton '91; academic). Another Alum felt that Denison definitely taught her to "value others' opinions and beliefs" ('66; academic). Respecting—or at least accepting—diversity encompasses having the ability "to interact, discuss, debate, and work with other individuals of (often) significantly different ethnic, cultural, religious, or other backgrounds; the ability to discuss and debate issues at an impersonal level; and the ability to exist in the real world and work with others who have differing goals and ambitions" (Grinnell '86; special).

Following diversity are the values of *Intellectual Rigor* and *Learning*. Intellectual rigor includes analyzing, testing, evaluating, and being intellectually honest. This does not mean the Alums see themselves as curious about everything, but rather that they believe that things can—and should—be figured out and understood. As one Alum ('81; public library) says, "Carleton taught me the importance of asking excellent and pertinent questions." Many commented that they value "learning to base decisions on good reasoning" (Macalester '96; academic). Common phrases from a number of the colleges include "analyzing," "using independent thought," "problem solving," and "the importance of asking the right questions." Kalamazoo Alums mention the "development of intellectual inquiry," the need to "evaluate situations and ideas beyond black [and] white thinking; to question [the] status quo," look for "the evidence for argument," and "value constructive debate and consensus-building" ('76 academic; '66 public; '91 special; '96 academic, respectively). An Earlham Alum feels she gained "the ability, even the duty, to combine intellectual inquiry with both pragmatic and value-driven concern for my fellow human beings" ('86; academic).

Along with intellectual rigor comes a healthy appreciation of *Learning*. This was most frequently expressed as "lifelong love of learning" or "learning for learning's sake" (Swarthmore '71 special; '86 academic). Continuous learning, lifelong learning, "the desire for knowledge and excellence" (Denison '62; public)—all illustrate this value. There is an assumption on the part of the Alums that learning—once one grasps its value—should never be allowed to stop.

Table 8: Values of the Alums (by College)

Concepts	Values	College							
		C	D	E	G	K	L	M	S
SELF									
	Critical Thinking	•		•		•	•		
	Moral Character	•	•	•			•		•
	Open Mind						•		
OTHERS									
	Diversity	•	•	•	•	•		•	•
	Friendship				•				
	Service			•	•			•	
	Tolerance	•		•	•		•	•	
	World View			•	•	•		•	
EDUCATION									
	Intellectual Rigor	•	•		•	•	•		•
	Learning	•	•			•	•		•
WORK									
	Hard Work		•		•				
	Quality Work		•						
	Work Ethic							•	

Tolerance is highly regarded by Alums from five of the eight colleges. They express this as being tolerant toward others, of their opinions, of their right to be themselves. To some degree, the Alums connect tolerance with having an open mind and respecting others (their opinions, views, and so forth, which also tie into the diversity theme). An Earlham '62 special librarian raised, as he writes, "in a conservative family," illustrates this concept:

> Earlham introduced me to liberal activists and a different way of looking at things. Being a Quaker school, it treated everyone equally and didn't discriminate against you if you were liberal or conservative. Everyone felt at home there. I was there at the beginning of the Vietnam War, so it was an interesting time. My experience at Earlham . . . was very eye-opening for me. I think Earlham prepared me well for the protests and the different opinions. It made me more tolerant.

The other attribute that is highly valued by a slightly different cluster of five colleges is what can be termed *Moral Character*. The CALS alums value being honest, fair, having integrity and forbearance. Even those respondents for whom it is not a "top 4" concept comment on it: a Lawrence '66 (academic) Alum speaks of learning about "personal and professional honor—ethics in all areas," while a Macalester '66 (public) Alum mentions developing "a broader sense of fairness." Overall, developing a good moral character seems to the Alums to include integrity and honesty, commitment and dedication in all that one does. A Grinnell Alum ('86; special) notes that she learned "independence of thought and action, with the realization of the impact my own expressions of thoughts have on others." And a Swarthmore Alum ('91; public) reflects the concept of moral character in comments about valuing "the desire to do good without being a do-gooder."

By college, the Alums' comments cluster this way:

Carleton: Self, Others, and Education
Denison: Self, Others, Education, and Work
Earlham: Self and Others
Grinnell: Others, Education, and Work
Kalamazoo: Self, Others, and Education
Lawrence: Self, Others, and Education
Macalester: Others and Work
Swarthmore: Self, Others, and Education

There are also cohort differences regarding which values rise to the top. Although diversity, moral character, tolerance, a world view, intellectual rigor, and learning are the highest rated in terms of frequency of occurrence, there are interesting clusters associated with different periods within the 39 class years that the CALS Alums represent. Table 9 displays those values identified most frequently in the comments of each cohort.

Three values are shared across at least six of the eight class cohort groupings: *Diversity*, development of a *World View* and of *Intellectual Rigor*. There are cohorts for which these three values have lesser strength, but in the main they are a constant from 1962 to 2000. Diversity shows as a steady value especially from 1966-95. A world view is important to all cohorts except for 1971-76, which is particularly focused on mental processes. Intellectual rigor is important for six of the cohorts, stretching from the class of 1962 through to the class of 2000. The 1996-2000 cohort seems focused on conceptual values that support their move from being students to being new practicing professionals. They are involved in the workplace and draw on *Self*, *Others*, and *Education* values to support their new role. In fact, comments of four CALS Alums from Carleton, Kalamazoo, and Swarthmore aptly represent the 1996-2000 cohorts:

Strong work ethic; Value in doing good work (Carleton '96; public)

Appreciation of a broad world view; Interest in lifelong learning; Critical thinking (Kalamazoo '96 public; '96 academic)

Table 9: Values of the Alums (by Cohort)

Concepts	Values	Cohort							
		62-	66-	71-	76-	81-	86-	91-	96-
SELF									
	Critical Thinking	•	•	•	•				•
	Moral Character		•		•	•	•	•	
	Open Mind							•	
OTHERS									
	Diversity		•	•	•	•	•	•	
	Respect	•							
	Service	•							
	Tolerance	•	•		•		•		•
	World View	•	•		•	•	•	•	•
EDUCATION									
	Intellectual Rigor	•		•	•	•		•	•
	Learning	•	•	•	•				•
WORK									
	Work Ethic								•
	Work Hard	•							
	Work Skills								•

> Social justice; Intellectual freedom; Work ethic; Work hard—play hard (Swarthmore '96; special)

As practicing LIS professionals, they see that their colleges helped provide them with a good work ethic and transferable skills. They find themselves applying critical thinking and intellectual rigor to understand and solve work problems. They are indeed in settings where they are continually learning. And the value for tolerance, along with the world view that they gained, helps them understand and work cooperatively with colleagues and users.

To summarize the cohort perception of values gained from their undergraduate college years:

1962-65: Self, Others, Education, and Work
1966-70: Self, Others, and Education

1971-75:	Self, Others, and Education
1976-80:	Self, Others, and Education
1981-85:	Self, Others, and Education
1986-90:	Self and Others
1991-95:	Self, Others, and Education
1996-00:	Self, Others, Education, and Work

It is interesting that only the 1962-65 and 1996-2000 cohorts, the "bookends," share appreciation for values that fall into all four broad conceptual categories. Other points include the focus within *Self* on critical thinking and moral character, the 1962-65 cohort's reference to hard work, and the 1986-90 cohort's focus on moral character, diversity, tolerance, and a world view.

Summary

After choosing a college perhaps familiar to them because of regional proximity, the CALS respondents were influenced by their college's academic and extracurricular structure and expectations, and by their own growth in intellectual, social, and psychological areas. While English and History were the most widely chosen majors, overall the Social and Behavioral Sciences accounted for 50 percent of all majors. The Alums used minors or concentrations either to add depth to their understanding of their major field of study, or as an opportunity to explore a secondary field of interest.

Just as they were exposed to a range of academic disciplines, the Alums also experienced a variety of curricular and extracurricular opportunities to adopt the college's values, especially those relating to service. For a majority of the Alums, the combination of curricular, extracurricular, peer, and individual experiences enabled them to identify and clarify their own values. The Alums and the college administrators agree that moral character, diversity of opinion and of background, tolerance, intellectual rigor and learning are important values. In addition, for the Alums, the values of intellectual rigor and a world view are strongly shared across the 39 years represented by the study. While the values within the concepts of *Self*, *Other*, and *Education* are fairly well-connected with their college experience, those values associated with the concept *Work* are, at this stage in the Alums' lives, the least recognized and developed.

CHAPTER 3

Career Choice

Upon graduation, the Alums faced the question of "what do I want to do with my life?" This chapter follows the career options they considered, the role of family in career choice, and the various occupations and careers the Alums experienced. Deeper exploration is made of the reasons why the Alums chose library and information science (LIS). The Alums were asked to identify the "ultimate reason" they actually enrolled in a graduate LIS program, and discussion of the concepts of *Family, Fit,* and *Opportunity* is an outgrowth of their answers. Finally, other studies were examined to determine how similar or dissimilar the CALS participants are from both other students and other LIS students, and four particular participants were followed to illustrate how the career choice question was answered by CALS Alums.

I. The Concept Called "Career"

In an expansive discussion of career development and career guidance, Boerlijst (1998, 283) bemoans the variety of theories and meanings given to terms such as *career, career planning, career guidance*, and *career development*. And it is true that the idea of career has changed over time. Prior to the 1970s, the words *vocation* and *calling* were used more frequently than career. In the 15th century, to have a vocation was to have a divine calling from God to engage in, usually, religious work. After that period, "vocation came to be viewed as a place in the structured daily undertakings of the work in society. All people were to be esteemed if they desired and strived to perform well in their primary office or vocation . . . All individuals called by God to practice any occupation or station were esteemed . . . They were called not to show unusual gifts but to do good in any ordinary station" (Rehm 1990, 116-117).

By the eighteenth century, in American higher education, the notion of "career" had taken on a slightly more pragmatic meaning: You attended college in order to be trained in law, the ministry, or perhaps medicine; then you entered into the chosen vocation. The intent was for you to do good works for the betterment of society through such professional activity. The idea of *vocation* and of *calling* broadened still further in the early nineteenth century. Bledstein (1978, 177) relates how a man of the times was no longer confined to

> a preestablished station in life, including a calling toward which sympathetic parents guided him. A man now actively chose his profession. . . The world of movement and expectation focused on the spirited individual, his specialized nature, his self-discipline, and the continuity of this rise rather, than [on] his humility, his self-subordination to the social order and his dependence upon God's will. In the steps of a career, an individual progressively discovered his potential.

According to Rehm (1990, 117), "By the twentieth century the sciences of psychology and economics had become at least as important as religion as social influences," and she quotes John Dewey's 1916 discussion of vocation in light of the American pragmatism and individualism of the time:

> A vocation means nothing but such a direction of life activities as renders them perceptively significant to a person, because of the consequences they accomplish, and also useful to his associates . . . Every person shall be occupied in something which makes the lives of others better worth living, and which accordingly makes the ties which bind persons together more perceptible—which breaks down the barriers of distance between them. It denotes a state of affairs in which the interest of each in his work is uncoerced and intelligent, based on its congeniality to his own aptitudes. (quoted in Rehm 1990, 117)

In other words, "to have a vocation" now meant working throughout one's life at something which, while supporting society's common good, also provided for personal gain.

Over the course of the 1950s-1980s, the term *career* more and more frequently took the place of vocation to describe the period of one's work life (McDaniels and Gysbers 1992). In 1976, Super defined career as "the sequence of major positions occupied by a person throughout his pre-occupational, occupational, and post-occupational life; includes work-related roles such as those of student, employee, and pensioner, together with complementary vocational, familial, and civic roles. Careers exist only as people pursue them; they are person-centered" (quoted in McDaniels and Gysbers 1992, 10). By the 1980s, the concepts of career, career choice, career development, and their associated processes were in flux. Indeed the 1980 edition of *Webster's New World Dictionary* defines a "calling" broadly—as "one's occupation, profession, or trade; an inner urging toward some profession or activity; vocation." It defines career as "one's progress through life or in a particular vocation; a particular profession or occupation which one trains for and pursues as a lifework."

Although career has been associated only with one's paid work, from 1980 to 1990 the concepts of career and career development began to encompass both the individual's work and "nonwork" roles—evolving so as to refer to one's "life work." The definition of career enlarged to the point that in 1985 the National Vocational Guidance Association changed its name to become the National Career Development Association. In the 1990s, according to McDaniels and Gysbers (1992, 3), "instead of being defined as job or occupation, career is increasingly being defined as the combinations and sequences of life roles, the settings in which life roles unfold, and the planned and unplanned events that occur in people's lives. Career development is being seen more and more as the unfolding and interaction of roles, settings, and events all through the life span."

Along with this evolution of career has come significant research on how an individual goes about choosing and then developing a career. Frank Parsons, in 1909, is credited with articulating "the first conceptual framework for career decision making" (Brown and Brooks 1996, 1). His model focused on knowledge of self and knowledge of the world of work (Hartung and Niles 2000). Parsons asserted that

> in the wise choice of a vocation there are three broad factors: (1) a clear understanding of yourself, your aptitudes, abilities, interests, ambitions, resources, limitations, and their causes; (2) a knowledge of the requirements, conditions of success, advantages and disadvantages, compensation, opportunities, and prospects in different lines of work; (3) true reasoning on the relations of these two groups of facts. (Parsons 1909, 5, as quoted in Brown and Brooks 1996, 1)

Subsequent theories about the career development process have come from both psychologists and sociologists, with the former focusing on the individual and the latter on social variables. To understand how individuals make career decisions, early career development researchers sought not just to measure and explain the traits of individuals, for example, but also to predict what would occur in the career development process (Brown and Brooks 1996). Current theories have tended to shift to more phenomenological approaches that look at cultural and social factors, including the individual's social class, gender, race and ethnicity. These factors are seen as influencers that either limit or expand the information, opportunities, and means available to individuals in moving from career awareness through career choice to career development and to the incorporation of their career into their overall life.

In their review of established career theories, Hartung and Niles (2000) discuss the more current psychological career choice and development theories: differential, personality-focused, developmental, and reinforcement-based. The *differential* approach focuses on matching traits such as "values, interests, aptitudes, and skills to educational or occupational factors that fit those traits" (Hartung and Niles 2000, 6). One of the best known theories to use this trait-and-factor perspective is Holland's Theory of Vocational Personalities and Work Environments (1959, 1985, 1997; see Spokane 1996). It uses a person-environment "fit" approach to describe various vocational personalities and work environments, and how they interact. According to McDaniels and Gysbers (1992, 28), the trait-and-factor theory

> describes individuals as having measurable traits (for example, interests and abilities). It also describes occupations in terms of the amounts and types of individual traits required. It further suggests that the traits individuals have can be compared with the amounts required by occupations. The goal of this comparison process is to provide individuals with a basis for making occupational choices.

This career development theory "asserts that people seek out jobs with requirements that are consistent with their personality traits" (Brown and Brooks 1990, 6). Parsons's early 1900s framework illustrates this approach, and the Strong Interest Inventory, one of today's most widely used interest inventories, incorporates Holland's model.

The *personality-focused* approach to the career development process "involves conceptualizing career choices and development as a function of early parent-child relationships, childhood memories, family dynamics, and the personal meaning of work and careers" (Hartung and Niles 2000, 6). Roe's (1956, see Roe and Lunneborg 1990) work on personality development during childhood and the role of parental influence illustrates this perspective. Her theory stresses "intrinsic personality needs as the primary determinants of choice. Thus people select occupations that satisfy important psychological needs" (Brown and Brooks 1990, 7). Roe's 1990 presentation of her theory regarding career choice incorporated specific factors into the decision-making process: these are gender, the general state of the economy, family background, learning and education, special acquired skills, physical capacity, chance, friends or peer group, marital situation, cognitive capacity, temperament and personality, and interests and values. And "the weights assigned to these factors . . . vary with time and circumstance" (Lunneborg 1997, 301; see Tinsley 1997 for a series of articles on Roe).

The *developmental* approach "involves examining and promoting individual progress through various career and life stages" (Hartung and Niles 2000, 6). It is exemplified by Super's life span—life space theory. "Life span" refers to the period from birth to death, which Super divides into five stages: Career Growth, Exploration, Establishment, Maintenance, and Disengagement. In each stage there are developmental tasks and issues to resolve. "Life space" refers to the particular roles a person plays at any given point in her or his life span (Hartung and Niles 2000). Super's theory is taken from "developmental, differential, social, personality, and phenomenological psychology and held together by self-concept and learning theory" (Super 1990, 199). Part of the career choice process consists of "developing a picture of the kind of person one is, and of trying to make that concept a reality" (Super 1951, 88). Thus, Super sees each individual as establishing her or his own personal concept of self. This self-concept is then tested out in different environments (e.g., familial, peer, collegiate, employment). Where the self-concept meets with approval of respected others, it is reinforced; where it is at odds with aspects of the environment, it undergoes adaptation. Gradually, over the stages of career growth, one's self-concept develops into one's professional and social identity. Or, as Hartung and Niles (2000, 12) express it: "The life span-life space perspective characterizes career choice and development as an attempt to implement one's self-concept in educational and occupational decisions. [For example,] college students feel more satisfied when they are able to successfully implement their self-concepts in their academic and career pursuits." For Super, career development is a lifelong process that changes and matures over one or more occupational and nonoccupational roles (Super et al. 1996).

Finally, the *reinforcement-based* approach stresses "how social learning and reinforcement patterns shape what [individuals] believe about themselves and the world of work" (Hartung and Niles 2000, 6). Here the emphasis is on understanding how one's observations about one's self and the world influence career aspirations, attitudes, beliefs, choices, and satisfactions. Proponents include Brown (1995, 1996), who asserts the importance of values in career decision making, and Mitchell and Krumboltz (1996), who invoke social learning theory. For Brown, values have affective, behavioral, and cognitive dimensions and serve as standards for evaluating one's own actions and those of others. In discussing Brown's theory, Niles and Hartung (2000, 35) use this example: "Working 80 hours a week for 50 weeks out of the year to earn a significant salary makes sense to the person who values materialism, but is hard to understand for the person who values spending time with family. Thus, values focus our behavior in specific directions and toward particular goals." Individuals are attracted to careers that appear to incorporate, reward, or share their values. Under Brown's theory, people are most comfortable, satisfied, and successful within a career that allows them to retain and express their personal values. A values-based life is one where a shared core of values underlies, and is expressed in, all aspects of life: career, family, leisure. This kind of life retains some of the traditional holistic connotations of vocation and calling.

A key part of Mitchell and Krumboltz's approach to career decision making is social learning theory, which "assumes that people's personalities and behavioral repertoires can be explained most usefully on the basis of their unique learning experiences while still acknowledging the role played by innate and developmental processes" (Mitchell and Krumboltz 1996, 234). Factors that influence career decisions include genetic background and special talents, environmental conditions (e.g., cultural or economic forces), learning experiences, and how the individual approaches carrying out tasks. These factors form a foundation underlying how individuals endeavor to generalize about themselves (i.e., their interests and values, their preferred ways of handling tasks) and thus create an individualized worldview (Niles and Hartung 2000, 25). Taking these factors into account, social learning theory says that individuals will prefer (or reject) a particular career or occupation depending on the following three conditions:

- They have succeeded (or failed) at tasks they believe are like tasks performed by members of that occupation.
- They have observed a valued model being reinforced (or punished or ignored) for activities like those performed by members of that occupation.
- A valued friend or relative stressed the occupation's advantages (or disadvantages) to them; they observed positive (or negative) words and images being associated with it, or both. (Krumboltz 1994, as cited in Niles and Hartung 2000, 26-27)

A career, then, might be seen as one's cumulative lifelong work. It can be as straightforward as "the combination and sequence of roles played by a person during the course of a lifetime" (Super 1980, 282). It may have characteristics of a vocation in the sense of work that "illuminate[s] a meaningful direction for developing one's gifts" (Rehm 1990, 118). Or it might be the result of a calling, in that the career has such an overarching purpose to it that its "activity and character . . . makes a person's work morally inseparable from his or her life" (Bellah et al. 1985, 66).

II. The Role of Family in Career Choice

There is substantial literature indicating that parents, and, to a degree, siblings influence children's conceptions of and interests in different careers. An excellent review of the literature is found in Bempechat (1990). She includes discussion of patterns of parent-child involvement that foster high academic achievement and center on the role of cognitive socialization, the development of basic intelligence; and of academic socialization, the development of attitudes and motives essential for school learning. Another welcome overview is found in Jodl et al. (2001, 1247), who note that "a consistent finding reported in the sociological literature is that parents' level of education and occupational status are associated with children's educational and occupational aspirations (e.g., Fitzgerald and Betz 1983; Hannah and Kahn 1989; Hill and Duncan 1987; MacKay and Miller 1982)." Jodl et al. (2001) also discuss Roe's (1956, see Roe and Lunneborg 1990) theory of the importance of the early parent-child relationship in career development; Holland's (1959, 1985, 1997) person-environment "fit" approach; and Super's (1951, 1990) life-space developmental theory that incorporates the family as a source of influence on self-concept and career maturity. Jodl et al. (2001) include Eccles's 1993 expectancy-value model, "which emphasizes parents as role models, sources of reinforcement, and providers of information, resources, and opportunities for their children," along with the work of Grotevant and Cooper (1988), Mortimer et al. (1986), and Schulenberg et al. (1984), which contains discussion of parents' role modeling, attitudes, and behaviors as contributory factors to career identification and choice (Jodl et al. 2001, 1247).

In addition, siblings play a role through their involvements with each other. Siblings model standards, work through the handling of emotions, interpret parental attitudes and behaviors, explore beliefs, and, for their younger siblings, lead the way in college choices and career avenues (Dunn 2002; Jacobsen 1999; Kerka 2000). But as DeRidder (1990, 3) explains, "Parents as daily models provide cultural standards, attitudes, and expectations and, in many ways, determine the eventual adequacy of self-acceptance and confidence, of social skills and of sex roles. The attitudes and behaviors of parents while working or discussing their work is what the children respond to and learn." For example, McCracken and Fails (1991) compared career plans of a group of 1985 and 1988 high school students in Ohio. They found that "in 1985 these youths, while in high school, had ranked the top four sources of influence on curriculum and career decisions as self, parents, friends, and counselors. In 1988, the youth who had graduated listed self, mother and father, friends, and teachers as the top influences." And a study by Otto (2000), which asked high school students about their parents' views on career choice, reported that 82 percent felt their career ideas were mostly or very similar to those their parents had for them. Otto also asked the students "how closely their ideas agree with their parents on 'the value of a college education.' Ninety-three percent say they hold views similar to their parents."

The Otto (2000) study also reveals that mothers are more aware than fathers of their children's career interests and abilities, and tend to hold higher educational expectations for their children. There is a body of literature that suggests that adolescents "are particularly influenced in the choice of career by same-sex parents" (Gates 2002, 3). There is disagreement about the degree to which mothers are more involved than fathers in the development of their children's career interests. Bradford et al.'s (2001) study of successful women in professional and upper level management positions found that both parents encouraged their daughters to meet high performance standards, get a good education, and become self-sufficient. Some of the difference in various findings may be the result of the educational level of the parents. For example, "Mortimer et al. (1992) report that parents with post-secondary education tend to pass along its importance to their children—a finding supported by other studies, [and] Marso and Pigge (1994) found that the presence of teachers in the family was a significant factor influencing teacher candidates' decisions to teach" (Lankard 1995). In an article on children of academics who also became academics, Alison Booth talks about her father, the renowned scholar Wayne C. Booth, and her mother, a psychologist:

> Some of my earliest memories are of my father's study . . . I remember index cards for [a particular book] spread across a big table in our flat in London, during the trip we took with Earlham College students one spring . . . Unquestionably, I liked the sense of my father as a teacher . . . By the time I was an adolescent, I was certain one should "make the world a better place" by becoming an educator or a psychologist (like my mother) or, even better, a great writer . . . My mother gave me the example of a bright, disciplined woman pursuing a career. My father showed me how to put your best into this particular profession [of teaching college English]. (Schrecker 1999, 22)

The Families of the Alums

To obtain information about who might have influenced the CALS Alums in their career choices, they were asked a number of questions about family members (i.e., mothers, fathers, sisters, brothers, and spouses or partners) (Q.IV-11-15). Ninety-four percent, that is, 420, of the Alums have siblings (Q.IV-11). The majority of that number have one or two siblings. Interestingly, almost half (47 percent) of the Alums are the oldest child in their family while 29 percent are the youngest and 24 percent are middle children. The terminal degree for 32 percent of the Alums' mothers is the bachelor's; for another 32 percent, the terminal degree is the master's or doctorate (Q.IV-13). For fathers, the figures are 27 percent and 50 percent respectively. Only 2 percent of mothers and 3 percent of fathers have less than a high school diploma.

CALS Alums were asked, "What kind of work did your parents do for a living when you were 18 years old?" (Q.IV-12). They were also asked to indicate the occupations in which their siblings spent the "greatest number of years." Some Alums gave very specific answers and others gave very general ones; thus concepts, occupations, and occupational domains, as well as specific jobs, were all noted. Analysis was done by grouping some answers into larger concepts

Table 10: Occupations Held by Family Members

Arts of All Kinds	Government (Local, State, Federal)	Office Work
Business	Health Professions	Religious Position
Computer Work	Higher Education	Sales
Construction, Installation and/or Repair Work	Homemaker	Science
	K-12 Education	Social (and Related) Service Work
Consultant	Law	Student
Engineering	Librarian/LIS Work	Unemployed
Farmer	Manufacturing/Production	Volunteer
Financial Work	Military	Writer

or fields, like Office Work, to represent a number of jobs (e.g., secretary; assistant; "a number of jobs in an office") and leaving others, like Engineering, where Alums used the exact word but provided no setting. In a few cases, a cluster of responses could be named by using *Occupational Outlook Handbook, 2004-05* categories. For example, "Construction, Installation, and/or Repair Work" (a combination of two *OOH* categories) provides a place for family members who are carpenters. Table 10 groups the work of family members into the range of broadly categorized occupations.

Brothers are the only family members represented in all 26 categories. Mothers are absent from Construction/Installation/Repair, Consultant, Farmer, Manufacturing/Production, Military, and Unemployed. Fathers are absent from Homemaker, Military, and Volunteer, and sisters from Consultant, Farmer, and Military.

As seen in table 11, there is some commonality between the occupations most frequently held by mothers and sisters, and those held by fathers and brothers. Although LIS work shows up as the third most frequent occupation held by mothers when the Alums were age 18, it is not a significant activity when the parents are grouped together. Overall, LIS work accounts for 5 percent of the occupations of Alums' parents (9 percent of mothers; 1 percent of fathers); and 3 percent of the occupations of siblings (brothers, sisters, and undesignated siblings).

Mothers

CALS Alums generally used "homemaker" or "stay-at-home mom" to refer to mothers who did not work outside the home. "K-12 Education" refers to employment in the field of education from kindergarten through the 12th grade, but is not restricted to teaching. "Librarian/LIS Work" covers professional and paraprofessional positions. "Office Work" refers to occupations that are clearly staff support in nature. Being a Homemaker was the most frequent occupation of Alums' mothers across six of the eight cohorts, the exception being the 1981-85 and the 1996-2000 cohorts (table 12).

Table 11: Most Prevalent Occupations of Family Members

Mother	Father
Homemaker	Business
K-12 Education	Higher Education
LIS Work and Office Work	Engineering
Sisters	Brothers
K-12 Education	Business
Health Professions	Higher Education and Computer Work
Homemaker	Engineering and Sales
Unspecified Siblings (not identified as brothers or sisters)	
Health Professions and K-12 Education	
Business	
Social Services	

Table 12: Most Prevalent Occupations of Mothers (by Cohort)

Mothers' Occupations	Avg. (%)	Cohort (%)							
		62-	66-	71-	76-	81-	86-	91-	96-
Homemaker	33	41	44	40	24	15	21	22	10
K-12 Education	17	25	16	20	22	8	14	11	20
Librarian/LIS Work	9	7	3	9	11	18	9	16	0
Office Work	9	10	12	6	11	8	2	5	40

While the 1962-75 classes showed a particularly high percentage of mothers who were chiefly homemakers, it is important to remember that the question asked the Alums for the kind of work their parent did when the Alums were 18 years of age—that is, at the beginning of their college years. So we can assume these 40-44 percent figures represent the period around 1958-71. During that time, career options for women were fewer than during, for example, the final ten years covered by the study. For the 1981-85 cohort, LIS Work was their mothers' most common occupation.

Alums from all eight colleges have mothers who were homemakers when the Alums were 18 years old. This was especially so at Denison, where 59 percent of Alums identified their mothers with that field; least so at Grinnell (22 percent). Alums from seven of the eight colleges have mothers associated with K-12 Education, the second highest ranked field; mothers of Lawrence Alums are more involved with Office Work and Sales than with K-12 Education. LIS Work is ranked second or third at Earlham, Grinnell, Kalamazoo, and Swarthmore. No Denison Alum indicated that her or his mother was a librarian.

Table 13: Most Prevalent Occupations of Fathers (by Cohort)

Fathers' Occupations	Avg (%)	Cohort (%) 62-	66-	71-	76-	81-	86-	91-	96-
Business	17	19	17	22	20	9	18	13	0
Higher Education	14	7	13	11	18	11	23	23	11
Engineering	10	11	12	9	8	11	5	8	22

Fathers

By cohort, Business was the occupation of the greatest number of fathers from 1962 through 1980 (table 13). This designation focuses on owning a business or being in a senior management position in business (as opposed, for example, to an academic deanship). Higher Education, generally a faculty position, was top ranked for a decade (1986-95), was split with Engineering in 1981-85, and was third after Engineering for the fathers of participants in the 1996-2000 classes. Higher Education was most popular during the late 1980s and early 1990s. With the exception of Business during the last cohort period, all three of the most frequently indicated occupations are found among the work of the fathers of Alums across all cohorts.

By college, Business shows a high to low range of 21 percent (Earlham) to 13 percent (Grinnell and Kalamazoo). The range for Higher Education is 25 percent (Grinnell) to Lawrence (6 percent). A high of 11 percent of the Alums (Earlham) have fathers who are engineers; no Alums from Grinnell are in this category.

Siblings

Most of the CALS Alums are members of families averaging three to four children; 90 to 93 percent of Alums with siblings indicate they had one to two brothers and one to two sisters. While a majority of the Alums indicated whether it is a brother or a sister who has a particular occupation, some indicated how many brothers and sisters they have but did not distinguish which ones do what kind of work. Where it has been possible to do so, brothers and sisters are separately analyzed. Taken as one group and also separately by gender, they provide interesting insights into the kind of family occupations which surrounded the Alums. Tables 14-18 describe the most prevalent occupations of the Alums' siblings.

In comparison with their parents, the Alums' siblings are represented in the largest array of occupations—all 26, so the percentage in any specific field is smaller. As a group, the top three occupations in which the siblings have spent the greatest number of their worklife years are K-12 Education, Business, and the Health Professions (table 14).

When brothers are specifically identified, however, they have an almost totally different set of occupations (table 15). Here Computer Work and Sales show up for the first time as widely reported occupations. And focusing specifically on brothers reveals a high degree of similarity with the occupational choice of their fathers, especially in Business, Higher Education, and Engineering.

Table 14: Most Prevalent Occupations of Siblings (by Cohort)

Siblings' Occupations	Avg (%)	Cohort (%) 62-	66-	71-	76-	81-	86-	91-	96-
Business	10	10	14	10	12	7	12	6	12
K-12 Education	10	12	12	12	6	3	13	67	0
Health Professions	8	7	8	12	8	7	3	4	8

Table 15: Most Prevalent Occupations of Brothers (by Cohort)

Brothers' Occupations	Avg (%)	Cohort (%) 62-	66-	71-	76-	81-	86-	91-	96-
Business	12	0	17	19	16	5	15	0	17
Higher Education	9	17	8	6	10	5	5	13	0
Computer Work	9	11	4	4	10	5	15	26	17
Engineering	7	11	5	9	6	14	5	4	0
Sales	7	6	12	11	3	5	0	4	0

A larger number of sisters than brothers are involved in K-12 Education (16 percent versus 5 percent), the Health Professions (11 percent versus 5 percent), and being a Homemaker (10 percent versus less than 1 percent) (table 16; appendix D: Q.IV-11). And in parallel with their brothers and fathers, sisters share Homemaker and K-12 Education fields of work with their mothers.

Undesignated Siblings

This term is used for instances where Alums indicated they had a number of siblings, but did not differentiate them into brothers and sisters. As seen in table 17, Business careers are held by 10 percent with K-12 Education and the Health Professions held by 9 percent of those siblings not identified by gender. Business is a particularly strong area for siblings in the 1962-65 and 1996-2000 cohorts.

Combined Groups

When brothers, sisters, and otherwise undesignated siblings are combined, Business becomes top ranked while a large number among sisters and undesignated siblings cause K-12 Education and the Health Professions to become second and third most prevalent occupations (table 18). In addition to being the top choice of brothers, Business is the work of 10 percent of undesignated siblings and 8 percent of sisters.

Table 16: Most Prevalent Occupations of Sisters (by Cohort)

Sisters' Occupations	Avg (%)	Cohorts (%) 62-	66-	71-	76-	81-	86-	91-	96-
K-12 Education	15	16	14	25	13	5	10	14	0
Health Professions	11	16	13	11	11	5	10	5	25
Homemaker	10	11	11	6	13	14	5	14	0

Table 17: Most Prevalent Occupations of Undesignated Siblings (by Cohort)

Undesignated Siblings' Occupations	Avg (%)	Cohorts (%) 62-	66-	71-	76-	81-	86-	91-	96-
Business	10	25	8	5	11	12	15	17	20
K-12 Education	9	17	14	9	3	4	15	0	0
Health Professions	9	0	8	17	6	8	0	8	0

Table 18: Most Prevalent Occupations by Siblings and by Group

Brothers	Sisters	Undesignated	Combined
Business Higher Education and Computer Work Engineering and Sales	K-12 Education Health Professions Homemaker	Business K-12 Education and Health Professions Arts	Business K-12 Education Health Professions

With regard to siblings' occupations overall, there are almost no differences between cohort and college findings, except for these instances:

- *Brothers:* The only significant difference from the cohort findings is that the top category for brothers of Denison Alums was Law (24 percent).
- *Sisters:* The top category of those of Carleton Alums was Science. For sisters of Earlham, Kalamazoo, and Lawrence Alums, Business was either the second or third most frequently mentioned career; but no Denison or Swarthmore Alums reported having sisters in that field.
- *Undesignated siblings:* The top category of those of Swarthmore Alums was the Arts.

Spouses/Partners

There are spouses or partners who work in each of the 26 occupations except Farming and the Military, so each field garners low percentages (Q.IV-8). Thus, their findings can be succinctly stated. The occupations in which the greatest number (52 percent) of spouses or partners work are

- LIS Work (11 percent)
- Higher Education (9 percent)
- Business, Computer Work, K-12 Education, and Health Professions (8 percent each)

Higher Education, the Health Professions, and the Arts (6 percent) are common occupations across all eight colleges for spouses or partners of the Alums. LIS Work and Business are the occupations of spouses or partners of Alums from all the colleges except Grinnell. And at the other end of the spectrum, only Earlham Alums have a spouse or partner in the Military or engaged in Farming (1 percent each).

Four conclusions can summarize the major findings on family occupations:

- The most common occupations of family members have, in general, held constant over the years. The 1996-2000 cohort is different in that it has more siblings still in school, and only their mothers are involved in K-16 education.
- There was a steep decline in the number of Alums who report their mother's occupation as Homemaker—that peaked with the 1966-70 Alums, and thus probably refers to the years of 1962-66.
- Business and Engineering are prevalent occupations for fathers, brothers, and undesignated siblings.
- Education is a constant: K-12 Education for mothers and sisters and undesignated siblings, Higher Education for fathers and brothers. In addition, although it does not occur with sufficient frequency to make it one of the three most common fields of work across the entire 1962-2000 period, a range of 2 to 10 percent of mothers and 4 to 15 percent of sisters are involved in Higher Education. Likewise, between 3 and 8 percent of fathers and 2 to 15 percent of brothers are involved in K-12 Education over that period. And finally, Higher Education and K-12 Education are also the second and third most common occupations of the Alums' spouses or partners.

It seems useful at this point to consider whether the CALS participants are particularly different from other students. Three studies are helpful: *The American Freshman, Twenty-five Year Trends, 1966-1990* by Dey, Astin, and Korn (1991) for comparison with other undergraduates; *Education, Careers and Professionalization in Librarianship and Information Sciences* by White and Macklin (1970); and *Occupational Entry: Library and Information Science Students' Attitudes, Demographics and Aspirations Survey* by Heim and Moen (1989) for comparison with other LIS master's students.

In terms of education, whereas 66 percent of the CALS participants' mothers have a college or graduate school degree, the range for Dey et al. (1991) mothers of first-year women students is 19-30 percent (1966-90). And while 77 percent of the Alums' fathers have a college or graduate school degree, the range for the Dey et al. (1991) fathers of first-year women is 29-38 percent.

Occupationally, the *American Freshman* study begins tracking fathers' work in 1967 and mothers' work in 1976. In the CALS study, mothers cluster into the occupations of Homemaker (an average of 33 percent from 1962-2000; 10 percent in 2000), K-12 Education (17 percent), and LIS work tied with Office Work (9 percent)—with Homemaker at its highest from 1962-80. Dey et al. (1991) found that, in 1976 with 20 occupations being tracked, Homemaker, K-12 Education, and Office Work were also the most common fields for the mothers of the first-year women students. LIS work was not tracked. In 1976, 34 percent of mothers in Dey et al. (1991) are Homemakers; by 1990, it is 16 percent. Across the 1976-90 period that Dey et al. studied, the percent of mothers of first-year women engaged in K-12 occupations ranged from 8-10 percent and those involved in clerical work held steady at 11 percent.

The three most prevalent occupations of the fathers of the CALS Alums over the 39 class years are Business (average of 17 percent), Higher Education (14 percent), and Engineering (10 percent). The three most common occupations of the Dey et al. (1991) fathers of female first-years are Business (with a year range of 32-26 percent), skilled and semi-skilled work (21-18 percent), and Engineering (steady at 7 percent). Over the 1976-90 *American Freshman* tracking period, K-16 Education is the work of just 3 to 4 percent of fathers of the first-year women students.

The educational and occupational disparities, especially for fathers, might be at least partially a function of parental income. Drawing upon the Morrison (1969) study, the CALS study asked in broad terms about the financial situation of Alums' families when the Alums were 21 years old (table 19). *American Freshman* uses salary dollar ranges so true comparison is not possible. However, if the reported ranges for first-year women are grouped to suggest those used in the CALS study, comparison of education, occupation, and wealth clearly demonstrates that the CALS Alums are very different from the freshmen women in the Dey et al. (1991) national study. The Alums' parents are better educated, are more apt to work in education, and appear to have higher incomes. (In both studies, this is self-report data—see appendix G for *American Freshman* detail).

III. Career and Occupational Interests of the Alums

In the course of the survey, the CALS participants were asked about their own career goals: first as a child and then when they started college (Q.III-1-2). They were also asked about occupations, other than LIS, that they had been interested in, had considered going into, or had experienced (Q.III-3-5).[19] The same 26 broad occupational terms (see table 10) were used in coding the results, so that comparisons could be made with the careers reported for family members. As before, the three most prevalent choices may appear to reflect small numbers of

---

[19]See appendix F for percentages associated with the most prevalent three goals/occupations for each of these questions (Q.III-1-5).

Table 19: Family Financial Situation

Family Financial Categories	CALS Alums: 1962-2000	Dey et al. (1991) 1966-90 period
Sometimes had difficulty getting the necessities	3%	13%
Had all the necessities but not many luxuries	45	38
Comfortable	50	41
Wealthy	2	9

Alums since, with this many categories, the overall percentage spread can be quite large (See appendix C: Q.III-1-5). Findings are reported by college. In addition to quoting various Alums, we follow four who were chosen to illustrate the thinking of Alums by decade and library type: Kalamazoo '66 (school), Grinnell '71 (public), Denison '81 (academic), and Swarthmore '96 (special).

"What were your career goals as a child?"

Trice et al. (1995, 320) find support for the idea that "identification with a parent's work is particularly strong among kindergarten, second-, and fourth-grade children, weakening somewhat among sixth-grade children . . . [And] that children's first and second occupational choices tended to fall within the same occupational cluster" as their parents. But young children also have interests outside those that are associated with parents and siblings. Thus at this point the list of 26 fields of their family members was enlarged as the Alums included pilot (2 percent of Alums), fireman (1 percent), letter carrier (less than 1 percent), outdoor work (such as gardening; 3 percent), sports (2 percent), being a vet (or working with animals; 4 percent), and being rich (1 percent; as a Carleton ('76; school) Alum put it "to be a mom and a millionaire") (Q.III-1). Some of the CALS Alums had very clear ideas: our school librarian (Kalamazoo '66) said "fireman" and our Grinnell ('71; public) Alum wrote "teacher or poet." Others were uncertain: our Denison Alum ('81; academic) said, "I don't remember having any, but I was always interested in service to others." And our Swarthmore Alum, representing the 1990s and special librarians, explained that "it depended on the day you asked me. My goals ranged from becoming a botanist to designing stage clothes for rock stars. My parents supported any ideas I had."

Analysis of all responding Alums' childhood views of desirable careers reveals that the most common three include two careers that we now associate with their families:

- K-12 Education (most common for Alums from five of the eight colleges)
- No Career Goals
- Health Professions

By CALS college, the top three choices of the Alums as children were

Carleton:	K-12 Education; None; Science/Math
Denison:	K-12 Education; (tie) None, Arts, and Health Professions
Earlham:	K-12 Education; None; LIS Work
Grinnell:	(tie) K-12 Education and None; (tie) Government Work and Writer
Kalamazoo:	(tie) None and Health Professions; K-12 Education
Lawrence:	None; Science/Math; (tie) Arts and K-12 Education
Macalester:	K-12 Education; Health Professions; (tie) None and Arts
Swarthmore:	Writer; (tie) None, K-12 Education, and Science/Math

Science/Math was the fourth most common career choice for Alums as they articulated their childhood preferences. The term *Writer* represents those CALS Alums who responded "being a writer," "writing books," "being a journalist," or "publishing magazines or books." "LIS" includes both "working in a library" and "working with books."

As children, 22 percent of Denison Alums were particularly interested in K-12 Education—the highest for any of the colleges. It appears that the Alums were modeling their mothers and sisters: 16 percent indicated their mothers worked in this occupation, and 25 percent of them indicated they had sisters associated with K-12 Education.

"What were your career goals when you started college?"

At the time they entered college, 22 percent of the CALS Alums had no career in mind (Q.III-2). This is higher than the Dey et al. (1991) national findings for freshmen, which display a 1967-90 range of 9.9 to 13.8 percent. However, it is supported by the comments of Deans Hornbach at Macalester and Gross at Swarthmore, who indicate that at their colleges "the largest 'intended major' [of incoming freshmen] is 'undecided'" (Hornbach interview, see Bibliography).

The percentage of Alums who, as freshmen, had no career in mind ranges from a low of 17 percent (Earlham) to a high of 60 percent (Grinnell). Those with career goals had a much smaller array in view than the total of 33 occupations they identified as their childhood interests. Now only 20 occupations attracted their interest. The Alums reported that their top three choices as first year students were

- None
- K-12 Education
- Science/Math

At this point in their education, a majority of the Alums felt generally undecided about a career. Although as children, Denison Alums were most strongly inclined toward K-12 education, at the beginning of college it is Kalamazoo respondents who were the most interested in that career. K-12 Education, however, was the top choice for those Alums who did have a career in mind. While Science/Math and the Arts shared fourth place as childhood aspirations, this area was of stronger interest when the Alums started college.[20] And at the beginning of their undergraduate years, 7 percent of the Alums were considering LIS a potential career; only Grinnell Alums report having had no interest in it.

By CALS college, the top three choices as a first year student were

Carleton:	None; (tie) K-12 Education and Science/Math
Denison:	None; (tie) Arts, K-12 Education, and LIS
Earlham:	None; K-12 Education; LIS Work
Grinnell:	None; K-12 Education; Writer
Kalamazoo:	K-12 Education; None; Science/Math
Lawrence:	None; Arts; K-12 Education
Macalester:	None; K-12 Education; (tie) Government, Health Professions, and Law
Swarthmore:	None; (tie) Higher Education and Writer

It may be helpful here to return to the four CALS Alums whose choices were noted above to see whether their career aspirations had radically changed or become clarified at the beginning of their undergraduate years: The Kalamazoo Alum, who had wanted to be a fireman, now planned to be a lawyer. The Grinnell Alum (teacher or poet) was "Uncertain—interested in and good at lots of different subjects in school." Our Denison Alum, who was uncertain but always interested in service, was still "undecided. I suppose [my career goal] was to find out what I wanted to do." And the Swarthmore Alum, whose early goals ranged from biologist to clothes designer, reported that her "career goals when I started college were vague at best. I thought I might become a teacher."

"In what other occupations or work have you been interested—in addition to or instead of LIS?"

Even after developing or beginning a career, there may be other fields of endeavor that a person may find attractive. The CALS Alums were asked if, after college, there were non-LIS occupations or work that interested them (Q.III-3). Fewer Alums responded to this, but for those who did, the top three careers were found to be

- K-12 Education
- Arts
- Writer

[20]Given that 78 percent of the Alums are women, it is worth noting that Pascarella and Terenzini (1991, 460) cite two studies that find that attending a liberal arts college enhances (1) "the choice of a sex-atypical major" and (2) "the likelihood of one's majoring in the biological sciences and choosing a career in typically male-dominated fields such as academia and the physical sciences."

K-12 Education was the most common response from Alums at all of the colleges except Earlham, which gave it second place. By CALS college, the top three non-LIS occupational interests were

Carleton:	K-12 Education; Writer; Health Professions
Denison:	K-12 Education; (tie) Arts, Sales, and Writer
Earlham:	Arts; K-12 Education; (tie) Science/Math and Social Services
Grinnell:	K-12 Education; (tie) Business and Social Services
Kalamazoo:	K-12 Education; Writer; Arts
Lawrence:	K-12 Education; Arts; Business
Macalester:	K-12 Education; Business; (tie) Arts and Writer
Swarthmore:	K-12 Education; Arts; Writer

Overall, at some point after leaving college, 9 percent to 31 percent of the CALS respondents still found K-12 Education to be an attractive idea as a career. For our four intrepid Alums, this question provided an opportunity to discuss work that might be a hobby or a potential second career. The Kalamazoo '66 (school) Alum who was first going to be a fireman and then a lawyer has also considered being "a historian, [or an] instructor of the learning disabled." The Grinnell '71 (public) Alum has regained a childhood interest in "teaching or counseling." The Denison '81 (academic) Alum acknowledged that, although she was undecided during childhood—but with a service interest—and undecided as a first year college student, she did once have a brief interest in "oceanography [or] marine biology." And the Swarthmore '96 (special) Alum has at times found "advertising [or] teaching" to be interesting ideas for an occupation. Teaching in some form is still of interest to three of the four.

"What other occupation(s) have you considered going into?"

Being interested in another field does not mean actually making the move to change careers, so the CALS Alums were also asked about other occupations which they have actually considered adopting over the course of their work life; that is, leaving LIS and changing fields (Q.III-5). Twenty-six fields were identified, and the three most frequently mentioned are

- K-12 Education
- None
- Writer

"None" was the first choice for Carleton, Earlham, and Lawrence Alums. If it is removed, then the list reads

- K-12 Education
- Writer
- (tie) Arts, Business, and Health Professions

K-12 Education is the first or second choice of Alums from all eight colleges. Writing is on everyone's list as first, second, or third choice of career with the range of interest in it varying from 7 percent (Kalamazoo) to 24 percent (Denison) of each college's Alums. By CALS college, the top three choices for alternative careers are

Carleton:	None; K-12 Education; Writer
Denison:	Writer; None; Doing Some Kind of Outdoor Work
Earlham:	None; K-12 Education; Writer
Grinnell:	(tie) Consultant and K-12 Education; (tie) None, Health Professions, and Writer
Kalamazoo:	K-12 Education; (tie) None and Business
Lawrence:	(tie) None, Health Professions, and Writer; (tie) Arts, K-12 Education, and Law
Macalester:	K-12 Education; Business; Writer
Swarthmore:	K-12 Education; Writer; Higher Education

For our Kalamazoo '66 (school) and Denison '81 (academic) Alums, there was no alternative career of interest that they would consider to LIS. Our Grinnell '71 (public) Alum is still thinking of teaching and counseling, but has also developed an interest in journalism. And our Swarthmore '96 (special) Alum is still attracted to "advertising [or] teaching."

"In what other occupations have you been involved over the course of your worklife?"

In terms of other occupations in which the Alums do have work experience, the top three are (Q.III-4)

- K-12 Education
- Business
- Office Work

For CALS members from five of the eight colleges, K-12 Education is the most common occupation in which they have experience; a range of two to 18 percent of the Alums (table 20). Business is one of the top three for Alums from five of the eight colleges. Office Work is one of the top three for six of the eight colleges. One new field shows up: Waiter/Waitress. Two percent of the CALS members, representing five of the eight colleges, say they have had experience in this area at some point over the course of their worklife. It is the one and only time this type of work is listed by the Alums.

By CALS college, the top three non-LIS occupations in which Alums have worked are

Carleton:	K-12 Education; Office Work; (tie) Business and Sales
Denison:	Office Work; Sales; (tie) Business and Social Services
Earlham:	Social Services; (tie) K-12 Education and Office Work

Table 20: Experience in Other Occupations

Other Occupations	Avg (%)	C	D	E	G	K	L	M	S
		Colleges (%)							
K-12 Education	13	12	2	9	11	16	18	15	16
Business	10	8	9	6	16	8	16	15	8
Office Work	9	10	16	9	11	10	5	5	13

Grinnell: (tie) Business, Social Services, and Volunteering; (tie) K-12 Education and Office Work
Kalamazoo: K-12 Education; Office Work; Business
Lawrence: K-12 Education; Business; Arts
Macalester: (tie) K-12 Education and Business; Sales
Swarthmore: K-12 Education; Office Work; (tie) Arts, Business, Higher Education, and Writer

All of the Alums from Grinnell have had occupations outside LIS. That is not true for Alums from the other seven colleges, where 4 to 12 percent have experienced only LIS as their career, with 12 percent being most common.

All four of the Alums we have been following have, at this point, worked in other fields. The Kalamazoo '66 (school) Alum has also done "teaching, historical research, house-parenting, bookkeeping, and water systems operations." The Grinnell '71 (public) Alum has been "a counselor in women's health education, a volunteer literacy tutor, [and] an interviewer (in Spanish) for community needs assessment for a neighborhood school/center." The Denison '81 (academic) representative has worked in retail, and the Swarthmore '96 (special) Alum notes that she has worked "with several nonprofits—fund-raising, programming, and volunteer management."

So what has been learned from this review of the Alums' career choices and intentions, from childhood through to their current status in the early twenty-first century? From childhood through college and into their work lives, the Alums moved through phases well articulated in the career choice literature. As children, they modeled professionals they encountered, such as doctors or nurses, or they wanted to be a teacher, like a parent or sibling (DeRidder 1990, Jodl et al. 2001; Mortimer et al. 1992). By the time they entered college, a number had become intrigued by the biological and physical sciences. As they moved from college into the workplace, creative interests were more fully articulated through the arts and in writing.

Finally, while there was significant similarity across the colleges in the Alums' various stages of career interest, there were also some differences (see appendix C: Q.III-1-5 and appendix F for more detail). For example:

- As children and as freshmen, more Carleton and Lawrence Alums showed particular interest in science and math (Q.III-1-2)

- At the start of college, Denison and Earlham Alums evidenced the greatest interest in LIS and in book-related fields (Q.III-2)
- The largest percentages of those interested and involved in business over the course of their work lives came from Grinnell and Macalester (Q.III-3-4)
- The largest concentration of Kalamazoo Alums have had, and continue to have, K-12 Education as an interest or personal involvement (Q.III-1-5)
- Writing was ranked among the top three interests (from childhood on) of Swarthmore Alums (Q.III-1-5)

In terms of previous occupations, both the 431 CALS Alums and the 3,516 LIS master's students in the White and Macklin study had experience in education, with White and Macklin (1970) noting that it "accounted for more than half the occupations mentioned if you count all levels of teaching from primary school to college." And Morrison (1969) reports that, of the 707 academic librarians he studied, one-third indicated that they had previous experience in teaching.

DeRidder (1990) believes that "parents have a pervasive and continual influence on their children's career development, beginning with early childhood and continuing as the child progresses through fantasy, exploration, tentative and trial stages of career development, and as the child responds to the question 'What do you want to be when you grow up?' " The basic conclusion to be drawn about career interests of the CALS Alums is that they were, and continue to be, attracted to involvement with education, especially K-12 Education—before, during, and after college. As seen in table 21, K-12 or Higher Education is one of the most common occupations for the Alums' family members, including spouses or partners. And beginning in their childhood and continuing through adulthood, K-12 Education has remained an interest of the CALS members.

Sixty-six percent of the CALS Alums have mothers, and 77 percent have fathers, with baccalaureate or post-baccalaureate education. A large number of the Alums also have parents, siblings, and spouses or partners who engage in education as an occupation. Given such an abiding interest (including experience) in education, what led the Alums to choose LIS for their career?

IV. The Alums Choose LIS

Morrison (1969) suggests that one reason precollege students consider teaching more than other fields is because they observe teaching earlier and more frequently (that is, through schooling) than other careers. In the CALS study, 19 percent of the Alums have parents with careers in K-16 education. Five percent have parents with careers in LIS work; 2 percent have siblings who work in the field. While 5 percent is only 42 Alums with parents engaged in LIS work, birth order is an intriguing factor to consider in why they chose the field: 55 percent of those 42 CALS Alums are either the only child or the oldest child in their family, and 26 percent are the youngest. In three cases, both parents are in the LIS field, and the Alum is the

Table 21: Most Prevalent Occupations and Interests

Mother	*Father*	*Siblings*	*Spouse/Partner*	
Homemaker K-12 Education (tie) LIS Work and Office Work	Business Higher Education Engineering	Business K-12 Education Health Professions	LIS Work Higher Education (tie) Business, Computer Work, and K-12 Education	
Alums' Interest in, or Connection with, a Field from Childhood Forward:				
Child	*College*	*Interested in*	*Considered*	*Experience with*
K-12 Education No Career Goals Health Professions	None K-12 Education Science/Math	K-12 Education Arts Writer	K-12 Education None (tie) Arts, Health Professions, and Business	K-12 Education Business Office Work

Alums: Frequency with Which a Field Appears from Childhood Forward:

Five times = K-12 Education
Three times = Business
Two times = Arts; Health Professions
One time = Science/Math (college); Writer (interest); Office Work (experience with)

oldest child in the family. An only child and first and last children tend to receive more parental attention, encouragement, career direction, and resources to support their decisions than do children "in the middle" (Kelly 2002). In our case, these particular Alums may have, from an early age, modeled their parents or been encouraged by them to see LIS in a favorable light.

Overall, 12 percent of the Alums were between ages 5 and 15 when they first thought about going into LIS work, 11 percent were 16-19, the majority (66 percent) were 20-30 years old, and 11 percent were 31-50 (Q.II-2). The LIS literature suggests that around 25 percent of LIS professionals consider the field prior to graduation from high school, and—depending upon the study—30-50 percent after college (Schiller 1969, Morrison 1969, White and Macklin 1970; Heim and Moen 1989). The CALS Alums and the White and Macklin (1970) studies are the most comparable in terms of age ranges. Table 22 shows that approximately 23 percent in each study considered the field prior to age 21 (K through college), and 77 percent postcollege.

In addition, even the more recent 1992 ACRL study found that 50 percent of the ALA and SLA respondents were 24 or younger when they decided to enter the field; 80 percent had decided by the time they were 30 with 25 as the average age (Scherdin 1994a).

To learn about the career "influencers" of the CALS participants, the survey questionnaire asked them to select from a prescribed list those factors that had led them to think that LIS would be an attractive career (Q.II-3A-D). The factors were drawn from the 1992 Farber/Bingham study of Earlham alumni who had entered LIS and were arranged in the following four broad categories:

Table 22: Age When First Considered LIS as a Career

CALS Alums: 1962-2000 time period (%)		White and Macklin: data collected from 1969 LIS students (%)	
age 5-15	12	17 and under	8
16-19	11	18-20	15
20-30	66	21-30	47
31-40	8	31-40	18
over 40	3	over 40	12

- General career-related factors (an area covering broad topics ranging from the love of reading through working conditions, image of the field, availability of a job, and length of the graduate program)
- Opportunities associated with the career
- Relationship to or encouragement from other people
- Experience in using or working in libraries

In all, the Alums had 47 items to consider, and they could checkmark any and all that they felt were applicable. In addition, they were asked in an open-ended question to list any other factors not covered by the 47 questions.

General Career Factors

Within this category, the three most frequently chosen reasons are ones long associated with the LIS field (Q.II-3A; table 23). The second choice (*Desire to work with/help people*) is an altruistic reason; the other two of the top three are individualistic in nature. By overall response and by college ranking, the Alums feel strongest about these eight general reasons (see appendix B and appendix C: Q.II-3A for the entire list).

Other choices, including those relating to *Salary*, the *Status/image of LIS professionals*, and *Receipt of written information on LIS as a career*, drew the fewest responses (1-2 percent) as factors that caused Alums to think LIS would be an attractive career (appendix C: Q.II-3A). By cohort, *Bibliographic instruction in classes taken at college* was selected by 1 to 4 percent of the Alums with the highest percentages beginning with the 1976-80 classes. However, when analyzed by college, it is clear that this selection was driven almost solely by Earlham respondents, who were exposed to classroom bibliographic and library instruction sessions beginning in 1964 (appendix C-D: Q-II-3A; Farber 1995).

Love of books/reading was clearly a strong value for the CALS members, making a field associated with these activities very attractive. For the Earlham and Grinnell Alums, the *Intellectual challenges of the field* were just as attractive, while Denison and Swarthmore Alums believed the field's *values* were similar to their own. Although the second and third reasons are tied when the colleges are taken together, table 23 shows the Alums varying in how

Table 23: General Career Factors (by College)

General Career Factors	Avg (%)	College (%) C	D	E	G	K	L	M	S
Love of books/reading	16	19	16	13	16	18	17	19	16
Desire to work with/help people	15	17	14	13	11	15	16	17	16
Fit with values/ideals important to me	15	15	16	13	11	16	14	17	17
Intellectual challenge provided by LIS	14	14	15	14	16	15	15	15	14
Working conditions	10	8	12	10	16	9	10	10	11
Availability of variety of job possibilities	8	8	7	8	11	9	9	6	6
Flexibility for better management of my other life commitments	7	7	10	6	11	6	8	4	8
Length/structure/requirements of LIS graduate programs	7	9	6	7	3	6	7	7	8

strongly they felt about wanting to work with or help people and how compatible the field was with their values or ideals. However, there is only a one to three percentage point difference for any of the colleges between their three or four most frequently marked general reasons; so the variation is small.

Table 24 presents these findings by cohort. The top ranking for the *Love of books/reading* held true over the 39 years represented by the Alums. Interestingly, the two groups that show the lowest support for *Desire to work with/helping people* are the bookends: the oldest (1962-65) and the youngest (1996-2000) cohorts.

Opportunities Associated with the LIS Field

The Alums felt a career in LIS would have a number of the listed Opportunity Factors associated with it (Q.II-3B). The main responses are shown in tables 25 and 26.

Aside from the clear belief that *Jobs* were available in the field, Alums were attracted to both *Learning* for themselves and learning in terms of *Educating* others. There was also interest in technology, although not enough Alums from any of the colleges marked it frequently enough for it to rank in the top three or four most common selections. The colleges broke into two groups on the *Technology* factor: 11-14 percent of Alums from Carleton, Denison, Earlham, Macalester, and Swarthmore favored the LIS field because of it, while only 1 to 9 percent of those from Grinnell, Kalamazoo, and Lawrence did. The idea of *Educating others*, as an opportunity within the field, appealed most to Earlham Alums and least to Swarthmore and Macalester Alums.

Table 24: General Career Factors (by Cohort)

General Career Factors	All (%)	Cohort (%) 62-	66-	71-	76-	81-	86-	91-	96-
Love of books/reading	16	18	17	16	16	14	16	16	14
Desire to work with/help people	15	13	15	15	16	14	16	16	13
Fit with values/ideals important to me	15	16	16	16	13	13	14	14	14
Intellectual challenge provided by LIS	14	15	14	14	14	13	17	15	14
Working conditions	10	10	9	9	9	11	12	12	13
Availability of variety of job possibilities	8	8	9	7	9	8	7	6	5
Flexibility for better management of my other life commitments	7	7	7	8	4	7	9	6	9
Length/structure/requirements of LIS graduate program	7	6	8	8	7	8	5	6	6

Table 25: Opportunities Associated with the Field (by College)

Opportunity Factors	All (%)	College (%) C	D	E	G	K	L	M	S
For a job	23	22	23	19	30	29	23	23	24
To learn to use/do research with a variety of information resources	19	19	24	19	4	18	17	19	18
To educate others	18	21	18	20	22	17	21	13	15
To combine LIS with some other area of interest /skill	16	13	9	17	17	17	17	14	18
For professional growth	14	14	15	12	22	14	13	17	15
Work with increasingly sophisticated information technology	10	12	11	12	1	5	9	14	11

By cohort, not unexpectedly, the availability of jobs was very important. Seven of the eight cohorts considered *Opportunities for a job* particularly influential in their career decision making (table 26). The 1991-95 cohort members, however, had just as much interest in *Learning to use/do research with a variety of information resources.* In fact, the majority of the classes placed it second in importance, with only the 1986-90 cohort finding it less compelling. The 1996-2000 cohort was equally interested in *Jobs*, *Working with information resources*, and *Educating others.* And for the 1986-90 cohort, *Educating others* and then *Jobs* were the strongest opportunity attractions of the field.

Table 26: Opportunities Associated with the Field (by Cohort)

Opportunity Factors	Avg (%)	Cohort (%)							
		62-	66-	71-	76-	81-	86-	91-	96-
For a job	23	26	25	22	20	25	24	20	22
To learn to use/do research with a variety of information resources	19	20	20	20	19	18	14	20	22
To educate others	18	20	18	16	19	17	26	17	22
To combine LIS with some other area of interest/skill	16	10	13	16	19	18	23	17	16
For professional growth	14	18	15	15	13	10	13	13	9
Work with increasingly sophisticated information technology	10	6	8	12	11	14	13	13	9

The CALS Alums were not asked to indicate whether they had experienced more than one career—only whether they had been involved in other occupations. In their comments, it is clear that some of that involvement prevailed for several years, some of it was summer-only work, and in many cases there is no indication of the length of the involvement. Thus, while 78 percent of the Alums have experienced work other than LIS, it is not known if it was instrumental in their subsequent choice of LIS as a career. A career in LIS as a way to *Combine interest areas/skills* might be of particular importance to two groups. It may have a higher value to those who desired to enter academic librarianship, where there has been progressive pressure for professionals to have a second master's degree. It might also have had a higher value to Alums who turned to LIS as a second career after many years of building skills and interests in another field.

Professional growth, as an opportunity within the field, was of less concern for most of the cohorts. The 1962-65 Alums valued it more highly—perhaps because they are now at the top of their career and have seen the benefits of it. And with the increasing commitment of LIS graduate programs to expand into *Information technologies*, it is noteworthy that the majority of Alums expressed such little attraction to it as a reason to select LIS as their career.

Relationship/Encouragement from Other People

Recall that Morrison (1969) suggests that one reason precollege students consider teaching more than, for example, LIS is because they observe teaching earlier and much more frequently than they do LIS. The Alums were asked if a librarian, family member, friend, or teacher had encouraged them in some way to consider the field (Q.II-3C; table 27).

Table 27: Relationship/Encouragement from Other People (by College)

Relationship/Encouragement Factors	Avg (%)	College (%)							
		C	D	E	G	K	L	M	S
A librarian during K-12 years	33	41	31	20	56	33	46	39	36
A librarian after college graduation	18	23	19	19	6	15	17	12	28
A librarian at college	16	12	11	25	11	21	7	15	5
A family member who was a librarian	10	10	11	8	6	11	11	13	9
A family member who was not a librarian	10	11	14	13	6	9	7	8	8
A friend	10	17	14	9	11	9	10	12	8
A teacher	4	6	0	6	6	3	3	1	5

While close to 100 percent of Alums indicated that reasons listed in the "General" or the "Opportunities" sections made LIS seem an appealing career, only 90 percent checked any of the reasons in the "People" category. Even so, for the CALS Alums of seven of the colleges, a *Librarian during their K-12 years* served as the major role model of LIS professionals or provided some impetus to consider the field. For Earlham Alums, a number of whom were already considering LIS work when they entered college, the importance of a *Librarian during K-12 years* ranked second. A school or public librarian was important to one-third (33 percent) of the Alums in their career decision making. Their interactions with such librarians were most noticeable during the elementary years and again while the CALS participants were in high school, with responses ranging from a low of 20 percent (Earlham) to a high of 56 percent (Grinnell). Without regard to library type, White and Macklin (1970) report that 25 percent of their respondents were influenced by librarians; Heim and Moen (1989) report 36 percent.

By cohort (see table 28), the importance of public or school *Librarians during the K-12 years* is indisputable, as it draws responses from the greatest number of CALS Alums marking this section across all classes. This table also clarifies the importance of a relationship with an *LIS professional at and after college*. Except for the earliest and the most recent classes, there is a clear connection between the Alums and a *Librarian after college graduation*. Comments from several Alums in the 1966-95 cohorts reveal that this connection was most frequently the result of (1) Alums working in libraries after college but before (or during) their graduate LIS education, or (2) LIS being a second career for the Alums who had interacted with LIS professionals while in their former career. However, for four of the cohorts (1962-65, 1966-70, 1986-90, and 1996-2000), the influence of a *Librarian at college* was as strong as that of a *Librarian after college.*

Table 28: Relationship/Encouragement from Other People (by Cohort)

Relationship/Encouragement Factors	Avg (%)	Cohorts (%)							
		62-	66-	71-	76-	81-	86-	91-	96-
A librarian during K-12 years	33	31	34	36	31	27	37	34	32
A librarian after college graduation	18	14	17	20	20	17	19	17	16
A librarian at college	16	14	17	13	16	15	19	16	16
A family member who was a librarian	10	9	7	11	9	14	10	8	21
A family member who was not a librarian	10	16	11	7	9	12	5	11	5
A friend	10	12	11	8	12	9	3	14	11
A teacher	4	3	4	5	3	6	7	0	0

The high ranking by 1962-65 Alums of a *Family member who is not a librarian* might reflect the more limited professional opportunities for women at that time. For example, if the CALS respondent did not want to be a teacher, family members may have suggested LIS work as a related, but also "appropriate," field for her. However, this suggestion is pure speculation. What seems to be more the case is the greater connection the Alums had with working, particularly in libraries where they might have interacted with LIS professionals. This is exemplified by the comment of a Carleton '62 respondent:

> Outside of work part-time for a year at the National Opinion Research Center when I was a Master's student, plus a summer of field work when I was 16, every job I've had has involved libraries, including all of my student jobs.

In fact, depending upon the nature of her NORC work, that too might now be considered simply one of the many variants of LIS work.

For CALS Alums from six of the eight colleges, *Family members* also served as significant influencers. This mirrors other findings in the career choice and development literature. Parents who have knowledge of higher education, who are in professional fields, and who stress education and achievement serve not only as important influencers but also as *value socializers* (Douglas and Guttman 2000; Freeman 2002; Astin 1984). Parents also have influence in their roles as "interpreters of reality and providers of experiences" for their children (Jodl et al. 2001, 1248). As Rosenberg (1957, 6) puts it, "Whenever an individual makes a selection from a given number of alternatives, it is likely that some *value* is behind the decision. An occupational choice is not a value, but it is made on the basis of values . . . When an individual chooses an occupation, he thinks there is something 'good' about it, and this conception of the 'good' is part of an internalized mental structure which establishes priorities." It is likely that the Alums included values gained from their parents, for example regarding education or educating others, when they began to think there might be something good about doing LIS work. On the

Table 29: Influencers in Rank Order

CALS Alums (1962-2000 data): Ranking	Heim and Moen (1988 data): Ranking
Pre- and post-college librarians	Pre-college librarians
Family members	Friends
College librarians	Teachers
Friends	College librarians
Teachers	Family members

overall question of people who influenced them, table 29 shows that Heim and Moen's (1989) MLIS students and the CALS Alums compare quite favorably.

Experience Using or Working in Libraries

We turn now to the question of what early experience in libraries the CALS Alums had, and the role that might have played in their coming to believe LIS might be an interesting career (Q.II-3D). Close to 95 percent of the Alums proffered multiple reasons in this category (table 30). The first three options that they could mark were about *using* a library; the second three related to *working* in a library. By college, a range of 23 percent (Denison and Lawrence) to 28 percent (Earlham) indicated that *Using their college library* influenced their ideas about LIS as a career. Earlham and Denison also serve as the low and high ends regarding whether or not *Using their high school library* is an influencing factor: the range is from 18 percent (Earlham) to 32 percent (Denison). In general, the percentage difference between the influence exerted by the Alums' college and their high school library appears to be small.

In responding to this question on "Experiences in Libraries," some Alums indicated the type of library they had used. Whether using or working in a library during high school, they most often indicated public libraries, then (in descending order) school, academic, and special libraries. However, for those who indicated they worked in a library between college graduation and entering a graduate LIS program, 38 percent were employed in academic libraries, 34 percent in public, 12 percent in school library media centers, and 17 percent in special or other LIS agencies (Q.II-3D). Heim and Moen (1989) reported that 28 percent of their respondents had worked in academic libraries, 35 percent in public libraries, 16 percent in school library media centers, and 21 percent in special libraries. The largest difference between the two studies is in the percentage of respondents who had worked in academic libraries: 38 percent of the Alums compared to 28 percent of the Heim and Moen students. More of the latter worked in school and special library settings than did the CALS respondents.

Table 30: Library Experience Factors (by College)

Library Experience Factors	Avg (%)	College (%) C	D	E	G	K	L	M	S
Using the library at college	26	25	23	28	24	26	23	27	27
Using a library during high school	23	25	32	18	24	22	25	28	23
Using a library after graduating from college	18	18	19	19	19	16	19	17	21
Working in a library after college but before entering a LIS graduate program	15	16	16	17	10	15	15	9	12
Working in the library at college	11	9	6	14	14	14	7	15	11
Working in a library during my high school years	6	6	3	5	10	8	10	4	6

It is clear that, by cohort, *Using the college library* was a consistently meaningful activity across the 39 years represented by the CALS Alums (table 31). Two cohorts are particularly interesting: the 1966-70 cohort, whose members felt as strongly influenced by *Using a library during high school* as they were by using one at college, and the 1996-2000 cohort where almost half of the CALS respondents found *Using the college library* to be influential.

In a closed-ended question, Heim and Moen (1989, 81) asked their MLIS students how frequently they used their college library. Seventy-two percent checked "one or more times per week," followed by 18 percent at "two to three times per month." It makes sense that as students get closer to considering what to do after college, they would also take more notice of work activity that is going on around them, including becoming more attuned to the work that the college librarians and other staff are doing (Morrison 1969).

In contrast to the Alums' use of libraries, *Working in a library*—whether during high school, at college, or prior to attending a graduate LIS program—proved not to be a significant influencing factor. Yet fully 33 percent of the respondents were employed in their college library (Q.II-5). The lowest percentage is from Denison Alums (19 percent); the highest from Earlham Alums (46 percent). And of that 33 percent, 79 percent were employed for two to four years (Q.II-5A). The most common place for student employment was circulation/access services (35 percent), followed by acquisitions/collection development (13 percent), and cataloging and reference (each at 11 percent) (Q.II-5B). Other service units included a broad range of special collections—a particular attraction for Lawrence, Macalester, and Swarthmore Alums. Fifty-five percent of the Alums indicated they initiated the quest for a job in their college library, 25 percent say a position was gained through work study assignments, 12 percent were approached by the library director, and 4 percent cite interaction with other library staff as the stimulus (Q.II-5C). The remaining 4 percent stated that a parent, friend, or professor knew someone on the staff who helped secure a student worker position. Those who indicated that the library director

Table 31: Library Experience Factors (by Cohort)

Library Experience Factors	Avg (%)	62-	66-	71-	76-	81-	86-	91-	96-
		Cohort (%)							
Using the library at college	26	28	24	26	25	27	27	26	45
Using a library during high school	23	25	24	24	23	23	17	25	23
Using a library after graduating from college	18	20	18	19	20	16	17	15	14
Working in a library after college but before entering a LIS graduate program	15	13	16	14	16	15	17	14	0
Working in the library at college	11	7	11	10	12	14	14	12	18
Working in a library during my high school years	6	6	7	7	5	5	9	7	0

sought them out are from only three of the eight colleges: Earlham (19 percent), Kalamazoo (24 percent), and Swarthmore (7 percent). The same three, plus Lawrence, had library staff who suggested the CALS Alums take student positions in the library.

The study's participants were then asked what they remembered about their college's library director (Q.II-6; table 32). Overall, 61 percent remembered nothing or felt neutral, 27 percent made positive comments, 4 percent made negative comments, and 8 percent of the Alums described their director in glowing terms. Not surprisingly, during the 39 years represented by the Alums, the directorship of all eight of the libraries changed. Some Alums who were in college when directors changed noted liking one and not another. Negative comments focused on the director not being involved in day-to-day activities, which troubled especially those Alums who were working in the library at the time. Neutral comments were generally from Alums who remembered nothing about the director, did not know who the director was when they were in college, or knew the director but had no interaction with her or him. In the cases of Lawrence, Macalester, and Swarthmore, some of the former directors taught non-LIS disciplinary courses and were remembered by members of those colleges' earlier cohorts more for their role as classroom faculty. Positive comments clustered into two groups: appreciation for the state of the library, which was attributed to the efforts of the director; and personal, rewarding interaction with the director. The Earlham, Kalamazoo, and Macalester Alums who made positive or outstanding remarks tended to use role-modeling words in their descriptions:

> Evan Farber seemed to create the kind of work environment I wanted to be in: supportive and intellectually challenging. (Earlham '91; public)

Table 32: Alums' Recollections of Their College Library's Director (by College)

College Library Directors	Avg (%)	College (%) C	D	E	G	K	L	M	S
Negative	4	3	4	0	25	5	4	3	5
Nothing/Neutral	61	86	92	17	76	55	80	69	90
Positive	27	11	4	62	0	30	16	21	5
Outstanding	8	0	0	21	0	11	0	8	0

> Dr. Chen taught me a lot about respect for people and respect for business needs in staffing. Eleanor Pinkham taught me a lot about working with, and expecting the best from, people. (Kalamazoo '66; special)

> We knew who he was—not hidden away. A rock band called "Dewey Decimal and the Librarians" was in honor of the library director! (Macalester '62; public)

The director can make a singular difference in the perspective students have of a profession, as the following comments about Earlham's Evan I. Farber illustrate:

> Very friendly and encouraging. Willing to work with students. Took the time to educate me about libraries and librarianship. ('62; special)

> Evan Farber was a wonderful librarian and his presence encouraged many students to go into librarianship. ('71; special)

> It seemed to me that even though Evan was the "director," he was a librarian first. He was as dedicated to helping the students and faculty learn how to use the library as all of the rest of the library staff. He was friendly and approachable. ('91; public)

The Nothing/Neutral reaction to directors was not surprising to the libraries' current directors. In interviews for this study (2004), all of them indicated that the opportunities they have to interact with most students have changed. Several who used to do reference work with students bemoan the fact that now they must either restrict that opportunity or forgo it all together. For an example of the role changes, consider the contrast Tom Kirk, Earlham College Library Director, makes between himself and Evan I. Farber, who was the library's director from 1962 to 1999:

> Evan met every student [in] every section of the Humanities [course] in the '70s [by] doing library instruction . . . I see all new students during orientation week and welcome them to the college. Evan did that and the Humanities [instruction],

> and he also did a lot of the instruction in English and History. I don't do that much because that is passed over to the librarians.

One reason much of the direct involvement is now the responsibility of the librarians is because, whereas earlier directors were responsible for just the library, the current directors may administer the library, the campus media service, and the institution's information technology unit. The library may also be a larger physical and organizational entity than in 1962. Or it may be part of a consortium, as in the case of Swarthmore where Librarian Peggy Seiden is engaged substantially in the work of the TriColleges (Swarthmore, Bryn Mawr, and Haverford). Whatever the cause for the expansion of responsibilities, the result is that the directors now have more interactions with administrators, faculty, and campus staff than with students—other than student representatives involved with those academic units and student library workers. Indeed, every director indicated that, as Denison Library Director Lynn Scott (Scottie) Cochrane puts it, "it is more important for the librarians as a group to be visible among the students. It is important that I be more visible among the faculty."

The Alums had clearer recollections of the working librarians, and those images were more favorable (Q.II-7; table 33). Comments revealed that this was partly because they interacted more frequently with the librarians than with the directors.

The negative comments centered on librarians who did not seem to want to help students, or who were not friendly or personable, or who were too rule-oriented. The Nothing/Neutral responses came from Alums who acknowledged knowing there were librarians around, but who either did not ask for assistance from them or simply recalled very little about them. Some respondents reflected that the librarians seemed "pleasant" but they had no real memories of them beyond that. Positive comments focused on how helpful the librarians were "such as when I was in my usual 'procrastinatory' panic" (Grinnell '86; special). The Alums who were positive about their college librarians described the latter as approachable, friendly, personable, very skilled and helpful, very knowledgeable, courteous, and supportive of students. One Lawrence Alum ('91 academic) recalled that the librarians were "very professional, yet pretty laid-back. Always concerned about the students—I always received excellent help from them." The 33 percent of Alums who were employed in the college library while undergraduates expressed appreciation for being able to work with the librarians. A Swarthmore Alum ('91; public) summed up her work experiences this way:

> Witnessing their excitement over/enjoyment in pursuing a reference question. The environment was warm—I got to do quite exciting (to me) things as a student worker in Friends Historical Library (handling centuries-old letters and minute-books). Folks seemed happy to be doing what they were doing.

A Macalester Alum ('76; public) noted that "the evening/weekend librarians were all new MLS graduates and were fun to work with even though they made sure we got our work done."

Table 33: Alums' Recollections of Their College Library's Librarians (by College)

College Library Librarians	Avg (%)	College (%) C	D	E	G	K	L	M	S
Negative	5	11	4	2	13	3	2	5	10
Nothing/Neutral	43	57	54	24	76	42	53	42	42
Positive	51	32	42	74	13	55	44	54	49

Other Factors

The CALS participants also had the opportunity to write in reasons beyond the checklist of 47 that factor into their belief that LIS might be an attractive career (Q.II-4). The most common reason was that they saw LIS as a pathway. As a field, they believed it would allow them to combine things they loved. A Carleton and two Kalamazoo Alums illustrate this approach to LIS:

> I knew that I wanted to work with books and children. After Carleton, I explored a number of options, including writing/editing, teaching, working in a bookstore, etc. I had always used the public library, especially as a child, and thought that perhaps library work would combine my interests. I loved and had a lot of knowledge of children's books and thought that a degree in library science might lead to a job more quickly than a master's in children's literature. (Carleton '91; public)

> I knew that I wanted work that connected me to the community, and I was not at all interested in social work, or religious work. (Kalamazoo '71; public)

> Exposure to breadth of subjects (always new and interesting). Nice way to combine History major and Computer Sci. minor. (Kalamazoo '91; special)

A second, fairly common reason was the intellectual pull of LIS, as noted by an Earlham ('81; special) Alum:

> I wanted, at a personal level, to feel that I had an understanding [of]—and to some degree, control over—information. It was like a continuation or expansion of my liberal arts education—what didn't I know and how would I be able to find out about it sometime in the future? Like being offered a magic key.

When subordinate factors (such as specific library type) are combined with main factors, 32 factors cluster into the five categories of general, opportunities, people, library experience, and other. Taken together, across college as well as cohort, the following represent the most significant reasons the Alums gave for thinking that LIS might be a good career:

- It fit with the values and ideals that are important to them, including their desire to work with or help people.
- They were attracted to the level and variety of intellectual challenge that the field provides, and it supported their love of reading or books.
- They could combine interests while working within the field.
- They found using libraries during high school and college to be positive experiences, and there were opportunities for a job.

The Alums' choices correspond closely to those of the 3,484 LIS master's students in the Heim and Moen (1989) study. The Heim and Moen respondents indicated how important each of 11 factors were in their decision making. Their top three reasons were "intellectual opportunities," "service orientation," and "variety of positions" available within the field.

The Ultimate Reason for LIS Graduate Work

For most people, the precollege and college years cover two of Super's *Life Span* stages: Growth and Exploration. By the age of 13 (end of growth) adolescents are becoming future oriented and are considering a large array of "what I want to be"; by age 24 (end of exploration) they have engaged in what Rosenberg (1957) calls the "*progressive delimitation of alternatives.*" During their childhoods, 5 percent of this study's participants considered becoming a librarian (Q.III-1). For the CALS respondents from six of the colleges, that figure rose to 7 percent upon entering college; it rose to 10 percent for Denison and Earlham Alums (Q.III-2). There were Alums who wrote of being "called" to the field in the sense that they were so passionate about it that they considered nothing else; others mentioned having friends or family members who were in the LIS field, and saw themselves enjoying it also. Yet, when asked what actually made them attend an LIS graduate program, 60 percent of the Alums' responses indicated that LIS was seen as meeting one or more of these needs (Q.II-9):

- It fit better than alternatives they had considered or experienced.
- There were opportunities for jobs.
- Its intellectual aspects were appealing.

Fit

In discussing their ultimate reason for choosing the career, 33 percent of the CALS Alums wrote about how the field fit their needs. This breaks into two groupings. Twenty-two percent of the Alums weighed other career options, or had already experienced other careers. They concluded that LIS was a better fit than the alternatives. A number indicated they wanted to use their undergraduate major—such as English or History—but could not find a satisfying job which allowed this. As an Earlham Alum ('76; special) put it: "I had a degree in English and I did not want to teach." Another set of Alums felt LIS allowed them to combine their multiple interests. A career-changing Lawrence Alum ('71; public) found that "a life in the theater was not for me and librarianship offered great play for my interests in books, children, and story-telling." A Grinnell Alum ('91; academic) noted that "I needed a change, love school, and wanted to try this profession which combines so many interesting skills." A Lawrence Alum ('76; academic) described wanting "to combine [my] background in music and foreign language in an academic setting." The second grouping related to "fit" was comprised of CALS Alums (11 percent) for whom LIS was quite simply the "right fit." A Kalamazoo respondent ('86; public) wrote: "Wanting to make a career out of library science—I just *knew* it was what I wanted to do" (emphasis in original). A Macalester Alum ('91; school) says, "it fit my personality." And a Carleton Alum ('71; public) commented that "I couldn't imagine doing anything else for work."

Opportunities

Twenty-one percent entered LIS programs for graduate study because the field proffered job opportunities. A number were already working in a library as support staff and wanted advancement into the professional ranks. In a few cases, their employer indicated that the library would help pay for the education. Others had seen or heard about available jobs. Yet another group, who have some level of LIS work experience, found that they truly enjoyed the work for more than "just a pay check." A Carleton Alum ('62; public), who in college weighed a career in LIS versus regional History, explained his ultimate reason this way:

> I spent three summers during college working in a public library. Since I was replacing staff on vacation, by the end of three summers I had done almost every possible non-administrative library job—if only briefly and badly—and I had a really good sense of what the career entailed. I've never regretted the choice.

It Seemed Intellectually Challenging

Nine percent of the Alums acknowledged the intellectual nature of the field. The CALS Alums seem to have viewed LIS as a career that includes *thinking* as a regular part of the work. Since many have commented favorably on the learning aspects of their undergraduate education, it is perhaps not surprising that being involved in work that continues to call for intellectual endeavor was appealing. A Macalester Alum ('91; public) illustrates this interest when she talks about wanting a career "that dealt with ideas." And a Carleton Alum ('76; academic) commented that he wound up going into LIS when he realized he was always "hanging around La Crosse [Wisconsin] Public Library with my 3-year-old daughter and wanting to know *everything*" (emphasis in original).

Beyond these three clusters of fit, opportunities, and intellectual challenge, there were assorted other reasons for enrolling in LIS graduate work. Some CALS Alums found they were conveniently near a university with an LIS school and, having thought about the field during their undergraduate years, they decided "why not?" Others wanted a profession and "not just a job" (Kalamazoo '71; school). At this preliminary stage in their involvement in the field, only a few focused on the service role of LIS—seeing providing information to others "as a tool to help people" (Grinnell '76; public). Role models or mentors played important roles in the ultimate decision for Alums from all the colleges except Grinnell. In particular, Alums from Earlham and Swarthmore cite:

- Parents who were librarians and felt they would find the field satisfying
- College or public librarians who mentored them
- Librarians whom they wished to emulate

Summary

The notion of having a career has evolved from being "occupied with something which makes the lives of others better worth living" (Rehm 1990:117) to that which encompasses "the combinations and sequences of [all of one's] life roles" (McDaniels and Gysbers 1992, 3). Along with the evolution of "career" came theories about how a person chooses and develops one. Of the current theories articulated in this chapter, the CALS participants appear to model aspects of the *personality-focused*, *differential,* and *reinforcement-based* approaches.

The *personality-focused* approach "involves conceptualizing career choices . . . as a function of early parent-child relationships, childhood memories, family dynamics, and the personal meaning of work and careers" (Hartung and Niles 2000, 6). We quoted DeRidder's (1990, 3) explanation that "parents as daily models provide cultural standards, attitudes, and expectations . . . The attitudes and behaviors of parents while working or discussing their work is what the children respond to and learn." Lankard (1995), Mortimer et al. (1992), and others also assert that parents with post-secondary education tend to pass along its importance to their children. Given that 66 percent of their mothers and 77 percent of their fathers have baccalaureate or post-baccalaureate degrees, it seems clear that a significant number of the CALS members were guided toward acquiring a college education. Also, some aspect of education was one of the three most common careers held by their parents and siblings—and a widespread consideration for many Alums at points prior to and during their pre-LIS work lives. Thus, engaging in some kind of a role connected with education, or educating, became a positive factor when the Alums considered their own career choice. There were Alums who said "I did not want to teach!" (Earlham '76; special), but there were also several like this career-changer who said, "I wanted to stay in secondary education, but not as a classroom teacher" (Kalamazoo '66; school).

The *differential* approach focuses on matching traits such as "values, interests, aptitudes, and skills to educational or occupations factors that fit those traits" (Hartung and Niles 2000, 6). Holland's theory of personalities and work environments is a person-environment "fit" approach that describes various vocational personalities and work environments, and how they interact. *Fit* in this context "asserts that people seek out jobs with requirements that are consistent with their personality traits" (Brown and Brooks 1990, 6). In their "ultimate reason" for selecting LIS, some Alums definitely illustrated this. They felt there was a fit between themselves and LIS. Thirty-three percent of the Alums who gave reasons for undertaking LIS graduate education indicated they saw LIS as meeting their needs, like the Denison Alum ('81; academic) who "wanted a career in which I'd be of service to others." Some felt the field matched their personality. Others concluded that it would allow them to combine interests, while those who had experienced other careers believed LIS provided a more appropriate place for their skills and aptitudes.

The *reinforcement-based* approach, as represented by Krumboltz (1994) and Mitchell and Krumboltz (1996), utilizes social learning theory, which says that individuals will prefer (or reject) a particular career or occupation depending upon certain conditions, seeing success or failure from the vantage points of having

- Performed some of its work tasks
- Observed a role model having positive or negative work experiences
- Seen positive or negative images of the occupation

Recall the respondent in the section on "Opportunities" (above) who felt, after three summers of public library work doing "almost every possible nonadministrative library job," that he had "a really good sense of what the career entailed" (Carleton '62; public). Clearly, he believed he knew what tasks comprised the work of the profession and had an idea of his ability to handle them. In terms of role models, many Alums had formed positive impressions of librarians while at their undergraduate college. Several also commented on librarians who seemed to "love their jobs" (Earlham '66; academic), and who seemed to have fun doing LIS work. Finally, K-16 LIS professionals, as well as family members, encouraged the Alums to consider LIS—lending a positive validation to the field's image. And, as this study showed, 21 percent of the Alums entered LIS programs for graduate study because they believed there were opportunities for employment.

The CALS participants, as children, modeled professionals they encountered, especially teachers. In college, a number became intrigued by the biological and physical sciences. As they moved toward the workplace, creative interests were more fully articulated through interests in the arts and writing. Yet this study found that, as undergraduates, the Alums were unlike the national group of first-year women students surveyed by Dey et al. (1991). The Alums' parents had more education, higher incomes, and a greater percentage were involved in some form of K-16 education. The parents of the Alums also had higher educational levels than MLIS students' parents in the 1989 Heim and Moen national study. The Alums and the MLIS students were similar, however, in having an awareness of the intellectual and service orientations of the LIS field, and in believing that there were opportunities for employment.

By cohort, the Alums did not exhibit much variation across the 39 years represented by their 1962-2000 classes, and the career-related LIS attractions that were significant for them continue to be important today. For example, both the Alums and a group of current LIS master's students shared the following as leading factors for choosing LIS as a career: love of reading/books, a good career fit, attraction of the intellectual aspects of the work, positive library experiences during childhood, and previous or current work experience within libraries (Kniffel 2004b). In addition, there are the practical reasons for "ultimately" enrolling in an LIS graduate program, as exemplified by the four Alums whose career interests and involvements have been followed throughout the chapter:

> I was accepted into an LIS grad program even though I hadn't finished my senior thesis, and I didn't make it into any grad schools for history, plus my experiential quarter experience [in a library] was very positive. (Kalamazoo '66; academic)

> I learned that getting a degree got you more money. I worked at Grinnell after graduation as a library assistant and getting my MLS basically tripled my salary. (Grinnell '76; academic)

> I wanted a career in which I'd be of service to others but didn't want the responsibility of being in a health-related profession [like my father, mother, and only sibling]. (Denison '80; academic)

> Two years after graduation, I started spending a lot of time at a public library in Thousand Oaks, CA. It was open and sunny with a very positive atmosphere. I loved being there and knew I would thrive in that sort of atmosphere. (Swarthmore '96; special)

So after contemplating an array of professions from teaching to journalism, and after experiencing work from being a library assistant to retail and office work, the CALS Alums have chosen to enter an LIS graduate program and seek the master's degree.

CHAPTER 4

Graduate School and the Profession

This chapter considers images of library and information science as a focus of graduate study and as a field, and of librarians as professionals. An occupational image usually contains "both favorable and unfavorable components" (Wilson 1982, 5). As the CALS participants moved toward LIS as a career, they carried with them an image of both the field and its practitioners. The focus of this chapter is on their changing perceptions as they take the views developed while in college into their LIS graduate programs of study. The Alums' perceptions had led them as far as a commitment to graduate education within a professional program of study. Discussion focuses on how their images evolved as they began their own evolution into professionals.

I. Graduate School

Pascarella and Terenzini (1991, 376) find evidence to suggest "that attending a private rather than a public college or university has a net positive influence on bachelor's degree attainment, plans for attending graduate school, and overall level of educational attainment." The CALS college deans or provosts note that 60 to 80 percent of their graduates go on to graduate school—but also that many do not do so immediately. Scott Bierman, Carleton's Associate Dean, says that "the vast majority will not go immediately on to graduate school. They'll try their hand at something for a year or two just to get out there in the world and do something apart from being enmeshed in an educational institution. Then they'll go back. They want a break" (interview; see Bibliography). Swarthmore's Dean Gross believes that students are increasingly "trying to take a year or two . . . A lot look for a non-profit berth for a while before they go to law school or medical school or whatever. I think the pure PhDs are likely to continue on directly. The kids going to professional schools are more apt to take some time" (interview; see Bibliography). This concurs with Dean Hornbach's observation that Macalester graduates may take time out because "they're not looking for a job, they're looking for a profession" (interview; see Bibliography). The Grinnell website illustrates the kind of post-college activity to which the deans are referring:

> Immediately after graduation, 30 percent of Grinnellians in recent classes have gone directly to graduate or professional school, 50 percent entered the workplace, and 20 percent engaged in public service pursuits, volunteer work, or travel. Many of those who do not go immediately to graduate or professional school do so later: ten years after graduation, over 50 percent of a class typically holds at least one advanced degree. (Grinnell website, see Bibliography)

It is commonly believed by LIS educators that their master's students "tend to be older than, for example, graduate students in the liberal arts or medical school students" (Stieg 1992, 130). Stieg goes on to state:

> Two factors are usually advanced in explanation, that librarianship is so predominantly female, and that librarianship is traditionally a second choice profession. The assumption is that women are busy with young families during their twenties and, after the children are in school, seek a qualification that promises genteel employment unlikely to conflict with family responsibilities. The other cause of the age distribution is that children do not grow up wanting to be librarians or archivists in the same way that they want to be doctors, lawyers, firemen, and teachers. Because the information professions are small professions that lack a high profile, young people simply do not know about librarianship, archives, or information science, unless they have a relative or friend who is an information professional or have worked in their school library. Many come to one of the information professions after they have tried something else and decided it was not for them, like classroom teaching, or after they have learned the hard way that they need something in addition to a liberal arts degree for gainful, interesting employment.

In discussing whether or not their students move directly into graduate school, some of the CALS college administrators do distinguish between disciplines, noting that, in particular, students majoring in the sciences, including premed majors, tend to advance from undergraduate laboratory experience into immediate graduate training. In terms of taking time between undergraduate and graduate education for devotion to their families, while few participants in the current study referred to delaying LIS graduate work because of having children, 35 percent did indicate there has been a point where they have interrupted their LIS (or other) career for family reasons (Q.IV-19). However, data from the Alums confirms Stieg's point that you have to encounter LIS to know that it might be the career for you: 5 percent of the CALS Alums have parents who are involved in LIS, and interactions with librarians (K-16 and after college) serve as a major inducement for Alums to consider the field. As discussed in the previous chapter, 22 percent of the Alums have weighed or experienced other career options. Certainly, the longer the gap between college and graduate education, the more likely it is that the Alums were experiencing other careers, including that of homemaker or support staff in a library. For example, a Carleton '86 Alum who entered an LIS program in 1994 after an eight-year gap explains that "I wanted a career change that would allow a more balanced lifestyle (I was very overworked), that would utilize my science background and allow for scholarly work, and that was still involved in education (I had been a science teacher)." For this Alum, a second career as an information professional was a good—and better—fit.

Stieg (1992) asserts that LIS students tend to be older than graduate students in some other fields. And, indeed, most of the CALS Alums followed the pattern noted by the deans and did not enter an LIS graduate program immediately after college. To be specific, they began LIS graduate education a "break" of varying lengths from higher education (table 34). However, the conclusions that can be drawn from the data change significantly depending upon how the clusters of years are combined. If we combine the first two groups (one year and two to five years), then 50 percent overall of the Alums were enrolled in an LIS graduate program within five years of leaving college, with Alums from Kalamazoo (at 44 percent) and Lawrence (at 41 percent) proving to be exceptions.

If the two to ten years groups are combined, then 69 percent of the Alums are represented including all of those from Grinnell. This combination allows more opportunity for LIS to have been chosen as a second career, or at least after some other kind of work had been experienced. Were the years one to ten combined, instead, then 78 percent of all the CALS participants are represented: ranging from a low of 62 percent (Lawrence) to a high of 100 percent (Grinnell). More significant, perhaps, is the fact that for seven of the colleges there is a range of 10-20 percent of the Alums who chose LIS after either extensive other careers or raising children. These are the Alums who had a gap of 11-20 years between college graduation and enrollment in an LIS graduate program.

It is also useful to consider the CALS cohorts. Since the Alums represent a span of 39 years, table 35 illustrates how the gap between college and graduate school closes as one moves from considering the oldest to the youngest cohorts. In 2000, the endpoint for this study, it is likely that a number of alumni from the eight colleges had not yet found themselves considering a career in library and information science, or were perhaps just beginning to investigate LIS graduate programs.

When asked about other occupations in which they might have been involved over the course of their worklife (Q.III-4), 78 percent of the Alums listed some type of other work—from a low of 71 percent (Earlham) to a high of 100 percent (Grinnell). By cohort, 69-81 percent of the CALS members have had some other kind of non-LIS work experience. However, since the Alums were not specifically asked to indicate how long they were involved in any non-LIS work, or whether they were engaged in it while also LIS professionals, the most that can realistically be said is that the CALS data lend general support to the college administrators' assertions that many of their students take some time out from education before entering graduate school. In

Table 34: Years between College Graduation and SLIS Enrollment (by College)

Years	Avg (%)	College (%) C	D	E	G	K	L	M	S
1	9	12	16	11	0	10	8	2	5
2-5	41	39	36	46	50	34	33	52	48
6-10	28	20	24	28	50	41	21	29	23
11-20	13	20	12	10	0	11	19	15	13
21-30	7	9	8	5	0	5	17	0	8
31+	1	0	4	0	0	0	2	2	5

Table 35: Years between College Graduation and SLIS Enrollment (by Cohort)

Years	Avg (%)	Cohort (%) 62-	66-	71-	76-	81-	86-	91-	96-
1	9	10	8	9	11	0	5	14	25
2-5	41	49	35	36	43	44	46	47	63
6-10	28	18	23	29	30	44	35	39	0
11-20	13	14	18	14	13	13	14	0	0
21-30	7	6	14	10	2	0	0	0	0
31+	1	4	2	1	0	0	0	0	0

addition, the data do not contradict Stieg's research findings that LIS professionals enter later than graduate students in some of the other professions.

II. Schools of Library and Information Science

Dey et al. (1991) report that students tend to select undergraduate programs on the basis of geographic convenience. Furthermore, sample statistical reports from the Association for Library and Information Science Education (ALISE) indicate that 75-78 percent of all LIS students attend an ALA-accredited graduate program in the same state as their residency (Sineath 1991, 1995). In chapter 2, it was reported that 85 percent of the Alums were residents of 15 states, including the seven CALS states. Together those states, represented in table 36, were home to 19-33 accredited LIS programs, depending upon the Alums' years of enrollment.

Table 36: ALA-Accredited LIS Graduate Programs in Alums' Home States (85 percent cluster)

State (*CALS State)	School and Years of Accreditation	
California	U/California at Berkeley, 1924-1994[21] San Jose State University, 1967-to-date	U/California at Los Angeles, 1960-to-date U/Southern California, 1936-1987
Connecticut	Southern Connecticut State University, 1970-to-date	
Illinois	Dominican University, 1936-to-date[22] U/Northern Illinois, 1967-1994	U/Illinois at Champaign-Urbana, 1924-to-date
Indiana*	Ball State University, 1978-1987	Indiana University, 1951-to-date
Iowa*	University of Iowa, 1969-to-date	
Kansas	Emporia State University, 1930-1958, 1964-to-date	
Massachusetts	Simmons College, 1924-to-date	
Michigan*	University of Michigan, 1926-to-date Western Michigan University, 1946-1984	Wayne State University, 1965-to-date
Minnesota*	University of Minnesota-Twin Cities, 1933-1986	
Missouri	U/Missouri - Columbia, 1967-to-date	
New Jersey	Rutgers University, 1954-to-date	
New York	Pratt University, 1924-to-date St. John's University, 1974-to-date SUNY - Buffalo, 1970-to-date Syracuse University, 1928-to-date	Queens College, 1968-to-date SUNY - Albany, 1930-to-date[23] SUNY - Geneseo, 1944-1985[24]
Ohio*	Case Western Reserve University, 1924-1987	Kent State University, 1962-to-date
Pennsylvania*	Clarion University of PA, 1974-to-date University of Pittsburgh, 1962-to-date	Drexel University, 1924-to-date
Wisconsin*	U/Wisconsin - Madison , 1924-to-date	U/W-Milwaukee, 1974-to-date

In actuality, the CALS Alums chose to obtain their LIS graduate education at 52 ALA-accredited programs in 31 U.S. states and two Canadian provinces (Q.II-10). However, the greatest number (45 percent) chose an LIS program in one of the five following states, with 37 percent of all of the CALS Alums enrolling in one of the specifically identified five institutions:

[21] U/C-Berkeley stopped participating in ALA accreditation in 1994.

[22] Formerly Rosary College with complete dates being 1936-57, 1960 to present.

[23] Complete dates: 1930-59, 1965 to present.

[24] Complete dates: 1944-59, 1966-85.

- Indiana (Indiana University, 9 percent of the CALS Alums). Chosen by Alums from six of the eight CALS colleges (excluding Grinnell and Macalester). The majority were from Earlham.
- Michigan (U/Michigan, 8 percent). Alums from all eight CALS colleges attended the U/Michigan with those from Denison, Grinnell and Kalamazoo especially favoring it.
- Illinois (U/Illinois at Champaign-Urbana, 7 percent). Attended by Alums from all the CALS colleges except Grinnell.
- Massachusetts (Simmons, 6 percent). Attended by Alums from all eight CALS colleges and favored by those from Carleton, Grinnell and Swarthmore.
- Wisconsin (U/Wisconsin-Madison, 7 percent). Attended by Alums from all the CALS colleges except Denison, and favored by Carleton, Grinnell, Lawrence, and Macalester respondents.

Indiana, Michigan, and Wisconsin are home to CALS colleges, and Illinois is nearby. Only Simmons in Massachusetts might be considered "far away" to all except perhaps Swarthmore Alums and those who grew up in the eastern portion of the United States. Each of the remaining 47 ALA-accredited LIS programs (in 28 states and provinces) garnered an average of 1 to 2 percent of the Alums. Stieg (1992) reports that, once resident in a state, many LIS students find it financially and personally more feasible to attend one of its graduate institutions than to move again, especially if one is place-bound for job or family reasons or wishes to minimize tuition costs. And indeed a number of the CALS Alums noted they attended an LIS program part-time because they had jobs or were caring for family members. In addition, for their graduate work, the Alums chose primarily public universities rather than continuing with private institutions. Of the five heavily favored institutions, only Simmons is privately operated.

The Development of LIS Programs: 1887-2000

Prior to 1887, librarians—in common with those in most occupations—were self-trained or trained on-the-job through apprenticeship programs.[25] Publication of professional journals like *The American Library Journal* in 1876 by the newly formed American Library Association helped, but were not sufficient for the education of those who wanted to be professional librarians. By this point in the 1800s, however, American higher education was experiencing a period of growth. The Morrill Land Grants of 1862 and 1890 made higher education more available, and graduate programs were being initiated at a number of American universities—including Johns Hopkins, Harvard, Princeton, Yale, Catholic University (Washington, D.C.), and the University of Chicago (Ostler et al. 1995). Chief among the graduate programs were those devoted to the law and to medicine, whose aspirants sought "professional training that combined the practical merits of the apprenticeships [with] the theoretical training from a rigorous academic experience" (Ostler et al. 1995, 11). So it was also with librarianship.

---

[25]This section is informed by the following works: Davis 1976; Gates 1990; Ostler et al. 1995; Roy 1998; Rubin 1998; Stieg 1992; *The Williamson Reports of 1921 and 1923*; Wilson and Hermanson 1998; C. M. White 1976.

By the late 1800s, there were more than 10,000 libraries in the United States (Gates 1990; Rubin 1998). Thus, when Melvil Dewey's School of Library Economy at Columbia College began in 1887 as the first American library school, its curriculum sought to address the organization of materials and concentrated on routine activities already being carried out in those libraries. The school was notable for being coeducational. As an occupation, librarianship was considered "suitable" for both genders. For women of the late 1800s, it presented opportunities to work on matters of detail in a quiet setting and to assist readers—characteristics appealing to cultured or well-educated women of the time (Roy 1998). It offered some women the opportunity to manage and administer enterprises at a time when the majority of women were employees, not employers. And for women seeking a career, it was a viable alternative to nursing or teaching. For men, the field offered second career opportunities, a place for quiet reflection and scholarly work, or "a higher calling and an area ripe for advancement in promotion and/or salary" (Roy 1998, 7 citing Garrison 1979 and Passet 1993).

Establishment of the Columbia school spurred the development of other academic programs as well as other formats for formal library education. Apprenticeship classes began being held in public libraries including those in Los Angeles, Denver, and Cleveland. Summer courses and seminars were offered by state library commissions in Wisconsin, Minnesota, Pennsylvania, and Indiana (Roy 1998). By 1890, the first specialization had been created: a training program for children's librarians at the Carnegie Library of Pittsburgh (Gates 1990). In 1915, the Association of American Library Schools was established as a vehicle for library program administrators to discuss standards for admission, instruction, and the curriculum (Gates 1990; Wilson and Hermanson 1998). The results of this array of educational possibilities were differing requirements, uneven teaching and course quality, and programs that required divergent lengths of time to complete.

By 1919 the Carnegie Corporation had become concerned about the wide array of programs and commissioned Charles C. Williamson, head of the Division of Economics and Sociology of the New York Public Library, to ascertain the state of the profession as found in its existing educational programs. Williamson's 1921 and 1923 reports established criteria against which to set and then measure standards for professional education programs in librarianship. Williamson found that, between 1887 and 1919, individuals could become library professionals through attendance at or correspondence courses with

- LIS schools offering one- and two-year programs
- Colleges giving summer courses only
- Libraries providing apprentice and in-service training
- Colleges and normal schools offering courses in practical aspects of library work
- Institutions of various kinds giving courses by correspondence
  (Gates 1990, 93)

If a core curriculum may be ascertained from the subjects allotted the most time, then Williamson found that, in the institutions he studied, the core consisted of cataloging, book selection, reference work, classification, and administration, with approximately half of the curriculum time devoted to the first four topics (*The Williamson Reports* [1921]). Beyond these, courses were essentially specializations—beginning with work with children and including such still common topics as the history of libraries, school libraries, and indexing. Having identified such curricular variety, and in an effort to eliminate programmatic weaknesses, Williamson laid out a course of recommendations that fundamentally changed library education.

Williamson saw librarians as professionals and library education programs as on a par with other professional schools such as engineering and architecture. Thus he asserted that, as opposed to the varying levels of library education that existed, library schools should be departments within universities and should only offer graduate education. In their new academic locations, schools should actively market library work to college students, and thereby increase the level of knowledge and sophistication of their resulting graduates. There should be uniform entrance requirements with emphasis placed on evidence of each student's education and ability to maintain a high standard of scholarship. In terms of the curriculum, he recommended a year of foundational studies followed by a year of specializations in areas including, but not limited to, school libraries, college and university libraries, library work with children, library administration, cataloging and classification, county and rural library work, and business libraries. Field work had a place in the curriculum, especially as he thought students should obtain a year of library experience during the course of their program. After students were employed as library professionals, the schools should provide them with continuing education for professional development. Williamson recommended that library school finances and faculty salaries be increased in order to improve programs, and that practitioners might teach minor or specialty courses. To ensure that all this occurred, and that the profession maintained high standards, he recommended establishment of a national certification board with responsibility for (1) certifying librarians, (2) accrediting library schools, and (3) being an effective central agency for the promotion of all types of library education and training (*The Williamson Reports* [1923, 136-145]). At least a college education, he notes

> is now required of the high school teacher in practically every part of the country. How can the library even in the smallest town be expected to serve intelligently the needs of all classes unless the librarian is at least as well equipped as the high school teacher? The librarian, indeed, should be equal in his educational and general equipment to the high school principal, the superintendent of schools, the minister, the editor, and all other educated persons upon whom the community depends for leadership. The librarian must be the intellectual equal of the best educated classes in the community if he is to live up to his opportunities. (*The Williamson Reports* [1921, 12-13])

In 1924, a year after publication of the second Williamson report, the American Library Association established the Board of Education for Librarianship, which formulated minimum standards for the various kinds of library education programs.[26] In 1926, the first list of ALA-accredited LIS programs included 14 schools, of which six were part of a college or university (Gates 1990, 94-95). Establishment of the University of Chicago Graduate Library School in

---

[26]Subsequently renamed the Committee on Accreditation (COA): www.ala.org/coa.

1926 is frequently cited as significant for three reasons. First, debate was at least temporarily ended on whether library education was training-focused or theory-focused; the latter was to be the case. Second, the faculty was multidisciplinary and its members brought from their respective fields research experience and associated expectations, such as that of scholarly publication. Third, the University of Chicago subsequently offered the first doctoral program in library science, which opened a path for university trained faculty to feed into other library education programs (Wilson and Hermanson 1998; Stieg 1992).

A 1951 revision of the accreditation standards limited accreditation to what was by then considered the basic professional preparation: a bachelor's degree plus the master's degree within the library science field. The standards were revised again in 1972 and 1992. Referring to the 1972 standards, but applicable to those of 1992, Gates notes that they

> describe the essential features of library education programs which prepare librarians for responsibilities beyond the narrowly local level. They identify these essential components of a graduate program of library education: program goals and objectives, curriculum, faculty, students, governance, administration and financial support, and physical resources and facilities. (1990, 95)

Since 1925, 86 American and Canadian LIS master's degree programs have been accredited by ALA (*ALA Historical List*). At the time of this study, the 57 current LIS master's programs accredited by ALA's Committee on Accreditation undergo reaccreditation every seven to ten years.

In reviewing the literature on the master's degree in a range of fields, Glazer concluded that, by the end of the 1960s, that tier of higher education had shifted from being grounded in the liberal arts to being

> practitioner oriented, emphasizing training in skills, career development, and pragmatic goals. It is linked to the needs of the student and the demands of the marketplace and driven by externally imposed standards, and it emphasizes practice rather than theory, skills rather than research, training rather than scholarship . . . The master's degree is overwhelmingly professional, it is largely terminal, and it is practice oriented. (Glazer 1986, quoted in Conrad et al. 1993, 16)

While LIS graduate schools, since their beginnings in 1887, had been practice-oriented, professional programs, the 1960s and 1970s reinforced an emphasis on practice. Those decades were, in general, a tumultuous time for U.S. higher education. The economy and all aspects of education expanded in the 1960s with the federal government investing especially heavily in higher education (Ostler et al. 1995). This largesse included LIS where federal monies "funded new library buildings, supported innovative programs, encouraged and subsidized the development of library services for minorities, and in library education itself, supplied fellowships both for doctoral study to produce needed faculty with advanced degrees and for minority students" (Stieg 1992, 28). Librarians were perceived to be in short supply. Thirty-seven new accredited LIS programs were established between 1960 and 1976 (*ALA Historical List*). By the early- to mid-1970s, however, federal funding was diminishing, economic growth was beginning to slow down, and, as some of the CALS Alums noted, "jobs hard to find" (Carleton '71; academic). Between 1976 and the recession of the 1980s, the LIS programs at Case Western Reserve, University of Denver, University of Minnesota, SUNY/Geneseo, University of Oregon, University of Southern California, Vanderbilt, and Western Michigan were discontinued; the University of Chicago school closed in 1991.

Library science programs also experienced an upheaval equivalent to the assault on the classical curriculum in the mid-1800s: the introduction of information science into their master's curriculum, beginning in the mid-1960s. According to Gates (1990, 201-203):

> Since the early 1940s, the increasing value and use of information as a commodity demanded the development of faster and more efficient facilities and processes for identifying, collecting, analyzing, evaluating, and disseminating it. . . . A major function of librarians has always been to organize whatever types of materials have been available at the time; to recover, find, or retrieve information and knowledge from these materials; and utilizing any and all available methods, to transmit them in some usable form to those needing or requesting them. However, when librarianship was not ready or able to satisfy all the additional needs involved in managing the tremendous volume of information, a new discipline began to emerge. First called information retrieval, then documentation, it is now known as information science.

Gates (1990) pointed out that while the basic objective of both librarianship and information science is the acquisition, storing, and retrieval of information for use, their approaches differ. Librarianship draws upon the humanities and social sciences to create user services centering on materials selection, reference work, and the organization and retrieval of information via cataloging and classification schemes (e.g., the Dewey Decimal and the Library of Congress classification systems). Information science, on the other hand, comes to the task from a multidisciplinary approach drawn from computer science, mathematics, information theory, management science, and linguistics. Both approaches incorporate aspects of psychology. In volume 1 of the *Annual Review of Information Science and Technology*, Robert Taylor (1966, 19) defined information science as

> the science that investigates the properties and behavior of information, the forces governing the flow of information, and the means of processing information for optimum accessibility and usability.

While librarianship is associated with a specific institution, the library, information science is concerned with the science of information without regard to any specific institution or environment (Gates 1990). Early information science research, and courses in LIS programs, dealt with the computerization of serials lists, acquisitions processes, and circulation functions—followed by the automating of library catalogs and the teaching of students to search online data bases. Such research and course work did not educate students about information per se, but rather about providing the means for users to find materials and to retrieve from those materials their own information. As the "Information Society" emerged, with it came two major realizations. First, awareness that "more than 50 percent of economic production in the U.S. is the producing and handling of information" (Williams and Zachert 1986, 228; see also Machlup 1962). Second, "a shift in emphasis away from the item that held the information to an emphasis on accessing the content of the information" (Rubin 1998, 22). By 1992, Stieg could write that infusion of computerization and information science into the curriculum meant in part that "cataloging via OCLC is taught in cataloging classes, online searching is considered part of reference, spreadsheets and relational databases are a part of management" (p. 30).

Library and Information Science programs increasingly shifted curricula so as to address both information services (the classical librarianship approach) and information technologies (the newer information science approach). With an expanded curriculum came philosophical changes that are reflected in program names. Beginning in the late 1960s, what had been mainly called graduate schools of library science gradually became schools of library and information science (LIS). In 1966, the Board of Curators of the University of Missouri authorized the establishment of its School of Library and Information Science (Van Fleet and Wallace 2002). In 1983, the Association of American Library Schools changed its name to the Association for Library and Information Science Education (ALISE). And by 1989, 84 percent of accredited library schools had the word "information" in their names (Gates 1990). The 1992 *Standards* for accreditation acknowledge this major development in the LIS field: the full title of the document is *Standards for Accreditation of Master's Programs in Library and Information Studies* (ALA website, see Bibliography). In a 2002 article titled "The I-Word," Van Fleet and Wallace noted that "Information" was now a part of the names of 98 percent of ALA-accredited LIS schools, and appeared in 50 percent of the official degree names awarded by the programs.

While the degree and program names changed, in general, the length of the MLIS program did not. In 1923, Williamson had recommended that master's degree programs within university settings be at least one calendar year in length. As LIS programs increasingly became university enterprises, one-year programs became the norm. These were master's degree programs with 36 or fewer required credit hours that could be completed in 12 months or two semesters and a summer. In the 1970s Canadian, and then U.S., schools, began to lengthen their programs (White and Mort 1990; Stieg 1992). While an increasing number of programs moved gradually to add enough credit courses to comprise two academic years, the requirements of just under half of the schools could still be met in one calendar year, even with an increasing number of information technology courses available to students. In 2001, a year after the last of the CALS cohorts had begun their programs, the five LIS schools attended by the majority of all of the cohort members exhibited the following range of minimum completion times (ALISE website, see Bibliography):

- University of Illinois at Champaign-Urbana: 9 months
- Indiana University: 18 months
- University of Michigan and University of Wisconsin-Madison: 16 months each
- Simmons: 12 months

The Graduate LIS Programs: Current Status

Given the foregoing discussion of changes in the LIS programs, it is interesting to find that the current status is one of general stability. In a 2004 article, Markey showed that the names of schools appear to again be set—almost no change of name was found since the 2002 Van Fleet and Wallace article. In terms of ALA-accredited program degree names, the acronym MLIS (standing for either Master's of Library and Information Science or Master's of Library and Information Studies) is now used by the largest concentration (35 percent) of programs. MLS (Master's of Library Science) is found in 17 percent, MS and MA in 17 percent and 10 percent (respectively), and MSLS in 9 percent of the professional degrees awarded to master's students. Another 8 percent of the degrees are some variation of the MLIS in that they incorporate "Information Studies" or "Information Science" into the name—with or without inclusion of the word "Library." Only 2 percent now award a Master's of Library Science degree that does not include the word "Information" in the degree name.

The graduate LIS programs most frequently chosen by the Alums illustrate the current array of institutional and ALA-accredited degree names:

- Illinois: University of Illinois at Champaign-Urbana, Graduate School of Library and Information Science (degree: Master of Science)
- Indiana: Indiana University, School of Library and Information Science (degrees: Master of Library Science; Master of Information Science)
- Michigan: University of Michigan, School of Information (degree: Master of Science in Information)
- Massachusetts: Simmons College, Graduate School of Library and Information Science (degree: Master of Science)
- Wisconsin: University of Wisconsin-Madison, School of Library and Information Studies (degree: Master of Arts)

All five now include "Information" in the school's name; four of the five also include "Library." One school awards two degrees; the rest award one. Two title their degree the "Master of Science"; one awards a Master of Arts. Two include "Information" in their degree name: Master of Information Science and Master of Science in Information. One awards a Master of Library Science degree.

Markey (2004) also found that 15 programs offered degrees beyond the ALA-accredited one, with the number of LIS schools offering dual master's degrees growing from 24 percent in 2000 to 57 percent in 2002. In 2002, 62 percent of the dual degrees were with humanities disciplines, 33 percent with the social sciences, and 5 percent with the sciences. Those degrees involving history most frequently support archives specializations, and most dual degrees regardless of the disciplines involved are of interest to academic and special librarians rather than public librarians and school library media specialists (Markey 2004, 322-333).[27] Markey

---

[27]See Van Fleet andWallace (2002) and Markey (2004) for lists of variant degree names. In this book, "MLIS" is used to cover the range of degree names.

concluded that Koenig and Hildreth (2002, 42) were right to say that "the day of the stand-alone LIS school with only one degree—the ALA-accredited master's degree—is over." Indeed, the latest expansion of LIS programs is the establishment of undergraduate majors, with Koteles and Haythornthwaite (2002) reporting the existence, at that time, of 16 majors, three minors, and two certificate programs being offered by LIS programs affiliated with the Association for Library and Information Science Education.

Although there is no field-wide required set of "core courses" for the master's degree, Markey (2004) finds that 81 to 85 percent of programs require a variable number of courses drawn from the areas of Organization of Information, Reference, Foundations, and Management. This compares with Williamson's 1921/1923 report of Cataloging and Classification (now part of Organization of Information), Reference, Administration (now Management), and Book Selection/Collection Development. (Markey notes that 20 to 30 percent of the present-day programs require collection development.) Required IT courses include "library automation, technical services, database management, system design, and general surveys of information technologies" (Markey 2004, 326). Examples of IT courses in the curriculum generally—that is, as required or elective—include courses with titles such as the following (Markey 2004, 331):

- Data Mining
- Data Security
- Digital Libraries
- Information Visualization
- Intelligent Information Agents

Core requirements have fluctuated over the 39 years represented by the Alums. Currently, the five schools most frequently chosen by the Alums require between two and five core courses. Organization of Information is the only common core area, with between one and three of the schools also requiring a course in Foundations, Reference, and/or Management. Each school has a dozen or more information technology-based courses listed in its master's program catalog. While Alums in the earliest cohorts did not have IT courses such as these available to them—beyond a few covering "automation," "database searching," and "information storage and retrieval"—from the 1970s forward, more and more CALS Alums were able to take courses in an increasingly wide array of Information Science and Information Technology areas.

Once they had entered an LIS graduate program, 78 percent of the CALS participants completed their program in one to two years, depending primarily on the number of months needed for meeting curricular requirements (Q.II-10-11). The remaining 22 percent of the Alums took three to seven years to complete their degree. It was mentioned earlier in this chapter that some Alums were place-bound (perhaps by virtue of jobs or family). Such individuals were welcome in graduate LIS programs, as part-time status is the norm for the majority of students in them. ALISE statistical reports regularly find that 65 to 69 percent of the LIS enrollment is part-time (Sineath 1991, 1995; ALISE website, see Bibliography). In some cases, the work that led Alums to part-time status was in libraries, either as part of an internship or as regular employment. Whereas 33 percent of the Alums worked as undergraduates in their college libraries, 75 percent of them worked in some type of library while in their LIS graduate program

(Q.II-12). The combination of LIS classroom and work experiences is reflected in their images of, and opinions about, LIS graduate education and LIS as a field.

III. Images of the Field

For this study, the CALS participants were asked how they regarded the field during two formative points in their movement toward an LIS career: when they left college and after they had finished their LIS graduate work (Q.II-8, Q.II-13). For the most part, the Alums were not knowledgeable at the point of leaving college about the field per se; they had formed impressions of libraries, but not of the profession itself. Of those who made comments, 59 percent recalled that, after leaving college, they had a positive image of the field, 22 percent had no image or were neutral, 13 percent were negative about the field, and 6 percent had mixed feelings about LIS (table 37). The largest numbers of respondents with positive images of the field came from Earlham and Lawrence; the image held by Carleton Alums was the most negative. Half of the Alums from Denison and Macalester acknowledged not knowing much about LIS as a field.

The following statements provide good representation of the views that most CALS Alums had about the field at the conclusion of their undergraduate education:

> *Positive:* A profession that would combine my love of literature and books with helping others find facts/information they needed. (Kalamazoo '66; special)
>
> *No Image/Neutral:* I really didn't have any idea of LIS. (Denison '86; public)
>
> *Mixed Image:* I thought it was a toss up between caring people and a lot of busy work. (Earlham '76; public)
>
> *Negative Image:* A profession that's female-dominated, probably primarily composed of introverts, with some potentially troubling shades of hierarchical decision-making. (Swarthmore '91; public)

Positive Image of the LIS Field

Table 38 reveals that the CALS participants had much clearer and stronger views of the profession after completing their LIS graduate education. Now positive views were expressed by 63 percent of the Alums compared to the previous 59 percent, a 4 percent gain (see tables 37-38). Carleton Alums registered the largest swing to a positive viewpoint: 34 percent. The focus of the majority of the Alums' comments was on two things: the variety of types of work available in the field and the technological developments. Respondents were pleasantly surprised by what they saw as the breadth and variety inherent in the field. They were impressed with the range of resources used within the field: print, nonprint, various electronic technologies. The

Table 37: Image of LIS after Baccalaureate Education (by College)

Image	Avg (%)	College (%) C	D	E	G	K	L	M	S
Positive	59	40	50	74	67	57	86	33	60
No/Neut	22	20	50	16	33	29	0	50	20
Negative	13	27	0	5	0	0	14	17	20
Mixed	6	13	0	5	0	14	0	0	0

Table 38: Image of LIS after Graduate Education (by College)

Image	Avg (%)	College (%) C	D	E	G	K	L	M	S
Positive	63	74	20	50	67	72	89	60	63
No/Neut	4	0	0	8	0	6	0	0	13
Negative	23	16	0	35	33	22	11	35	13
Mixed	9	11	80	8	0	0	0	5	13

heterogeneity of either the range of people served or those who would be their peers contributed to their reactions. A number of the Alums singled out the variety of libraries and work opportunities as impressive. The positive image seems to reflect the Alums own broadened awareness of the field.

Neutral or No Image of the LIS Field

At the conclusion of their graduate work, a significant number had learned enough about the field to no longer feel neutral, a rating which drops from 22 percent to just 4 percent—disappearing entirely for Carleton, Denison, Grinnell, and Macalester Alums. (Comments demonstrate that the Macalester participants in particular had an enormously expanded understanding of what the field encompasses.) The Earlham, Kalamazoo, and Swarthmore Alums who still left with neutral feelings had comments such as this one from a Swarthmore Alum ('66; public): "No specific image; seemed like a creative career." These respondents were, in other words, at ease with the field but not particularly interested in or excited by it.

Mixed Image of the LIS Field

The number of Alums who expressed both positive and negative views of LIS rose from 6 percent after college to 9 percent after graduate work. There are two dominant concerns. One was a realization that LIS professionals might not command high salaries. The second was that "LIS was not an intellectually challenging program but still exciting because of the subject matter, [and] librarians were interesting" (Earlham '62; public).

Negative Image of the LIS Field and of LIS Education

The largest change in viewpoint (10 percent) overall is found in the negative category; this shift was registered by respondents from Earlham, Grinnell, Kalamazoo, and Macalester. For Earlham there was a 30 percent increase in Alums who viewed LIS negatively. Grinnell Alums moved from neutral to negative. After college, none of the Kalamazoo Alums felt negative about the field; however, after their graduate program 22 percent of them did. And the percent of Macalester Alums who felt negative had doubled from 17 percent to 35 percent.

Whereas the positive, neutral, and mixed comments have been about the LIS field, 70 percent of the negative impressions were of LIS education: 48 percent about the program and 22 percent about the faculty. A Macalester ('76; public) Alum said she "thought the MLS program was very poor—the course work was like being back in high school." And this is a very representative view of those who fault the graduate schools for a lack of rigor in what is expected of students and for a general lack of challenge in the program as a whole. Several of these Alums used "boring" and "dull" to describe their disappointment with their graduate education. In reflecting upon their graduate program, the remaining Alums recalled finding some portion of their LIS professors "unable to connect the day-to-day reality of library work to the classroom" (Grinnell '86; public) and "too detached from the service orientation" (Earlham '76; public) that the Alums, as undergraduates, had begun to associate with the field.

IV. Criticisms of and Suggestions for LIS Education

Cavanaugh (1993, 107) states that "criticism of professional education's performance in preparing graduates for professional practice environments is wide-ranging [and] long-standing." She goes on to cite a range of studies from various professions in support of her statement, including one that "described mismatches between education program content and the nature of professional demands in first-year practice as perceived by graduates in medicine, business administration, and engineering" (Cavanaugh 1993, 107). She notes that, for their part, educators regularly fail to address or appreciate the "different nature of nonacademic, service-oriented, practice environments" (Cavanaugh 1993, 108). On the other hand, Houle (1967, quoted by Stieg 1992, 113) seems to represent educators in his description of the friction between alumni and their institutions:

> The voice of the aggrieved alumnus is always loud in the land and, no matter what the profession, the burden of complaint is the same. In the first five years after graduation, alumni say that they should have been taught more practical techniques. In the next five years, they say they should have been taught more basic theory. In the tenth to fifteenth years, they inform the faculty that they should have been taught more about administration or about their relations with their coworkers and subordinates. In the subsequent five years, they condemn the failure of their professors to put the profession in its larger historical, social, and economic contexts. After the twentieth year, they insist that they should have been given a broader orientation to all knowledge, scientific and humane. Sometime after that, they stop giving advice; the university has deteriorated so badly since they left that it is beyond hope.

When asked "What suggestions do you have for improving LIS education?"(Q.VI-2), 77 percent of the CALS Alums made suggestions. Ten percent of the comments focus on LIS schools themselves.

Some considered the programs in general, such as the Grinnell '76 academic librarian who felt "most of the programs are too short to produce competent practitioners." Others had comments about specific schools and their master's degree programs. However, it is well to remember that 88 percent of the Alums had previously said they would encourage students graduating from their own college to enter the LIS field. The criticisms and the Alums' most frequent suggestions cluster into three areas that are familiar within LIS education as far back as the Williamson 1921 and 1923 reports:

- The need for specific, named courses
- Changes in the curriculum in general
- The need for more frequent or required internships/practica

Overall, 51 percent of all the Alums' comments addressed these topics, which garner the highest number of comments in each college and in each cohort. Table 39 presents analysis of participants' comments by the three topics and the type of library they were employed at during the time of this study.

Courses

On the matter of courses, the most frequent need identified by Alums from all library types was for ones relating to management. Examples include managing personnel and patrons, communication (oral, written, and behavioral), and financial management. Related but broader areas include strategic planning, operating as a nonprofit, business best practices, customer service, and political acumen. In addition, there are "issues" associated with some comments, such as gaining a better understanding of (and how to deal with) economic issues, social issues, and public policy. An Earlham '76 public librarian suggested that LIS schools should look to "schools of Social Work and Public Administration, [which] generally seem to do a better job and could be used as models." A Lawrence '81 special librarian recalled her former boss, a

Table 39: LIS Graduate Program Areas Generating Most Frequent Suggestions

LIS Program Areas	Library Type Employing CALS Alums (%)			
	Academic	Public	School	Special/Other
Courses	47	41	39	57
Curriculum	25	25	39	11
Internships/Practica	28	35	22	32

public librarian, saying "there wasn't enough on managing the patrons—vagrants, unattended children, unruly teens, perverts. It's a big part of the job in a public library. Also the legal issues involved with dealing with problem patrons." Other Alums noting similar public problems indicated that an understanding of these difficulties is needed by librarians at all levels in many different kinds of libraries.

The second largest number of comments is devoted to cataloging, including concerns about the lack of courses on classification and indexing. Several Alums connect the need for cataloging and classification with current technologies, including digitization. A Lawrence Alum ('66; academic) sums up these sentiments when she says, "Fewer librarians with cataloging skills and course work is a bad omen." She would like to see LIS programs more actively involved in teaching and conducting research on metadata and the organization of electronic information. Or, as a Carleton '86 special librarian puts it: "Don't neglect cataloging. In its modern guises and applications, it is what will keep libraries relevant in an electro-centric world."

Of course there are other course recommendations that Alums feel are just as necessary to keep libraries relevant and librarians current and involved in both their work and profession. The core areas of collection development and reference are judged as central to the field with Alums stressing the need for more rigor in reference education. A Swarthmore Alum ('62; public) found it "appalling how many inadequately trained reference librarians are sitting behind desks shortchanging the public." The very practical needs of mid- and upper-level managers and administrators include grant-writing, fund-raising, PR, and marketing (from academic, public, and special librarians). The concerns primarily of public librarians, but also of school library media specialists, about more youth-related knowledge is quite specific: Classes in early childhood and teen development, parenting education, curriculum development, as well as pedagogical techniques to help children and young adults "extract, understand and apply information" (Carleton '66; school, and Carleton '91; public).

There is the expectation across all library types that LIS education will address a whole raft of information technology topics including web design/development, systems and network thinking, and database design/searching/management. Academic librarians stress the need to know not just teaching skills but also learning theory. The comments of a Macalester Alum ('81; academic) illustrate why course- and research-related teaching is such a strongly felt need by academic librarians: "much of the challenge we face with proselytizing for Information Literacy on our campuses stems from a lack of background in learning styles, pedagogical theory, etc." And there are academic, public, and special librarians who believe LIS students must be grounded in the history and traditions of the profession. Two Carleton Alums ('62; academic; '71; public) stress that such grounding allows for "comparison to the situations today and how the values and skills of the LIS profession apply" because "this is what is common to all libraries. I can teach my staff how to do things but there is nothing that replaces having thought about the reason for and the place of libraries in our communities, our world."

Curricula

Fewer Alums wrote about the curriculum in its entirety. However, several academic librarians suggested increasing interdisciplinarity and lengthening the program. And some public and school librarians focused more on LIS students. Two Alums emphasized attributes that students should have:

> Expect students to work smarter, not harder. (Carleton '62; public)
>
> We need people who can analyze, think critically, manage projects, always move toward the future, write and speak articulately. Be sure to emphasize these in the curriculum. (Earlham '76; public)

Two Macalester Alums in classes ten years apart stress being flexible:

> People coming out of LIS programs now need to be tremendously flexible to adapt to and shape the changing information environment. (Macalester '81; school)
>
> Encourage flexibility and teach other ways to use library skills for when jobs are scarce and budgets are tight. (Macalester '91; public)

Two Kalamazoo graduates, now school library media specialists, feel that "mind set is important":

> [Teach them] how to think logically, how to generalize or move toward more specificity. ('62; school)
>
> Teach them to analyze their practices and procedures in terms of whether they benefit the ultimate users. ('66; school)

Alums from all four library types share a concern about broad curricular and programmatic change. Among the academic librarians, an Earlham Alum ('96; academic) expresses this common focus: "LIS is a long-standing field of study, and should not be changed idly," and a Denison Alum ('71; academic) writes of the need to keep "core principles and processes." A Lawrence '76 special librarian urges LIS programs to "set the foundations, the goals of, and purposes for, library science. Concentrate on those ideals that are permanent because the 'wrappings' (e.g., software, mediums, format) are changing so quickly." Or, as a

Swarthmore respondent ('71; academic) phrases it, "develop students' enthusiasm based on values, not as much on techniques."

Internships and Practica

The CALS Alums view internships, practica, and other forms of real-life exposure to the enormous variety of LIS work as being singularly important. One word describes their suggestions for improving LIS education in this area: "more." Some Alums would require work experiences, others just want students to have as many opportunities as possible to gain some experience. Most recognized that many LIS programs do provide internship/practica opportunities, and that schools and students must work together to find times within a student's program for this to occur.

Everyone who commented in depth on this topic indicated that they themselves had gained significantly from the exposure to new ideas, opportunities, types of work, and to seeing LIS professionals "in action." Combining the words of Kalamazoo, Earlham, and Macalester Alums from the classes of 1962 through 1991, here is a blended view of the value of practica and internships:

> If students could experience academic vs. public vs. archival, etc., it would be easier to choose a concentration. They would have some experience, and they would know what suits them better. Interning in different settings allows students to see how different institutions handle different situations. The professionals (e.g., directors, seasoned reference librarians) who gave me direct access to themselves enhanced my education immeasurably by giving me a feel for the actual work life (and situations) common to a professional. Whether paid or volunteer, for a short or a long period of time, this experience will help the student (1) get a job, and (2) be ready to work independently. Those students not currently working in a library, or having no previous library work experience, especially benefit from experiencing the variety of work available with an LIS degree—how else are they ever going to know?

Two Other Topics of Concern: Theory-Practice and "Rigor"

Some CALS respondents linked comments on internships/practica with comments on "theory and practice." Usually, the two concepts are connected by "versus," not "and"; however, of the 333 comments made about LIS programs and education only 30 are devoted to the theory-vs-practice topic. Participants who linked internships/practica and theory-practice issues conceived of work experience while enrolled in graduate LIS education as prime opportunities to integrate the two:

> I have always wanted practice to be integrated more directly into LIS theory. Everyone in LIS programs should have a job in the library while studying information science. (Kalamazoo '62; academic)

> Internships should be mandatory. There needs to be more opportunities to put theory into practice. (Carleton '96; public)

> The best way to really understand what you are learning is to apply it while you are learning it. (Carleton '91; special)

There is also this slightly different suggestion: "[The curriculum] should always include an internship or a case study (conducted through interviews, not just a literature search) so as to give a taste of the realities of LIS in a particular setting—usually quite different from the idealistic way they're taught in library school." (Macalester '62; special). An Alum who, perhaps because she looked at her LIS graduate work as "training" rather than "education," felt that

> my training was both not practical enough, not specific enough, yet not theoretical enough. I see the value of exploring both ends of the spectrum. The practicums were the most valuable experience (working alongside working librarians) and were extremely valuable in obtaining my first job. (Carleton '76; public)

Yet, a Grinnell Alum ('76; public) sought both, saying that "theoretically grounding [the] values of profession, ethics, principles will serve well in the long term, but you also need to include practical components. I am amazed how much of my job can involve dealing with politics or with building and grounds maintenance." Jarvis (1999, 40-41) points out that learning is "the process of creating and transforming experience into knowledge, skills, attitudes, values, emotions, senses, and beliefs . . . [and that students] have to try out their knowledge in the practice situation before they can trust it." A Lawrence '81 public librarian backs this up when he suggests that LIS graduate programs "have more opportunities for students to observe professionals on the job to see how the theories they are learning are actually used (or not) in 'real life.'"

A second small set of comments focused on a perceived lack of rigor within the graduate program, with several Alums pointing out that "LIS education should demand more of its students" (Kalamazoo '91; special). For example, an Earlham ('76; academic) Alum's thoughts tied rigor to the theory or practice discussion: "It seems a bit contradictory, but I think [LIS education] would benefit from being more intellectually rigorous *and* more experiential/ practical. Hands-on and intellectually demanding" (emphasis in original).

Between 3 percent and 6 percent of all comments from all the colleges except Lawrence, and from all cohorts, focused on wanting LIS education to be "harder," "more rigorous," "academically more challenging," "more thought-provoking." Most of the comments suggested that lack of rigor encouraged a negative view of the profession. Some Alums coupled their comments with the disapproving note that they had worked harder at their undergraduate institution. However, a Carleton '86 Alum felt that distinctions between the two forms of education were appropriate:

> Library degrees are professional, *not* intellectual degrees! (Get a subject master's for that!) To think otherwise is to delude yourself. The liberal arts I got at Carleton was a *very* different experience (i.e., it was intellectually challenging) than library school, but that is how it should be. (emphasis in original)

That sentiment was echoed by a Swarthmore '71 Alum, who felt that to talk seriously about the curricula, the courses, or the value of practica had become hackneyed, noting that

> everyone I talk to is bored silly in programs these days. They do it to get the credential so they can work in the field, not because the program is inherently interesting or intellectually challenging. And that's fine. What I tell people is that you become a librarian because of the honesty and integrity of the work, because the book world is endlessly fascinating, and because you encounter many fine, smart, interesting people along the way. For those reasons it's worth doing.

V. Advice to New Practitioners

Given such sentiments about LIS education, how did the Alums answer the CALS survey question that asked them, based on their LIS (or other) career and experiences, what advice they would offer individuals who were just entering the work place as LIS professionals (Q.VI-1)? A majority of the Alums speak directly to the new practitioners, using "you" in their responses. And they have much to suggest—making comments that usually cover two or more topics. Their remarks cluster into these areas:

- Flexibility, learning, and change (27 percent)
- Approaching the job (16 percent)
- Fit—skills, knowledge, abilities, and values (14 percent)
- Technology (9 percent)
- Users and community members (7 percent)
- Professional development (7 percent)
- The LIS profession itself (7 percent)

In addition to these is an assortment of comments that urge MLIS students, prior to beginning a first professional position, to undertake practica, internships, paid employment, or volunteer hours "in as many settings as possible . . . in order to get a sense of what you might like to do" (Kalamazoo '71; special) (appendix C: Q.VI-1). There is also advice regarding work in specific kinds of libraries and specific kinds of work. For those interested in academic libraries, several Alums recommend getting a second master's degree. For public librarians, an Earlham Alum ('71; public) suggests "while in grad school, work in a library that specializes in an area in which you are profoundly ignorant." For school library media specialists, the belief is that "you should definitely teach in the classroom setting first" (Earlham '71; school). Even so, argues a Carleton '71 school librarian, "choose the focus [within the broader field] you love most, first: children's literature, music, art, government documents, academic, etc. And the environment second [because] there is so much variety within the profession." And "if you are looking at special librarianship, get some management and business fundamentals classes" (Macalester '66; special). A Grinnell '86 special librarian also points to the benefit of exposure to more than one kind of LIS arena:

> If you are going to pursue a career emphasizing work in digital information resources, be sure to get a good foundation in not just the core library subject matter (cataloging, reference, management, etc.) but also gain a firm understanding of the basic archival concepts. Archives provide a much more robust concept of electronic information, in many cases, than do traditional library models. Collections, folders, "groups" in the archives world better describe web resources and databases, in many ways, than does the item-level description of the library world. Further, the librarians of the world understand information and its users far better than do the programmers of the world so be sure to learn how librarians perform reference interviews and interact with customers. The form of those interactions may differ in the digital world, but the role and result of the interactions [are] no less important.

Basically, says a Lawrence '71 public librarian:

> Experiment with different kinds of library work to find the best fit. Libraries and LIS vary tremendously and no one is suited for everything. What I thought I wanted in lib. school is not what I ended up doing and loving.

This is reinforced by a special librarian (Earlham '66) who heads a newspaper library. She urges LIS graduates to "look around a lot—I had no idea newspaper libraries even existed when I was in school."

Flexibility, Learning, and Change

The concepts of *flexibility, learning,* and *change* are emphasized in 27 percent of the Alums' comments and are characteristics integral to every kind of LIS work. Almost 100 responses focused on the issue of *Flexibility*. The Alums mean it initially in terms of one's choice of an LIS (or non-LIS) library type and kind of position. Then they see flexibility as crucial to handling the tasks within one's job, including relationships with users and with one's colleagues. Two Alums have related recommendations: that new practitioners "keep [their] options open and be aware of all kinds of opportunity in all kinds of organizations, not just traditional libraries" (Earlham '91; special) "especially if you can be geographically flexible" (Carleton '86; academic). An Earlham '76 academic librarian suggests that new practitioners need to "be willing to work in a location that may not be perfect in order to gain experience for somewhere better." "Be flexible on entry positions," says a Carleton '81 public librarian, adding that "loyalty still counts and jobs will open up and grow with you." And a Kalamazoo '62 academic librarian's advice is to "work diligently; be flexible and open to new opportunities and experiences; have a good sense of humor; exercise 3 times/week if not daily; [and] don't worry obsessively!"

A Kalamazoo '71 academic librarian says, "Prepare to be as flexible as possible, and expect to continuously learn." Indeed, the CALS respondents believe that if a new practitioner does not enjoy continuous and lifelong *learning*, she or he should not go into the LIS field. Mention of the importance of such learning comes from Alums in every kind of LIS agency, across all the colleges and cohorts. The CALS Alums point out that assuming a first professional position means learning about

- One's job
- The broader field of LIS
- Users and one's community
- The work of one's colleagues
- Trends that might affect one's library—its internal and external environment
- And especially, one's own responsibilities as a practitioner and a member of the profession

A Denison '66 academic librarian believes "you [also] must know your own strengths and weaknesses—ask for help when you need it (and you will)." An Earlham special librarian ('66) wants new practitioners to "be open to new opportunities, training, [and] people; be humble; don't expect instant answers; have realistic expectations about organizations, especially in your first job ([where it may seem] easy to be super critical)."

Other comments illustrate the range of thought:

> Stay abreast of changes in the profession so you can maintain the traditional aspects of the field: such as no cost information and excellent customer service while embracing new technology and other innovations. But be open to new directions you may not have anticipated or had a previous interest in. (Earlham '71; public)
>
> Seek out other librarians [and] libraries that you admire, find out how they do things and how you can use their ideas to improve services at your library. (Grinnell '86; public)
>
> Stay current throughout your career. (Kalamazoo '71; academic)
>
> Be eager to learn; expect the profession to change. (Macalester '71; academic)

Change has been rampant within LIS for several decades. Both new and seasoned LIS practitioners already know of the importance of being "open to change," "prepared to work in a rapidly changing field" and able to "think broadly about the future" on a regular basis. The Alums go beyond those exhortations. They alert new practitioners to "expect your job functions to change continually" (Denison '76; public). New practitioners should be ready and able to change their work tools, and perceptions of how things ought to be; and, as a Macalester '62 special librarian puts it, should

> expect some frustrations and lots of rewarding experiences. Expect that, even if you stay in the "same" job for 5 years, it will be a very different job by the end of that time.

And finally, as an appropriate underpinning for handling flexibility, learning, and continuous change, a Kalamazoo '71 special librarian says "make sure you love your work, or switch to what you truly love."

Approaching the New Job

Sixteen percent of the respondents' comments center on how to handle the first professional job. On the general approach to being a new employee or professional, the Alums make such points as:

> Listen before you speak. Learn before you do. Acclimate yourself to the culture of your new job. Don't expect them to change due to your arrival on the scene. (Macalester '66; public)
>
> Come with an open mind and a desire to learn as much as possible. Be open to advice from everyone. Learn *why* you are doing your job and make it your goal to be the best you can. (Carleton '66; special; emphasis in original)
>
> Be imaginative. Consider LIS solutions in nontraditional LIS applications. Keep aware of the problem you are trying to address and be willing to change your tools. Improve yourself. Be a person you respect. Find the good part of a job/position or make/find a new one. Believe in yourself. Use all that you learn. (Kalamazoo '66; special)
>
> Realize that a good librarian looks at the large concepts and not the particulars of the concept. Realize that "know-how" is more important than gathering facts. Try to see the world from more than one's own point of view. (Lawrence '66; academic)

Several Alums also suggest that, once in their first position, new practitioners are smart to begin by "work[ing] in a range of basic assignments" (Macalester '66; academic), while "developing some specialized skills (Lawrence '66; public). And some Alums note there is a political aspect to most professional work, with a Kalamazoo '71 school library media specialist recommending that "you choose the projects you want to do and battles you want to fight carefully." Finally, two Earlham '76 Alums who are in academic libraries point out that new practitioners need to be aware that, regardless of library type, "management will probably be a part of your job to some degree." So "if you have *any* inkling that you could be, or want to be, a director or administrator, take advantage of every opportunity to develop the necessary knowledge base and skills. It seems that there is a coming shortage, and you will most likely be called upon to move into such a role, possibly very soon [after obtaining your degree]" (emphasis in original).

Fit—Skills, Knowledge, Abilities, and Values

Fourteen percent of the comments dealt with personal attributes, and the majority of responses addressed skills, knowledge, and abilities revolving around the topic of "fit." These comments seem associated with those concerned with how to approach a new position, and the importance of continuing to learn, accepting change, and being flexible. Is this field, this job, right for a new practitioner's skills, abilities, and interests? Do they fit together well? As a Carleton '71 public librarian says, "It's important to find an area of LIS work which interests you and suits your talents." A Macalester '76 public librarian urges, "Make sure that this is truly work that you are suited to."

Sometimes the question of "fit" simply refers to personal attributes. Eight percent of the Alums whose comments clustered in this category make suggestions for what kinds of personal traits are needed to be successful in the field. A Carleton '62 public librarian says, "If you love books or computers, but hate people, do not become a public librarian." And an Earlham '66 public librarian asserts that "this is *not* necessarily a career for those introverts wishing to avoid public contact. Learn to love being political!" (emphasis in original). Along with liking books, computers, people, and politics, Alums believe new practitioners should have a sense of humor, and "be positive, friendly, and social so that you get along with coworkers and project a good image," says a Carleton '76 school library media specialist. Another media specialist speaks directly to the subject of values, saying "believe in yourself and the value of your work, and what you can contribute to others" (Grinnell '66). A Swarthmore '71 academic librarian urges new professionals to "develop strong core values aligned with those of the profession and be able to articulate them."

Values are particularly important for some Alums, who want new practitioners to "be kind and think of the other person. But swim against the tide if need be to follow your values" (Swarthmore '66; public). Others, like a Carleton '71 special librarian, believe LIS practitioners are expected to be "generous, smart, thoughtful." The list of personal attributes various Alums believe that new practitioners need (and that the field expects them to have) include

- Being proactive
- Believing in oneself
- Having a positive attitude
- Being able to exercise patience with yourself, coworkers, and users
- Being courageous, open, and thoughtful
- Being a good listener

A Swarthmore '71 special librarian recommends that "[you] make your behavior in the workplace be something others want to emulate." Or, in the words of a Kalamazoo '71 special librarian: "Don't be a critic unless you are an actor too." Suggestions from two Carleton Alums both illustrate the diversity of thought among the Alums and provide an interesting reflection on Carleton:

> Beware of arrogance. ('76; special)
> Be arrogant. ('91; academic)

However, as a Kalamazoo '86 public librarian points out, "There is an angle of LIS for all learning and personality types."

Technology

Nine percent of the CALS Alums focused on technological concerns. While stressing that new practitioners "must be highly computer literate" (Kalamazoo '66 academic), many would agree with this Carleton '96 public librarian who voices a common concern: "Computers may be the wave of the future, but they can't replace good, friendly service." She adds, "It's important to know how technology works, but ultimately it's good service that is remembered." As much as some Alums worry that technology is displacing "good books" and good reading, they also assume that new practitioners will be knowledgeable about the most current technologies that affect the libraries and other information-based agencies in which they might work. A Swarthmore '62 school library media specialist concludes that "LIS is [a] huge field with a niche for everyone, except [the] technology phobic." Perhaps this Carleton '62 public librarian has found the balance:

> Do not allow the advent of new technologies [to] make you lose sight of earlier goals: love and value of reading, the creation of an informed citizenry. Select and use technology to make libraries still greater builders of democracy and gathering places that build social capital.

Users and Community Members

Seven percent of the Alums believe new practitioners must be as knowledgeable and as current as possible about the community they work in—whether that community is an academic institution, a school, a town, or an office setting. The goals of knowing and then serving one's community were encapsulated by this Swarthmore '71 special librarian:

> Libraries are in business to serve users. User services are the reason you open the door in the morning. Throughout your career, drop whatever you're doing to assist users. Be interruptible.

A Kalamazoo '76 public librarian points out that in working with users

> there will be a lot of routine day-to-day activities but there will also be some unusual things that will keep it interesting: a fascinating patron, an interesting

> reference question, a chance to use some piece of knowledge to help someone answer their question.

A Lawrence '66 special librarian exhorted new practitioners to "take a broad view of your work. Don't *over* identify with being a 'professional' but think in terms of service and contribution to the community" (emphasis in original). An Earlham '91 public librarian encouraged new practitioners to "keep in mind that library work is *people-focused,* not books, computers, etc.; librarians help people find what they're looking for and make it easier to find. Our commitment [is] of service to people" (emphasis in original). For, as a Carleton '66 public librarian noted, "librarians can have a significant social role and presence in their community," or as an Earlham '66 public librarian phrased it, "Know that what you do changes lives."

Professional Development

Part of being a professional is keeping current with one's field and specialization. Seven percent of the CALS respondents stress that new practitioners need to begin a continuing education program of some sort as soon as possible after leaving their MLIS graduate program. They suggest involvement in professional associations, developing work and social friendships with other LIS professionals, and engaging in various forms of information sharing (i.e., conference papers, posters, publishing). As will be seen more fully in chapter 5, these Alums believe that some form of continuing education and involvement is necessary in order to learn new skills and update existing ones, stay current with technologies, share knowledge and expertise, and "keep abreast of development in the field" (Macalester '91; academic). A Kalamazoo '71 academic librarian concludes that the easiest way to go about professional development is to "be alert to opportunities for professional growth. [And] accept assignments or projects that will challenge, stretch, and enhance [your] skills and knowledge." An Earlham '76 public librarian urges new practitioners to "simply take every opportunity available to develop appropriate skills, through workshops, conferences, classes, etc."

The LIS Profession Itself

The last of the clusters of advice the CALS participants proffered to new LIS professionals concerned the profession itself. It may not be often that one hears of a profession being described as "fun," yet several of the 7 percent of CALS Alums who advise new practitioners to become engaged in LIS use the term. An example is the Macalester '71 Alum who is currently using LIS skills in work outside the field:

> LIS is a great field—lots of opportunities; Focus on the user; Fun is part of the profession—You can enjoy your work and feel fulfilled.

Most of the Alums who write about the profession itself described LIS as being "enjoyable," "challenging," "dynamic"—"a good field, worth your time" (Earlham '96; academic). Several Alums speak to the change that is constant within the field, noting that "as with all occupations, it's evolving as the times change" (Lawrence '66; school). A Denison '71 academic librarian recommends that new practitioners "find vacuums and fill them. LIS is so wide open and there are so many changes, that the scope for making valuable contributions is endless. Create your own niche." Other Alums focus on the challenges within the field. A Macalester '96 academic librarian encourages new practitioners to "consider it as a place where your skills can really be put to the test and where your broad interests can be useful to you."

Two concluding quotes. The first provides a good summary of a majority of the advice the Alums have for new practitioners; the second welcomes them into the profession:

> Be flexible—get as many different kinds of experience as [you] can. Have strong technical underpinnings, but focus on the customers. Build relationships. Get involved in a professional society. Grow. Learn something new every day. (Lawrence '66; academic)

> I would just say "congratulations—you've made an excellent choice of career." I have found this to be a very satisfying life—keep looking for a niche that capitalizes on *your* strengths. There are so many possibilities within this field. (Swarthmore '66; school; emphasis in original)

VI. Images of Librarians: After College

The rest of this chapter follows up discussion of the Alums' image of the field of library and information science by considering their image of librarians. Table 40 shows that, as they graduated from college, 57 percent of the participants indicated that they had a positive image of librarians—ranging from a low of 36 percent (Carleton) to a high of 74 percent (Earlham) with 60 percent being the median (Q.II-8). Twenty-five percent either had no "image" or were neutral about librarians (as in "they were OK"). Twelve percent had a negative image and 6 percent were mixed in their impressions. An example of the latter is the Carleton '62 Alum who says, "I had a very mixed image. I very much liked the public library directors with whom I had worked, but I had also begun to meet some librarians with rotten service attitudes."

As table 40 demonstrates, Earlham respondents had the highest "positive" impression (74 percent) and the lowest "negative" impression (2 percent). Carleton had the largest "none/neutral" at 38 percent, followed by Swarthmore at 31 percent. Swarthmore also had the largest "negative" and "mixed" views of LIS professionals at 21 percent and 10 percent, respectively. By cohort, the 1971-75 cohort had the lowest number (46 percent) of respondents holding a positive image of librarians. The 1996-2000 cohort had the highest number (86 percent) with four of the eight cohorts in the 61 to 69 percent range (see appendix D: Q.II-8). Eight to 15 percent of the members of the eight cohorts held a negative image of librarians at the conclusion of their undergraduate college years.

How did the Alums express their views? That is, what did they say that led to the assignment of one of these four terms? The following composite sketches offer insight into the images the CALS respondents had of "librarians" at that point in their lives (appendix B: Q.II-8).

Table 40: Image of Librarians after Undergraduate Education (by College)

Image	Avg (%)	College (%)							
		C	D	E	G	K	L	M	S
Positive	57	36	60	74	67	62	57	59	38
None-Neutral	25	38	20	17	17	22	30	24	31
Negative	12	17	16	2	17	14	11	8	21
Mixed	6	9	4	6	0	3	3	8	10

Positive Image

Summary comments: Helpful and intelligent. Well-educated. Knowledgeable about their field. Hard-working professionals. Someone who is willing and capable of helping you in your research. Problem-solvers. Learning centered.

Fifty-seven percent of Alums viewed librarians favorably at the conclusion of their undergraduate years. The most common descriptive words were "helpful" and "intelligent," which were often used together. "Helpful" was the most frequent word used to describe librarians with just under 30 percent of the comments using the exact word. For example:

Librarians were helpful people (Denison '71; academic)

They were extremely helpful people (Earlham '96; public)

Helpful and intelligent (Kalamazoo '66; school)

Knowledgeable and helpful (Macalester '62; special)

Very helpful (Swarthmore '81; academic)

As undergraduates, the Alums saw librarians as "intelligent," "smart," and "knowledgeable." A school library media specialist (Macalester '71) says, "They had the power of knowing where to find answers." A Kalamazoo '91 (special) Alum's image was of professionals who were "Smart—worked magic—they knew neat things and could quickly find answers." Alums who made positive comments saw librarians as professionals who exhibited traits that the Alums, as undergraduates, were being exposed to on their college campuses: being smart, working hard at one's endeavors, helping others in some fashion. An Alum from Earlham '91 (public) says, "The [Earlham librarians] made me realize the value of helping people learn how to use libraries and find the information they need/want." As a Swarthmore '81 (special) Alum put it: "They perform a useful service."

Several Alums used the word "dedicated":

> Librarians were dedicated to assisting people in finding information and enjoyment from books. (Kalamazoo '71; academic)
>
> Dedicated, knowledgeable, service-oriented. (Lawrence '71; public)

For other CALS Alums, librarians were seen as an "important part of education" (Denison '62; special), as "making a large impact on the educational experience" (Earlham '81; academic), and "as instruments necessary for success of academicians" (Lawrence '76; public). Two respondents from the 1991-95 cohort mention technology: A Carleton Alum ('91; special) was impressed with "the reference librarians and the technology that was being used for research" and a Lawrence Alum ('91; academic) felt that "we were on the cusp of the Internet explosion. I saw librarians as being on the forefront of that." Among those with librarians for parents are two Macalester Alums, who remember feeling this way:

> I knew because of parents, who were both librarians, that librarians came in all shapes and sizes ('76; academic)
>
> Since my parents were librarians, librarians were family friends over for dinner, etc., librarians were pleasant adults who often seemed interested in hearing what I was doing. ('71; special)

The overall positive image of librarians was of professionals "who cared and wanted to help others to learn, to enjoy the libraries, and to find what they needed for information" (Kalamazoo '71; special).

No or Neutral Image

> *Summary comment*: "I never thought about librarians." (Denison '66; academic)

Thirty-two percent of CALS Alums indicated that as undergraduates they had either no image of librarians or felt basically neutral about them. Several base their lack of an image on having had little contact with LIS professionals. Others note they did not use their undergraduate college library enough to form an impression of those who worked there. A Grinnell Alum ('66; school) sums up this perspective on librarians' image: "A neutral one. I hadn't thought much about it. I was not planning to be a librarian."

The few Alums who commented beyond just saying "no image" or "neutral" generally recall "remember[ing] the library and its material resources, not the library staff" (Lawrence '66; special).

A Mixed Image

> *Summary comment*: "Helpful but . . . " (Earlham '66; special)

Nineteen percent of the Alums report having formed an image that contained both positive and negative elements. Just over 40 percent of that number employ a "helpful but" type of phrase. Some remember librarians as "pleasant, helpful, somewhat boring" (Swarthmore '62; public). A Macalester Alum ('91; public) reports that

> I had a range of images. My image of school librarians (elementary and junior high) was very positive—helpful, interested, and friendly. My image of academic librarians was fairly nonexistent to mildly dull.

In contrast, an Earlham Alum ('76; academic) notes that

> my early experience with public and school libraries was mixed, largely negative, including both facilities and staff—these both tended to be barriers to the collections themselves, so I was never able to evaluate the latter effectively. My first very positive experience with a library and its staff was at Earlham.

Finally, this detailed reaction to the question of image from a Swarthmore Alum ('66; school):

> I had the vague sense that, "in the real world," librarians had an old-fashioned, unglamourous, or humble image but that in an academic community they were respected for the contributions they made to the pursuit of education and of academic inquiry. I sensed that the college librarians were probably doing important work but I found them a bit remote. I was aware that some but not all professors held librarians in high regard as colleagues worthy of faculty status. In relation to being a college professor or to other careers that some Swarthmore students might eventually pursue, I had the notion that those interested in LIS careers might be considered mistakenly, in the eyes of some, to have less professional status.

Negative Image

Summary comment: "Not very exciting people" (Earlham '76; special)

Eight to 15 percent of the members of the eight cohorts held a negative image of librarians at the conclusion of their undergraduate college years. The kinds of words that these respondents used included dull, unglamorous, quirky, stodgy, nerdy, bookish, passive, and uninteresting. Two Lawrence Alums specifically said that as undergraduates they saw librarians as "clerks" ('71; academic, and '81; special). Close to 20 percent of the negative comments referred to "the stereotype."

Alums who employed a stereotype as part of a librarian's image tended to add these as attributes:

- Old maid librarian
- Nerdy bookworm

Table 41: Image of Librarians after College and after Graduate LIS Program

Image	After College (%)	After LIS Program (%)
Positive image	57	70
None/Neutral image	25	7
Negative image	12	8
Mixed image	6	15

- Prim, teacher demeanor
- Bun-wearing, etc.

A Kalamazoo Alum ('62; academic) said, "I didn't know about the 'bun and tennis shoes' image of librarians until quite a bit later. At the time I thought librarians were just regular people (which they are!)." And a Macalester Alum ('66; special) noted that, while she thought librarians were professionals, she "was aware that their public image was not good (my academic advisor pushed law school and discouraged library school)."

VII. Images of Librarians: After LIS Graduate Education

To determine whether their LIS education had changed their image of information professionals, the Alums were asked what image of librarians they held after finishing their LIS graduate program (Q.II-13). Table 41 (above) shows there was a 13 percent increase in positive images (from 57 percent to 70 percent), and a 17 percent decrease in the number of Alums who had no or neutral impressions (from 25 percent down to 7 percent). So for a large number of Alums, LIS graduate work helped clarify their view of librarians. However, while there was a 4 percent decrease in those who saw librarians in a negative light, there was also a 9 percent increase in those who—as they started their own careers as LIS professionals—now regarded librarians with a mixed image. When analyzed by college, changes in the image Alums held of librarians after college and after completion of their graduate LIS program are more clearly seen (table 42).

Positive Image of Librarians

After concluding their graduate education, from 15-34 percent of Carleton, Kalamazoo, Lawrence, Macalester, and Swarthmore Alums had a positive image of librarians. Carleton Alums showed a remarkable 51 percent increase in the number who, after finishing their LIS graduate education, saw information professionals in a positive light. Conversely, the number of Denison and Earlham Alums who had favorable impressions dropped by 6-10 percent. Denison Alums became very much more ambivalent about the question of image. Earlham Alums

Table 42: Image of Librarians after College and after Graduate LIS Program (by College)

Image	Avg (%)		College (%)															
			C		D		E		G		K		L		M		S	
	U	G	U	G	U	G	U	G	U	G	U	G	U	G	U	G	U	G
Positive	57	70	36	70	60	54	74	64	67	67	62	79	57	80	59	74	38	63
No/Neut	25	7	38	9	20	12	17	10	17	0	22	7	30	7	24	0	31	3
Negative	12	8	17	11	16	15	2	11	17	0	14	3	11	5	8	5	21	11
Mixed	6	15	9	10	4	19	6	15	0	33	3	11	3	7	8	21	10	23

became both more negative and more mixed about librarians. Grinnell Alums also clarified their impressions—moving from predominantly neutral and negative to predominantly mixed.

What happened? Although Carleton Alums, for example, had an enormous change in perspective, their comments can serve to represent Alums from the other colleges who became positive:

> I had discovered that they were indispensable professionals, highly intelligent, with great knowledge of many fields. ('66; special)

> There are many, many, many different kinds of people in the world. Why had I only encountered the unfriendly ones before??? Librarians are diverse in ability, outlook, interests, background, and I welcomed this new perspective. ('91; public)

> Tech savvy; Strong values: democracy, intellectual freedom, etc. ('76; special)

> Very diverse group of, for the most part, intellectuals—most quite dedicated to the world of information. ('81; public)

It is likely that, during their graduate work, the CALS respondents who already had a positive image found others who were like the LIS professionals they had previously encountered. In addition, they and those Alums who developed a positive image of librarians found images of themselves in their classmates, LIS faculty, and practicing librarians they met. For example, the image held by a Macalester '91 public librarian after college was of "the stereotype most of the world has: boring job, bun-wearing, etc." Her image of librarians after LIS graduate education: "Dedicated; Enthusiastic; Rebellious; Brave; Intelligent." That is, those Alums with a positive view after their master's work had found a comfortable community that shared their own beliefs, values, and perspectives—a community that was familiar to them (Hyman 1968; Merton and Rossi 1968; Kemper 1968; Weidman et al. 2001).

Negative Image of Librarians

Those Alums who, as undergraduates, had previously been negative, were prone to make comments like this one from a Swarthmore respondent ('66; academic): "Still stodgy!" And what of the Earlham Alums who, after their LIS education, were less positive, more negative, and more mixed in their impressions? These Alums enrolled in LIS graduate programs with very high expectations of librarians—based in large measure on experiences they had with librarians at Earlham. This comment from an '81 academic librarian is typical of their image of librarians prior to the Alums' LIS graduate experience (Q.II-8):

> I assumed that the way (attitude) that Earlham librarians did their job was pretty much the way it was done in higher education or at least at small liberal arts colleges around the country.

In commenting on what they remembered about their college's librarians (Q.II-7), many Earlham Alums singled out individual librarians by name for particularly positive comment. Several clearly saw one or another Earlham librarian as a role model or "exemplar." In their graduate classes, they encountered the much broader range of students who would become their professional peers. Or, as a '62 (special) Alum phrased it, "in other words, a cross-section of life." Macalester Dean Hornbach could have been describing these Earlham Alums when he referred to students who live in a "bubble." That is, during their college years, some students only vaguely realize that they

> are sort of living inside this wonderful, unique environment where a lot of people think like they think (progressive, out there on things) but without realizing there is another world out there where people aren't going to think like they think. (interview; see Bibliography)

After meeting their soon-to-be professional peers, a number of Earlham Alums became more aware of the diversity of professionals in the LIS field. One reflected that he came to realize that "there are nerds and wonderful people in every profession, and that some librarians are more helpful than others" ('91; public).

Mixed Image of Librarians

After finishing their LIS graduate program the number of Alums from all eight colleges who had become mixed in their perceptions grew from 6 percent to 15 percent. Many of these Alums had no (or a neutral) image when they graduated from college. Others previously had positive images. And some had held negative images. In other words, they moved away from all three of those categories. As a Denison Alum ('66; academic) puts it: "Positive: Highly educated and intelligent. Enjoy the work they do. Negative: Defensive about their image. Often socially inept." And a Lawrence Alum ('76; academic) succinctly observed that "librarians could be the full range from fools to the sublime." A Macalester Alum ('86; public) said by the time she had finished her graduate program the image "varied with the type of librarian (school, special, public)." This last comment gives an indication of what was happening to many of these Alums. Having finished their graduate program, they were beginning to identify and distinguish each other by the type of library in which they wanted to work as professionals.

Summary

Within ten years of completing the baccalaureate, 78 percent of the CALS members had begun an LIS graduate program. Forty-five percent enrolled in programs in states within close proximity to their undergraduate college. As had been the historical pattern for schools of library and information studies since the first program opened in 1887, the education they found there was a mixture of theoretical and practical library matters with a focus on the latter. In the 1980s, the introduction of information science gradually shifted the program focus from solely a user service approach based in one specific kind of building, to an uneasy balance between that approach and one which emphasizes characteristics and attributes of information itself with a much less focused regard to setting or clientele. From the 1970s forward, more and more Alums found an increasingly wide array of courses stretching from the history of the field to digital libraries and data mining.

Once enrolled in an LIS graduate program, 78 percent of the Alums completed their program in one to two years. Initially, 59 percent had a positive impression of the field, 22 percent were neutral or had no image, and 13 percent had a negative image. After finishing their graduate program, 63 percent had a positive impression. Respondents were pleasantly surprised by what they discovered as the breadth and variety inherent in the field. Those with a neutral or no image of the LIS field had dropped from 22 percent to 4 percent. However, those with a negative impression had increased from 13 to 23 percent. More than two-thirds of the negative impressions were related to LIS education: the program and the faculty. Seventy-seven percent of the CALS respondents made suggestions for improving LIS education in the areas of specific courses, the curriculum as a whole, and the use of practica and internships.

The advice Alums gave to new practitioners dealt with practical matters, such as how to approach one's first professional position, users and community members, professional development, the field itself, and three conceptual areas integral to every kind of LIS work: the need for flexibility, continuous learning, and embracement of change.

When the participants graduated from college, 57 percent of them had a positive image of librarians—just slightly lower than the percentage with a positive impression of the field. At the end of their graduate education, those with a positive view of librarians had risen to 70 percent. Also showing an increase, however, was the percentage of CALS respondents who had a mixed image of librarians; that percentage had risen from six to 15 percent. These respondents had moved away from the positive or neutral or negative impressions they had formed while in college. Their comments suggested that as they began to see themselves as workplace-located librarians, they also began to be more critical of their professional peers.

CHAPTER 5

The Alums at Work

This chapter is centered on the library workplace—the environment in which the vast majority of Alums have chosen to make their careers. First there is a review of the various types of libraries, since to discuss libraries in the twenty-first century does still evoke the traditional definition of a *place* containing books and other materials for people to access and use.[28] That discussion is followed by an overview of how the CALS respondents spread themselves among the library types. In-depth consideration is then given to the nature of LIS work: what it is that the Alums as LIS professionals actually *do*.

I. The Four Traditional Types of Libraries

Traditionally, libraries have been divided into four types, based largely on the population being served: academic, public, school, and special libraries.

Academic Libraries

Every institution of higher education—from small community college to research university and all types in between—possesses one or more libraries. Academic libraries are

---

[28]The following draws upon Gates (1990), Schuman (1992), Bierbaum (1993), Gertzog and Beckerman (1994), Rubin (1998), and the ACRL, PLA, AASL, and SLA websites (see Bibliography).

generally established as part of the founding dictates of an institution.[29] The Association of College and Research Libraries' "Standards for Libraries in Higher Education" states that such libraries "should establish, promote, maintain, and evaluate a range of quality services that support the institution's mission and goals" (ACRL 2004, 538), which may cover student enrollments from 200 to well over 60,000 and faculty disciplines (and related curricula) from the basic arts, humanities, social sciences, and sciences to over 100 disciplinary specialties.

Organizationally, academic libraries may either be standard hierarchies (e.g., units, departments, divisions) or team-based and cross-functional. The collections and staff may be all within one facility or they may be spread across one or more campuses in divisional or departmental buildings. Most academic libraries are members of consortia established for the purpose of sharing the expertise of librarians and the expenses of acquiring and processing materials. Funding is based on institutional programmatic needs and comes primarily from institutional resources and, for some libraries, from external granting agencies. Titles for the heads of academic libraries vary widely; among the more common ones are Dean of the Library (or Libraries), Library Director, and increasingly titles that represent expanded responsibilities beyond just the library, such as Vice-President for Information Services. The head of the library usually reports either to the institution's president or to the institutional officer responsible for academic programs. In terms of staffing, these libraries can vary from one librarian and one supporting staff member to hundreds of each. The most recent National Center for Education Statistics report for academic libraries identifies 3,527 academic libraries in the United States including 2,148 in baccalaureate and graduate institutions (U.S. DOE, NCES 2003). The average staff size of an academic library headed by a CALS participant is 106 (appendix H). However, this figure is skewed by one institution. If that unusually well-endowed library, with a staff of 600, is removed, the average drops to 60 full- and part-time professional and support staff, a figure that would be more typical of academic libraries in the community college through smaller university range.[30]

Public Libraries

Whereas the users of academic libraries are generally 17 years and older, and are focused on formal educational endeavors, those of the public library vary from infants to centenarians with needs that span all topics. Just identifying common local community interests illustrates the array of potential users (Gertzog and Beckerman 1994, 85):

---

[29]In early American history, appeals for gifts of library materials were common, and many libraries were established by gift—the most notable example being that of John Harvard's collection of some 400 volumes, bequeathed in 1638 (Hamlin 1981).

[30]It should be noted that these figures do not include student employees, who are a substantial factor in almost all U.S. colleges and university libraries, working an average of 12-15 hours/week.

- Business and Professional
- Cultural
- Educational
- Environmental/Conservation
- Fraternal
- Health-related
- Political/Governmental
- Recreational
- Religious
- Youth-/Child-focused

American public libraries are often spoken of as "the cornerstone of democracy" (Block 2001, 65). They are public institutions, usually authorized by state law and "supported by general public funds or special taxes voted for the purpose; and administered on the basis of equal access to all citizens of the city, town, county, or region which [maintain them]" (Gates 1990, 139). Public libraries are, in essence, created and controlled by, and responsible to, the people within a set geographic boundary. These libraries are considered "free" because they do not charge admission, and materials may be used within the facility without charge. Ancillary services, such as photocopying, may carry a charge. Among the earliest free public libraries in the United States is one in Peterborough, New Hampshire, where citizens voted in 1833 to use state funds and local tax assessments for a library. Between 1849 and 1872, the state legislatures of New Hampshire, Maine, Vermont, Rhode Island, Connecticut, and New York passed laws that enabled towns to levy taxes in support of public libraries (Gates 1990, 70, 72).

The function of a public library is

> to provide the printed and non-printed materials to meet the individual and group needs of its constituency for information, education, self-realization, recreation, and cultural growth and for assistance in carrying out their duties as citizens and members of the community. The library organizes, interprets, and guides citizens in the use of these materials and makes them easily, freely, and equally available to all citizens. (Gates 1990, 146)

The range of subject matter in the collections, and the services provided, reflect the following:

- The interests of the public being served
- The values, concerns and politics of the community
- The size of the library's budget

Working within its budget, a public library may respond to identified community interests and values by offering to its community services such as the following (Nelson 2001, 146):

- Basic literacy
- [Community] commons
- Consumer information
- Current topics and titles
- General information
- Business and career information
- Community referral
- Cultural awareness
- Formal learning support
- Government information

- Information literacy
- Local history and genealogy
- Lifelong learning

The library may be a single-building entity or a system with one or more branch libraries. Its chief administrative officer may report to a board of elected or appointed community members or to a city manager, who is technically and functionally responsible for the library. In 2003, there were 9,211 single facility and system-size public libraries in the United States (Chute et al. 2005). The average staff size for public libraries directed by a CALS Alum is 43 (see appendix H); if the one largest library in the group, with a staff of 300, is eliminated from consideration, the average staff size becomes 27—more typical of the majority of U.S. public libraries outside major metropolitan areas (Lynch 2003a).

School Library Media Centers

These libraries are established and governed by local school district boards. School libraries were introduced first into secondary schools, and then into primary schools. In communities without school libraries, students are expected to either use the public library or a collection of materials developed by their classroom teacher that relates to the subjects she or he is teaching. As recently as the 1940s, the local Parent-Teacher Association or classroom teachers would raise funds to buy the library's materials. In addition to locally raised funds, foundations and the federal government have injected monies into school library media centers since the mid-1960s. In 1960, there were libraries in 31 percent of U.S. elementary schools and 94 percent of U.S. secondary schools; by 1991, the figures were 97 percent and 95 percent respectively—holding at 97 percent overall in 2002 (Gates 1990; Rubin 1998; Scott 2004). Local school boards must be convinced by superintendents, principals, teachers, and parents that students and teachers are limited intellectually without an on-site library.

School libraries have also been known as media centers, school library media centers (SLMC), and instructional materials centers, in acknowledgment of the variety of materials and formats that they contain. The library is an "integral part of the educational program of an elementary or secondary school providing materials and services that meet the curricular, information, and recreational needs of students, teachers, and administrators" (NISO standard 2.1.12, NISO website; see Bibliography). The heads of many SLMCs are information professionals. Still, it is not at all unusual for a classroom teacher to be assigned the library as part of her or his teaching responsibilities. While many states may require that school library media specialists be credentialed as teachers, teachers who manage SLMCs are not necessarily required to be information professionals with LIS graduate course work. In 2006, the American Association of School Librarians (AASL) reported that "almost one-quarter of public schools and four-fifths of private schools lack a paid school library media specialist" (AASL website; see Bibliography). If there is an information professional heading a school library media center, she or he may report to a district school library media specialist, to the curriculum administrator of her or his school, or to the school's principal. In 2002, there were 62,364 state certified librarians working in public school library media centers and 3,909 in private schools (US DOE, NCES 2002). In 2003-04, there were 110,953 SLMCs—of which 82,569 were in public schools and 28,384 were in private schools (US DOE, NCES 2006a-b). The average total staff size of a media center directed by CALS respondents is two, most commonly the information professional and a clerical "library aide."

Special Libraries

The National Information Standards Organization (NISO), a nonprofit association originally founded in 1939 to identify, develop, maintain, and publish technical standards, defines a special library as[31]

> a library within a business firm, professional association, government agency, hospital, research institution or other organized group; a library maintained by a parent organization to support a specialized clientele; or an independent library that may provide materials or services or both to the public, or to other libraries. Scope of collections and services are limited to the subject interests of the host or parent organization and usually have depth within those subject areas. (Standard Z39.7-2004; NISO website, see Bibliography)

Many people's image of a special library is of one located in a business enterprise. There are, however, scores of different kinds of special libraries. Gates (1990, 197) lists their typical homes:

> historical societies; newspapers; schools of law, law firms, and state bar associations; . . . agencies of federal, state, county, or municipal governments; airlines; medical schools, hospitals, and medical societies; divinity schools, churches, and religious organizations; museums; military installations; prisons; learned societies; music organizations; banks, insurance companies, advertising agencies, publishing firms, and other businesses; and industries, large and small.

The mission of the special library is to provide those materials and services that have application to the specific work of the parent body. Special libraries are very pragmatic and serve narrowly defined purposes and clienteles. For example, a company that manufactures soap would expect its library to focus on materials relating to soap chemistry and manufacture, not on general recreational reading (Schuman 1992; Bierbaum 1993). The library may be an independent support unit within the organization, or part of a larger research division; in some cases it *is* the research division. The head of a special library may report to a division manager or a vice president, but less frequently to the organization's chief executive officer. As can be seen from appendix H, the size of the collections, populations served, and staff of the special libraries directed by CALS Alums varies widely. The average total staff size of a special library headed by a CALS Alum is four; the most frequent number of staff members is one.

---

[31]NISO is accredited by the American National Standards Institute and draws membership from the fields of libraries, publishing, media, and information technology.

Table 43: LIS Organizations Employing the Alums (by College)

LIS Organization	Avg (%)	College (%) C	D	E	G	K	L	M	S
Public	34	34	45	35	29	26	40	39	25
Academic	33	27	28	32	43	38	32	26	41
Special	23	26	24	26	14	21	14	22	27
School	11	12	3	7	14	15	14	13	7

II. The Libraries of the CALS Alums

The CALS Alums are found in each of the four types of libraries (Q.II-16A); the distribution by college is presented in table 43 (above). The largest number is employed in public libraries, followed by academic, special, then school. Respondents from Carleton, Denison, Earlham, and Macalester mirror the overall average ranking. Almost half of all Denison Alums are working in public libraries, whereas similarly high percentages of Grinnell and Swarthmore Alums are in academic libraries. Lawrence Alums generally follow the pattern of public and academic employment; beyond that, as many are working in school libraries as in special libraries. Approximately a quarter of Carleton, Denison, Earlham, and Swarthmore respondents are special librarians. The lowest percentages (3 to 15 percent) of the CALS Alums work in school libraries—a finding more clearly seen when considering employment by cohort (table 44), which shows that none of the responding Alums in the 1981-85 and 1996-2000 cohorts work in school libraries. In fact, school library media specialists are the least represented in all the class groupings. The 1971-75 and 1991-95 cohorts have a higher number of CALS respondents working in special than in academic libraries, so their rankings are public, special, academic, then school. Alums in the cohort of 1996-2000 work only in academic and public libraries.

It is worth noting that 55 percent of the Alums have worked in more than one library type over the course of their careers (tables 45-46; Q.II-16B). This is especially true for Earlham, Kalamazoo, Lawrence, and Swarthmore respondents. On the other hand, half of Grinnell Alums have worked in only one type of library. The majority of Carleton, Denison, and Macalester Alums have worked in only one type of library, although they may have changed jobs within their type of library. Table 46 shows that, when viewed by cohort, the majority of Alums in those covering the years 1962-75 and 1981-90 have worked in different types of libraries (Q.II-16B).

The fact that a number of respondents have worked in more than one type of library raises the question of whether or not the majority of CALS Alums have moved regularly from one to another kind of library. The answer is no, as the total number of libraries—of any kind—that they have worked in is small (table 47; Q.II-14).

In fact, close to half of the Alums have worked in only one to two libraries over the course of their LIS careers. As one might expect, more of those in the older 1962-65 and

Table 44: LIS Organizations Employing the Alums (by Cohort)

LIS Organization	Avg (%)	Cohort (%) 62-	66-	71-	76-	81-	86-	91-	96-
Academic	33	36	31	27	45	31	38	24	38
Public	34	31	30	34	31	34	36	42	63
School	11	12	19	11	10	0	2	3	0
Special	23	21	20	28	14	34	24	30	0

Table 45: Percent Who Worked in More Than One Library Type (by College)

More than One LIS Organization	Avg (%)	College (%) C	D	E	G	K	L	M	S
No	45	54	59	40	50	42	36	70	38
Yes	55	46	41	60	50	58	64	30	62

Table 46: Percent Who Worked in More Than One Library Type (by Cohort)

More than One LIS Organization	Avg (%)	Cohort (%) 62-	66-	71-	76-	81-	86-	91-	96-
No	45	40	44	44	57	42	33	52	75
Yes	55	60	56	56	43	58	67	48	25

Table 47: Number of Libraries Worked In (by Cohort)

Number of Libraries	Avg (%)	Cohort (%) 62-	66-	71-	76-	81-	86-	91-	96-
None	2	0	1	1	4	0	3	11	0
1-2	48	36	40	48	56	45	56	57	100
3-5	38	49	41	34	33	45	36	29	0
Over 5	13	15	18	17	8	9	5	3	0

1966-70 cohorts have worked in three or more libraries. These two cohorts comprise 38 percent of all the study respondents, and they have been longest in the workforce. From the 1971-75 cohort forward, the largest concentration of Alums has worked only in one to two libraries. The exception is the 1981-85 cohort in which 90 percent of it members split evenly between one to two and three to five libraries.

III. The Nature of the Work

The 1962-2000 class years covered by this study were a period during which LIS work and work places changed significantly and yet in important respects stayed essentially the same. Three quotes illustrate this. The first two are from young adult books in the 1960s; the third from the 2004-05 edition of a major U.S. government publication:

> A library, says the dictionary, is a place to keep books. And so the question "What does a librarian do?" should be easy to answer: a librarian looks after books. But who would expect to find a librarian at an Army or Air Force missile base? Yet that is where you might find today's librarian. . . . What *doesn't* a librarian do! Wherever there is a library there will always be a librarian. . . . The librarian never forgets her primary purpose—to bring books and people together. (Busby 1963, 6, 63)

> Libraries today are not simply places where books are collected . . . They are centers of information. . . . Essentially, the librarian's job is to make available to each patron the information that he seeks. . . . The exact work of the library depends to a great degree on the size of the library for which [a librarian] works. . . . Librarians must keep up with all that is happening in the world. They must be intelligent, like to learn, and be curious about what is going on around them. (Splaver 1967, 22-31)

> The traditional concept of a library is being redefined from a place to access paper records or books to one that also houses the most advanced media, including CD-ROM, the Internet, virtual libraries, and remote access to a wide range of resources. Consequently, librarians, or information professionals, increasingly are combining traditional duties with tasks involving quickly changing technology. Librarians assist people in finding information and using it effectively for personal and professional purposes. Librarians must have knowledge of a wide variety of scholarly and public information sources and must follow trends related to publishing, computers, and the media in order to oversee the selection and organization of library materials. Librarians manage staff and develop and direct information programs and systems for the public, to ensure that information is organized in a manner that meets users' needs.
>
> Most librarian positions incorporate three aspects of library work: user services, technical services, and administrative services. Still, even librarians specializing in one of these areas have other responsibilities. Librarians in user services, such as reference and children's librarians, work with patrons to help

> them find the information they need. The job involves analyzing users' needs to determine what information is appropriate, as well as searching for, acquiring, and providing the information. The job also includes an instructional role, such as showing users how to access information. For example, librarians commonly help users navigate the Internet so they can search for relevant information efficiently. Librarians in technical services, such as acquisitions and cataloguing, acquire and prepare materials for use and often do not deal directly with the public. Librarians in administrative services oversee the management and planning of libraries; negotiate contracts for services, materials, and equipment; supervise library employees; perform public-relations and fund-raising duties; prepare budgets; and direct activities to ensure that everything functions properly. (*Occupational Outlook Handbook, 2004-05*:118-119)

Although the variety of tasks and the tools used by information professionals (as librarians are increasingly known today) changed enormously, LIS work retained its essential character: connecting people with information they believe they need. Information professionals share some kinds of work regardless of library type. They are responsible for acquiring, organizing, and providing access to an array of materials (i.e., acquisitions, cataloging and classifying, storage, circulation). They offer resource identification and information-seeking services to their users (i.e., reference, referral, and research support). They teach users, focusing on how to identify and find what the latter indicate they need. But the work of information professionals is also shaped by the kind of community their library serves.

Academic librarians believe in the virtue and value of education. Many see themselves as teachers of students and colleagues of faculty, a characterization more or less apt depending upon the particular institution. As described in chapter 1, the types of U.S. higher education institutions range from community colleges (two-year programs) through four-year colleges to internationally renowned research universities—and from private to state-supported. Thus, as the particular mission or focus of a type of institution varies, so does the particular focus of its academic librarians.

The majority of academic librarians focuses on collection development, library instruction, and reference and research activities; a smaller number focuses on the organization of the information either held in or accessed through the library. Those working primarily with undergraduates need broad curricular subject knowledge, skill in identifying and appraising resources that relate to both course curricula and student knowledge levels, an understanding of learning pedagogy, the ability to teach simple and complex search strategies using a range of technologies, and the personal attributes to handle one-on-one and group interactions, along with student needs frequently driven by shorter-than-desired deadlines for a paper or project. Librarians who also work with graduate students and research-oriented faculty must have these same skills and abilities plus specialized knowledge of one or more "subject fields, languages, materials of instruction and special types and forms of materials, reader guidance, research, and all forms of technology. They must be competent both as librarians and as educators," especially as the number of course areas and disciplines found on a campus increases (Gates 1990, 180; see also Schuman 1992, 71-72). The more complex the academic institution, the more specialization there is in the work of academic librarians.

The Association of College and Research Libraries' "Standards for Libraries in Higher Education" (ACRL 2004, 540-541) states that academic librarians

> should have a graduate degree from an ALA-accredited program . . . should be responsible for and participate in professional activities, [and be] covered by a written policy that clearly establishes their status, rights, and responsibilities. This policy should be consistent with the ACRL "Standards for faculty status for college and university librarians."

Academic librarians are normally considered either professional staff or faculty. If the former, they may have continuing employment agreements that place them between nonprofessional staff and faculty members. If the latter, they are held to teaching, research and publication, and service standards that are the same as, or similar to, those of the classroom and research faculty. The number of academic librarians varies by each institution's size (i.e. students, faculty, staff), the number of academic and other programs offered, the size and character of the library's collections and of the services available, the physical organization and number of library facilities, the structure of the library as an organization, and the funding.

Public librarians must be prepared for, and must deal with, the broadest possible range of user information needs. Thus, Bryan wrote, they should be "comparable in intellectual caliber, education, and personal qualifications with other social and educational leaders in the community" (1952, 6; see also *The Williamson Reports [1921]*, 13). What was true then is true today. In small public libraries the information professional (and there may be only one) handles everything; in large systems, librarians specialize in one or another area. Where academic librarians focus on students and faculty, public librarians devote considerable time and effort toward developing collections and programming for specific age groups: children, young adults, adults, seniors. Librarians may also develop collections, services, and programs for specific clienteles in their community—most frequently local businesses or newly established ethnic groups. The number and specialties of public librarians depend significantly on the socioeconomic, educational, and cultural diversity of the community, and on the roles the library has chosen to emphasize within its community. The information professionals "serve in leadership positions, direct departments, plan and develop new programs, assign execution and maintenance of ongoing programs to others, and utilize their special skills to fulfill the information needs of the library's clientele. Librarians are expected to apply theory and expertise to solving library problems" (Gertzog and Beckerman 1994, 438-439). For public librarians, those "problems" may be local political issues and individuals, financial limitations in the face of public pressure to provide current materials and services, requests to censor specific materials and access tools (such as the Internet), and what kinds of tailored services to develop to meet the needs of multicultural populations.

Public librarians who work with children need to know children's literature, child psychology, current social issues, methods for teaching reading, and the subject matter of the local school curriculum (Oakes 1970, 63). In working with young adults, librarians need to know those things and also, according to Oakes, need to be "creative and imaginative. Flexible and 'unshockable' . . . Outgoing. Intellectually curious. Socially conscious. People-oriented with a *genuine* affinity for young people" (ibid., pp. 69-70). Public librarians whose users are primarily adults need to have a different set of roles. Among them are these, offered by Block (2001, 66):

- [Public] librarians are keepers of our shared history, reminding communities about why and how they came to exist.
- A building cannot defend someone's right to know, but the librarians who sustain the institution can and do. . . . We serve the cause of informed citizenship.
- Because we share our founding fathers' belief that people can be trusted to form their own opinions, we do our bit to keep the First Amendment a living, breathing reality.
- Buildings do not live by a code of ethics, but librarians do. If people trust us, it's because we alone among a competing cacophony of voices have no ideological axe to grind.
- Helping people realize their potential is something librarians routinely do.
- Librarians build upon the cornerstones of democracy inherent to American libraries.

School library media specialists are also commonly called school librarians, media specialists, or teacher-librarians. In the United States, to be a school librarian one must follow a specific LIS graduate program curriculum. Many states prefer that a librarian also be credentialed as a teacher. School librarians provide the leadership and expertise required to ensure that the school library media center is an integral part of a school's learning environment. In 1988, ALA's American Association of School Librarians (AASL) and the Association for Educational Communications and Technology (AECT) released *Information Power: Guidelines for School Library Media Programs*, which defined three roles for school library media specialists: information specialist, teacher, and instructional consultant. The AASL website (see Bibliography) notes that

> [t]he role of the school library media specialist has changed radically since 1980. Library media specialists are instructional staff and school libraries are "classrooms." Library media specialists teach students as well [as] teachers about topics as diverse as copyright, plagiarism, taking useful notes, topic selection, evaluating web sites, citing sources, research skills, information literacy, technology skills of all kinds, and audiovisual operation and production to name a few.

The overall mission of a school library is to support its school's curriculum. School librarians do this formally by working collaboratively with teachers and curriculum specialists on course design and modules. Within their centers, their goal is to work with individual children and with groups to stimulate their imaginations, promote critical thinking, and expose them to diverse points of view on topics being studied (Rubin 1998). School librarians need to know educational psychologies and pedagogies appropriate to the age ranges of students in the school in addition to the resources (print, nonprint, and online) relevant to both teacher needs and student learning levels. There are four broad concerns which school librarians and public librarians share: ensuring that the library is integral to its community, keeping current with technological advances, retaining sufficient funding, and dealing with efforts of (primarily) parents to censor materials.

Special librarians go beyond identifying and obtaining relevant information for users to working with the information itself on behalf of the client. These librarians typically are "action-oriented, seeking out the information needs in the parent organization and providing the solutions to those needs" (Bierbaum 1993, 1). By identifying, retrieving, summarizing or otherwise presenting the information in a format other than as citations or raw data, special librarians add value to the information. They are, for example, in the lead in working with the emerging "knowledge management" systems being adopted by many of the larger U.S. businesses. This level of responsibility and liability differs markedly from the role of librarians in other types of libraries. The special librarian "is an employee of the organization first, then a librarian. . . . The corporate librarian is not expected to set aside professional principles nor ethical standards; but in the corporation, the corporation comes first. A necessary corollary is that the library that does not contribute to the corporation's goals is a likely candidate for extinction" (Bierbaum 1993, 8, 65). Because the focus of the special library is often as much on creating information as it is on collecting information, Bierbaum (1993, 9) asserts that the special librarian is in the information communication business, and is expected by her or his organizational users to have the following:

- A thorough knowledge of the mission and goals, organizational structure, and cultural and political climate of the parent organization
- An understanding that the library's mission and goals should be congruent with those of the parent organization
- An assumption of responsibility for supporting and enhancing the work of the parent, whether it is producing weapons or delivering health services
- A determination to communicate with the library's clientele and the management of the parent organization in order to serve both better and—not at all incidentally—to protect and enhance the position of the library within the organization

Since 1997, the Special Libraries Association has periodically updated a set of professional and personal competencies for information professionals who are special librarians. Professional competencies focus on areas of specialized or expert knowledge, products, and services. Personal competencies stress effective and appropriate skills in essential activities. (See appendix I for an executive summary of the 2003 competencies.) A fundamental difference between special librarians and the other three types is the need that special librarians have to justify the existence of their libraries, themselves, and their staff. Like most other units within a parent organization, annual survival of the special library is dependent upon its demonstrating that it enhances, directly or indirectly, the organization's bottom line regardless of whether that is a product or a nonprofit service. Thus, in the industrial and for-profit sectors, special libraries often charge other units of their own organization for services rendered, and are expected to show a profit at the end of each fiscal year (Schuman 1992). Special librarians do not have tenure or continuing appointment. Except for governmental agencies they rarely have civil service job rights. They are generally considered middle management and thus have no union protections. Their continued employment each year is dependent upon how successful they and their services are as seen by the organization's senior officers.

The CALS Alums' Work Responsibilities

With the foregoing as a general context, we now consider the nature and types of work that the study respondents report doing. Fifty-three percent of all the CALS Alums have spent two to 10 years in their current position (Q.II-16E). Of the rest, 9 percent have spent one year, 26 percent have spent 11-20 years, and 12 percent have spent 21 or more years in their current position. Alums in the earliest cohorts have moved frequently by virtue of advancement into management or administrative positions; for those in the more recent cohorts, changing positions is due as much to simple job or library change as to promotion. To identify their major LIS work areas, the Alums were asked about the responsibilities they have in their current position (Q.II-16D). They were given a list of 15 areas and asked to checkmark all those that applied to them. The list is an expanded version of the one used in the 1992 ACRL study (Scherdin 1994a):

- Administration/management
- Automation planning, design, and coordination
- Cataloging/classification/indexing/abstracting/thesaurus construction
- Circulation/access services
- Collection development and management/Acquisitions
- Conservation/preservation
- Database searching
- Group activities (e.g., curriculum development, instructional consultant, library instruction, storytelling)
- Interlibrary loan
- Outreach services
- Publicity/public relations/fund-raising
- Records management/archives
- Reference/reader services/information and referral
- Website development and/or maintenance
- Other

The first 14 areas cover only the broadest categories of LIS work—but are those in which a majority of the Alums might be expected to have responsibilities. *Other* was included in order to catch specializations that might otherwise be missed, such as Alums who might handle rare materials or who have major systems responsibilities.

Table 48: Most Common Responsibilities of CALS Respondents (by Cohort)

Most Common Responsibilities	Avg (%)	Cohort (%)							
		62-	66-	71-	76-	81-	86-	91-	96-
Reference/Reader Services/ Information and Referral	13	13	11	13	11	13	14	14	19
Collection Development and Management/Acquisitions	12	12	12	11	13	11	11	12	12
Database Searching	11	11	9	11	10	11	11	14	9
Administration/Management	10	12	11	12	10	8	8	6	2
Group Activities	9	8	8	9	8	11	11	11	14

Reference service was either the first or the second most frequently checked responsibility for CALS Alums from all the cohorts (table 48 above; see appendix D: Q.II-16D for the entire list of responsibilities). *Collection development and management/Acquisitions* shows the least variation across the cohorts, perhaps because it is a mainstay of all libraries. Beginning with the 1976-80 cohort, *Administration/Management* is ranked lower and lower by each successive cohort, reflecting the added responsibilities that typically come with increased experience. *Database Searching* was also a prevalent activity for Alums from all of the colleges (see appendix C-D: Q.II-16D). It is most closely associated with *Reference Service*, and is distinct from *Website Development and/or Maintenance*, which 6 percent of Alums indicated is a current responsibility.

Among other less common responsibilities, by cohort, *Website Development/ Maintenance* was an obligation of 2 percent of the 1962-65 CALS Alums, rising to 10 percent for 1986-90 respondents (see appendix D: Q.II-16D). For the 1996-2000 cohorts, Web responsibilities follow *Reference, Group Activities* (like library instruction and curriculum development), *Collection Development*, and *Database Searching* and *Outreach Services*. Eight to 14 percent of the CALS Alums are involved in group activity, a type of work most frequent among academic and school respondents. In addition, library instruction is extremely common in academic libraries, and it is undertaken by librarians from all parts of the library. School library media specialists engage in curriculum development with classroom teachers and commonly have classes come to the library for group work. The smaller involvement of earlier cohorts in *Website Development/Maintenance* and *Group Activities* is likely influenced by their movement out of "front line" positions and into managerial work.

The Most Time-Consuming Responsibilities

The CALS Alums were also asked to indicate the two responsibilities on which they spend the most time (table 49; Q.II-16D). Five tasks accounted for 73 percent of the responses, with four of the five being the same as those identified as the most common in table 48. The

Table 49: Most Time-Consuming (by Cohort)

Most Time-consuming	Avg (%)	Cohort (%) 62-	66-	71-	76-	81-	86-	91-	96-
Reference/Reader services/ Information and referral	25	21	19	23	29	35	33	31	40
Administration/Management	17	18	21	19	19	12	15	5	7
Collection development and management/Acquisitions	14	13	19	14	14	12	14	9	7
Group activities	10	10	10	11	7	12	8	14	7
Cataloging/Classification	7	11	8	5	10	10	6	2	0

remaining nine activities on the LIS responsibilities list (including *Other*) were selected by three to 6 percent of the Alums (see appendix C-D: Q.II-16D).

While *Reference* is a responsibility for 13 percent of all the CALS Alums, table 49 shows that it is where 25 percent of them spend most of their time. All cohorts place it first except 1966-70, and it takes increasing amounts of the time of Alums in the 1981-85 through 1996-2000 cohorts.

Administration/Management, which was listed by 10 percent of the Alums as one of their responsibilities, is however a major area of time-consuming work for 17 percent of them—it is in second place on the "major time-consuming" list contrasting with its fifth place on the "all responsibilities" list. And as would be expected, the older the cohort the greater the percentage of Alums who indicated that it takes a large proportion of their time. However, it is interesting to find that this level of work is done by a range of 12 to 21 percent of the 1962-90 classes. There is anecdotal, and some empirical, evidence that information professionals become supervisors, managers, and administrators fairly quickly after their LIS graduate work. As noted earlier in this chapter, this is more obviously the case with school and special librarians, but can also be true for academic and public librarians.[32] In 2002, an ALA survey of its members found that among LIS professionals the greatest percentage had administrative responsibilities, followed in order by reference/information, a cluster of activities identified as "school library media specialist work," youth services, cataloging/classification, automation/systems, collection development, and adult services (Lynch 2003b). (ALA membership is composed essentially of academic and public, and school library media specialists. Special librarians are most likely to be members of the Special Library Association or of disciplinary associations such as those for medical or law librarians.)

School librarians were the only group of CALS Alums who had great difficulty identifying only two responsibilities as those consuming the most time. Recall that previously it was found that the average staff size in a school library media center is one (the Alum)—

---

[32]There is, for example, Alice Hirshiser, who had worked in a public library before attending graduate school and who was hired as a public library director three months after receiving her MLIS (Nelson 1997).

although some have the help of a library aide. Thus, as a Swarthmore '66 school librarian explains, "I'm basically responsible for all aspects of library service."

Other Responsibilities

Aside from those just discussed, each of the remaining responsibilities are time-consumers for one to 3 percent of the Alums:

- Automation planning, design and coordination (3 percent)
- Circulation/access services (3 percent)
- Conservation/preservation (1 percent)
- Interlibrary loan (1 percent)
- Outreach services (1 percent)
- Publicity/public relations/fund-raising (3 percent)
- Records management/archives (1 percent)
- Website development and maintenance (3 percent)

If *Automation* and *Website* activities are combined, they make up 11 percent of all the responsibilities of all CALS Alums and the two most time-consuming areas for 6 percent of them. However, in a great many libraries, these activities are carried out by separate staffs, so they have been treated separately in ranking the Alums' work roles. By cohort (see appendix D: Q.II-16D2), it is interesting to note that two to 6 percent of the CALS respondents invest significant time in Web activities except for the 1962-65 and 1996-2000 cohorts, none of whose Alums included it.

In addition to these remaining responsibilities, four to 6 percent of the CALS Alums identified work activities under the *Other* designation. These ranged from attending meetings, fund-raising, and grant-writing, to facilities management and exhibition/curatorial work. The following illustrate the kind of specialized work that is often not found when looking at only the common types of libraries and areas of responsibility:

> I am a product strategist—I work on software design for all aspects of library automation with special expertise in cataloging. I have been president and co-founder of an ILL product company . . . I am active in current/developing library standards, too. (Kalamazoo '66; special)

> Special projects librarian including development of a Doc[ument] Del[ivery] program, a research project on library serials, and helping with analysis for staffing levels. (Macalester '96; special)

Activities on Which CALS Alums Would Like to Spend More Time

When the Alums were asked, "If you could spend more time on one work activity, which one would it be?" (Q.II-16I), 53 percent of all the activities listed related to

- Work with the Public (22 percent)
- Collection Development (11 percent)
- Computer Work (11 percent)
- Reference Work (9 percent)

Work with the Public was mentioned by respondents from every cohort and every college. *Collection Development* and *Computer Work* are already among the top five responsibilities of the respondents, yet many Alums would like to spend more time on each of them. In addition, some CALS members lament that new responsibilities have taken the place of these, as is pointed out by an Earlham '62 public library director:

> I regretted giving up collection development and work with the public when I became Director. Now, after all these years, I feel I've lost my skills at reference and would be a duck out of water working with the public services.

In terms of *Computer Work*, the Alums tended to indicate specific areas, like the Grinnell '86 special librarian who wrote in "web-based information service development" and described that as "project management, planning, implementation, [and] information architecture." Recall that *Reference Work* is already a major responsibility for the greatest number of Alums and also where 25 percent of them spend the most time. Clearly, it is also an area—along with work with the public in general—that is particularly attractive and one that libraries are increasingly stressing.

Aside from these five significant areas, there are 19 other activities on which the Alums would like to spend more time (see appendix C: Q.II-16I). A Denison '82 public librarian illustrates how hard it was for some CALS Alums to restrict themselves when asked to identify only one work activity, saying, "I enjoy cataloging to the exclusion of all else—but could always spend more time with computers." And 1 percent of the Alums feel similar to the Lawrence '76 Alum who wrote, "I actually wouldn't change my current balance."

IV. Work Attributes

Salaries

In the CALS survey demographics section, the Alums were asked to indicate their "current salary" within given ranges (Q.IV-3). The Alums' responses were distributed as follows:

- Under $20,000 9 percent
- $21,000-30,999 9 percent
- $31,000-40,999 14 percent
- $41,000-50,999 24 percent
- $51,000-75,999 32 percent
- $76,000-90,000 6 percent
- Over $90,000 6 percent

In 2002, nationally, the average starting salary of new LIS graduates was $37,456 (Maatta 2003). The present analysis defines *beginning librarians* as those CALS Alums who had been employed from one to three years in LIS work.[33] Twenty-four Alums who fit this definition provided their actual 2003 ("current") salary figure in response to question IV-3 (table 50). The 24 alums come from six of the eight cohorts (not 1962-65 and not 1976-80). Almost half (10) are members of the 1991-2000 cohorts. The 2003 salaries reported by the Alums were compared with 2002 *beginning librarians* to allow for the fact that, at the time of the CALS study, the Alums had between one and three years of employment.

In table 50, the average salary for the Alums who work in schools and special libraries is found to be slightly higher than the average for the 2002 national group of *beginning librarians*. The salary average of Alums who are academic librarians is slightly lower than their counterparts. The greatest difference between the new practitioner Alums and those of the 2002 group is seen in public librarianship, where the average salary of the national group is $3935 higher than that currently attained by the public library-based Alums. It might be that the CALS members are employed in smaller libraries or are in geographic areas that do not command the higher average salary.

By area of activity, table 51 shows that only the CALS respondents who are beginning professionals with *Administrative* responsibilities are earning average salaries near to that of their 2002 national counterparts. Within the other three work areas, the Alums' average salary is 8 to 9 percent lower than their counterparts.

Table 52 displays the salary ranges of all the CALS respondents—from beginners to those approaching retirement. The Alums who are academic librarians have ranges that reflect, at least in part, their academic status. Academic librarians may be considered faculty and paid at that level, or they may be considered professional staff and paid somewhat lower (table 52; Q.IV-3).

Public libraries employ more part-time librarians than do the other kinds of libraries, which may partially account for the 25 percent of the public librarians in the CALS group earning less than $31,000. In addition, public libraries are also dependent upon direct local tax and gift support, and many are located in rural areas of the country; both considerations may contribute to the fact that 51 percent of respondents are earning less than $41,000. In contrast,

---

[33]Two percent of the Alums who responded to this question have less than one year of LIS work, but none provided actual salary data so the *beginning librarian* definition reflects respondents with one through three years of LIS employment.

Table 50: Average Beginning Salaries (by Library Type)

Library Type	Alums with 1-3 Years of Experience in 2003	National Group for 2002 (Maatta 2003)
Academic	$36,000	$36,610
Public	28,000	34,065
School	41,000	40,171
Special	40,000	39,484

Table 51: Average Beginning Salaries (by Activity)

Area of Work	Alums with 1-3 Years of Experience in 2003	National Group for 2002 (Maatta 2003)
Administration	$38,500	$38,463
Automation/Systems	33,533	38,243
Collection development	32,214	35,700
Reference	30,227	37,680

Table 52: 2003 Salaries of Alums (by Library Type)

Salaries	Avg (%)	Library Type			
		AL	PL	School	Spl
Less than $31,000	18	14	25	19	16
$31,000-40,999	14	12	26	10	5
$41,000-50,999	24	25	16	34	25
$51,000-75,999	32	35	28	36	31
$76,000-90,000	6	4	4	0	14
over $90,000	6	9	2	0	9

one reason that 70 percent of the school librarian Alums are in the $41,000-75,999 range is that they may be categorized as "teachers" during salary negotiations, may be part of the same educational union as teachers, or may be managerially responsible for a school's library system. The range of special librarians' salaries reflects the extremely diverse kinds of organizations in which they work.

Across the cohorts, 55 percent of the CALS Alums earn between $41,000 and $75,999. Table 53 indicates that the largest percentage of such Alums is found in the cohorts covering

Table 53: 2003 Salaries of the Alums (by Cohort)

Salaries	Avg (%)	Cohort (%)							
		62-	66-	71-	76-	81-	86-	91-	96-
Under $20,999	9	14	10	11	8	13	8	22	30
$21,000-30,999	9	11	12	8	10	10	8	3	20
$31,000-40,999	15	8	12	12	6	26	18	38	40
$41,000-50,999	23	16	18	20	22	23	46	25	10
$51,000-75,999	32	38	42	33	45	16	21	6	0
$76,000-90,000	6	5	7	8	8	6	0	3	0
over $90,000	6	8	9	8	0	6	0	3	0

1962-80 and 1986-90. The greatest concentration of Alums earning in the $31,000-40,999 range is in the 1996-2000 cohort, followed by the 1981-86 cohort. The most recent cohort (1996-2000) has only one Alum with a salary higher than $40,999; however, all the other cohorts have Alums in every one of the salary categories—from under $20,999 to over $90,000.

Position Titles

Rather than listing job titles and asking the CALS Alums to identify those associated with their positions, the participants were asked to state their own position title (Q.II-16F). The array of titles thus received from the Alums was then analyzed and similar titles clustered together. There is both commonality and difference across the four types of libraries. For example, respondents from all of the library types report some Administration/Management positions along with corresponding titles; all four types also have Reference positions and use Reference-related titles. Title clusters identified by the greatest percentage of respondents are presented by each type of library.

Academic Library

The following titles account for 88 percent of those reported by respondents who are academic librarians:

- Collection Development or Subject Specialist (23 percent)
- Reference, Public Services, or Research and Information Services (20 percent)
- Management, including Team Leader (17 percent)
- Cataloger, Metadata Librarian, or Technical Services Librarian (11 percent)
- Director, Library Director, or Dean (10 percent)
- Electronic Resources Librarian, IT Librarian, or Systems Librarian (7 percent)

The remaining titles (12 percent) are associated with unique situations (e.g., Night Librarian, and Visiting Librarian) or these areas of work: Archives, Interlibrary Loan, Library/Bibliographic Instruction, Outreach, Preservation, Special Collections, and Special Projects. A majority of the nonmanagerial/administrative titles end in the word "Librarian," as in Reference Librarian or Systems Librarian.

Given their mission of supporting the educational needs of students and faculty, it follows that academic libraries should be heavily invested in both reference and collection development positions. With regard to the technology-related titles, the 7 percent of respondents with such titles represent only a portion of those whose work includes technology. Recall from Section I of this chapter, that (for example) while 10 percent of the Alums indicated that their work responsibilities included database searching, only 5 percent spent significant amounts of time doing it. This difference illustrates that while a particular task can be a major activity it can also be subsumed under a Reference or Public Services Librarian's title, rather than that of an IT or Systems Librarian's title.

Public Library

The following titles account for 83 percent of those identified by respondents who are public librarians:

- Reference, Adult Services, Readers Advisory, or Public Services (21 percent)
- Manager, Coordinator, Deputy or Departmental Director (21 percent)
- Young Adult or Youth Services (12 percent)
- Director or Library Director (11 percent)
- Library Assistant/Associate, Librarian I/II/III, Senior Librarian (10 percent)
- Children's Services (8 percent)

The remaining titles (17 percent) either refer to subject areas or to functions:

- Subject areas (Business, Foreign Languages, Genealogy, Music, Sociology) (5 percent)
- Functions (Aide, Archivist, Business Manager, Cataloger, Circulation, Collection Development, Human Resources, Interlibrary Loan, Periodicals, Planning-Special Projects, Preservation, Technical Services) (12 percent)

Public libraries, more than other library types, appear to utilize two kinds of generic titles. The first is Library Assistant or Library Associate: these are common though somewhat confusing, as some libraries use these to refer to paraprofessionals and others use them to refer to information professionals. The second is Librarian I, Librarian II, Librarian III, and Senior Librarian. These information professional positions tend to be in libraries with civil service-mandated personnel systems. If clustered together, 10 percent of the Alums working in public libraries have one or the other of these generic kinds of titles.

As in academic libraries, public library titles frequently end in "Librarian." Here they are most commonly Reference and Young Adult/Youth Services position titles. The "YA" librarians are different from Children's Services Librarians. Although the exact age division varies from library to library, in general, "children's services" encompass infants through age 12 and "young adult"/"youth services" ages 13-17 (AASL and YALSA websites, see Bibliography). Public libraries are heavily invested in managerial/ administrative positions. This is especially due to the widespread existence of multibranch public library systems. Branch facilities, headed by branch managers, have their own administrative hierarchy and services in parallel with those of the main library facility in the system.

School Library Media Centers

The following titles account for 76 percent of the CALS Alums employed in school libraries:

- Library Media Specialist (23 percent)
- Librarian (17 percent)
- School Librarian or Teacher-Librarian (15 percent)
- Media or Technical Generalist/Specialist (15 percent)
- School Library Media Specialist (6 percent)

The remaining titles fall into three groups:

- K-12 Levels (High School Librarian, Prep School Librarian, Secondary School Media Specialist, and School District Department Head) (12 percent)
- Technology (Director of Information Technology Services, Information Specialist/Webmaster, Library Technician) (6 percent)
- "Library Aide/Library Assistant" (6 percent)

Most, if not all, of the Alums who hold *any* of the above titles direct and administer their library. Thus these titles are all variants of Administer/Manager/Director/Head Librarian/ Librarian position titles. Even Library Aide/Library Assistant, which sounds like a nonprofessional title, may be an official school title held by an MLIS librarian who is responsible for the school's library. There is an average staff size of two in the school library media centers in which these Alums work (appendix H). None of them has a staff larger than four, with one staff member being most common.

In the list of general responsibilities, the majority of the 11 percent of CALS school librarians checked all 15 possible responsibilities (including "Other"). And more of them than Alums in other library types commented, "I do it all!" When selecting the two activities in which they spent the greatest amount of time, school librarians most frequently chose "Group Activities (curriculum development, library instruction, etc.)" followed by Administration/ Management, Reference, and Other. Those marking Other again tended to write "I do it all" as their sole most time-consuming responsibility.

Special Library

These librarians have the most diverse position titles. The following account for 70 percent of those identified by CALS special librarians:

- Manager, Director, Head Librarian (23 percent)
- Librarian (16 percent)
- Specialist (14 percent)
- Reference or Instruction Librarian (7 percent)
- Cataloger (5 percent)
- Health Science/Medical Librarian (5 percent)

The CALS special librarians work in libraries with an average staff size of four, with most having only one staff member (appendix H). Thus, as with school librarians, Alums in special libraries are most likely to be the heads of their libraries. The first three position titles given above account for 56 percent of the special library Alums, and most if not all represent information professionals who manage or administer their libraries. The second three titles in the list denote the most common functional responsibilities, with the rest being:

- Archives/Records Management (3 percent)
- Automation/Electronic Services Librarian (3 percent)
- Law (3 percent)
- Outreach Services (1 percent)
- Resource Librarian (1 percent)
- Technical Services (2 percent)
- Technology/Systems Librarian (4 percent)

Indeed, even some of these titles also may designate an Alum who heads her or his library. It is not unusual, for example, for law libraries to have only one person holding the position of Law Librarian—and that is the director of the library. If there are additional information professionals there, they will have position titles like Reference Librarian or Collection Development Librarian.

Five titles (8 percent) are difficult to "fix" within the special library's organization but could indeed relate to functional positions:

- Business
- Consultant
- Market Research Program
- Special Operations
- State Aid/Data Collection

The last 5 percent of the special librarian titles are Professional Staff or Library Assistant, and most probably indicate nonadministrative positions.

Although CALS respondents from all four library types report position titles that denote Administration/Management responsibilities, senior organizational titles are most common among school library media specialists and special librarians because of the all-encompassing nature of their work. The majority of those Alums associated with academic and public libraries do not hold administrative or managerial titles. (This was also borne out in this chapter's earlier description of most common job responsibilities; see table 48.) The above findings suggest that those whose chief desire is to administer a library will reach that goal most quickly if they seek school library media specialist or special librarian positions.

Full-Time and Part-Time Work

Regardless of the type of library in which they work, or their specific position, 61 percent of Alums average 40 hours or more a week doing their LIS work (Q.II-16G). Twenty-five percent spend 30-39 hours a week at work, and 8 percent spend 20-29 hours. These rankings also held true across the cohorts from 1962 through 2000. If full-time work is defined as 20+ hours per week (especially typical in public libraries), then 94 percent of the Alums have the equivalent of full-time positions.

The CALS Alums were asked, "In addition to LIS work, do you do other types of work part-time?" (Q.III-6). In some cases, a part-time LIS position and a part-time non-LIS position comprise an Alum's work life. A perhaps surprising 26 percent of Alums report having part-time, second jobs in addition to full-time LIS work. While the majority of respondents from seven of the colleges do not work part-time, among Grinnell Alums 57 percent do hold second jobs.

Of the CALS members who indicated the nature of their part-time employment, 25 percent work in business (table 54; appendixes C-D: Q.III-6). This may be in their own small business, as a partner with a spouse, or as an employee of a business. After business, there are large concentrations of Alums who engage in arts activities, teach part-time, and work as nonpaid volunteers. These combined four areas comprise 77 percent of all Alums who work part-time. Only teaching and volunteering drew CALS respondents from all eight colleges. Aside from these activities, a range of one to 6 percent of Alums are engaged in other kinds of work roles.

Some specific examples of part-time activities:

> Elementary school teacher; HS English teacher. (Carleton '76; school)
>
> Substitute teaching. (Denison '66; public)
>
> I do contract original cataloging for small public libraries in the area, but that is minimal work. (Earlham '71; special)

Table 54: Part-Time Employment (by College)

Employment	Avg (%)	College (%)							
		C	D	E	G	K	L	M	S
Arts	16	7	20	22	25	11	15	0	24
Business	25	27	20	28	0	14	45	0	29
Caretaker	3	7	0	0	0	7	5	0	0
Coach/Instructor	2	7	0	3	0	0	0	0	0
Computer work	5	7	0	6	0	7	0	14	0
Farming/Gardening	3	0	0	8	0	4	0	0	0
LIS (other than own job)	5	0	0	6	0	7	5	0	6
Ministry	1	0	0	3	0	0	0	0	0
Teaching	19	13	40	8	25	29	15	43	18
Volunteer	17	27	20	14	25	14	5	43	18
Writer	6	7	0	3	25	7	10	0	6

Part-time ILL for a research library and a medical hospital library. Also 8 hrs. a week cataloging government documents and websites at two other institutions. (Kalamazoo '62; academic)

Volunteer webmaster; volunteer archivist for two different nonprofit organizations. (Swarthmore '86; academic)

By cohort, both teaching and volunteer work is done almost entirely by the 1962-80 classes (appendix D: Q.III-6). Of the 26 percent of CALS Alums who have part-time work, 78 percent are in the 1962-80 cohorts, 23 percent are in the 1981-2000 classes, indicating that the bulk of this kind of work is being done by older Alums.

Professional Development

As they had indicated to new practitioners (see chapter 4), the Alums believe that part of being a professional is keeping current with one's field and specialization. They have generally followed their own advice about membership in professional organizations (Q.IV-23). As table 55 shows, ALA and state associations claim the greatest number of Alums. The American Library Association, founded in 1876, is the oldest LIS professional association in the United States with most of its members based in academic, public, and school libraries. While 78 percent of the Alums are associated with those three types of libraries, 74 percent of the Alums are members of ALA (Q.II-16SA; Q.IV-23). Typically, in the United States there are state library

Table 55: Major Professional Associations

Professional Associations	Participation (%)
American Library Association	74
State library association	55
Regional LIS association	30
Other LIS-related organizations	25
Special Libraries Association	21

associations; however, as with ALA, membership is generally voluntary on the part of individual LIS professionals although directors feel a strong compulsion to participate. It is not unusual for LIS professionals to hold memberships in both ALA and their state association, or in some other combination of LIS-related associations.

Regional associations often hold joint meetings with state associations – providing opportunities for practitioners to meet with colleagues across state boundaries. Special Library Association membership of 21 percent is just 2 percent less than the 23 percent of the Alums who are special librarians. The "other" organizations that Alums named include international, national, and local LIS-related organizations, along with specialist groups. The most frequently identified such organizations include the following:

- American Association of Law Libraries
- American Society for Information Science and Technology
- Medical Library Association
- Music Library Association
- National Association to Promote Library and Information Services to Latinos and the Spanish Speaking (REFORMA)
- Seminar on the Acquisition of Latin American Library Materials (SALALM)
- Society of American Archivists

Professional involvement with their associations varied (see appendixes C-D: Q.IV-23). Twenty-five percent of the respondents indicated that they also belong to professional associations other than ones that are focused on LIS. These tended to be related either to an Alum's work, such as the American Sociological Association for an academic librarian doing collection development in sociology, or to a non-LIS activity in which the Alum is involved, like a teachers' union.

Authorship by Alums was not as robust as membership in professional organizations (table 56; Q.IV-21). The survey questionnaire asked CALS participants if they had been involved with one or more of six different forms of publishing. Depending on the type of publication, a range of 16 to 88 percent of the 431 CALS members indicated they had published. Those who had published in one format (for example, book reviews) had usually also published in a second format (such as journals). An increasingly common format for publication is the Internet. The

Table 56: Alums Indicating Authorship by Type of Publication

Publication Type	Authorship (%)
Book reviews	37
Journal articles	37
Web publications	26
Conference papers	26
Other	16
Monographs	10

Table 57: Alums' Authorship (by Cohort)

Publication Type	Avg (%)	Cohort (%)							
		62-	66-	71-	76-	81-	86-	91-	96-
Book reviews	45	44	42	39	33	38	40	14	20
Journal articles	42	40	46	35	43	38	31	17	0
Web publications	34	20	18	22	35	32	43	33	30
Conference papers	32	22	34	25	33	18	7	11	10
Other	17	15	14	13	30	9	21	11	20
Monographs	13	11	12	8	13	18	7	0	0

"Other" category includes work manuals, government documents, newspaper columns, and conference papers and posters.

Of those Alums who stated that they had authored in each of the six formats, a larger percentage of the 1966-70 cohort had published journal articles and conference reports than those in other cohorts, although that cohort also reported the smallest percentage who had published on the Web (table 57 above). Age, however, is not necessarily a useful indicator for predicting which cohorts have the greatest number of members involved in authorship. An example of this is seen with monographs: The two cohorts with the greatest number of years in the field (i.e., 1962-65 and 1966-70) have fewer members with monographic publications than the 1981-85 cohort. In no case did 50 percent or more of the members of any of the cohorts answer "yes" to authorship within one of the publication types. Another aspect of publication activity is service on editorial boards. Over 50 (12 percent) of the CALS respondents indicated they had engaged in this form of professional involvement (Q.IV-22).

Aside from LIS educators, the only LIS professionals who, as a group, may have research and publication as part of their job requirements are academic librarians. Beginning in the 1960s, an increasing number of colleges and universities provided their academic librarians with tenure or continuing status of some kind. However, most of those institutions then also required that the librarians engage in varying forms of publication as part of the tenure process (see DeBoer and Culotta 1987; Huling 1973; DeVinney 1987; and "Faculty Status and Collective Bargaining Statements" 2001).

V. Job Satisfaction

There is an enormous literature devoted to studying job satisfaction, including a plethora of instruments to measure and assess it. Studies have been carried out on various occupations and professions, including LIS. Beginning in the 1970s, there has been research about "general job satisfaction, job satisfaction in specific types of libraries, job satisfaction within library units and occupational groups, job satisfaction and work schedules, job satisfaction and management style, job satisfaction and attitude, job satisfaction and age and tenure, and job satisfaction and gender" (Thornton 2001, 144). Van Reenen (1998, 24) analyzed a number of LIS job satisfaction studies and drew these conclusions from them:

- Older workers were more satisfied than younger workers.
- Experienced employees were more satisfied than those with less experience.
- Those who planned to be working in the same library five years hence were significantly more satisfied than persons with other plans.
- Those lacking supervisory responsibilities had the lowest satisfaction while department heads were the most satisfied.
- Acquisitions department employees had significantly higher levels of satisfaction than employees of any other department, with Reference second.
- Professional librarians were more satisfied than nonprofessional staff.
- The factor that consistently scored the highest satisfaction rates was working directly with customers.

Van Reenen (1998) compared information professionals who attended workshops he conducted in 1995-97 with an *Inc.*/Gallup 1996 survey of American workers. He found that 80 percent of the information professionals were satisfied to extremely satisfied with their workplaces, and he noted that this was 11 percent lower than the national group of workers.[34] However, another 1996 study, reported by St. Lifer, phrased the job satisfaction question differently and found that 90 percent of the LIS respondents said "they enjoy what they do," and that the top three job satisfaction factors were *working with users, helping people find what they need*, and *having a variety of job responsibilities* (St. Lifer 1996, 20), a good example of the fact that findings are conditioned by how the question is asked.

---

[34]This 91 percent "average worker" figure was also reported in *The 1997 National Study of the Changing Workforce*, which surveyed a nationwide cross section of 2,877 adult employees.

Table 58: Levels of Job Satisfaction

Aspects of Job Satisfaction	Categories (%)			
	Not Satisfied	OK	Satisfied	Very Satisfied
Responsibilities	5	11	48	36
Working hours	8	14	45	33
Range of people employed in my library	14	22	42	22
Salary	18	25	39	18
People I work most closely with	5	12	38	45
Supervision/Feedback	21	25	36	18
Opportunities for development/promotion	22	29	34	14
Opportunities to use my skills and abilities	10	11	29	50
The autonomy I have to do my own work	5	7	28	60

The Alums were asked how satisfied they were with nine aspects of their current positions (table 58 above; Q.II-16H). Seven of the nine aspects were the same as those used in the ACRL 1992 study. One of the remaining two dealt with autonomy and the other with the library staff as a whole. The rating categories used in the CALS survey were *Not Satisfied, Satisfied, OK*, and *Very Satisfied*. The *OK* response was equivalent to being "accepting but not thrilled" or "somewhat satisfied" and was designed for those respondents of surveys who are not totally comfortable indicating they are completely "satisfied" with the state of something. The ACRL (1992) choices were Dissatisfied, Neutral, and Satisfied; van Reenen (1998) used a five-point scale from Extremely Dissatisfied to Extremely Satisfied. The intent of the CALS question was to identify broad satisfaction ranges without exaggerating (as in "Extremely . . . "), while still teasing out the extent of satisfaction.

Table 58 arranges responses from high to low using the *Satisfied* column for ranking purposes (see appendixes C-D: Q.II-16H). It is clear from the table that, within their current positions, the great majority of CALS respondents are *Satisfied* to *Very Satisfied* with these nine aspects of job satisfaction. Even where there is double-digit lack of satisfaction, it is expressed by less than 25 percent of the Alums.

Regardless of the cohort, *Satisfied* or *Very Satisfied* was the first or second choice (out of the four degrees of satisfaction) for five of the nine aspects (see appendixes C-D: Q.II-16H):

- Working Hours
- Responsibilities
- Opportunities to Use My Skills/Abilities
- People I Work Most Closely With
- Autonomy

Table 59: Job Satisfaction (OK, Satisfied, Very Satisfied) by Cohort

Aspect of Satisfaction	Range (%)	Cohort (%)							
		62-	66-	71-	76-	81-	86-	91-	96-
Responsibilities	90-100	100	95	93	100	94	90	90	100
Opportunities to use skills and abilities	90-100	93	86	89	94	94	88	90	100
Autonomy	86-100	94	96	94	96	100	95	94	86
Working hours	85-100	100	93	85	89	86	95	94	100
Range of library personnel	80-100	90	82	92	81	82	89	80	100
Coworkers	75-100	96	95	95	92	97	100	90	75
Salary	74-87	74	83	85	87	84	83	76	75
Supervision/Feedback	70-81	78	81	81	80	77	79	76	70
Development/Promotion opportunities	62-89	81	74	86	80	62	89	68	75

The Alums chose either *Satisfied* or *OK* to indicate their degree of satisfaction for three aspects:

- Supervision/ Feedback
- Opportunities for Development/Promotion
- Range of People Employed in My Library

On the topic of salary, seven of the eight cohorts gave a *Satisfied* rating to this aspect. The most recent 1996-2000 cohort felt their salary deserved the even lower *OK* ranking.

Satisfied

Table 59 (above) combines the *OK, Satisfied,* and *Very Satisfied* categories to more clearly illustrate the degree of job satisfaction being expressed by the CALS Alums in their current positions. The table is arranged from high to low by the minimum percentage of each job aspect's overall average.

Not Satisfied

"Opportunities for Development/Promotion" drew the highest number of *Not Satisfied* responses (22 percent), followed by "Supervision/Feedback" and "Salary" (table 60; appendixes

Table 60: Percent "Not Satisfied" by Aspect and Cohort

Aspects of Satisfaction	Avg (%)	Cohort (%)							
		62-	66-	71-	76-	81-	86-	91-	96-
Development/Promotion opportunities	22	19	26	114	20	38	11	32	25
Supervision/Feedback	21	22	19	19	20	23	21	24	30
Salary	18	26	17	15	13	16	18	24	25
Coworkers	5	4	5	5	8	3	0	10	25

C-D: Q.II-16H). Regarding salary, 18 percent of Alums indicated they were *Not Satisfied*; however, another 18 percent had indicated they were *Very Satisfied* with their salaries. In general, and not unexpectedly, those who checked *Very Satisfied* regarding salaries were in higher-level positions.

The 1996-2000 cohort was the most dissatisfied of all the cohorts regarding supervision (30 percent were *Not Satisfied*) and also with their close workmates (25 percent). This may provide support for van Reenen's (1998) conclusion about older workers being more satisfied than younger ones. Or it may simply indicate the adjustment new professionals frequently must make between their previous view of a field and their experience after entry into it (Becker and Carper 1956a; Bledstein 1978; Ashforth and Saks 1996; Cooper-Thomas and Anderson 2002). It is worth noting that no one in either that cohort or the 1962-65 one is dissatisfied with her or his working hours. Nor are they, along with the 1976-80 cohort, dissatisfied with the responsibilities they have.

Comparisons

The largest percentage of CALS Alums gave "Autonomy" and "Opportunities to use my skills and abilities" a *Very Satisfied* response: 50 percent and 60 percent respectively (see appendixes C-D: Q.II-16H). By cohort, although the most recent 1996-2000 classes may be unhappy with supervision, feedback, and close workmates, 71 percent of them are *Very Satisfied* with the amount of autonomy they have in doing their work, and 63 percent are *Very Satisfied* with the opportunities they have to use their skills and abilities. These are higher than for any other cohort. Information professionals, like all professionals, want work that ensures that they will be able to use their knowledge, skills, and abilities—and in the ways that they themselves deem appropriate. Freidson (1986, 14) states that autonomy is "the minimal characteristic of the professional." Asher (1995, 72) believes that autonomy "is the single most important predictor of people's degree of satisfaction with their work." And Hackman and Oldham (1980) consider autonomy to be the way through which professionals take responsibility for their work. One difference between professional and nonprofessional positions is that in the latter you may be given the autonomy to do your work, but that work may not utilize your particular skills and abilities. Information professionals expect to find in their LIS positions both autonomy and the

Table 61: Percentage Job Satisfaction by Alums and 1992 ACRL Study

Aspects of Satisfaction	CALS Alums (%)	1992 ACRL Study (%)
Responsibilities	90-100	86
Working hours	85-100	82
Range of library personnel	80-100	not asked
Salary	74-87	54
Coworkers	75-100	76
Supervision/Feedback	70-81	56
Development/Promotion opportunities	62-89	54
Opportunities to use skills and abilities	90-100	86
Autonomy	86-100	not asked

opportunities to utilize their skills and abilities (Watson-Boone 1998). Indeed, this belief may be yet another reason why members of the newer cohorts dislike the supervision they are experiencing: they expect to function independently while their supervisors believe they still need guidance in the particulars of "the way we do things here." Comparison between the CALS Alums and the ALA and SLA participants in the ACRL 1992 study shows that, with the exception of feelings about coworkers, the Alums are clearly more satisfied with their jobs (table 61 above).

This table shows that both the CALS respondents and the ACRL participants cited the issues of *Salary* and *Advancement Opportunity* as causing their lowest levels of satisfaction. Scherdin (1994a, 85) comments that as far back as Bryan's (1952) study "inadequate financial return and insufficient opportunity for advancement were the two most frequently checked reasons for dissatisfaction with library work." A 1984 survey on career development conducted by the ALA Office for Library Personnel Resources found that 80 percent of LIS professionals from all library types were not satisfied with the advancement opportunities available at their workplace (Bernstein and Leach 1985). The present study finds that Alums from the classes of 1962 through 2000 confirm that salaries and advancement opportunities are still matters the field needs to address. In 2001, ALA created a separate, but associated, organization called the ALA Allied Professional Association to address this issue nationwide. The ALA-APA provides

- Certification of individuals in specializations beyond the initial professional degree
- Direct support of comparable worth and pay equity initiatives, and other activities designed to improve the salaries and status of librarians and other library workers. (ALA-APA website, see Bibliography)

The issue of advancement is now, in some ways, more difficult for newer LIS professionals than for those of the 1962-80 cohorts. Previously, the hierarchical structure of libraries as organizations meant one could advance from entry level librarian to director either within one's current library or, more frequently, by moving from library to library in ever ascending positions. Among the Alums, for example, 48 percent have worked in only one to two libraries in the course of their LIS career. The classes of 1962-70 have moved around the most and more members of those classes hold high positions. Since the 1990s, many academic and some public libraries have restructured themselves away from unit, department, and divisional organizations into system-focused, team-based organizations in which there are likely to be fewer levels of hierarchy—in some cases, few or no departments or divisions. Teams have a team "leader" who leads by articulating the organization's vision and purpose in concrete team-specific terms (Senge 1990). While being a successful team leader is akin to being a successful manager or administrator, the flatter organizational structures of team-based libraries means that to advance within the LIS field, it is now even more likely that the information professional must move from one library to another.

Summary

This chapter has focused on the library as workplace. When discussing libraries it is usual to talk of librarians in almost generic terms. However, description of academic, public, school, and special libraries as places of employment—along with responses from the CALS Alums to questions concerning their jobs—reveals distinctions in job responsibility, salary range, and position title by type of library. Of particular note is the expansiveness of the responsibilities of school library media specialists and of special librarians. Based on the information provided by this study's respondents, both academic and public librarians have greater opportunities to specialize within their positions.

Respondents illustrated the greatest commonality when they were asked to indicate levels of satisfaction with workplace factors that affected their specific jobs. Between 75 and 100 percent of the CALS participants indicated they felt *OK* or were *Satisfied* to *Very Satisfied* with those aspects which impinged most closely on their personal daily activities: their working hours, specific job responsibilities, opportunities to use their skills and abilities, job autonomy, and colleagues with whom they worked the closest. Those satisfaction factors that drew concern focused on advancement. The 1962-65 and the 1991-2000 cohorts were the most disturbed about their salaries. The older cohort members may be considering the effect of their salaries on retirement options, while the younger members may be seeking raises in order to support young families or to pay off education loans. The other advancement issue dealt with development and promotion opportunities. Here it is possible to speculate that the low satisfaction accorded by the 1966-70, 1981-85, and 1991-95 cohorts reflects a feeling that the time has come for "a step up" in the form of promotion, additional responsibilities, or greater involvement beyond their specific job area. Some of these Alums may feel that they have reached mid-career; others may believe that the skills and abilities they have demonstrated are not being appreciated. These assessments of satisfaction have centered on the Alums' most immediate focus, their jobs.

Beyond that is the larger arena in which their jobs are set: LIS work as a whole and satisfaction with it as having been the right career choice.

CHAPTER 6

Satisfaction with Work and Career

This chapter expands on the theme of job satisfaction by considering how the CALS respondents viewed not just LIS work in general, but also their career in the field. In addition, challenges they have encountered and those endeavors that have given them great pride are described, along with discussion of their personal and professional hopes for the future. As seen in the previous chapter, the CALS Alums were, overall, satisfied with their jobs in terms of responsibilities, opportunities to use their skills and abilities, degree of autonomy, working hours, range of library personnel, and their close coworkers. Even though they were not as satisfied with development and promotion opportunities, supervision and feedback, and their salaries, these were regarded as at least acceptable aspects of work life. It seems, then, that the Alums should be fairly well satisfied with not only their LIS work but also the career of library and information science.

I. Satisfaction

In discussing social learning theory as a way of understanding career choice, Niles and Hartung (2000) refer to Krumboltz's belief that people will prefer (or avoid) an occupation if these three conditions apply:

- They have succeeded (or failed) at tasks they believe are like tasks performed by members of that occupation.
- They have observed a valued model being reinforced (or punished/ignored) for activities like those performed by members of that occupation.

- A valued friend or relative stressed the occupation's advantages (or disadvantages) to them, they observed positive (or negative) words and images being associated with it, or both. (Krumboltz 1994, as cited in Niles and Hartung 2000, 26-27)

In line with Krumboltz's (1994) three conditions, the Alums continue as LIS professionals because they have succeeded at tasks associated with the field, they have been rewarded for their performance within the field, and they have seen others express value for the work of the field.

The LIS literature indicates that most librarians are indeed satisfied with both work and career. Morrison (1969, 65) found that 87 percent of the 707 academic librarians he studied in 1958-59 expressed satisfaction with their careers. In 1966, Schiller (1969, 55) asked 2,282 academic librarians "To what extent has your library career fulfilled your expectations?" Their response was that the career was

- Much more satisfying that expected (27 percent)
- More satisfying than expected (25 percent)
- About as expected (37 percent)
- Somewhat disappointing (10 percent)
- Very disappointing (1 percent)

The 1992 ACRL study found that 93 percent of the ALA and SLA members who responded were satisfied with their work. A 1994 survey of 935 readers of the *Library Journal* reported that 85 percent of them were satisfied with their jobs (St. Lifer 1994). And a 2002 survey of 770 school library media specialists found that 44 percent were "Very Satisfied" and 46 percent were "Somewhat Satisfied" with their work (Lau 2002).

The CALS survey questionnaire asked the Alums what they liked most and least about their work, and most and least about LIS as a career (appendix C: Q.II-16J-K and M-N). Asking information professionals about their likes and dislikes resulted in reams of paper. A broad spectrum of comments emerged from these open-ended questions, enriching the quantitative responses presented in chapter 5. Every CALS respondent had something to contribute to these questions. The comments were compared with each other using the constant comparative method of analysis. The result for each question was a set of concepts that reflected related, more individualized comments.

II. "What Do You Like Best about Your Own Specific LIS Work?"

In answering this question about the "best" aspects of their own specific work, the Alums' comments first sorted into 32 topics, which when concentrated resolved themselves into three concepts: *Functions* such as reference or cataloging, *Activities* like problem solving, and the *Work Environment* including being in a workplace where the autonomy to do one's work is valued (appendix C: Q.II-16J).

Table 62: Best Part of Job: Functions

Functions	Comments (%)
Collection development	23
Reference	17
Children through young adult years	16
Management/Administration or working with library staff	14
Cataloging/Indexing	10
Outreach/Liaison	9
Programming	7
Readers' advisory	3
Archives	1

Functions

CALS participants whose comments related to "Functions" described what they liked best through using terms that define LIS specialties. Table 62 (above) presents the top functions mentioned in the 115 comments (19 percent of all comments) made by these respondents. Most Alums indicated functional areas by writing in single terms, such as "reference" or "programming." Some were more descriptive, like this Earlham '71 public librarian's comment: "I have a YA math club [for] at-risk teen girls. I am helping them to become library users."

Activities

The Alums were more expansive when they identified as "best" those things that might be considered as task areas. Here they are actively engaging in the work. Table 63 presents the top ten most favored activities.

A fundamental mission for LIS professionals is to bring people and information together. Here it is clear that these Alums see that as the best part of their work. Those who specifically said *Empowering users* are separately categorized since "empowering" means giving people power to accomplish something they desire, which is stronger than merely helping someone with an information need. The meaning behind *Helping patrons* is illustrated by these comments:

> I like it best when I help someone for whom the outcome of our collaboration means a lot to them, be it finding research for a school project, medical information, or business information. (Carleton '81; public)

Table 63: Most Favored Activities

Activities	Comments (%)
Helping patrons/users/people	42
Seeking and finding information/doing research	15
Instructing/teaching	8
Doing creative things	8
Continuing to learn	8
Technology-related activities	6
Problem solving	5
Service expansion/improvement/implementation	5
Affecting the organization	3
Empowering users	1

> Connecting the user with the information that's right for the moment - and helping her or him use that information and evaluate it. (Grinnell '66; school)

> The satisfaction of *assisting* the user and *teaching* the user how to find resources. (Macalester '76; academic; emphases in original)

> Special Collection library with enormous interface with public = Heaven. (Kalamazoo '66; academic)

Anyone who feels very satisfied when *Seeking and finding information* for users (or themselves) can identify with the thoughts of these Alums:

> The excitement of a "treasure hunt" search for obscure information. (Carleton '81; special)

> Working with patrons on difficult or broad or deep or specific or general *genuine* reference questions. (Earlham '62; public; emphasis in original)

Recall that special librarians, in particular, spend significant portions of their time compiling and then analyzing information for users as part of their job. Thus it should be no surprise to find that *Seeking and finding information* is heavily favored by them. It is a large part of what attracted them to special libraries in the first place. The 5 percent of the CALS respondents who wrote about enjoying the *Problem solving* parts of the work might also fit here.

Instructing/Teaching and *Doing creative things* seem familiar. They continue the thread of what the Alums were exposed to as children and valued about their undergraduate experience. *Instructing/Teaching* is especially enjoyed by academic librarians and school library media specialists. Both kinds of information professionals spend considerable amounts of time teaching students how to be information literate. In public libraries, teaching has gradually shifted to giving users lessons on how to navigate the Internet and do e-mail; otherwise public librarians most frequently provide users with the answers to their information-based questions. In special libraries, information professionals provide answers and do selective teaching. By being creative or "doing" creative things, the CALS Alums mean—as explained by a Lawrence '86 public librarian—"that I enjoy the opportunities for creativity. Adult programming is my primary responsibility off [the reference] desk. Planning and providing free innovative programs are very enjoyable and rewarding." A Grinnell '86 special librarian writes that she likes best "the opportunity to conceive, implement, and launch innovative web-based information services." Note that both respondents use the word "innovative," which may be the key to how they see LIS work as creative.

Although for all Alums, *Continuing to learn* has high value, for Swarthmore respondents it is particularly significant. *Continuing to learn* tied for third place for all Alums, but is tied for second place with *Seeking-finding* for Swarthmore Alums. A 1971-75 cohort special librarian talked of having "opportunities to learn medicine," a '91 public librarian of "learning from patrons," and a '86 academic librarian noted (perhaps wryly) that the best part of her job is "getting to learn about many subjects without having to write the paper!"

Finally, the ideas of *Service Expansion, Improvement, or Implementation* and of *Affecting the organization* come mostly from Alums who have major management or administrative responsibilities. Two examples from public librarians:

> The ability to influence the programs and services made available to library customers/patrons. (Macalester '66)
>
> I do acquisitions and outreach to the fast growing Latino population. It's very satisfying to grow a collection and programs that this new group finds useful and to create an atmosphere where they feel welcome. (Earlham '66)

Work Environment

The largest number of comments (42 percent) dealt with the topic of *Work Environment*. These are not just tasks that Alums associate with their LIS jobs; they are essential—albeit subjective—ingredients that make the difference between having an "OK job" and a "great job." Comments cluster into four attribute categories and represent 80 percent of the responses (table 64). The remaining 20 percent cover having an overall positive work environment that includes good hours and the opportunity to work with specific materials (13 percent), receiving appreciation from users (3 percent) and, at 1 percent each, having expertise, being respected, having a sense of accomplishment, and having a sense of "fit" with the setting.

Table 64: Most Favored Work Environment

Work Environment Attributes	Comments (%)
Variety	32
Autonomy/Authority/Freedom	21
Great colleagues/Boss/Users	15
Intellectual challenges/Using my mind	12

These four attributes are crucial to satisfaction with work within the information professions. While helping users is fundamental to the description of LIS work, aspects such as variety, autonomy, and intellectual challenge are core to being satisfied with one's life as a working professional. While definitions of "profession" differ, commonly ascribed components include specialized knowledge, autonomy in making judgments, an ethical code, and the employment of one's knowledge in service to others and to the greater social good. Authority over one's own work is central in many definitions, as is having expertise in the work (Abbott 1988; Bledstein 1978; Freidson 1973, 1994; Richard and Emener 2003). Some would add that a profession also exhibits a distinctive culture (Goode 1957; Hart and Marshall 1992; Wilensky 1964). As Hughes (1962, 656) boldly states, "Professionals *profess*. They profess to know better than others the nature of certain matters, and to know better than their clients what ails them or their affairs. This is the essence of the professional idea and the professional claim" (italics in original). The importance to the Alums of these characteristics as "best" parts of their job suggests that, without them, the respondents would feel less a part of a profession.

Variety

Entire books could be written about the importance of variety to information professionals. However, these comments serve to make the point:

> The chance to do so many different things—collection development, supervision, scheduling, indexing, reference, readers services, etc. (Carleton '91; public)

> I love the variety—selecting books, cataloging them, helping people find information, organizing library programs. (Kalamazoo '71; public)

> Never a dull moment—varied, interesting work with people and library materials. (Macalester '81; school)

> The variety—reference and cataloging are very logical; programming and displays can be very creative. (Lawrence '86; public)

> It's never boring. There's always something to learn about [the] subject matter, new technologies, and how to deal with people. (Macalester '62; special)

Autonomy/Authority/Freedom

The importance of *Autonomy* has been discussed in the previous chapter. Here it may be sufficient to note that many Alums simply wrote in the word "autonomy" as their choice for what is "best" in their jobs. Others combined it, as in "variety and autonomy" (Earlham '66; public). Two basic elements of autonomy are found in this comment by a Carleton '76 academic librarian: "Autonomy—there is great flexibility within the organization to work on interesting projects and [to] collaborate with colleagues." Academic librarians in particular, across the colleges and cohorts, find that having autonomy is integral to their identity as members of the academy.

In elaborating on what they meant by *Autonomy*, the CALS Alums stressed having decision-making authority and "having a sense of freedom to do my job as I see fit" (Swarthmore '71; academic) in terms of arranging, developing, and handling their responsibilities. A number said "I get to do it all" with reference to making decisions on all sorts of matters. This was frequently coupled with enjoying the variety that comprised their work. An Earlham Alum '76 school librarian wrote of being "able to develop the collection from scratch!" A Kalamazoo '62 special librarian explained that it was important that she have "the ability to . . . control and enhance information access." A Macalester '62 public librarian appreciates that she has "the power to effect change."

Great Colleagues/Boss/Users

Having good coworkers enables the Alums to feel more productive and effective. A Denison '86 public librarian notes that he values "the people in my department. We have a very good work relationship. The department works well together." A Kalamazoo Alum ('62 academic) reiterates the point when she says that "there is satisfaction in working with people who work well together." A Carleton '62 academic librarian represents several respondents who all used the same phrase in identifying "high quality colleagues" as the most important aspect of their own LIS work. Likewise a great boss is important for some Alums, including the Swarthmore '86 special librarian who values her boss for "the encouragement to be creative."

On the other hand, a Lawrence '81 special librarian believes her users are most important: "I work with attorneys who have knowledge, motivation and a goal—the best possible reference desk customers!" Other Alums describe a range of users whom they enjoy; a Denison '76 public librarian, for example, finds "working with a diverse and continually evolving clientele" to be most satisfying.

Intellectual Challenges

Some of the typical ideas behind regarding *Intellectual challenges/Using my mind* as outstanding parts of the job are articulated by these two Alums:

> The challenge of working with bright people. (Kalamazoo '66; special)

> The opportunity to embrace new challenges that will test and stretch my talents. To solve challenging research questions. (Kalamazoo '71; academic)

A Carleton '86 Alum who works in an agency providing special services to libraries identified "having mental acuity" as one of his strengths, and added "I enjoy having a special expertise in my corner of LIS, and being able to share that knowledge through training and support of library staff." And a Grinnell '76 public librarian saw using her mind as one way in which "I have an impact on [my] organization." A number of Alums simply spoke of liking the "puzzles" that came across their desks each day.

Ultimately, it seems that the combination of "helping people and using my brain" (Denison '81; academic) in a setting where there is variety and autonomy is irresistible to the majority of the Alums. When all of the attributes found in the three concepts of Functions, Activities, and Work Environment are combined and ranked as one list, these four rise to the top and comprise just under 50 percent of all the attributes:

- Helping patrons/users/people
- Variety in my work
- Autonomy
- Seeking and finding information/doing research

III. "What Do You Like Best about LIS Work in General?"

Asking what the Alums liked best about LIS in general returns us to what brought them to the profession: work with the public and satisfactions found with the field itself (Q.II-16M). The greatest number of comments (74 percent) about LIS at large dealt with these four areas:

- Service to others/Helping people/People focus (33 percent)
- The intellectual challenge (19 percent)
- Variety in the field: positions, kinds of activities (11 percent)
- Access to materials, technologies, information (11 percent)

The remaining 26 percent of comments were on these topics:

- Continuous learning
- Ethics, values, and mission of the profession
- Positive work environments in LIS
- Career flexibility
- Fit between LIS and me
- Specific jobs: archives, cataloging, reference
- The colleagues one encounters
- Being able to teach/train others
- Autonomy

Service to Others/Helping People

Career publications, such as Busby's 1963 children's book *What Does a Librarian Do?* through to the U.S. Department of Labor's *Occupational Outlook Handbook* (2004), point out that "librarians assist people in finding information and using it effectively for personal and professional purposes" (*Occupational Outlook Handbook* 2004, 218). If one does not enjoy being around people, either coworkers or library users, it is difficult to find satisfaction with LIS work. The raison d'être of the many different kinds of LIS agencies and work is, ultimately, to bring people and information together in some way. More CALS Alums from all eight colleges and cohorts made positive comments about serving others than about any other aspect of LIS. Alums value their interactions with users, the myriad of opportunities to help users find what they are seeking, the gratitude users express at receiving such help, and the focus on people that the LIS field exhibits. The difficulty some Alums (and other information professionals) have with people almost always relates to the behavior of some portion of a library's community of users: lack of respect for those who are there to help them, rudeness, anger, crankiness, "the 'entitlement' attitude of some who take the 'servant' part of public servant a bit literally" (Earlham '76; public). This balancing act between enjoying work with their library's public and handling that portion of it who are not respectful and courteous is well expressed by this Swarthmore '76 academic librarian:

> *What I Like Least about LIS Work*: Working with patrons.
> *What I Like Best about LIS Work*: Working with patrons.

Comments about helping others tend to focus on supporting the user as well as on the role of public service work and libraries within the larger picture of a community and the country. The following reflect the perspective of most of the Alums who found helping others to be the "best" aspect of LIS:

> Knowing (believing) that the work I do makes life easier for lots of people, including library staff and patrons. (Carleton '86; special. Parenthesis in original)

> When I get a chance to help a person find the info they need and many come back and tell me "I found a job," "I passed the test," "I located my father," it is great! (Earlham '71; public)

> The knowledge that I have helped people with their problems. (Carleton '71; special)

> I like the public service nature of the work. It makes my work feel worthwhile, since I'm *not* working just to make a profit for a company. What I do here has an immediate positive impact on individual people and the community." (Lawrence '86; public; emphasis in original)

> I like that public libraries are a part of our democratic society's commitment to having an informed citizenry. (Earlham '91; public)

> I feel like I'm making a positive contribution to society at large. Better researchers and better thinkers mean (I hope) better citizens. (Carleton '86; academic)

The other three characteristics of LIS that the CALS Alums like "best" illustrate a desire to be intellectually engaged in work that provides them with a variety of opportunities, and preferably in a setting where that engagement includes firsthand involvement with certain materials, technologies, or information resources.

Intellectual Challenge

The "thinkwork" or mental nature of the field is valued by many CALS Alums. Use of abstract and practical knowledge is inherent to LIS and, notes a Denison '71 academic, "It is fun to think." A Grinnell '66 school librarian finds that the field "has a genuine intellectual base." Some of the activities Alums cite to illustrate the idea of LIS work being intellectually challenging include:

- Problem solving
- The investigative nature of the work
- Creativity
- Rigor of thought

These respondents used variations of the phrases "intellectually stimulating" or "intellectually challenging" to denote what they liked best about the field. Several spoke of the intellectual challenge of the work in combination with having variety in their work life and with helping others. An Earlham '62 public librarian, for example, wrote of the "intellectual stimulation gained from library materials used in concert with colleagues and patrons." A Carleton '66 academic librarian expresses pleasure in what is mentally required "in creating collections and [then] working to help people make sense of those collections." Two other sets of comments reinforce the connection between the service aspect and the intellectual aspect of LIS. One group of Alums described the satisfaction they received in acquiring, using, and sharing their knowledge with library users. Another group expressed their pleasure in doing research, or knowledge building—for others, or for themselves—in their nonpublic related LIS activities:

> Learning how to find out what I or patrons need to know, and sharing this knowledge with patrons. (Carleton '76; public)

> I like working with people who need information that I haven't researched before, especially if the user is involved in the topic. (Denison '66; special)

> I love knowing how to find a tremendously broad range of information and using that skill to help a very interesting public. (Earlham '66; public)
>
> Having the opportunity to indirectly further knowledge. (Earlham '96; academic)
>
> Having an intellectual base and the opportunity to help people learn how to think. That's exciting. (Grinnell '66; school)
>
> Helping people–sharing my expertise to help them learn and grow. (Kalamazoo '86; public)

Variety

To the Alums, this word means that the field is one in which "no two days are alike" (Earlham '81; public) for there is "diversity of experience within a routine—the basic shape of each day is more or less the same, but it is always different" (Kalamazoo '66; public). Variety also means that one finds within LIS "a variety of job opportunities from traditional library settings to companies to consortia agencies, etc." (Kalamazoo '66; public)—"that is, there's an opportunity to match almost any kind of interest to a relevant job" (Lawrence '71; academic).

Access to Materials

Recall from chapter 1 that a "love of books/reading" was a major reason why CALS Alums felt LIS might be an attractive career (Q.I-3A). Others believed the field offered them opportunities to "learn to use and do research with a variety of information resources" and to "work with increasingly sophisticated information technology." In considering what they like best about LIS, some Alums come back to those reasons:

> Working in a venue where information and information access are *the* reason for the work. (Earlham '76; academic; emphasis in original)
>
> Working with books and information technologies and feeling that I am part of a profession which helps people enrich their lives through reading/learning. (Kalamazoo '66; school)
>
> The connection with technology and advances in information technology. (Swarthmore '81; special)
>
> The combination of working with books (for future) and people (for now). (Carleton '86; academic)

Other Comments

For 6 percent of the CALS respondents continuous learning is one of the best aspects of the field, evoking comments about "opportunities for learning" (Carleton '66; academic) and "learning something new every day" (Earlham '62; special). Overall, the Alums view libraries as places with a positive work environment, cooperative and interesting colleagues, and career flexibility. The last consideration was noted not just in terms of job opportunities, but also because many library administrations and managers have been supportive of LIS as "an easy career for a woman to leave and come back to [as she] works around a family" (Kalamazoo '66; school). Whether in terms of flexible scheduling, part-time employment, or reintroduction into the LIS workplace after some time out for child rearing, the field in general has accommodated the needs of families. Thirty-five percent of the CALS Alums have interrupted their LIS career for family reasons—reflecting Alums from every cohort except the most recent (1996-2000, Q.IV-19). Fifty percent of these 139 respondents expressed positive reactions to the interruption, and 47 percent of those were parents caring for young children. Another 11 percent had mixed feelings about it, generally expressed in terms such as these of a Carleton '66 special librarian:

> My longest absence from the workforce (10 months after first baby) resulted in a new job with [a] higher salary and better prospects. But I think my long period of part-time work after each additional baby compromised my professional, dedicated image.

Those who reacted negatively to the interruptions cited missing the intellectual camaraderie, lack of subsequent career progress, lower salaries over the subsequent years, or loss of expertise. Those who reacted positively mentioned "treasur[ing] those years I was home with the girls" (Earlham '62; public), libraries that were "flexible and didn't penalize me for being home" (Lawrence '71; public), and "being able to interrupt my career for child-rearing was one of the things that appealed to me about librarianship" (Lawrence '71; public). It should be noted that of all four library types, respondents indicated that public libraries have the strongest history of work flexibility. A Denison '66 public librarian commented that the interruption was "*Great!* How flexible I have found library work to be whenever I needed to work part-time, or not at all, for a few years. *Family* has easily come "first" before *work*. In many other careers this would never have been possible" (emphases in original). For many, this has allowed them to have a viable career and a balance between career and family life.

One additional set of comments on what the CALS Alums found "best" about LIS as a career deserves discussion. Four percent focused on the ethics, values, and mission of LIS. One group of those Alums finds that the field provides them with "a 'right livelihood.' I'm *proud* of the services we offer to the public" (Carleton '66 public; emphasis in original). Most of the comments came from Alums in public and academic libraries. Some comments were personal, such as these:

> Providing ready access to information supports one of my most important values. (Carleton '62; academic)

> [I] feel like I am doing something worthwhile with my life. (Kalamazoo '86; public)

> It's honest work, serving the public. (Macalester '76; public)

> A congruence of professional ethics with my personal values. (Swarthmore '71; academic)

> It is really a positive profession—there is no ethical dark side to it. (Earlham '86; academic)

Other comments expressed appreciation for the values espoused by the field, although the particular values cited differ:

> The values of the profession: service, literacy, intellectual freedom, lifelong learning. (Lawrence '76; public)

> The values that are espoused (and hopefully promulgated) by the profession: promotion of learning; information access; critical thinking; non-censorship; information preservation. (Swarthmore '86; academic)

A Swarthmore '71 special librarian remarked on "the integrity of the work." It is, a Lawrence '71 public librarian wrote, "a noble profession" with, as a Macalester '86 public librarian sees it, "a positive social impact." Some of these sentiments reflect support for intellectual freedom; others note that part of the mission of libraries (especially public ones) is to assist everyone—a feature that reflects the values of information professionals and their communities.

IV. "What Do You Like Least about Your Own Specific LIS Work?"

Where there are likes there are bound to be some dislikes. Given the job features that the Alums particularly favored, some of their dislikes are predictable. Here comments coalesced into five concept clusters (appendix C: Q.II-16K):

- Job-Related (42 percent)
- Working Conditions (33 percent)
- People (internal and external to the library) (19 percent)
- Lack of Respect (3 percent)
- Wrong Fit (3 percent)

Table 65: Least Liked Job-Related Activity

Activity	Comments (%)
Paperwork, busywork, or non-LIS work	23
Not enough time to fulfill work responsibilities	17
Managing/Administering	11
Lack of variety	11
Specific tasks	10

Job-Related

As might be expected, the greatest number of the CALS respondents wrote about aspects of their specific job responsibilities. Table 65 (above) presents the most frequently reported job-related comments.

Paperwork and *Busywork* were common words that the Alums used when responding to this question. *Non-LIS work* was identified as "too much time spent on nonprofessional tasks which could be done as well by a clerical worker" (Macalester '62; school), or "the tedium of clerical duties associated with public use of the Internet" (Earlham '66; public). In all cases, the respondents consider such kinds of activities to be nonprofessional in nature.

Not enough time to fulfill work responsibilities does not imply a lack of desire to carry out one's responsibilities, but rather a sense of being "overwhelmed" with the amount of work the responsibilities require:

> Too often I feel overwhelmed by the amount of work I need to do, and at the lack of control libraries have in dealing with vendors. (Carleton '66; academic)

> I often feel overwhelmed and overworked because there is not enough time to get all the work done which needs to be done. I bring a lot of work home. (Kalamazoo '81; public)

> Not having enough time to do everything that needs to be done—I deal with 700 students every week (2 schools) and have 1 full-time aide and a few volunteers—that doesn't really count services provided for teachers! (Lawrence '71; school)

Managing/Administering is undesirable work for those Alums who feel uncomfortable with such roles, but who, for one reason or another, are constrained to perform them. This ranges from Alums who supervise at the unit level to those who find themselves in upper level administration—as in the case of a Carleton '66 public librarian:

> Unfortunately, I dislike most of [my job]! When I changed careers I was hoping to escape from management, but I got sucked right back into it.

However, most of the Alums who indicated that this area was their least favorite part of work limited themselves to writing in just the word "Management," or "Administration," or "Supervising." In some cases, the possibility exists that the Alum is uncomfortable in a team-based setting, as with the Kalamazoo '62 academic librarian who dislikes "correcting other librarians' work." Given the high levels of autonomy often held by academic librarians, this kind of activity would be neither frequent nor normally welcomed by one's colleagues.

Lack of variety covers "boring" work, "tedious" work, and according to Alums like this Earlham '62 public librarian: "Answering repetitive, unproductive questions." This is balanced, however, by the 3 percent of Alums who complained of "too much variety" in their work, such as the Lawrence '66 special librarian who talked of there being "too much fragmentation because work covers so many fronts." And a Kalamazoo '66 academic librarian found, "so much is changing, technologically, that it is hard to stay on top of what we need to know."

Finally, the category *Specific Tasks* covers two contradictory sets of CALS Alums. One set misses work for which they no longer have responsibility: "I miss reference" from a Carleton '76 school librarian and "lack of contact with customers" from an Earlham '76 public librarian —both are now administrators. The other set of Alums would like to discard certain aspects of their current work: "technical troubleshooting with network, computer and printing issues" (Macalester '66 academic librarian, whose major work is reference and outreach) and "collecting money from patrons and discussing problems with that" (Swarthmore '71 public librarian whose main responsibility nevertheless includes this aspect of circulation/access services).

Working Conditions

Thirty-three percent of the comments made by CALS Alums pertained to work conditions, and subdivide into external and internal working conditions that the respondents consider difficult. *External conditions* refers to "politics," and budgetary issues, such as having to justify one's request to higher level authorities, or needing regularly to engage in fund-raising or grant-writing.

Internal conditions covers the following:

- Job constraints (e.g., not enough hours/week, night and weekend work schedules, and too much time or travel away from family; lack of advancement possibilities)
- Organizational bureaucracy/structure
- Lack of staff, including an inability to hire needed staff
- Lack of sufficient salary/benefits
- Poor work environment

Internal working conditions overlaps in one regard with the *Job-related* category: feeling "isolated." This was expressed in particular by special and school librarians. For example:

> Right now I am very isolated, being a solo librarian, and I have to work at networking with other librarians. (Carleton '91; special)
>
> Isolation from other librarians—no one on-site to ask questions. (Swarthmore '66; special)
>
> Isolation from people with similar interests. (Kalamazoo '66; school)
>
> As sole practitioner in my small library branch, I was tied to my desk during open hours with little opportunity for collaboration with teachers. It sometimes felt like jail. (Macalester '81; school, regarding a previous job)

As indicated earlier in this chapter, special and school librarians are most apt to have a total staff of one to four people, and they are likely to be the only professional. The lack of close professional colleagues is one cause for seeking other positions or work in other types of libraries. A previous unpublished study of LIS Alums found that special librarians moved more frequently than information professionals working in other library types, and that they tended to go from special into academic librarianship (Watson-Boone 2000b).

People

Those comments that identified *People* as the source of what the Alums liked least about their jobs also fell into internal and external categories: people from inside the library and people outside of it. The former related primarily to dealing with personnel problems. These Alums were usually managers or supervisors. Most did not decry having that role, but spoke of the few staff members who are "difficult and time-consuming to goal direct" (Earlham '62; academic). Some Alums identified colleagues or their boss as the source of discouragement. Patrons who are rude, incompetent, naive, inexperienced, or classed as "problems" or as "difficult people" were also strong sources of frustration for Alums. "Dealing with problem patrons—those who feel they deserve super special treatment" (Carleton '96; public) represents one end of the spectrum. In-between are "cranky people" (Macalester '91; public) and "constantly monitoring student behavior and having to discipline unruly students" (Kalamazoo '66; school). At the other end of the continuum are the "homeless and/or mentally ill patrons (Earlham '76; public). Most of the CALS Alums who described difficulties with the public are employed in public libraries. Some Alums working in academic or school libraries did have issues with students being disruptive or lazy. Alums in special libraries expressed very few patron-related concerns.

Lack of Respect

Although this was a concern to only 3 percent of the Alums, it is singled out as a cluster because it relates a lack of respect the respondents have felt from administrators to whom they report, or from the public with whom they work. Sometimes the phrase was simply "Lack of respect from administration" (Carleton '81; special); other times it was more specific:

> Receive criticism more often than thanks. (Earlham '76; public)
>
> Not appreciated as a professional. (Kalamazoo '66; special)
>
> Other staff think it's an easy job (even if they don't say so). Other staff and admin. really don't understand what I do. (Macalester '62; school)

Wrong Fit

This final cluster included Alums who felt they were in the wrong job or that they would do better in a different type of library. An example of the former is the Carleton '76 special librarian who wrote that "I don't have a great memory so reference can be frustrating for me." And a Denison '66 public librarian expressed frustration about "being forced into children's services and management." A Lawrence '96 academic librarian illustrates a wrong-type-of-library fit in her description of the project orientation of her current position: "It's too business-related—not at all like traditional information work."

V. "What Do You Like Least about LIS Work in General?"

There was a 74 percent overlap in the areas which the CALS Alums disliked about their own specific work, and about LIS work in general. The categories of *Job-Related*, *People (Internal and External)*, *Respect*, and *Wrong Fit* were all found in Alums' responses to both questions, along with the "Job Constraints" portion of *Working Conditions*. In terms of the least enjoyable aspects of LIS work in general, 48 percent of the comments dealt with four topics (Q.II-16N):

- Lack of respect from others (16 percent)
- Lack of understanding regarding the field (15 percent)
- Paperwork/Busywork/Non-LIS work (10 percent)
- Lack of variety in LIS work (7 percent)

Lack of Respect from Others; Lack of Understanding regarding the Field

Lack of respect and *Lack of understanding* share elements and combine to comprise 31 percent of all the comments Alums made about disagreeable aspects of LIS work in general.

Comments came from Alums across colleges and cohorts, and in proportion to their representation within the study (that is, the most from academic and public librarians, then special librarians followed by school library media specialists).

One group of comments concern specifically "the library" and bear upon the Alums' frustration with what they perceive as a "lack of realization [and knowledge] on the part of the public about what libraries could do for them" (Macalester '91; public and Denison '62; public). Alums are frustrated with "the low value society seems to place on libraries" (Carleton '86; special), and specifically about a "lack of public understanding of what libraries mean to culture" (Carleton '85; academic) or to the "overall cultural/economic 'matrix'" (Swarthmore '71; public). An Earlham '66 public librarian mused that perhaps "libraries and education in general are not being properly valued" in the United States. There is some thought that "the Internet is often viewed as a replacement for librarians and libraries" (Macalester '76; academic). And one Alum bemoaned the "perception that all information is now available free on the Internet, with no concern for organization and validity" (Lawrence '62; academic). For several Alums there is a direct connection between understanding about libraries and providing budgetary support. Thus, it is easy to see why a Grinnell '96 public librarian indicated that her greatest frustration has been consistently "having to explain to people why the library is an important institution, the importance of *access* to information, and the importance of monetarily funding the public library" (emphasis in original).

Another cluster of comments on the *Lack of Respect/Understanding* theme focuses on the work and professionalism of information professionals. Here the views of both the public and employers are seen as the source of difficulty. Several Alums commented on a lack of regard for LIS work by colleagues who are attorneys, marketers, academic faculty, teachers, and "also by public school administrators for what I do for students and teachers" (Grinnell '66; school). There is "a lack of understanding of our professionalism by those outside of the LIS field" (Carleton '81; public and Lawrence '91; academic). Part of the difficulty, Alums feel, lies in "the perception that we just check out books!" (Macalester '62; school). If you listened in on a conversation of some of the Carleton Alums, you would hear the following kinds of comments:

> There is a lack of respect by those I help - they don't comprehend how hard everyone works—they just want more of everything without understanding budget and time constraints. ('96; public)
>
> Part of the problem is answering to administrators who know nothing about librarianship. ('91; academic)
>
> I believe there is a lack of appreciation from society in general. We are underpaid, undervalued, and overworked. ('76; special)
>
> [Yes, and] they assume we can't do things! ('91; special)

> I find the most difficult thing about LIS work in general is that the entire field of expert information management constantly struggles to be recognized as valuable to institutions and society. ('86; special)

Were CALS Alums from the other colleges to enter the conversation, comments might turn to the activities that information professionals actually perform, versus what employers or the public think LIS work entails:

> I wish the public had a greater respect for and knowledge of our work. (Denison '86; public)

> Why do they view it as simple, repetitive [and] routine when it is actually complex and intellectually challenging?! (Carleton '62; academic)

> People don't understand our skill set so we aren't involved as frequently as we should be in helping to solve important problems.(Carleton '66; special)

> There is the assumption that a MS-degreed librarian and library clerk are the same. (Earlham '62; special)

> Certainly my principal and other teachers don't understand the complexity of the job. For example, they don't realize that the new federal testing requirements impact every part of the school—including my efforts to help ensure that students are knowledgeable. (Earlham '66; school)

Even Alums not in such situations are aware of it. For example:

> I am fortunate to work for a city that strongly supports its library system in a community that *uses* the library. I think that if I worked for another library system, I would least like the lack of support given to many library systems and the general lack of understanding of librarianship as a profession. (Lawrence '86; public; emphasis in original)

In perhaps the saddest sounding comment, a Lawrence '71 academic librarian simply said, "We are not valued by others." Unfortunately, this is not entirely an incorrect statement. A 2001 survey of 1000 U.S. adults found that only 38 percent were aware that librarians typically hold the master's degree, even though "respondents realized that strong research skills (75 percent) and expertise in computers (70 percent) are prerequisites to becoming a librarian" ("Public Unaware of Librarians' Education" 2001, 10).

Paperwork and the Lack of Variety

These two topics continue to be problematic for the CALS Alums. They are topics that some Alums feel adversely affect both their specific jobs and their career. The respondents tend to be quite specific about *Paperwork*:

> Excessive paperwork, especially pointless required studies which are annoyingly frequent. (Carleton '62; special)
>
> Buried in paperwork. (Kalamazoo '62; academic)

On the topic of a *Lack of variety*, either the phrase "lack of variety" or derivations of the word "repetition" were common—as in the responses of a Carleton '81 special librarian who notes "the monotony/repetition" of her work, and of a Swarthmore '81 public librarian who feels that "often the work is repetitive, and sometimes boring."

VI. Challenges, Pride, and Professional and Personal Goals

In order to add depth to the CALS respondents' views on likes and dislikes, they were asked also about challenges they had met and about their professional and personal goals for the upcoming five years (Q.III-8-10).

Challenges

Some of what the CALS Alums thought of when asked what they liked least, reflected challenges they had experienced since becoming LIS professionals (Q.III-8). Thirty-five percent described difficulties with a boss, coworkers, users, handling a new project, or general work conditions. For example, a Carleton '66 school librarian pointed out that she had had to learn "to deal patiently with high school students," and a Kalamazoo '66 public librarian reported that "reconstruction of a burned periodical collection" had taken a lot of fortitude. Another 30 percent identified the need for new skills as challenging. Assumption of managerial responsibilities required "learning how to supervise [and] becoming a leader" (Denison '71; academic). The need for developing competence in, keeping pace with, or updating technology-related skills was pointed out by 13 percent of all Alums. A Swarthmore '71 public librarian wrote, "I started when catalog cards were manually typed, and have had sole responsibility for turning them into an active, clean database." Regardless of age, for some information professionals the influx of electronic technologies since the 1960s has been tremendously exciting, while for others it has been a career-long challenge. Fifteen percent of the Alums noted that simply adjusting to a new job or a new library type had been their greatest challenge thus far. Comments from these Carleton and Lawrence respondents serve as illustrations:

> Working for the first time in a public library as a Youth Services Librarian with a hostile youth services assistant, a dictatorial director, no vacation for the first year, and [a] preschool storytime schedule of 6-8 programs a week! (Carleton '91; public)

> Being hired as manager of a technical training department—which I knew nothing about—in a very competitive corporate market. As it turns out, I like managing a service organization, but I'm not very interested in profit. And the hours and travel were much too demanding. (Carleton '66; special)

> Finding a job where my abilities are used to the fullest. And I've found one! (Lawrence '71; public)

Some respondents in stressful work environments, as well as some of those approaching retirement, wrote that "staying motivated" was their greatest challenge. Others have found it difficult to balance work and family. Still others have been faced with severe budgetary situations and the challenge of keeping library services functioning with reduced staff.

Proudest Of

Interestingly, when asked to identify what they are proudest of in terms of their career or work (Q.III-10), the Alums did not write about overcoming challenges such as the above. Instead, they described being proudest of:

- The use they have made of their LIS skills and the quality of their work (30 percent)
- The recognition they have received from others (12 percent)
- Helping users (12 percent)
- Having made a difference in their library or community (8 percent)
- Their library itself (8 percent)

Skills

Alums who are proudest of the use they have made of their LIS skills and the level of their work most often speak either of the complexity or the high quality of their work. A Carleton '66 special librarian illustrates the former:

> I'm pretty good at entering new situations, analyzing the problems and opportunities, and developing solutions. I'm a pretty good project manager, and not a terrible line manager. I've been credible serving some very diverse users groups. I'm also proud of understanding the impact/potential/adoption path for new technologies. And I'm proud of the storytelling I did when I was a public librarian.

Many special librarians were initially hired into organizations in fields about which they were ignorant. So they were most apt to express sentiments similar to those of this Earlham '62 Alum:

> Proud to have worked successfully in a medical library. I knew *nothing* about medicine when I started there. (emphasis in original)

In terms of high quality work, an example is the Kalamazoo '91 academic librarian who wrote that she is proud "of my student reviews—I teach a for-credit class and get excellent evaluations from my students." And a Swarthmore '91 special librarian pointed to her prospect research, which "is a fairly new field, and I think I'm excellent in it. The people I work for always think I do magic. I get a lot of praise (as do my fellow researchers here)." Six percent of these Alums noted that they see "good results" from their work in terms of successful outcomes, valued services, or user response.

Recognition

In an earlier part of this chapter, we presented responses of Alums bemoaning the lack of respect they, as professionals, and their field receive from the public. Here many of them, along with other Alums, also speak of respect in terms of their pride in "the recognition of my work within my institution" (Carleton '71; special) and of being "well respected for what I know and do" (Kalamazoo '66; public). An Earlham '96 public librarian writes that, "I feel proud that I work for a library and that I have been given the responsibility of assistive technology, [and] technology liaison to the Reference department." Thus recognition may be for the individual alum's expertise, knowledge, level and type of responsibility, or for contributions to the work of one's colleagues. Several Alums echoed this Earlham '76 public librarian, who says she feels recognized "when people I helped return to thank me or refer people specifically to me." Others noted being awarded honors by professional groups within and outside LIS, such as the Carleton '71 public librarian who received "the CAYAS Visionary Award for exemplary service to youth in Washington State" and several school librarians who received the School Media Specialist of the Year Award in their district or state. Two Alums have been pictured on the cover of LIS professional journals.

Helping Users

In the context of being proud of one's work or career, this phrase covers a range of comments from "helping health personnel find information that helps their patients" (Denison '71; special) to "having touched the lives of more than a few kids" (Grinnell '66; school). Service to users is central to LIS and to the Alums' views of their work and careers. For 12 percent of the CALS Alums, "helping" is reflected in how they carry out their work with particular user groups or in their sense of serving society. This last view is exemplified by a Carleton '71 public librarian who is proud "that I am providing library services to people who do not have easy access to the library because of language, culture, geography, or time," and by an Earlham '66 public librarian who feels proud "that I truly serve people—all ages, sizes, and intellects." And it isn't just public librarians who feel this way, as seen by the comment of a

Kalamazoo '66 academic librarian whose proudest achievement is her "instruction of future lawyers and law librarians."

Making a Difference

This means seeing the tangible results of one's work in the understanding or lives of users. "I made a difference," said a Carleton '96 public librarian, "in the lives of the kids I've helped. I've helped them learn better research skills—and their parents too!" Some Alums wrote that they know they've made a difference "because I get thanked all the time" (Kalamazoo '91; special). Other CALS respondents specifically referenced the mentoring they do, as when an Earlham '62 academic librarian expressed how proud she was of "mentoring two excellent library staff who grew—matured—into excellent adults."

My Library

Eight percent of the Alums said they were proudest of their library itself, and only about half of these Alums are directors. Sometimes "my library" was all they wrote; other times they went on to discuss building expansions or renovations, or the difference they made in their library's quality and community standing, as in these two typical examples:

> I took a poor library and made it a good one. (Kalamazoo '62; school)

> Turning around a library that had 9 budget defeats in the previous 12 years and poor community support. After 10 years there as Director—budget increased substantially, library became the most *treasured* institution in town. (Macalester '62; public; emphasis in original)

Other

Three other sets of comments ought to be mentioned. Two percent of Alums are proudest of simply having persevered. A Carleton '71 academic librarian described how she "started library school at the age of 40, while working full-time, two kids, and a husband out of town three to four nights a week." Others reflected on going back to school for the degree after being widowed (with young children), or on struggling through difficult working conditions, budget situations, and job demands. A Swarthmore '66 school librarian wrote of being "proud to have vigorously defended children's access to library materials and a specific book during a grueling, protracted book challenge/censorship case."

A small group of Alums (1 percent) specifically expressed pride over having maintained their values. All but two of them were from Kalamazoo:

> My values are solid and inform my professional beliefs, especially with regard to intellectual freedom. (Kalamazoo '96; public)

> I cherish my two careers—law and librarianship—and do them both proud. I live an honorable life; I know others think that about me. (Kalamazoo '71; special)

> Being able to maintain my moral and ethical values within my profession. (Swarthmore '66; academic)

This last quote leads to the final set of comments about what the Alums were proudest of regarding their work or career. Six percent chose to say they were proud of serving their profession; 66 percent of those being academic librarians. Some, like a Carleton '71 academic librarian, were direct in saying, "I have made a modest impact/contribution to the profession." Others noted their work for ALA, state library associations, and consortia as committee participants or office holders, and in "leadership roles in professional organizations" (Kalamazoo '71 academic). These activities were seen as giving back to the field. There were Alums who reflected on the larger value of their activities: "My contribution to the profession is through creating quality [cataloging] records" (Kalamazoo '86 academic). And certain accomplishments seem particularly expressive of the LIS field, such as the Earlham '71 academic librarian who wrote of being proud of

> developing one of the first technical services pages on the Web. And of creating an apprenticeship method for advancing paraprofessionals through the ranks.

The Kalamazoo Alum ('66; school) who felt proud that "my colleagues and the students in my high school have a positive image of libraries and librarians," and the Swarthmore '81 academic librarian who said he was "most proud of being in a service profession" are typical of many.

What Do You Hope to Accomplish Professionally in the Next Five Years?

Two percent of respondents wanted to continue just "enjoying my job" (Kalamazoo '81; public), whether that is working with children, managing part of a library, or just carrying out their current responsibilities. The rest have specific goals in mind, six of which account for 78 percent of the comments (see table 66, and appendix C: Q.III-9 for detail).

Expand/Improve Systems, Services, Facility

Not all 22 percent of the CALS Alums who described projects they plan to expand or improve are currently managers/administrators. While only 17 percent of the Alums count such responsibilities among their major tasks, LIS professionals typically have a lot of control over their own work—something that is illustrated here. The range of projects and ideas is quite varied. A subset of 4 percent of the comments focused directly on building, expanding, or renovating library facilities; 15 percent dealt with services of various kinds; and 4 percent related to technologies. Overall, the goals range from the very tailored (to one's current work) to the sweeping, in their inclusion or intent. The former include these examples:

> Develop a database of MARC record sets for electronic packages. (Kalamazoo '62; academic)

Table 66: Professional Accomplishments—Next Five Years

Accomplishments	%
Expand/Improve systems, services, facility, etc.	22
Professional/Personal development	18
Get/Change jobs	12
Stay employed/Motivated	10
Get promoted/Become a manager or director	9
Retire	7

> Upgrade the collection/weed/repair/start a paperback collection. (Lawrence '71; school)

> Greatly reduce processing problems. (Swarthmore '62; academic)

Larger scale intentions bear upon entire service points as well as technology-related projects:

> Reinvent our interlibrary loan service to serve students-at-a-distance. (Carleton '76; public)

> Develop a well-balanced electronic collection to match our print one. (Kalamazoo '66; academic)

> Improve the Media Center website and training modules for students. (Macalester '66; school)

Goals with broader organizational implications include:

> Successfully build a Homeland Security Digital Library as a national asset. (Carleton '62; academic)

> Create a library district out of six independent libraries. (Earlham '76; public)

> Align information literacy skills with all subject area curricula in my school. (Lawrence '86; school)

> Negotiate major salary upgrades for all staff. (Lawrence '86; public)

Finally, an Earlham '86 academic librarian reveals the passion behind her thinking when she says her goal for the next five years is to

> increase the teaching/learning opportunities in my library. I long to develop a library where Web pages, printed "pathfinders," etc. are *engineered* to teach students more about using the library, embed information fluency skills, etc. *every time* they engage the library staff or me for help. I want time to think strategically about ways to design and implement such things, and make it impossible for a student to use the library without learning something—yet still use it efficiently. (emphases in original)

Professional/Personal Development

Alums from all the colleges and all the cohorts spoke of their desire for further development of their skills and abilities. Many talked of becoming "more proficient" and "more knowledgeable," and of adding depth, sophistication, or knowledge to their discharge of current duties. For example, a Kalamazoo '71 school librarian wrote that she wants "to become a technology expert." On the larger stage, a Carleton '81 public librarian aims to "up my profile in the children's literature community," and a Grinnell '86 special librarian wants to "increase my responsibility and role in the information service profession; do more public speaking at conferences." For some Alums, professional development is an immediate need, as with the Macalester '66 public librarian who is about to become Assistant Director at a large urban library and needs "to improve my understanding of the impact of diverse populations on professional practice." Others are looking further ahead and seeking to prepare themselves to advance professionally, like this Swarthmore '91 public librarian: "Get broader experience within or beyond this library system. Become more independent/well capable of managing children's services at a branch library."

"Staying on top of the field," or being more proficient in a subject area, is the goal for some Alums, who spoke of the desire for continuing education, another master's degree, and the "desire to continue learning, both formally and informally" (Denison '66; academic). Twenty-four percent of CALS respondents already have a second master's degree, 4 percent have another professional degree (such as the JD, EdD, and MD), 4 percent hold a Ph.D., and 3 percent have specialist degrees or advanced certificates (appendixes C-D: Q.IV-16, and appendix J). Thirteen percent of the Alums are currently enrolled in non-workshop courses: for personal interest (54 percent), for continuing education (30 percent), or to obtain another degree (16 percent) (Q.IV-17). When asked if they would like to go back to school in the future, 39 percent of all Alums said yes (Q.IV-18). The areas of greatest interest are education, history (including art history), language and literature, and LIS.

Get/Change Jobs; Stay Employed/Motivated; Retire

These categories are distinct but also overlap, and together they comprise 29 percent of the comments regarding plans for the future. Of the 12 percent of respondents concerned with *Getting or changing jobs*, 38 percent are special librarians—most of whom feel they would rather be in academic libraries. As noted earlier, special librarians tend to change library types more than other kinds of librarians (Watson-Boone 2000b). Most of the 28 percent who are public librarians hope to find full-time positions in public libraries, although one Earlham '71

Alum has as her goal "to learn to be a reference librarian and then find a job within a museum combining [reference and museum work]." Another 28 percent are academic librarians, who are divided between considering special librarianship, preferring part-time work, and just seeking "a great place to work, with great people, doing great things" (Grinnell '91; academic). Only 3 percent of the school librarians are thinking of a job change, perhaps because it is most typical of them to have already chosen LIS as their second career—after having had a classroom teaching position.

Ten percent of the CALS Alums are focused on *Staying employed or motivated* in their current positions. A Carleton '91 public librarian, for example, writes of the "struggle to be a middle manager," and an Earlham '76 academic librarian expresses concern about whether his work "is stimulating enough over a long period of time to keep me interested." In terms of continued employment, a Denison '66 special librarian worries about "the possible 'contracting out' of my job," a Kalamazoo '76 academic librarian hopes to "get tenure," and an Earlham '66 special librarian just hopes "to make it to retirement—the State Library is in a precarious position right now because of the state budget." This last respondent is one of the 7 percent who made comments about *Retirement*. These preretirement Alums were all from the 1962-80 cohorts. Most of the comments focus on "planning my retirement," "will be retired," or on being in the midst of finishing projects prior to retirement—like the Macalester '62 school librarian who said she wants to "open a remodeled and expanded library next year, and then retire." Others talked about finishing projects, wrapping up loose ends, or keeping a hand in but "working less" (Kalamazoo '66; public). The latter situation is illustrated by an Earlham '71 academic librarian who explained, "I would like to retire from administration and take a cataloging or indexing job without the administrative responsibilities."

Get Promoted; Become a Manager/Director

For academic librarians, *Getting promoted* initially means receiving job security or tenure in some form. Throughout the 1970-90s, increasing numbers of colleges and universities provided their academic librarians with some form of tenure. While tenure was welcome for the acknowledgment it gave of one's stature as a member of the general faculty, it also required allocating one's "second 40 hours" to the necessary work of writing, publishing, and presenting. Failure to receive tenure meant you moved on to another institution, which might or might not also have such requirements for its librarians (Watson-Boone 1998; Huling 1973; DeBoer and Culotta 1987). For some academic librarians, working on tenure takes them away from their primary (and most enjoyable) work. For others, like this Carleton '86 Alum, tenure and subsequent promotion allow them to do work that they want to do:

> I look forward to publishing at least one monograph, preferably two, on route to full professor.

Becoming a manager or a director in any type of library, on the other hand, requires demonstrating both evidence of and potential for intellectual and policy leadership in personnel, facilities and budget management, along with political and social skills inside and especially outside of the library itself. Several Alums who are unit or department heads hope to "take on more control over larger library programs" (Kalamazoo '96; public), increase the range of their responsibilities, and begin the process toward directorships.

Other Comments—Writing; Family

Five percent of CALS Alums plan to do research, write, and publish—and these are not academic librarians who are working toward tenure. All of the Alums who spoke about nontenure-related writing or publishing were from Carleton, Denison, Earlham, and Swarthmore:

> A Carleton '71 school library media specialist plans to "research and publish on topics related to several projects."
>
> A Denison '71 academic librarian expects to "publish a defense of retaining (or reinstating) input specifications in library standards."
>
> An Earlham '71 special librarian plans "to become a writer."
>
> And a Swarthmore '71 special librarian expects to "finish up research/writing on the subject of provenance/ownership."

Finally, 35 percent of the CALS Alums have taken career breaks, with the majority of those being to raise children (Q.IV-19). Many of them singled out the career-family flexibility of LIS work as the "best" feature of the field for them. In discussing goals for the next five years, 1 percent of Alums wrote that they sought a balance between work and family. For some this means taking a part-time rather than full-time position:

> I am actually expecting my first child, and am going from full-time to part-time. I expect that to last for the next five to 10 years while I raise my kids. (Kalamazoo '86; public)

Others, like this Macalester '91 public librarian, hope to "find work I can do from home or a job which I can integrate into parenting demands."

What Do You Hope to Accomplish Personally in the Next Five Years?

Regardless of college or cohort, the greatest number of comments regarding personal goals revolved around family matters. The following areas comprised 68 percent of the Alums' goals (table 67; appendix C: Q.III-9).

Retire and *Travel* are self-explanatory. *Build savings* refers to saving up to buy a house, pay off a mortgage, or to create funds for their children's college expenses, or for special projects. Alums working in all library types mentioned planning to continue their education with the general sentiment being to "continue to study and grow" (Kalamazoo '62; school). The

Table 67: Personal Accomplishments—Next Five Years

Accomplishments	Comments (%)
Family	25
Improve personal skills	9
Retire	9
Travel	8
Build savings	6
Continue education	6
Self-fulfillment goals	5

topics of *Family*, *Improve personal skills*, and *Self-fulfillment goals*, however, deserve some additional discussion.

Family

Seventy-five percent of the CALS Alums are married or have partners (Q.IV-8). Another 10 percent are divorced, separated, or widowed. Sixty percent have children with 96 percent being within the U.S. norm of one to two children, and most have both a son and a daughter (Q.IV-9). Forty percent of the sons and 39 percent of the daughters are between the ages of one to 18, and 94 percent of these children live at home with the Alums.

The CALS respondents indicated the occupations of 79 percent of their spouses or partners (Q.IV-11). As noted in chapter 3, spouses or partners work in 24 different occupational areas with the largest percentage associated with LIS, higher education, business, computer technology, and K-12 education. It can be surmised that most respondents are in households where both parents or partners are working. It is not surprising, then, to find that the largest number of comments about personal goals (25 percent) relate to the family.

The preceding subsection of this chapter concluded with discussion of Alums who want a balance between work and family. While some who had mentioned it before spoke of it again here, several others seemed to see creating this balance as a personal goal rather than as a professional one. Comments about family focused on

- Having children; creating a family
- Raising healthy and happy children who will be good citizens
- Seeing that their children receive a good education, or getting them through college
- Spending more time with spouses or partners and children
- Doing things together as a family

A Grinnell '86 public librarian states such a family-focused goal in terms that reflect the sentiments of many of these Alums. In combination with valuing the flexibility she sees as inherent in LIS work, her goal for her personal life is to "provide a stable, fun and peaceful home life for my family."

Several Alums spoke of their children's adolescence, like the Kalamazoo '76 academic librarian who plans on "guiding my daughter through her teenage years." A Denison Alum ('86; public) is focused on "continuing to improve spiritually and as a father and husband." A few now look at the next five years with some trepidation, as they have become widowed, have a spouse or partner with age-related health problems, or must deal with very unwelcome news. One example:

> My personal life has recently changed as my husband has been diagnosed with lung cancer. My goals as of now are to be able to support our family of four children by myself. (Kalamazoo '91; special)

Improve Personal Skills

The CALS Alums are interested in enhancing their proficiency with, or learning more about, a broad array of pursuits and activities (Q.IV-11):

- Art work, including painting, drawing, stained glass, and woodworking
- Book arts
- Bridge, including becoming a Life Master
- Carpentry
- Computer literacy, programming, website design and construction
- Dancing
- Gardening
- Genealogy
- Language fluency, including in German and Spanish
- Music, including instrumental and vocal performance
- Photography, especially digital aspects
- Quilting and sewing, including quality sufficient for prize winning in the former
- Reading as an individual and as a member of a book club
- Sports, including tennis, swimming, tai chi, rock climbing, and competing in rowing regattas

As a separate question, the Alums were asked, "What two activities do you enjoy when not working at your LIS or other regular job?" (Q.III-11). This was an open-ended question, and most of the Alums said they could not list just two enjoyable leisure activities. Word and phrase analysis identified these 26 activities:

The Arts	Games	Outdoors	Sports
Cinema	Gardening	Pets	Technology
Club Activities	Genealogy	Photography	Travel
Cooking	Hand Work	Puzzles	Volunteer Work
Exercise	Home Improvements	Quilting	Writing
Financial Management	Learning	Reading	
Friends	Mentoring	Speaking	

The Arts, Gardening, Quilting, Music, Reading, and *Sports* categories appeared on both the lists of personal skills to improve and on the lists of enjoyable leisure activities. The ACRL 1992 study also asked this question, but those respondents were required to select leisure activities from a prescribed list (Scherdin 1994a, 89). The seven options receiving the highest concentration of responses in the ACRL study were

- Reading
- Attending artistic events
- Spending time with friends or family
- Nature related activities
- Engaging in artistic activities
- Playing individual sports (golf, tennis, cycling)
- Gardening

Leisure activities that both the CALS Alums and the ACRL respondents share were

- Reading
- The Arts (attendance at, as well as performance of)
- Gardening
- Outdoor, nonorganized sport activities

Reading and *The Arts* were the top two choices of both the CALS Alums and the ACRL respondents. *Reading* was the most frequently noted activity of Alums from all eight colleges and across the cohorts. *The Arts* revealed Alums who are painters, film buffs and symphony attendees, and those with part-time jobs as musicians. CALS Alums also favor *Exercise, Travel,* and *Hand Work*, which do not appear on the tables in the Scherdin (1994a) article that reports on the ACRL study. *Hand Work* refers to sewing, tatting, knitting, and quilting with the last being a particular favorite of Carleton, Earlham, Lawrence, and Macalester Alums. Smaller numbers of Alums favor *Cooking*, working with *Computers*, *Photography*, doing *Puzzles* of various kinds, and playing with their *Pets*. *Learning, Writing, Volunteer Work*, and *Mentoring* round out the list of major leisure activities for the Alums.

Self-fulfillment Goals

This phrase brings together the personal goals of 5 percent of the CALS respondents. It expresses the desire to "figure out what I want to do with the rest of my life" (Carleton '71;

Table 68: Satisfaction with LIS as a Career (by College)

Satisfaction	Avg (%)	College (%) C	D	E	G	K	L	M	S
Very satisfied	69	71	79	62	71	69	73	72	65
Moderately satisfied	26	26	14	30	29	27	24	21	34
Very dissatisfied	5	3	7	8	0	4	4	6	5

public). It is not related to job or career dissatisfaction. Where it is obviously related to retirement planning, Alums respond in broad brush strokes, such as "planning a new life" (Denison '66; special). However, in general, these Alums' essential wish and goal is to "be happy," to "find ease and serenity in an increasingly chaotic world" (Denison '66; academic), to have a "peaceful inner and outer life" (Kalamazoo '76; special)—or maybe "to run away to a very rural place in Hawaii" (Swarthmore '62; public). Interestingly, all the respondents who mused about life goals were from the 1962-76 cohorts. Some may indeed be contemplating retirement life, but not expressing it as such.

In answering the question about leisure time (Q.III-11), a few wrote about family and friends as important parts of their lives. While focused on family, the Alums' personal goals range widely—from improving personal skills to establishing life goals. Within that framework, some goals reflect difficult situations that are at present unsettled, like the Lawrence '76 public librarian who plans to "heal from divorce; raise daughter; re-reinvent [my]self." Others, while also focusing on family, are in a more optimistic position to identify goals. This Macalester '91 public librarian articulates a set of personal goals and leisure involvements that might form a composite of the desires of many Alums:

Help raise happy, healthy family; Travel; Learn; Read

VII. Satisfaction with LIS as a Career

After the previous expressions of likes and dislikes, challenges, pride, and professional and personal goals, it should be no surprise that a strong majority of CALS Alums voiced support for LIS as a career and for continuing to be an LIS professional (Q.II-L; Q.II-O). Alums from all colleges and cohorts indicated satisfaction with their career choice. By college, between 92 and 100 percent (low, Earlham; high, Grinnell) of the Alums are moderately to very satisfied with their choice of LIS as a career (Q.II-L) (table 68 above).

If the *Very satisfied* and the *Moderately satisfied* categories are combined, then 95 percent of the CALS Alums are satisfied with their choice of LIS as a career. This compares quite favorably with Morrison's (1969) 87 percent rate and Schiller's (1969) 89 percent rate for academic librarians in the studies that were noted earlier. This is further supported by the 1992

Table 69: Satisfaction with LIS as a Career (by Cohort)

Satisfaction	Avg (%)	Cohort (%) 62-	66-	71-	76-	81-	86-	91-	96-
Very satisfied	69	70	66	72	71	53	75	69	88
Moderately satisfied	26	23	28	24	27	38	20	28	12
Very dissatisfied	5	8	6	4	2	9	5	3	0

Table 70: Likelihood of Continuing as an LIS Professional (by Cohort)

Likelihood of Continuing	Avg (%)	Cohort (%) 62-	66-	71-	76-	81-	86-	91-	96-
Very likely	78	62	79	82	82	72	85	72	100
Moderately likely	12	8	8	13	10	22	15	16	0
Very unlikely	11	31	12	5	8	6	0	13	0

ACRL study, which found that 93 percent of the ALA and SLA members studied were satisfied with their work (Scherdin 1994a).

The lowest percent of satisfaction with LIS as a career was expressed by the 1981-85 cohort; the highest by the 1996-00 cohort (table 69 above). Although the 1981-85 cohort members expressed the most concern about their choice of LIS as a career, they have more positive feelings about the future. As seen in table 70, they feel it is also moderately to very likely that they will remain within the field. When asked about continuing as an LIS professional in the future (Q.III-16O), several members of the 1962-65 cohort noted they were already retired or were planning to retire in the near future. Otherwise, 72 to 100 percent of the Alums plan to continue as members of the field.

Table 71 displays these findings by college, and 71 to 94 percent of the Alums (low, Grinnell 71 percent; high, Carleton and Lawrence at 94 percent) responded that they are moderately to very likely to stay within the field. Again, current retirees and those anticipating it form the higher percentages of Alums who say it is unlikely they will stay in the field.

Another indicator of satisfaction is encouraging others into a career path in the same field. The first question in the survey's section on "Librarianship, LIS Education, and LIS Work" (Q.II-1) asked respondents, "Would you encourage today's [college] students to enter the library and information science (LIS) field?" The CALS Alums were asked to answer by checking "Yes" or "No," and were asked to explain their choice (table 72). A number wrote in "Maybe." In the analysis of results, "Maybe" was accepted as a legitimate choice. By college, 80-96 percent said Yes, 0-14 percent Maybe, and 0-13 percent No.

Table 71: Likelihood of Continuing as an LIS Professional (by College)

Likelihood of Continuing	Avg (%)	College (%)							
		C	D	E	G	K	L	M	S
Very likely	78	82	86	74	71	75	80	76	79
Moderately likely	12	12	7	13	0	9	14	13	14
Very unlikely	11	6	7	14	29	16	6	11	7

Table 72: Encourage Students to Enter the LIS Field

Encourage	Avg (%)	College (%)							
		C	D	E	G	K	L	M	S
Yes	88	86	96	88	86	87	92	80	96
No	7	9	4	8	0	9	4	13	0
Maybe	4	5	0	4	14	3	4	6	4

Table 73: Encourage Students to Enter the LIS Field (by Cohort)

Encourage	Avg (%)	Cohort (%)							
		62-	66-	71-	76-	81-	86-	91-	96-
Yes	88	90	85	84	91	89	100	89	100
No	7	6	11	11	4	3	0	9	0
Maybe	4	4	5	5	6	9	0	3	0

Across the cohorts, 84-100 percent of the Alums agree that they would encourage students to become LIS professionals, 0 to 9 percent say maybe, and 0 to 11 percent would not encourage current students to enter the field (table 73).

Of the Alums who were negative, 21 percent (the largest group) believe it "depends very much on the person" (Grinnell '66; school). They simply feel it is a matter of individual choice, and while they themselves might (or might not) enjoy the profession, they are uncomfortable "pushing" it on others. For another 18 percent of these Alums, the response was spurred by knowing communities or situations where there are few jobs. This was a particular concern of Alums in the 1971-80 cohorts, who had received their MLIS during a period of recession in the United States, and other respondents who were seeing public and school library budgets under stress as the national economy began a downturn. A Kalamazoo '62 school librarian, for example, cited reduced budgets in local schools: "I would like to [recommend LIS], but not in the current environment here in Oregon with cutbacks everywhere." Another 15 percent cited "low pay" as their reason for not recommending LIS as a career. A Lawrence '81 special librarian said, "I'd be surprised if it weren't the lowest paying profession for advanced degree-holders." And 5 percent stressed a need for gaining library experience beforehand—stressing that "this is a very personal decision and one best made after working in libraries" (Carleton '76; academic).

Among the 88 percent who are positive on this topic, close to 33 percent described the LIS field and the array of work possible within it. Twenty-seven percent wrote of the opportunities available for liberal arts graduates to use their education, skills, and abilities. Another 18 percent focused on how well a liberal arts education meshes with LIS and how their undergraduate college in particular exemplifies this.

Characterizations of the Field of Library and Information Science

CALS Alums described LIS as a field that is expanding in the areas it covers, the tools it uses, and types and locations of jobs within it:

> The information explosion certainly did happen! Not only is knowledge power, [but] access to knowledge is power. LIS should become ever more exciting—at the same time, it's still a career that is family-friendly. (Carleton '71; public)

> Librarianship is the last bastion of the generalist—the one field where broad knowledge is more greatly valued than in-depth study. (Grinnell '86; special)

> I would recommend the field because it's a wonderful microcosm of our world in so many exciting and marvelous aspects. Technology, information (traditional and otherwise), all kinds of people (patrons and library professionals), current events, etc. are daily experience for most librarians. Working in a library is a continuing educational experience from the moment you walk in the door to 5 p.m.—or whenever you leave the building. I love the fact that I will never know everything about my library or the library field in general, but will learn all the time, whether I'm on the job, at a library conference, or participating in formal continuing education. (Earlham '66; public)

Opportunities

Some of the Alums who recommended LIS as a career felt it is "a great career for liberal arts students who are interested in a variety of disciplines. It allows you to stay in touch with various fields, to continue learning, to be creative, and to work with and for interesting people" (Swarthmore '66; school). A Denison '71 academic librarian sees the field as "a liberal arts student's dream: providing the opportunity to interact with people and ideas in all disciplines." Other Alums spoke of LIS as being "a satisfying form of community service," and "a great way to keep learning forever and to apply everything you've ever learned—often in unexpected ways" (Swarthmore '86; special; Macalester '62; special). Another Swarthmore Alum ('71; public) summed the opportunities up this way: "It's a wonderful field for people who like to do research, who have eclectic interests, who are bright and want to help people." In addition, some Alums felt that, despite the fiscal constraints currently being felt by libraries, there are and will be significant job opportunities for today's graduating students. Given that "lots of librarians will be retiring soon," "there will be a great need for LIS professionals and, therefore, many opportunities" (Carleton '91; academic; Denison '66; academic). With continuing expansion of the "information" technology sector within LIS, one Kalamazoo '86 special librarian believes that "this is, arguably, the most 'open' field in terms of potential employment in just about *any* industry" (emphasis in original).

The Liberal Arts Education; The Liberal Arts College

Several Alums focused on the "liberal arts ideals of knowing a bit about everything and being able to communicate well" as being a perfect match with LIS work (Lawrence '91; academic). They noted the traits of inquisitiveness, of being open-minded and nonjudgmental, and of service to others as values in both the liberal arts college and in LIS. An Earlham '66 public librarian noted that both

> value social change. Librarians are on the front line in the battle for social change, as we empower a huge cross section of people, many of whom are among the less privileged, to become educated, informed, productive, self-confident, and successful in their lives.

She feels that liberal arts graduates already have this understanding and approach to society, and that this makes them particularly valuable to the field. The following Alum speaks directly of the benefit of graduating from a particular liberal arts college. However, if you were to substitute "my college" for "Carleton," all of the CALS Alums who spoke positively about LIS and liberal arts colleges would likely say she is evoking their colleges and their views of the LIS field as well:

> As a librarian, you are not necessarily expected to know something about everything (though that certainly helps), rather, you need to know where to begin and how to navigate the search. Carleton not only encourages students to broaden their interests and their knowledge, but also demands that students learn how to think. Learning how to think requires creativity, open-mindedness, the ability to listen, respect for differing points of view, the willingness to learn and change your mind, an appreciation for the unexpected (to name just a few). Doesn't this sound like a job description for a library and information professional? Also, Carleton professors take their roles as teachers very seriously. They are excellent models for Carleton students who are constantly teaching each other, either formally (as tutors, volunteers in the community, as athletic assistants, as members of study groups and student organizations) or informally (on the Frisbee field, in the dorm kitchens, during late-night conversations). I see librarians as being informal teachers, teachers who have some ideas on how to access the

> world of information or the world of literature, and know how to share their expertise with people of all ages, backgrounds and abilities. The Carleton students I know also have the requisite energy, enthusiasm and curiosity that is crucial to the health and well-being of an LIS professional. (Carleton '91; public)

Summary

Studies from the late 1950s into the twentieth-first century have repeatedly found that a majority of librarians are satisfied with their jobs (Morrison 1969, Schiller 1969, ACRL 1992, St. Lifer 1994, Lau 2002). This chapter delved deeper into the details of why 95 percent of the CALS respondents indicated they were "moderately" to "very" satisfied with LIS as a career. Across colleges and cohorts, those indicating they were very dissatisfied with their LIS career ranged from zero percent (Grinnell and the 1996-2000 cohort) to 8 percent among the colleges (Earlham) and 9 percent (1981-85) among the cohorts. Only 11 percent indicated they felt it was very unlikely that they would continue as an LIS professional, and many of those were in the earliest cohort and contemplating retirement. Finally, the level of satisfaction with one's career may also serve to encourage others to enter the same career. A range of 80 to 96 percent of the Alums said they would encourage today's students to enter the field of library and information science. A particularly positive indicator for the future is the finding that 100 percent of the 1996-2000 cohort said they would encourage current undergraduates to make LIS their career.

When asked what they liked "best" about their own specific LIS work, 70 percent of the comments from Alums alluded to library *functions:* collection development, reference, work with children through young adults, and management or administration of a library and its staff. Fifty-five percent of the comments from those who identified library *activities* focused on the enjoyment of helping others and of seeking or finding information through doing research. And 80 percent of the comments clustering around *work environment* aspects of one's job specified the importance of variety, autonomy, intellectual challenges, and having a great boss, users, or colleagues. The kinds of involvements respondents liked least were, most frequently, job-related activities and working conditions.

There was notable overlap between what the respondents disliked about their specific jobs and what they disliked about their career. The comments of 48 percent of the Alums coalesced into four areas of concern that were also found in the previous chapter's discussion of job dissatisfaction: lack of respect from others, lack of understanding about the field by those outside LIS, paperwork/busywork, and lack of variety in LIS work. However, in this chapter these frustrations are balanced against four categories that reflect the greatest number of positive comments about the field: providing service to others, meeting intellectual challenges, experiencing variety in the field, and having personal access to materials, technologies, and information.

As information professionals, the CALS participants noted they were most proud of the use they had made of their skills, the recognition they had received from others, of helping users, of having made a "difference" in their library or community, and of their library itself. This did not mean they were permanently content, however. When asked what professional accomplishments they planned for the upcoming five years, the largest number described projects to expand or improve their library. In response to being asked to indicate personal goals planned for that same future period, regardless of college or cohort, the greatest number commented about family matters followed by the desire to improve personal skills in areas such as art work, carpentry, dancing, language fluency, photography, and sports.

Overall, the CALS respondents described LIS as a career with which they were satisfied, a profession in which they planned to remain, and as a field that continues to diversify in the areas it covers, the tools it uses, and the types and locations of jobs within it. Many expressed appreciations that echoed a Denison '71 academic librarian's comment that LIS as work and career was "a liberal arts student's dream."

CHAPTER 7

Ways of Expressing a Service Orientation

This chapter looks at the CALS Alums not in terms of their college or their cohort, but in terms of their predisposition toward service. Chapters 1 and 2 established that service is a fundamental part of the ethos of the eight liberal arts colleges—and an important value the colleges hope and intend to pass onto their students. Subsequent chapters determined that LIS also has fundamental values that are service oriented. But are the Alums like other LIS professionals, and do they express a service orientation in ways other than just through their work? The answer to the first question can be found by comparing the behavioral preferences of two groups: the CALS Alums and the respondents to the 1992 ACRL study. The answer to the second question lies in how the Alums answered three service-related survey questions about their participation in civic, religious, and mentoring activities.

I. Behavioral Preferences

The 1992 ACRL national study of 1,697 ALA academic, public, and school librarians, and of Special Library Association members, included administration of the Myers Briggs Type Indicator forms. For the present study, the MBTI® was sent to one of every four CALS Alums at each college except Grinnell, whose numbers were too small for them to effectively participate.[35] The MBTI® is a widely used personality and career guidance tool based on Jungian psychology. It is grounded in the belief that individuals have distinct personality orientations for

[35]I am indebted to Dr. Mary Jane Scherdin for her analysis of the Alums' data and for her construction of the "Characteristics of MBTI® Preferences" table (Scherdin 1994b, 127).

looking at—and for behaving within—both the world of work and the world at large (Myers et al. 1998). This approach asserts that individuals feel most comfortable in occupations that have orientations similar to their own. Analysis of the data from the CALS Alums finds that they and the 1992 ACRL study respondents have very similar personality orientations. In this regard, the Alums fit the national profile of LIS practitioners.

The MBTI® terminology for the four preference scales needs some explanation as it does not correspond to average dictionary definitions. The MBTI® identifies eight basic personality preferences (i.e., orientations) set within four bipolar scales:

- Direction of focus, source of energy: Extraversion/Introversion
- Ways of taking in information: Sensing/Intuition
- Ways of coming to conclusions: Thinking/Feeling
- Attitudes toward the external world: Judging/Perceiving

In the Extraversion (E) and Introversion (I) scale, *Extraversion* in the MBTI® context describes someone who is outgoing and gregarious. This label is the closest of all the MBTI® terms to the common definition of the word. The MBTI® term *Introversion* (I) means that the "main interests [of individuals] are in the inner world of concepts and ideas" (Scherdin 1994b, 126). Such individuals tend toward internal lives—to have depths of interests, to be reflective, and to work problems through before expressing themselves. Key differences between the two terms are that Introverts generally are not as spontaneous as Extraverts and that while the latter gain their energy from external sources Introverts gain it from within themselves.

The *Sensing* (S) and *Intuition* (N) scale refers to ways of gathering information. Scherdin (1994b, 126) describes Intuitives as being "oriented toward the future, [they] like to exercise creativity, tend toward independent rather than traditional views, and are inclined to see the overall picture," whereas Sensors are "practical, conservative, dependable, precise, and methodical." "Sensing (S) types are drawn to occupations that let them use their practical skills, where they can deal with facts. Intuitives (N) like situations in which they look at possibilities, think independently, and problem-solve at a systems level," says Scherdin (1994b, 134). Sensors tend to respond to facts and like to deal with specifics, but also to utilize all five senses in gathering information. Intuitives tend to use insights and consider possibilities, including hunches, while seeking a general, overall picture of something. Sensing types are patient with details; Intuitives are patient with complex situations (Scherdin 1994b, 127).

The *Thinking* (T) and *Feeling* (F) scale refers to different ways of reaching conclusions. Thinking individuals tend to arrive at decisions through critique and reason, have fairly strong principles, and may be described by others as "firm but fair." Feeling types approach decision making more subjectively, and consider the circumstances surrounding issues. Scherdin (1994b, 126) notes that "it has been said that Thinking types make decisions with their heads and Feeling types with their hearts." The final part of the preference equation is the *Judging* (J) and *Perceiving* (P) scale, which deals with the external world. Judging-type individuals like to be organized, like to control life, and tend to set goals. Perceiving types are flexible, like to let life happen, and are more interested in process than in goal setting. People have the ability to use all eight of the preferences but, as Scherdin (1994b, 128) explains, "one preference on each of the four scales is more natural and feels more comfortable. These inborn preferences will be used more often and trusted more implicitly."

Analysis of an individual's responses on the MBTI® instrument yields one preference out of the two comprising each of the four scales. The individual's resulting four preferences are then combined into a four letter acronym or "type." Thus 16 different preference combinations ("types") are available.[36] In the ACRL study, the greatest concentration (28 percent) of information professionals had Introversion, either Intuition or Sensing, Thinking, and Judging preferences—an assignment to which the letters INTJ and ISTJ correspond. An additional 8 percent of the ACRL survey participants had Introversion, Sensing, Feeling, and Judging (ISFJ) preferences. The greatest concentration of CALS Alums, 32 percent, is split evenly between the INTJ and ISTJ types; the next highest concentration (13 percent) is found to have the ISFJ type. The Alums cluster even more strongly than the ACRL study participants around these three types.

With 45 percent of the CALS respondents concentrated in the INTJ, ISTJ, and ISFJ types, their behavior in their work, and toward their users and their colleagues, demonstrates the tendencies of or preferences for:

INTJ: 16 percent	*ISTJ: 16 percent*	*ISFJ: 13 percent*
Introversion	Introversion	Introversion
Intuition	Sensing	Sensing
Thinking	Thinking	Feeling
Judging	Judging	Judging

Introversion (71 percent of Alums) and *Judging* (68 percent) are the strongest aspects in all three of the Alums' behavioral preference types; followed by *Intuition* (63 percent) and *Sensing* (38 percent), and then *Thinking* (54 percent) and *Feeling* (46 percent). Drawing upon Scherdin's (1994b) material for guidance, we can say that the CALS Alums have the following behavioral characteristics or preferences.

The Alums are considered *Introverts* because their main interests and energies come from the world of concepts and ideas, an inner world. They are inwardly directed and favor reflection and concentration. They like to pursue things in depth; they value deep friendships. They think things through before acting on them.

Intuition and *Sensing:* Some of the CALS Alums take in information through insights (*Intuition*); others by relying on facts (*Sensing*). Some are ingenious, imaginative, and visionary (*Intuitives*), while others are practical, methodical, and dependable (*Sensors*). Some Alums seek a general, overall picture of upcoming projects, activities, or situations (*Intuitives*) in contrast to those who seek a more specific and precise understanding of what is involved before committing themselves (*Sensors*). Intuitive respondents are "oriented toward the future, like to exercise

---

[36]For a complete description of the 16 MBTI® types see, Hammer and Macdaid (1994), Myers et al. (1998), and Scherdin (1994b).

creativity, [and] tend toward independent rather than traditional views" (Scherdin 1994b, 126), while Sensing respondents are grounded in present reality.

Thinking and *Feeling:* The largest concentrations of CALS Alums (INTJ, ISTJ; 32 percent) fall into the *Thinking* preference area with a secondary group of Alums (13 percent; ISFJ type) displaying a *Feeling* preference. Thus, it is fair to say that a significant portion of the Alums make decisions through a logical, analytical approach. They lean toward conclusions based on reason and critique. They are comfortable working within established principles. As individuals they may be described as "firm but fair" and are objective in their approach. In contrast, there are those respondents who make decisions based on how those decisions affect people. Their decision processes include subjective elements, acknowledge circumstances or situations in effect, and place a high value on harmony. These respondents are described as "compassionate" and "personally involved."

The Alums *Judge* in the sense that they deal with the outer world by giving it order. They prefer order in their lives and in their workplace. They tend, therefore, to be systematic in their approach to problems and to activities. They are comfortable with the idea of setting goals for themselves or the projects in which they are involved. The idea of planning and scheduling activities is fine with them. They prefer a good deal of structure in their lives inside and outside of work.

Comments from randomly chosen Alums regarding what they like best about their job and career contain hints of these behavioral preferences. A Kalamazoo '66 school library media specialist illustrates the humanistic ISFJ (Introspective, Sensing, Feeling, Judging) type when she says that "books and young people and my library aide" are what is best about her job. That type is also found in a Carleton '96 public librarian, who describes what was best about LIS work this way: "Working with other professionals—we learn from each other."

The ISTJ (Introspective, Sensing, Thinking, Judging) type with its stronger preference for analytic processes is seen in a Swarthmore '81 special librarian, who feels that "guiding patrons through the process of historical discovery" is the best part of her job, while the best part of LIS as a career is "the connection with technology and advances in information technology." Finally, the INTJ (Introspective, Intuitive, Thinking, Judging) type is evident in Alums who prefer to think before they speak, who enjoy learning new skills and solving new problems through reason and analysis, and like an ordered environment. For a Denison Alum ('81; academic), for example, the best part of her job is "helping people and using my brain." Of the CALS Alums who were randomly chosen for review of their comments on what they liked best about their job and about LIS, 50 percent identify working with users in one way or another as the best part of their job. Indeed, when discussing preferred aspects of their job or of LIS as a career 63 percent of those who exemplify the ISFJ type cite working with or helping users.

Scherdin (2003 personal correspondence) found two statistically significant differences (both at the .05 level) between the sample of CALS Alums and her 1992 respondents. In the first instance, 53 percent of the CALS sample (as compared to 43 percent of the ACRL respondents) had *Introverted* and *Judging* preferences. In the second instance, 6 percent of the ACRL participants were found to be of the ESTJ (Extroverted Sensing Thinking Judging) type in contrast to less than 1 percent of the CALS Alums. Yet on the broad-based dichotomous scales, the two groups show general comparability (table 74).

Table 74: MBTI® Preferences (by CALS and ACRL Participants)

Preferences	CALS (%)	ACRL[37] (%)
Extraversion	29	37
Introversion	71	63
Sensing	38	41
Intuition	63	58
Thinking	54	60
Feeling	46	40
Judging	68	66
Perceiving	32	34

Although cohorts were not analyzed, seven of the eight CALS colleges were.[38] Scherdin notes that the following are statistically significant differences (all at the .05 level except as indicated; Scherdin 2003 personal correspondence) between the Alums of the different colleges:

- Carleton, Earlham, and Lawrence have no significant differences between each other or with the other colleges.
- Kalamazoo has a significantly higher percentage of Alums who had Sensing+Feeling preferences (that is, ways of taking in information plus ways of coming to conclusions).
- Macalester has significantly more Intuitive+Feeling and more Intuitive+ Perceiving Alums (that is, ways of taking in information plus ways of coming to conclusions, and ways of taking in information plus attitudes toward the external world).
- Swarthmore has significantly more Intuitive+Judging and Introverted+Intuitive Alums with the latter at the .01 level (that is, ways of taking in information plus attitudes toward the external world, and direction of focus plus ways of taking in information).
- Swarthmore has significantly more Introverted-Intuitive-Feeling-Judging (INFJ) types than the other colleges.
- Denison has significantly more Extroverted-Intuitive-Thinking-Perceiving (ENTP) types than the other colleges.

It is also illuminating to analyze the MBTI®results by the type of library in which the Alums have experience (table 75). Four of the 16 type combinations reflect 56 percent of the

---

[37]Scherdin (1994b:131) and personal correspondence.

[38]Due to their small number, Grinnell respondents were not asked to complete the MBTI®.

Table 75: MBTI® Preferences (by CALS Alums' Library Type)

Preferences	Avg (%)	CALS Alums' Library Type (%)			
		Academic	Public	School	Special
ISTJ	17	23	13	0	0
INTJ	17	23	8	25	20
ISFJ	13	10	13	13	15
ENFJ	9	3	15	13	0

CALS sample. The largest concentrations of Alums working in school and special settings are of the Introverted Intuitive Thinking Judging (INTJ) type. The largest numbers of Alums in academic libraries are split between the INTJ and Introverted Sensing Thinking Judging (ISTJ) types. The CALS respondents in public libraries are the only group that formed a substantial Extraversion cluster. The MBTI® descriptions of INTJ and ISTJ (Scherdin 1994b, 130) do sound characteristic of the Alums, especially as they expressed themselves regarding work and career likes and dislikes in chapter 5:

> INTJ: Usually have original minds and great drive for their own ideas and purposes. In fields that appeal to them, they have a fine power to organize a job and carry it through with or without help. Skeptical, critical, independent, determined, sometimes stubborn. Must learn to yield less important points in order to win the most important.

> ISTJ: Serious, quiet, earn success by concentration and thoroughness. Practical, orderly, matter-of-fact, logical, realistic, and dependable. See to it that everything is well organized. Take responsibility. Make up their own minds as to what should be accomplished and work toward it steadily, regardless of protests or distractions.

The INTJ and the ISTJ types together represent 34 percent of the sample Alums. The ISFJ type represents 13 percent, and is described as follows (Scherdin 1994b, 130):

> ISFJ: Quiet, friendly, responsible, and conscientious. Work devotedly to meet their obligations. Lend stability to any project or group. Thorough, painstaking, accurate. Their interests are usually not technical. Can be patient with necessary details. Loyal, considerate, perceptive, concerned with how other people feel.

CALS Alums with the ISFJ type characteristics of stability, patience, and concern for others are spread through all of the library settings. Alums in all four library types have some of the tendencies of the ISFJ type, and CALS respondents in academic, school, and special libraries

Table 76: MBTI® Dichotomous Scales (by Alums' Library Type)

MBTI® Scales	Alums Library Type (%)			
	Academic	Public	School	Special
Introversion over Extraversion	100	60	60	66
Intuitive over Sensing	60	50	80	66
Thinking over Feeling	60	50	80	66
Judging over Perceiving	80	75	60	66

are strongly INTJ types. However, only 9 percent of the Alums demonstrate the more socially responsive ENFJ type, and two-thirds of them work in public libraries:

> ENFJ: Responsive and responsible. Generally feel real concern for what others think or want, and try to handle things with due regard for the other person's feelings. Can present a proposal or lead a group discussion with ease and tact. Sociable, popular, sympathetic. Responsive to praise and criticism (Scherdin 1994b, 130)

When MBTI® types with the greatest concentrations of Alums are analyzed by the two letter dichotomous scales, it is clear that the Alums share behavioral preferences across library type (table 76 above).

One additional comment needs to be made regarding the CALS Alums and the Myers-Briggs Type Indicator. As noted earlier in this section, the Alums and the American Library Association and the Special Library Association participants in the 1992 ACRL study are similar. However, both groups are different from the general U.S. population. Given the similarity of the Alums and the ACRL information professionals, it can be assumed that what Scherdin (1994b, 132) says about her respondents regarding Introversion and Intuition would also pertain to the CALS Alums:

> Librarians are the opposite of the general population on Introversion (I) and Intuition (N) . . . A partial explanation for these differences lies in the fact that while Introverted Intuitive types are relatively infrequent in the general population, their numbers are more frequent at higher educational levels. A preference for Intuition indicates a theoretical orientation that is associated with interest and comfort in college and university settings. Since librarians are among the most highly educated people in the population, their placement in this category seems appropriate.

II. Civic Involvement

In addition to behavioral preferences, civic, religious, and mentoring activities influence expression of service orientations. The question of civic engagement drew a response from 39 percent of the Alums—one of the smallest responses on the survey instrument (Q.III-24). An additional 24 percent indicated that, while they had formerly held memberships in one or more such groups, they were no longer actively engaged in them. The majority of this latter group come from the 1962-70 cohorts. The Alums who did respond to the question held membership in common—across all eight colleges and cohorts—in only three types of organizations: cultural, religious, and fraternal. Beyond those three, there are differences by college and by cohort. Cultural and religious involvements comprise 24 percent of those listed by respondents (see appendix C: Q.IV-24 for detail). *Cultural organizations* include musical, local history, and quilting groups. Eleven percent of the responses identify a *Religious organization* or a specific church (e.g., Presbyterian Church; my church). Table 77 presents the top eight categories of involvement by college. (Religious beliefs of the respondents are presented in more detail later in this chapter.)

Environmental groups range from garden clubs to the Sierra Club, while membership in *Library-related* organizations means involvement as a "Friend of the Library" or a seat on the local public library's board of trustees. *Fraternal* groups encompass a wide variety of organizations from lodges, to the Rotary, the Daughters of the American Revolution, and sororities and fraternities. The most commonly cited *Political organizations* are the major national parties (i.e., Democrats, Republicans), and the League of Women Voters. The local Parents-Teachers Association (PTA) and groups such as the Boy Scouts and Right-to-Life comprise the *Child-related* activities of Alums. *Municipal* engagement includes groups such as the Junior League and the Optimists.

These eight categories account for 72 percent of the responding Alums' civic involvements. A further 13 percent of Alums have connections with alumni associations, book clubs, charitable organizations, educational groups (like the American Association of University Women), and neighborhood associations (see appendix C: Q.IV-24 for detail). Nine percent hold membership in peace-centered organizations (such as Peace through InterCommunity Action), social groups, and unions. And 4 percent are members of sports clubs. In general, the Alums are nominally involved in civic activities. In this regard, they seem typical of those Americans whom Putnam (2000, 63) discusses in *Bowling Alone: The Collapse and Revival of American Community*:

> Organizational records suggest that for the first two-thirds of the twentieth century Americans' involvement in civic associations of all sorts rose steadily, except for the parenthesis of the Great Depression [of the 1930s]. In the last third of the century, by contrast, only mailing list membership has continued to expand . . . At the same time, active involvement in face-to-face organizations has plummeted, whether we consider organizational records, survey reports, time diaries, or consumer expenditures. We could surely find individual

Table 77: Civic Organizations/Involvements (by College)

Involvements	Avg (%)	College (%)							
		C	D	E	G	K	L	M	S
Cultural	13	12	21	15	25	8	19	7	15
Religious	11	8	5	4	25	20	16	15	6
Environmental	9	12	16	11	0	2	0	15	12
Library-related	9	6	0	6	0	18	10	7	9
Fraternal	8	4	21	8	25	4	13	11	3
Political org.	8	12	0	9	0	4	6	7	12
Child-related	7	8	11	6	0	14	6	4	0
Municipal	7	8	0	6	0	4	10	11	9

exceptions . . . , but the broad picture is one of declining membership in community organizations.

III. Religious Activities

While civic involvement drew responses from only 39 percent of the study's participants, there was a 93 percent response to the question "What was your religion while at [College]?" and a 96 percent response to the follow-up question "Has it changed over time?" (Q.IV-25). Overall, 78 percent of the Alums who responded to the initial question indicated they had a religion while at college; 72 percent of them were affiliated with a religion at the time of this study (table 78).

There has been a 6 percent decrease overall in the number of respondents who now have a religious affiliation. Alums from six of the colleges showed this change (i.e., from having a religion at college to not having one now): Carleton (a drop of 5 percent), Denison (two percent), Earlham (1 percent), Kalamazoo (13 percent), Macalester (17 percent), and Swarthmore (10 percent). Percentages did not change for Grinnell and Lawrence Alums. Less than 1 percent of Grinnell Alums indicated they had changed their religion, while 10 percent of those at Lawrence noted that the religion they practice now is different from the one they observed while at college.

Table 79 shows that five of the eight cohorts showed a decrease in religious affiliation. The largest decrease (15 percent) is in the 1991-96 cohort. The 1976-80 cohort shows no decrease, while two cohorts showed a greater number of Alums having a religious affiliation now than is reported for their college years: 7 percent more of the 1981-85 cohort, and 2 percent more in 1986-90.

Table 78: Religion While at College and Religion Now (by College)

Religious Involvement	Avg (%)	College (%) C	D	E	G	K	L	M	S
Religion at College									
Religion is given	78	75	81	77	88	79	74	88	73
Had/listed no religion	22	25	19	23	13	21	26	12	27
Religion Now									
Religion is given	72	70	79	76	88	66	74	71	63
Have/list no religion	28	30	21	24	13	34	26	29	37

Table 79: Religion While at College and Religion Now (by Cohort)

Changes in Religion	Avg (%)	Cohort (%) 62-	66-	71-	76-	81-	86-	91-	96-
Religion at College									
Religion is given	78	80	78	76	77	77	77	80	89
Had/listed no religion	22	20	22	24	23	23	23	20	11
Religion Now									
Religion is given	72	71	67	68	77	84	79	65	78
Have/list no religion	28	29	33	32	23	16	21	35	22

A larger number of CALS Alums responded to the question of whether their religion had changed over time (Q.IV-25) than responded to the question of whether or not they had a religious affiliation while in college. Of the 96 percent who answered the "change" question, 64 percent indicated they had not changed their religious affiliation. Of those who had changed religious affiliations, 33 percent indicated they had changed their religious affiliations at least once, and 4 percent indicated they now have no formal religion. Four percent of the respondents who had no religion while at college indicated they now have a religious affiliation. This means that for all the CALS Alums, 64 percent have not changed the religion they observed while at college and 36 percent either have changed religions or have become religious.

While undergraduates, 95 percent of the Alums were affiliated with Christianity across the eight colleges: the percentage ranged from a low of 90 percent (Swarthmore) to a high of 100 percent (Grinnell). The 4 percent of the Alums who professed Judaism were found in four colleges: Kalamazoo (3 percent of Alums), Lawrence (3 percent), Earlham (8 percent), and Swarthmore (10 percent). The remaining 1 percent of those with a religion indicated they were Baha'i, Pagans, or Pantheists (see appendixes C-D: Q.IV-25 for detail by name of the religion or denomination as provided by the Alums). When asked to name their current religion (if any), the Alums provided fundamentally the same affiliations: Christianity, Judaism, Baha'i, Pagan, Pantheism.

Quakers attended primarily Earlham and Swarthmore, while the majority of the Alums who were Baptists attended Denison and Kalamazoo. But fundamentally, the same religious groups the Alums were associated with during their college years are those they profess today. Both during college and now, Catholics and Methodists are found among Alums in all of the CALS colleges. Methodists are found in each of the eight cohorts. Quakers along with Alums who listed their religious affiliation as "Christian" or "Protestant" are found in all but the most recent cohort. The remaining religious groups are scattered amongst the colleges and the cohorts.

Between their college years and the time of this study, there were one to 4 percent increases in the adoption of eight religious affiliations by Alums: Baptist, Catholic, Christian, Episcopal, Evangelical, Jewish, nondenominational, Protestant, Quaker, and Unitarian-Universalist. By contrast, a one to 4 percent decrease was found among Congregational, Lutheran, Methodist, and Presbyterian denominations.

The Alums were also asked about what importance religion had for them at college and what importance it has for them now (Q.IV-25). Analysis of their comments resulted in the identification of five frameworks through which the CALS respondents expressed their engagement with religion: *Cultural, Grounding, Intellectual, Spiritual,* and *Ambivalence* (some respondents included more than one approach in their comments). A Carleton '66 public librarian draws on the *Cultural* approach when he says that while at college, he saw his religion "as a cultural focus of reference." An Earlham '76 special librarian described it as signifying "equality of all people, regardless of age, race, income, etc." For a Lawrence '71 public librarian, religion at college and now is "purely cultural." Such Alums, both at college and now, see religion in terms of socially oriented values and behavior. Those for whom it is a *Grounding* express their sentiments through that and similar terms: "it recharges me weekly and centers me" (Denison '66; school), and "it is central to my consciousness" (Kalamazoo '66; special). The view of religion as *Intellectual* is articulated by a Grinnell Alum ('76; academic), who sees it "as a foundation for exploration," and in a Lawrence '71 academic librarian's description of her religion as "very important as a practice and [as] a philosophy." Alums who experience their religion in a *Spiritual* sense speak of "nature-based spirituality" (Swarthmore '66; special) or as providing "spiritual food for thought—nothing formal" (Macalester '91; special). Finally, there are Alums who feel *Ambivalent* about their religion. A Carleton '66 public librarian illustrates this approach:

> I do not believe that a teleological belief system is necessary to ethical behavior, and I certainly feel that organized religion (churches as social institutions) has a lot to answer for through the course of world history. I do, however, believe that faith is important to life.

Table 80: Alums' Approach to Religion (by College)

Approach		Avg (%)	C	D	E	G	K	L	M	S
Religion at College	Cultural	39	33	20	41	50	53	33	38	31
	Intellectual	24	33	40	21	50	24	11	25	23
	Grounding	16	17	40	21	0	6	33	0	8
	Spiritual	11	8	0	7	0	12	0	13	31
	Ambivalence	11	8	0	10	0	6	22	25	8
Religion Now	Cultural	29	16	0	39	67	35	14	40	21
	Spiritual	24	26	13	13	0	30	36	40	29
	Grounding	21	11	50	24	0	15	36	10	21
	Intellectual	20	26	38	18	33	20	7	10	21
	Ambivalence	6	21	0	5	0	0	7	0	7

Between their college years and the time of their response to this study, the Alums' preference for one of these five general approaches to their religion has experienced some change (table 80 above).The percentage of Alums expressing religion in *Cultural* and *Grounding* terms decreased—along with those who were previously *Ambivalent.* The percentage of Alums who have a *Spiritual* view of their religion doubled. A Carleton '76 school librarian who described her views of religion while in college in terms of the *Cultural* model, now uses the *Spiritual* approach. She says:

> I'm not active in a specific church right now, but I think of my faith as what holds the rest of me together in all situations. I've gotten less "specific religion"-based and find spiritual guidance from a variety of sources.

And an Earlham '76 public librarian now considers religion "much more important," adding:

> I continue to develop spiritually; I am very active in my church community. I am still (and will always be) culturally Christian, but I believe in a spirituality (and religion) of works, not words. Words are important and lovely, but I believe it's how you live your life that counts.

The increase in the percentage of Alums who demonstrate a *Spiritual* approach, and comments such as the above, may reflect the same considerations of religion as were found in a 2005 survey of 1,385 Catholics, Protestants, Jews, and Muslims aged 18-25. This online poll found that a majority said "that religion and spirituality are an important part of their lives, but [that they are not] following the religious establishment" ("Gen Y Questions Formal Religion" 2005, D5).

While the comments of a majority of respondents provided little from which to infer the level of importance that they associate with their religion, some Alums did follow up on the question's use of the word "importance." Two Kalamazoo Alums provide examples of this:

> Not important, but both then and now, I have been interested in religions and consider myself a spiritual person. (Kalamazoo '76; special)

> Important (civil liberties, human rights, spiritual life). (Kalamazoo '66; academic)

A conservative reading of the comments on the issue of importance suggests that a majority of the Alums feel their religion was of some importance during college and of somewhat greater importance now. Because of the subjectivity inherent in the comments, no attempt was made to rank "importance." However, there is some indication that members of the 1962-71 cohorts accord their religion more importance than do members of the 1976-96 cohorts.

Putnam (2000, 67) states that "religiosity rivals education as a powerful correlate of most forms of civic engagement." He also sees positive correlations between the degree of religiosity and the degree of volunteering, philanthropy, and altruism. As with civic involvement, Putnam (2000, 72) finds that "actual attendance and involvement in religious activities has fallen" from the 1960s forward. Some of the decline can be accounted for by generational differences, and some by an increase in an individualized approach to religion—that which is reflected in the *Spiritual* approach of the Alums and seen in the Gen Y survey's finding of appreciation for religion, yet distance from its more organized forms. Yet Putnam also notes that religion remains today, "as it has traditionally been, a central fount of American community life" (72). Overall, analysis of the Alums' civic and religious activities finds them moderately involved in both areas, although they give more importance to religious than to civic engagement.

IV. Mentoring

Questions about mentoring were included in this study because the work-related literature points to mentoring as a very common form of service through which the new professional is socialized into not only a specific work setting but, more broadly, into a field of work. From Levinson (1978) through Kram (1985) to the work of Allen (1997a-b, 1999, 2003), mentoring is spoken of as a relationship within an organization between a newcomer and a more senior member through which the latter helps the former learn the ways of the organization. Some mentoring is formal; that is, it is sanctioned by the organization. Most mentoring, however, is an informal occurrence that reflects "spontaneous relationships that occur without external involvement from the organization" (Russell and Adams 1997, 4). Many people, including some CALS respondents, do not use the word *mentor* to describe people who inform and enrich their work lives (Q.V-1-12), nor are they always comfortable describing themselves as enacting that role (Kram 1985; Wiltshire 1998); that is, seeing themselves as either "mentees" or "protégées"—the two most common terms for the recipients of mentoring.[39] Yet this relationship between someone with seasoned professional experience and someone just gaining that kind of experience does work to provide practical knowledge (as opposed to schooled theory) to the newcomer, and the Alums support this view. Wiltshire (1998) divides mentoring into *instrumental* and *classical*. Instrumental mentoring occurs within the workplace and serves career development; classical mentoring occurs, she believes, both within and outside of the workplace. Most research on mentoring is set within the organization. In her seminal work on mentoring within the organization, Kram's (1985, 22) review of the research concludes that mentoring serves two broad groups of functions: career functions and psychosocial functions:

> Career functions are those aspects of the relationship that enhance learning the ropes and preparing for advancement in an organization. Psychosocial functions are those aspects of a relationship that enhance a sense of competence, clarity of identity, and effectiveness in a professional role.

She goes on to indicate how such functions occur:

> Career functions are possible because of the senior person's experience, organizational rank, and influence in the organizational context . . . Psychosocial functions are possible because of an interpersonal relationship that fosters mutual trust and increasing intimacy. (Kram 1985, 23)

While mentoring relationships are recognized as an important aspect of career development, they are also "key sources for ensuring the continuation of knowledge" within the organization and the profession (Allen 2003).

Levinson (1978) identified a set of functions that are referred to in much of the subsequent research on mentoring. Using Barondess's (1995, 17) paraphrasing of Levinson's functions, the present study asked the CALS Alums if (1) they had been mentored and (2) have been or are a mentor with "mentor" defined as any one or more of the following (Q.VI-1-12):

- A teacher who enhanced my skills and intellectual development.
- A sponsor who used her or his influence and contacts to facilitate my entry into, and possible advancement of, my career(s).
- A host and guide who helped initiate me into a new occupational and social world, acquainting me with its values, customs, resources, and cast of characters.
- An advisor who provided counsel, moral support, and direction.
- An exemplar who illustrated virtues, achievements, and actions that I admired.

---

[39]Murray (1991) lists *mentee, candidate, apprentice, aspirant, advisee, counselee, trainee, student, follower, subordinate, applicant, hopeful*, and *seeker* as common terms. In the following discussion, *recipient* is used to denote someone who is being mentored.

Thirty-six percent of the CALS members did not respond—perhaps neither having had a mentor nor having mentored anyone (Q.V-1-12). Approximately 5 percent of the Alums declined to respond because they felt the definitions were "too loose." However 59 percent felt comfortable enough with the terms to indicate they have received mentoring, and 46 percent described mentoring they have given to others. All of those (100 percent) who consider themselves mentors have also been the recipients of mentoring. At least some Alums from every college and cohort have been mentored and have mentored others.

Kram (1985) divides the mentoring experience into four phases: *Initiation*, *cultivation*, *separation*, and *redefinition*. In the initiation phase, the relationship starts either informally or as the result of a formal program that pairs the two individuals, and they begin to identify personal and professional commonalities. If the relationship is to become one of genuine mentoring, however, it must be cultivated. That is, "the [two] learn more about each other's capabilities and optimize the benefits of participating in the mentorship" (Chao 1997, 16). This is when the mentor truly teaches and promotes the recipient, and the latter receives the greatest socialization benefit from the former. Because of the growth that occurs during this phrase, the recipient becomes knowledgeable enough to develop a deeper understanding of (for example) her or his position requirements or of the LIS field, and perhaps the ability to move into a new position. One of the assured outcomes of the cultivation phase is that the recipient begins to act independently of the mentor. The faster independence develops, the earlier the separation phase subsequently occurs (Kram 1985).

In a formal program, separation typically happens when the Alum has developed enough knowledge and skill to be independent. Sometimes the structure of a program is such that separation could be premature, and mentor and recipient must decide if they want their relationship to continue outside the program. Formal programs contribute to the successful socialization of newcomers. However, because of their structured nature and their explicit goal of professional socialization, this means that the relationship often ends simply because it is time for the mentor to take on a newly assigned newcomer (Allen et al. 1999). Depending upon the structure of the formal program, it could be argued that true mentoring relationships can begin only at this point; that prior to this conscious decision the relationship may be more one of advisor-pupil than of mentor-recipient.

Table 81 indicates how long mentoring relationships have lasted for the CALS Alums (Q.V-7): Those who have had one to three years or "still continuing" relationships include Alums from all the cohorts, but they are most commonly from the 1991-2000 classes (see appendixes C-D: Q.V-7). The greatest percent (30 percent) of those whose relationships have lasted over five years come from the 1962-65 cohort. For the cohorts covering 1966-2000, the largest concentration of Alums in each cohort has experienced a relationship that either lasted two to three years or is still continuing. Table 82 shows that when a mentoring relationship ended it was most frequently for one of two reasons: one of the participants changed positions or the mentor retired (Q.V-8).

Table 81: Duration of Mentoring Relationship: Alums as Recipients

Mentoring in Years	Alums (%)
1 year	13
2-3 years	31
4-5 years	14
Over 5 years [but then ended]	16
Still continuing	26

Table 82: Mentoring Relationship by Reason Ended

Reason Ended	Alums (%)
One of us changed positions	39
Other: my mentor retired	28
We became peers	16
The formal program ended	14
One of us changed careers	3

It is not unusual after a year or so in an informal relationship for the two individuals to find that the newcomer is now comfortably socialized into the organization or position, and the result is that "our relationship changed to one of more equality—less mentoring" (Earlham '71; school).

This act of separating can be difficult for the mentor or for the recipient. Stopping a relationship in which each party has benefited is always a psychological break, and for many it is a physical break as well. The latter is especially the case for those who have experienced career advancement by either moving to a different organization or to another geographic location within the same organization (Kram 1985; Chao 1997).

The last part of the mentoring process is the redefinition phase. Here, mentor and recipient find themselves in a position of informal contact perhaps via e-mail or at conferences (Chao 1997). The two may now see themselves as peers, but it is not unusual for the Alum to feel "adrift for a while" (Earlham '62; academic). A significant number of the Alums (28 percent) found the relationship ended because their mentor retired and was uninterested in continuing in this kind of engagement with the field.

For the rest of this discussion of Alums and mentoring, generally "mentored" (past tense) is used, as 74 percent indicated the relationships have now ended—an acknowledgment that the cohorts with the largest number of CALS Alums span 1962-1980, and many now themselves serve as mentors (see appendixes C-D: Q.V-7).

Table 83: The Value of Mentoring Received by Alums (by College)

Value	Avg (%)	College (%)							
		C	D	E	G	K	L	M	S
Very valuable	65	62	62	67	50	61	82	69	54
Some value	35	38	38	33	50	39	17	31	46

Table 84: The Value of Mentoring Received by Alums (by Cohort)

Value	Avg (%)	Cohort (%)							
		62-	66-	71-	75-	81-	86-	91-	96-
Very valuable	65	65	52	71	69	68	80	62	83
Some value	35	35	48	29	31	32	20	38	17

The Alums: Being Mentored

Of the 255 CALS Alums who reported having been mentored, 65 percent found it *Very valuable* to their career and 35 percent considered it to be of *Some value* (Q.V-1). By college, Lawrence Alums are particularly pleased to have received mentoring, while Grinnell Alums find differing strengths of value in it. Five of the colleges approximate the overall valuation given to mentoring. However, all of those who have received mentoring perceive it to be valuable (table 83 above).

Table 84 presents the findings by cohort. The greatest number of Alums who find being mentored to be *Very valuable* are in the 1986-90 and 1996-2000 cohorts. The latter group represents respondents who are, in general, the newest to the profession. They may feel mentoring is particularly helpful as they find their way in the field. The high number in the 1986-90 cohort may represent Alums who have been (or are) in the midst of major career advancement years. Members of the most recent cohort are likely to be in Kram's (1985) initiation or cultivation stages of the mentoring experience, where they are receiving the most direct benefits of the relationship. The older 1986-90 cohort respondents may have completed the mentoring process or be in the redefinition stage, where the relationship "either evolves into a completely new form or ends entirely" (Kram 1985, 48). The fact that the Alums in this cohort give "being recipients of mentoring" such high value suggests that they have had successful transitions throughout the mentoring phases, or that they have received promotions into managerial levels and are now in a new (mid-career) mentoring relationship with a still more senior person.

As is typical of most mentoring situations (Kram 1985), the majority (74 percent) of these Alums had mentors who were five or more years older than they were (Q.V-6). However, 20 percent of the CALS Alums and their mentors were the same general age, and 6 percent of the Alums were older than their mentors. (The latter is particularly true for Alums who have chosen LIS for their second career.) And as is also typical, a majority (74 percent) have had individuals from within LIS as their mentors (Q.V-3). Fifty-nine percent of the CALS women and 41 percent of the men have had more than one mentor (Q.V-2). For 33 percent of the CALS Alums, their mentors have been their boss; for 18 percent it has been someone other than their boss, and 49 percent have had at least one mentor who was their boss and one who was not (Q.V-4).

There is a significant literature calling for or describing LIS-based mentoring programs. It covers all library types and a wide array of LIS professionals and positions. Examples focusing on library type include Hardesty (1997; academic libraries), Chatman (1992; public), Buddy (2001; school), and McGreevy (2001; special). The role of department heads or seasoned professionals toward new professionals has given rise to its own literature, exemplified by Fulton (1990) and Nofsinger and Lee (1994). From Cargill (1989) through Cole (2003), material can be found that discusses mentoring for professional development. Henderson (1996) covers mentoring over the Internet while Ritchie and Genoni (2002) consider group mentoring. Harcourt and Neumeister (2002) describe having specific sets of LIS professionals (in this instance, cataloging librarians) mentor LIS graduate students while the latter are engaged in related course work. And an excellent example of a formal program is found in Pollack et al. (1992). While there is, in the LIS field, great interest in mentoring to socialize new professionals, to advance careers, and for professional development, the CALS Alums demonstrate that in general those on the receiving end of mentoring believe it "just happened" to them. While 13 percent say they picked their mentors and 17 percent were selected for mentoring, 67 percent indicated that they "fell into" a mentoring relationship (Q.V-5). Kram (1985), Wiltshire (1998), and others point out that informal mentoring may be the most common kind. However, it may not be immediately recognized as such by the recipient. An Earlham '62 public librarian writes of her mentor, "She began her career earlier than I started mine and offered her experience and help so graciously that I have realized only this minute that she was my mentor! (We never worked together.)"

The CALS Alums were asked to list two or three benefits that they saw from the mentoring they received (Q.V-9). Table 85 presents their responses, using Levinson's (1978) characterizations of a mentor as *Teacher, Sponsor, Host/Guide, Advisor,* or *Exemplar.*

Mentors who may be characterized as *Teachers* are described as providing training and as enhancing the Alums' skills and intellectual development: "[they] have helped me learn about all aspects of the field" (Swarthmore '81; public). Teachers focus on the individual's knowledge, skills, and abilities as these are used within the field. They perform extremely important socialization roles with regard to new professionals. A Grinnell '76 public librarian would turn to his mentor for "mental challenge—critical thinking, [and] discussion of ideas." A Lawrence '66 academic librarian "learned how one puts theory into actual practice." A Carleton '66 special librarian began to understand "the importance of precision and accuracy in cataloguing; the importance of good interpersonal relations." Mentors who are teachers push Alums to do more, to stretch themselves, and to become less naive and more practiced. Teachers "took my stupid questions" (Kalamazoo '91; special); they "demanded more" (Swarthmore '66; academic); they "[taught] me not to accept the status quo but [to see] what's possible in my chosen area of work" (Macalester '81; school).

Table 85: Roles Held by Alums' Mentors as Seen by CALS Alums

Mentor's Role	CALS Alums (%)
A teacher	31
An advisor	26
A sponsor	20
An exemplar	13
A host/guide	11

Alums who saw their mentors as "an *Advisor* who provided counsel, moral support, and direction" describe them as "support—intellectual and moral," "someone to call on for advice," or "a sounding board for my plans—and personal encouragement" (Earlham '62 academic; Grinnell '86 public; and Lawrence '71 academic, respectively). Clearly, these mentors were offering organizational or professional knowledge as well as belief in the Alums' abilities to handle their work. The mentors appear to span counseling and caring—some providing "helpful advice" (Kalamazoo '66; school); others expressing "confidence in my growing abilities in the field" (Lawrence '71; academic).

A *Sponsor*, on the other hand, uses "her [or] his influence and contacts" to facilitate the new professional's entry into the field, and possibly the advancement of the Alum's career. While sponsorship is important in bringing a new professional into an organization, it is more common in settings where upward career advancement is strongly competitive. Sponsorship resonates with terms like "old boy" or "old girl" networks, and "having connections." Those CALS respondents who identified mentors as sponsors remarked frequently about being introduced to "her peers—three movers and shakers" (Carleton '66; public), or seeing their mentor as "being a source of professional contacts" (Lawrence '62; academic), or helpful in arranging "key interviews" (Lawrence '66; public). Alums have seen sponsors frequently use their "contacts for my advancement in the field" (Kalamazoo '91; special) and for "securing recommendations for invitation only workshops" (Swarthmore '76; academic). Sponsors squire Alums around at conferences ensuring that they meet others who can get them on committees or increase their visibility within the field.

Exemplars "illustrate virtues, achievements and actions" that CALS Alums admire and would like to emulate. Many of the 14 percent of Alums who view their mentors this way write of seeing them as role models and of being inspired by them. The benefits were tangible for this Carleton '81 public librarian: "I had the opportunity of observing people I really respect do their work. Interacting with them regularly really improved my work." For an Earlham '76 public librarian, this amounted to "help[ing] me learn to behave as a professional, as opposed to a college student." Two Swarthmore Alums described their mentors this way:

> They provided living examples of qualities I sought to develop. ('71; academic)

> They broadened my horizons; gave me great examples to aspire to. ('62; academic)

Finally, mentors can be *Hosts or Guides* for new professionals. In this role they help initiate freshly graduated MLIS information professionals into a new occupational and social world, "acquainting him or her with its values, customs, resources, and cast of characters" (Barondess 1995, 7). An almost purely professional socialization activity, this form of mentoring acknowledges the significant distinctions between knowledgeable mentor and novice practitioner. These mentors "shared insight into the culture of the profession" (Kalamazoo '91; special) and provide "initiation into a new world" (Swarthmore '71; public). The host or guide serves to introduce the organization and the new professional to each other: "They helped me feel connected and in a way cared for—it helped me feel very quickly that I was an integral part of the library system staff" (Earlham '91; public). In some cases mentors were bosses who "allowed me to work at a variety of jobs within the library to see what I liked" (Denison '71; special). In other cases, the usually sharp political acumen of hosts and guides was particularly useful, as a Kalamazoo '86 public librarian found out: "They have inside knowledge of library systems and who has the power to do what." This is echoed by a Lawrence '86 public librarian who believes that having such mentors is "the quickest way to be acclimated to a new workplace. They ease the adjustment to a highly bureaucratic system."

Teacher, advisor, sponsor, exemplar, host—these are the positive descriptions of mentors of the CALS Alums. But what drawbacks, if any, do the Alums see in such relationships? Twenty-four percent of those who write about being mentored identify difficulties with the mentor-Alum relationship. Their range of concerns is shown in table 86 (Q.V-10).

Within the socialization context, the more experienced mentor has knowledge that the new professional does not have. Levinson (1978) likens this to a parent-child relationship. That is, unless the mentor and the recipient are already essentially peers in terms of position or rank, there is always some degree of unequal power at work in the relationship. This unequal power lies behind many drawbacks to a mentoring relationship (Kram 1985; Levinson 1978; Merriam 1983; Morton-Cooper and Palmer 1993). Disagreeing with one's mentor is not always easy. Basically, some Alums find, "it can be hard to explain why you don't want to take advice or follow [in] their footsteps" (Carleton '66; special). For the 33 percent of Alums who have their boss for a mentor, there are "expectations that I would always follow recommendations" (Lawrence '66; academic), so disagreeing can lead to the risk of being "seen as insubordinate" (Lawrence '71; public). Learning "only one person's procedures/philosophy" (Earlham '66; special) can limit development of one's own ideas; you "can get stuck in the mold of the mentor's approach" (Carleton '76; school). Not fully developing one's own philosophy, approach, thoughts and skills means "you can end up mimicking their style, etc., which may not be good" (Earlham '66; special) in part because that "can also have a negative impact on your career goals" (Carleton '66; special). This can have particularly unfortunate ramifications if the Alum's career plans differ from "the job [your mentors have] set up for you" (Kalamazoo '86; special).

There are situations where mentors cannot provide what Alums need. For some CALS recipients, it is simply that "mentors often do not have enough time to spend on mentoring"

Table 86: Drawbacks Reported by Alums as Recipients

Mentoring Drawbacks	Alums (%)
I couldn't disagree easily with my mentor	22
Mentor held down my ideas	15
Mentor stalled my career plans	14
I couldn't get what I needed from my mentor	11
Wrong match of two people	11
I couldn't meet my mentor's expectations	10
I was never seen as an equal	7
Others viewed the relationship negatively	7
Organizational structure hampered relationship	3

(Earlham '76; academic). In other cases, the Alum's need is too great, as with the Carleton '81 public librarian who has found that, thus far, "none have helped me conquer my fear of leading others." Drawbacks to formal mentoring programs include the following:

- The match between mentor and new professional is too artificial.
- The two have such different styles as to be incompatible.
- When the program is run by a professional association, the Alum may feel "the relationship was based on the library association's desire to build itself up rather than on me as a professional." (Macalester '76; academic)

A few Alums have felt unequal to the tasks set by mentors, as with the Swarthmore '66 special librarian who writes: "I may never live up to her ambition for me." Others have come to believe they will never be seen as peers with their mentors. Here the disappointment comes as Alums realize they have outgrown their mentor or that "as [my] career progresses, it is difficult to place the relationship on a more equal footing" (Carleton '86; special). For others the realization that they have moved on with their careers or knowledge of the work they do also means realizing they and their mentors have come to exist in such different areas that they will "never become personal friends" (Kalamazoo '71; school). The outcome of the shift in status seems to trouble them equally whether it is from newcomer to peer in knowledge or in career advancement.

In both the formal and the informal relationship, some CALS members have found that being the recipient of a mentor's attentions is viewed negatively by the Alums' peers or colleagues: "other colleagues see the relationship as favoritism" (Carleton '91; public) or the new professional "as 'teacher's pet'" (Swarthmore '66; academic). This is especially true when the mentor is the Alum's boss. Other respondents, like this Earlham '66 public librarian, found that "some people could not understand my great admiration for someone they did not consider so special." And occasionally, the organization's structure inhibits the mentoring relationship. This happens especially in formal mentoring situations if the mentor and new professional are in different departments and "mentors are not attuned to [the] administrative expectations" of the Alum's actual boss (Swarthmore '81; academic).

Overall, the CALS Alums believe the benefits of being mentored significantly outweigh the limitations. Mentoring provides benefits for both the new professional and the mentor, but both must adjust to the realities of the relationship (Kram 1985). Sometimes the new professional finds it is necessary to dampen his or her expectations, as with a Lawrence '66 academic who writes that she unrealistically found that when she gained a mentor: "I expected my own library work would immediately be on the same plane as that of the veteran's." Sometime it is the mentor who discovers that it is not always easy to bring newcomers into the field and to advise, teach, sponsor, or guide them.

The Alums: Being a Mentor

Forty-six percent of the CALS respondents have served as mentors. Of these Alums, 74 percent mentored someone within LIS; the other 26 percent served as a mentor for someone outside of the field (Q.V-11A). Sixty-six percent of those the Alums have mentored are female; 34 percent are male (Q.V-11F). The Alums generally mentor more female than male newcomers: 14 percent of those mentoring men have helped three or more of them, while 44 percent of those mentoring women have mentored three or more (Q-V-11F). All the CALS participants who are mentors had previously been recipients of mentoring, confirming a consistent finding in the literature that "those who have engaged in mentoring activities in the past report greater willingness to mentor others" (Allen et al. 1997a, 71).

The Alums were asked how they became mentors (Q.V-11B). Two reasons stand out: they see it as part of their job, or they were asked by either a boss or a newcomer (table 87). As a Macalester '66 academic librarian put it, "Supervising relationships sometimes become mentoring relationships." Most of the CALS members who believe that mentoring is part of their job "as a boss" (Kalamazoo '66; special) also indicate that they hire or see staff members who have needs or untapped potential. They then initiate a mentoring relationship. Conversely, the second large concentration of Alums became mentors because they were asked to do so. In almost all cases the newcomer makes the request, although on a few occasions it comes from a senior administrator who asks an Alum to mentor a newcomer. Most CALS Alums indicated that they were asked by the other person, and some respondents reveal the circumstances that led to that. Some examples:

> By chance. People would hear me at a workshop or work for me and then seek me out for advice. I've sent/encouraged at least five people to library school! Role model. (Carleton '86; academic)

Table 87: Reasons Alums Became Mentors

Reasons for Mentoring	Alums (%)
It is part of my job	32
I was asked	28
It just happened	12
It was part of a formal program	11

> I have become someone that newer library directors in our area tend to turn to [to] help them learn the legal aspects of their job—just because I've been in the job [as director] a long time. (Earlham '62; public)

> One was long-distance—when I was contacted by a novice high school librarian who had read one of my articles. We emailed and I know I helped her through her first year. We did meet once. (Grinnell '66; school)

> Through working together with this colleague on a special project. (Macalester '81; school)

In those instances where Alums feel the relationship "just happened," the comments tend to show something within the Alum that might attract others. A Denison '71 academic librarian demonstrates this when she says that they "just started—struck up friendships. I don't think of it as anything special, but friends helping each other." And an Earlham '66 public librarian describes herself as "the person in the reference department who acts in the mentoring role. I think because it comes naturally to me." Where formal programs are in operation, a number of Alums will volunteer to mentor. The programs may be within the organization or initiated by a state, regional, or national association. A Macalester '66 special librarian notes that she started mentoring through "the Medical Library Association program [and] also in a consultant role on grants." A Swarthmore '71 academic librarian was invited by her LIS program's alumni association to mentor master's students. And an Earlham '71 public librarian explains that mentoring resulted because she is part of a group that "organized a mentoring program" for newcomers.

In a study of informal mentoring at five different organizations, Allen et al. (1997b) found that the reasons mentors gave for their willingness formed two clusters: Other-focused and Self-focused. The Other-focused factors are the desire to

- Pass information on to others
- Build a competent workforce
- Help others in general
- Help others succeed

Table 88: Alums' Reasons for Mentoring

Mentoring Categories	Alums (%)
It is part of my job	29
To give back to or recruit for the field	17
It just happened	12
I saw potential in someone	12
I was asked by the newcomer	11
It was part of a formal program	7
Altruistic: "to help others"	7
Other	5

- Benefit the organization
- Help specific groups (e.g., minorities, women) move through organizational ranks

The Self-focused factors are

- Gratification in seeing others succeed and grow
- Free time for other pursuits
- Personal desire to work with others
- To increase one's own personal learning
- Pride
- Desire to have an influence on others
- To increase the respect of others toward the mentor

When the CALS respondents' reasons for mentoring are placed within the Allen et al. (1997a) categories, the results demonstrate that almost all of the Alums' reasons are Other-focused (table 88 above; Q.VI-11A).

Whereas the majority of the Alums "just fell into" being mentored and 12 percent believe it "just happened" that they became mentors, the largest concentration say that they actually became mentors because it is "part of my job." An organizationally based, socializing reason, this is reflected in comments such as: "mentoring is part of supervising" (Carleton '66; public); "because I believe this is an apprenticeship profession" (Earlham '91; public); "it is the right thing to do—I see it as a natural part of my supervisory responsibilities" (Macalester '81; academic). Here there is no sense of there being a value in seeing newcomers grow within the job or the field or of a personal desire to work with others. These Alums feel most comfortable describing themselves as teachers. They see their mentoring as a training or teaching activity associated with bringing new professionals into full understanding of their job responsibilities within the organization. This is not a situation where the Alum has a choice to mentor; rather it seems to be "part of the job description" (Denison '62; special) to do so.

In contrast, some of the 17 percent who write of "giving back" or recruiting others into the field see mentoring as "a service to the profession" (Earlham '62; academic). Others do it believing there is a need "to guide outstanding people to the LIS profession" (Kalamazoo '86; public). And another group echoes the sentiment of this Carleton '71 public librarian: "I valued the support and advice I was freely given and wanted to share the experience with someone else." These CALS members may see themselves as hosts and guides or as sponsors. Their actions are directed partially toward making potential professionals aware of the field and partially toward benefiting the field by ensuring a supply of new entrants.

Alums who mentor as a result of seeing the potential in someone tend to take on the advisor or host/guide role. These Alums see "talent and commitment" (Denison '71; academic) in someone or they "knew women who would make wonderful librarians" (Lawrence '71; public), and were not content to just suggest the field. Such CALS participants are activists mentors. They look both for newcomers to the organization and for members of their own departments who "have talents that could be used and channeled" (Carleton '66; public) into the field or who could be guided toward better positions, new career tracks, or a more rewarding avenue for professional or personal growth. The 11 percent of the Alums who have been asked by newcomers to mentor them also fit the description of "advisor": they provide counsel as well as direction. Having been approached by an MLIS student, or a new professional, or by a paraprofessional who is considering taking the next step, these Alums most frequently say "my advice was sought; my senior position led to it" (Earlham '86; academic). A Kalamazoo '62 academic librarian illustrates such a situation: "I like the person who asked me to be her mentor. A library school student who works with me wanted a mentor. She asked. I agreed."

For CALS respondents in a work setting near a graduate LIS program, the most common type of formal program may be the internship or practicum arrangement. Alums might agree to be "shadowed" by a student, have a student work in their department or unit, or add an MLIS student to a project they are supervising. For some Alums the relationship created by these kinds of formal programs concludes at the end of the semester; for others the relationship continues and grows into a more encompassing mentorship. And as noted earlier in this chapter, formal programs for new professionals within the work setting are often reported in the LIS literature. Many of these are found in academic libraries where, as in the case of a Swarthmore '76 academic librarian, "I was recently elected promotion and tenure coordinator at my library and am thus de facto chair of the newly formed P&T Mentoring Committee." In work settings, the Alums who mentor as part of a formal program may exhibit any of the five Levinson (1978) roles of advisor, exemplar, host/guide, sponsor, and teacher.

Finally, there are the 7 percent of CALS respondents who mentor for altruistic reasons. Allen (2003, 136) writes that serving informally as a mentor "is a volitional activity that goes above and beyond the mentor's formal job requirements . . . [it is] prosocial behavior." This kind of behavior is a collection of traits that predispose a person toward helpful actions, and Allen (2003) notes that other researchers have suggested it has two dimensions. The first is other-focused empathy; the second is helpfulness. Aryee et al. (1996, cited in Allen 2003) have linked altruism with the motivation to mentor. Here the Alums are acting with a conscious or unconscious intent of "using my experience to help others" (Kalamazoo '66; academic).

Recall from the beginning of this discussion of mentoring as professional socialization that Kram (1985) identifies two basic functions to the mentoring process: career and psychosocial. Psychosocial functions are "those aspects of a relationship that enhance a sense of competence, clarity of identity, and effectiveness in [the newcomer's] professional role" (Kram 1985, 22). But the mentor also benefits from the relationship (Levinson 1978), and in the most successful relationships those benefits are also career-related and psychosocial. In the career sense, mentors may develop skills that lead to their own career advancement, wider supervisory or managerial responsibilities, or placement on teams or projects that depend on the same supportive and developmental skills they used in their mentoring activities. In the psychosocial context, mentors provide role modeling, acceptance, confirmation, counseling, and friendship to recipients (Kram 1985; Chao 1997). In return, mentors receive affirmation of their professional skills, knowledge and abilities, and the intrinsic satisfaction of seeing others grow and develop. In their study of mentors in five organizations, Allen et al. (1997a) found the following to be positive benefits of mentoring:

- Development of close relationships and friendships
- Offers potential for protégée payback
- Loyalty of protégées
- Satisfaction in seeing others grow and succeed
- General satisfaction in helping others
- Helps mentor do her or his own job
- Increases mentor's own learning and knowledge
- Increases mentor's organizational visibility
- Provides organizational recognition of the mentor
- Ensures the passage of knowledge to others
- Builds a competent workforce

The CALS respondents identified benefits that cluster into five areas (table 89; Q.V-11C). An Earlham '66 public librarian addressed professional benefits:

> Mentoring helps me focus my own ideas about the profession, the field, and specific responsibilities and skills I sometimes take for granted—as well as opening me up to new potentials gleaned from those I work with.

Other Alums echoed these sentiments. Several confirm Kram's (1985) claim that supporting newcomers this way helps "redirect creative energies" in mid-career mentors. The following examples illustrate both this redirection and other benefits of mentoring that the Alums could utilize in their work as managers, colleagues, and members of the LIS profession:

> Helps me articulate values, goals. (Carleton '62; public)

> It's given me an understanding of the ways to teach and encourage new librarians. (Carleton '66; special)

Table 89: Benefits Received by Alums Who Mentor

Benefits	Alums (%)
I gained professionally	46
I gained individually	22
Altruistic: Proud of recipients	21
We became friends	7
I learned how to mentor by mentoring	4

> I now more clearly define my goals, objectives, practices, and skills for myself. (Earlham '62; public)
>
> It's inspired me to try new things in my library. Recharged my passion and creativity and assertiveness in my work. [I've] learned new ways to approach people and tackle issues. (Kalamazoo '71; school)
>
> It has increased my feelings of responsibility to my job and affection for my workplace and coworkers. (Lawrence '81; special)
>
> Helped me think about my own career and potential. (Macalester '66; public)
>
> I stay in touch with current practice. (Macalester '71; special)
>
> It helps me feel I'm part of a living network—that I've contributed to the positive energy in the organization; Helped the workplace become more of a community. (Swarthmore '91; public)

Alums who feel they have gained personally write of increased self-confidence, patience, and a sense of individual accomplishment. Some CALS respondents have also found, as with the case of this Grinnell '85 public librarian, that "it made me reassess myself: was I exhibiting the behavior I wanted my mentees to follow?" Being proud of the recipients and their efforts was generally expressed in an altruistic fashion. Alums spoke of feeling proud of the recipients' accomplishments, their growth as individuals and as professionals, and "the joy of the student's 'aha' of discovery" (Swarthmore '81; academic). For some, the most profound benefit has been deep and lasting friendships as well as feelings of mutual respect. An Earlham '66 public librarian notes that "they stay in touch with me and have told me how much [my mentoring] helped them." And Alums from Carleton, Earlham, Kalamazoo, and Lawrence felt they learned how to mentor through the act of mentoring. For example, an Earlham '91 public librarian feels "I have improved my ability to know how and when to help" while a Carleton '71 academic

Table 90: Major Limitations to Mentoring

Limitations	Alums (%)
Lack of sufficient time to give to it	26
Lack of experience	24
Feelings of failure	21
Limitations of authority	9
Organizational structure is a hindrance	7

librarian comments, "I learned you need to get to know someone before giving him your full support."

The mentoring process can be perceived by the mentor to have limitations, and table 90 (above) lists the major ones expressed by CALS respondents (Q.V-11D). Most Alums who commented on the issue of lacking sufficient time simply indicated, like this Lawrence '86 public librarian, that "the most severe limitation is *time*" (emphasis in original). An Earlham '81 public librarian explains that "the difficulty is understanding the time commitment in a nonstructured mentoring relationship—I spent too much time." When they chose to write more than just the word "time!" under the survey question asking about limitations, the respondents noted they feel they (or the recipients) cannot devote as much as would be helpful. This especially limits their influence, effectiveness, and their ability to teach, sponsor, groom the recipient, and cultivate the relationship.

Twenty-four percent of the respondents expressed frustration or discouragement over what they perceived as their lack of experience in mentoring. Some find they do not have the breadth of experience that would be helpful. A Carleton '96 public librarian, for example, feels restricted: "I'm lacking a ton of experience. I've only worked full-time for one library and know there's a ton more to learn. All I can offer as a mentor are experiences based on one library situation!"

"Feelings of failure" (Allen et al. 1997a, 82) arise from two reactions that mentors have to the mentoring relationship: mentors may come to believe that they and the recipient are a "wrong match," or they may also find it "difficult to accept differences" between what they and a mentored individual believe the latter should do about some situation. In either circumstance, the mentor ultimately concludes that the relationship has not been cultivated as it could or should have been. A Carleton '81 special librarian notes, "I can be judgmental and have not learned very well how to mentor someone I personally dislike." On this point, researchers such as Kram (1985) and Allen (2003) would say that a mentoring relationship is not possible if it is not consensual. And it is here that organizationally established mentoring programs must be particularly careful in matching individuals. In other cases, "people have wanted more from me than I could give" (Denison '81; academic). The converse can also be problematic, that is "balancing their need for knowledge and growth with my urge to say too much at times" (Earlham '62; public). As Levinson (1978, 99) notes, "The mentor represents a mixture of parent and peer; he must be both and not purely either one."

Nine percent of the Alums, like the following two academic librarians, noted that mentoring can require more than they are able to provide. Most of these respondents cited lack of sufficient authority as the reason for feeling limited:

> I can't always open doors, only suggest direction, because I don't have the authority necessary. (Denison '71)
>
> I don't have enough clout to help someone actually land a job. (Kalamazoo '66)

A Grinnell '86 public librarian also clearly wants to be able to do more as a sponsor, guide and host for younger newcomers:

> I am unable to provide [enough] financial support for my mentees to attend conferences and workshops and thus make connections with other professionals and be exposed to other thoughts and ideas.

For a few of the CALS Alums, the organizational structure is a hindrance in that it constrains the amount of time available, even in formal mentorship programs. For others, the structure becomes a hindrance when the mentor finds there are few ways to promote the new professional or that "there is no recognition from the administration that mentoring is beneficial" (Grinnell '66; school).

The final two questions the Alums were asked regarding mentoring others covered what they saw as the most important contributions they had made to the newcomers (Q.V-11) and how they would like others to describe them in their mentoring role (Q.V-12). Data on contributions were gathered using Levinson's (1978) five characterizations with the definitions rephrased on the questionnaire just enough to make them resonate with the CALS participants in their role as mentors:

- A teacher in enhancing someone else's skills and intellectual development.
- A sponsor in using your influence and contacts to facilitate someone else's entry and possible advancement in their field or work.
- A host and guide in helping initiate someone else into a new occupational and social world, acquainting him or her with its values, customs, resources, and cast of characters.
- An advisor providing counsel, moral support and direction.
- An exemplar through your own virtues, achievements and actions.

Contributions

As shown in table 91, the CALS participants describe their contributions primarily as *Advisors, Teachers*, and *Sponsors* (Q.V-11F).

Table 91: Contributions by Alums as Mentors

Contributions	Alums (%)
Advisor	32
Teacher	31
Sponsor	24
Host/Guide	8
Exemplar	3

Advisor

Some Alums fulfill an *Advisor* role as they "provide practical advice," "listen to their questions/problems/situations," and "give position feedback and constructive advice" (Carleton '76 school; Denison '81 academic; Kalamazoo '71 school, respectively). Others offer "counseling when they hit a wall" (Denison '71; academic) and "my skills when necessary" (Swarthmore '91; public). But for the majority of the CALS respondents the *Advisor* contributions are in the form of "moral support as they [the recipients] make choices" (Carleton '71; special), supporting them as they "build self-esteem" (Earlham '81; special), giving them "a shoulder to cry on" (Lawrence '71; public), and "convincing them of what they have to contribute—of their own unique strengths" (Earlham '66; academic). Some of this moral support may be solely from a professional perspective, but some may come from moral concerns in the spiritual or religious sense. (Recall that 72 percent of Alums describe themselves as having a religion.) The range of *Advisor*-related actions is illustrated in this comment from a Swarthmore '66 academic librarian: "I provide a sounding board and advice; professional networking; and motivation and encouragement."

Teacher

Some CALS participants feel they have "provided specific skills and know-how" (Earlham '76; public) in specialties (such as cataloging, reference, and collection development) or in more basic fundamentals. An example of the former is found in a Carleton '66 special librarian who feels that her most important contribution is that "I have shown new catalogers how to do their work carefully, thoughtfully, and with regards to the audience they are serving." An example of the "basics" comes from a Swarthmore '62 public librarian who says she has taught those she has mentored "to read, think, and use language independently—[and] to write creatively." Other Alums focus on the personal attributes of those they have mentored, such as a Grinnell '86 public librarian, who believes she has "helped them gain more self-confidence in job skills, and encouraged them to keep improving and striving to do a better job." Then there is the Earlham '66 public librarian who believes the recipients of her mentoring have "learned that rules can be broken and that a workplace can be a fun place." Another Earlham Alum ('76; public), however, reflects a slightly more serious tone when she writes that her greatest contribution is "probably my attitude of professionalism and belief in *service*" (emphasis in original).

Sponsor

In this role, the Alums have done everything from "getting [recipients] interested in the field" (Carleton '76; academic) to "opening doors," "providing career paths," "securing work promotions," and "helping them achieve tenure" (Carleton '71 academic; Denison '62 special; Earlham '71 public; Lawrence '66 academic, respectively). A Kalamazoo '66 academic librarian feels particularly proud of having helped "one college student go to library school, come back to work for me, supervise her original supervisor, [and] move on to another library. She is now an AUL [assistant/associate university librarian]!"

Exemplar and *Host/Guide*

The 11 percent of Alums whose comments fall into these two categories emphasize "modeling philosophical and practical behaviors in the profession" (Lawrence '71; public), and "being an exemplar of expertise and of values" (Macalester '81; school). Hosts talk of "helping [recipients] see the abundance of opportunities available" in the field (Earlham '66 special), and of "providing content and technical knowledge to help people move through" and "navigate the organizational terrain" (Carleton '66; public and Kalamazoo '86; public, respectively).

CALS Alums as Recipients and as Mentors

As table 92 shows, the Alums clearly have a bias toward the *Advisor* role both in terms of how they view themselves and how they view their own mentors (Q.V-11F and Q.V-9). Akin to Kram's (1985) "Counseling" function, *Advising* is a psychosocial characteristic. The Alums looked to their own mentors for advice, counsel, feedback, moral support, and active listening. As mentors, the CALS Alums find themselves now performing these same roles. It makes sense, therefore, that they would feel positive about being seen this way. The *Advisor* role most closely parallels what they have experienced in both aspects of the mentoring relationship.

Next in frequency, the CALS Alums see their own contributions to be *Teaching* followed by *Sponsoring*. And in the Alums' eyes, their mentors' role as teacher is especially strong. Levinson's (1978) "Teaching" function is akin to Kram's (1985) career characteristics of "Coaching" and "Challenging Assignments." Here the Alums see their mentors as focusing on the immediate work to be done by the Alums and on the competency levels the Alums are developing. Kram (1985, 31) finds that especially through giving the recipient challenging assignments, the mentor is able to see the recipient "develop essential technical and managerial skills through work that encourages learning." As recipients of a mentor's teaching, the Alums gain knowledge not only in their work tasks but also in areas that prepare them for career advancement. When the CALS Alums become mentors, they see how teaching newcomers enables the latter to become more competent and grow. In addition, they and the newcomers begin to share ideas and insights, which enables the Alums-as-mentors also to continue to grow within the field.

Kram (1985, 25) claims that *Sponsorship* "is the most frequently observed career function." In many kinds of organizations, including the various types of libraries, sponsorship

Table 92: Rankings of Contributions and Descriptions by CALS Alums

CALS Alums Contributions as Mentors to Others			CALS Alums' View of Their Mentors	
Type of Mentoring	%	Rank	%	Rank
Advisor	32	1	26	2
Teacher	31	2	31	1
Sponsor	24	3	20	3
Host/Guide	8	4	11	5
Exemplar	3	5	13	4

opens the way for the new professional to move out of the newcomer role and into an "up-and-coming" or seasoned role within the organization. As several respondents have noted, their mentors used contacts to get the Alums on committees, involved in professional associations, and into new positions. When the Alums became mentors, they in turn found themselves wanting to "open doors" (Carleton '71; academic) in the same way for those they were now helping. In contributing through sponsorship to the growth of new professionals, the Alums are socializing the newcomer into positions where they may be seen as viable candidates for handling greater responsibilities.

The remaining mentoring function in Kram's (1985) typology that is similar to those of Levinson (1978) is "Role Modeling"—what Levinson calls the "Exemplar" function. Where *Sponsorship* is the most frequently observed career function, *Role Modeling* is the most frequently reported psychosocial function: The newcomer finds in a mentor "a particular image of who he can become" (Kram 1985, 33). As they observe their mentors, they see traits they admire in how to handle difficult situations, daily work life, and novel experiences. For some Alums, this may include taking on attributes of their mentors, such as certain behaviors and personal values. For other Alums, mentors in management positions essentially provide insights into what it would be like to be a manager, thus allowing these Alums to develop a sense of whether becoming a manager might be a desirable career move. When the CALS Alums began mentoring, they probably became aware that some of their recipients looked up to them in this fashion. But given its last place ranking among the Alums' sense of contributions, it is clear that they are not totally comfortable with this kind of situation. The idea of being a role model is flattering, but it can also be awkward. For example, if the recipient of the mentoring is a new hire within the Alum's own department, such role modeling by the newcomer can lead other staff to see her/him as the boss' favorite, or "teacher's pet" (Swarthmore '66; academic).

The role of *Host/Guide,* although dealt with by Levinson (1978), is not a part of Kram's (1985) typology. However, it is likely that this activity occurs during what Kram (1985) terms the "initiation phase," when the newcomer first moves into the new occupational and social world of the organization and the field. During this phase the Alums experience their greatest uncertainty about their choice of career and their work: it is all very new. Their mentors help

Table 93: Ranking of Contributions and Description by CALS Alums and Their Mentors

Contributions	Alums as Mentors to Others		How Alums Would Like to Be Seen		Alums' View of Their Mentors	
Description	%	*Rank*	%	*Rank*	%	*Rank*
Advisor	32	1	23	1	26	2
Exemplar	3	5	21	2	13	4
Host/Guide	8	4	21	2	11	5
Teacher	31	2	21	2	31	1
Sponsor	24	3	13	5	20	3

show them "the ropes" by sharing "insight into the culture of the profession" (Kalamazoo '91; special). According to Kram's (1985) research, this period lasts six months to a year. Jarvis (1999, 16) also believes that an initial period of professional socialization happens quickly; it can be conceived of as the Alums' "probationary period" when they and the organization learn about each other and determine if the Alum has been appropriately placed. During this time, the mentor serving as *Host/Guide* helps the Alum gain both content knowledge and process knowledge. Once they become mentors, the CALS Alums also move their own newcomers fairly quickly through this phase. Most of the weight of the probationary period is on the newcomer's shoulders with the Alum mentoring her or him along with enough socialization both to impart necessary organizational knowledge and to assess the quality and quickness of the newcomer's response. If the response is sufficiently good and the relationship has developed, both Alum and newcomer then move into the cultivation phrase where true advising, teaching, and sponsorship roles are initiated.

How the Alums Would Like Others to Describe Them as Mentors

It is intriguing to find (table 93 above) that while the CALS participants downplay the roles of *Host/Guide* and *Exemplar* in discussing their contributions (ranked fourth and fifth out of five), they would indeed like others to describe them that way (Q.V-11F; Q.V-12; Q.V-9). Four of the five mentoring characteristics are essentially tied (i.e., *Advisor, Exemplar, Host/Guide,* and *Teacher*), especially in contrast with the 13 percent who choose *Sponsor.*

Other than agreement on a preference for the *Advisor* role, there are significant contrasts in terms of ranking between Alums' mentoring of others, and how they wish to be seen. In the survey, the CALS respondents identified their contributions through an open-ended question which was then analyzed using the Levinson (1978) characteristics. In describing their contributions, they used words, phrases, and sentences that strongly reflect enhancing recipients' skills (*Teacher*), helping to bring or advance them in the field (*Sponsor*), and providing them with moral support, counsel, and direction (*Advisor*). This suggests that the Alums find it more difficult to make statements along the lines of "my greatest contribution is that they all take after me" (*Exemplar*).

Table 94: How Alums Would Like to Be Seen as Mentors (by College)

Mentoring Characteristics	Avg (%)	College (%)							
		C	D	E	G	K	L	M	S
Advisor	23	20	28	22	19	23	24	27	23
Teacher	21	22	21	22	18	21	18	21	23
Exemplar	21	22	28	21	31	21	22	19	18
Host/Guide	21	21	21	21	19	21	25	18	16
Sponsor	13	14	3	13	6	12	11	12	18
Other	1	0	0	0	6	1	0	3	3

As for the low ranking of *Host/Guide* in terms of contributions, recall that Jarvis (1999) claims that once socialized into their profession, the Alums become less and less aware of all they have learned. Thus, it is possible that many simply do not consider mentoring as a socialization process where they, as more seasoned members of the profession, have indeed been introducing newcomers to the values, customs, resources, and cast of characters in the field. That is, they may see their contributions as more locally centered on immediate work and work practices where advising, teaching, and then sponsoring have the most immediate applicability in helping newcomers become full practitioners within the local setting and the field.

The Alums could checkmark as many of the five mentoring characteristics as they wished. By college, those who would like to be seen as *Advisors* range from 19-28 percent (low, Grinnell; high, Denison) with Carleton, Grinnell, and Lawrence Alums ranking it lower than first (table 94 above).

Carleton, Earlham, and Kalamazoo Alums are most favorably disposed to being seen in one of four roles: *Teacher, Exemplar, Host/Guide*, and *Advisor*. Denison Alums prefer *Advisor* and *Exemplar*, and are the least interested of all the college respondents in the role of *Sponsor*. Grinnell Alums place significant emphasis on being seen as *Exemplars*. Lawrence Alums would like to be seen as *Hosts/Guides* and as *Advisors*. Macalester Alums emphasize the *Advisor* role. And Swarthmore Alums, while favoring being seen as *Advisors* and *Teachers*, express the highest interest of respondents from all the colleges in being seen as *Sponsors*. While few Alums made comments in the "Other" category, the majority of those who did suggested that "Friend" should be part of the typology, and hoped they themselves would be seen that way.

Advisor is a desired characterization by Alums in four cohorts: 1971-75, 1981-85, 1991-96, and especially 1996-2000 (table 95). The focus of CALS Alums in the 1996-2000 cohort on being seen as *Advisors, Hosts/Guides*, and *Sponsors* may reflect what they have either experienced or wish to receive from their own mentors. At least at this stage in their careers, these Alums appear to have no interest in being described as *Teachers* or *Exemplars*—roles which they may feel require more LIS career experience than they currently possess: the 1962-65 and 1981-85 cohorts, however, do wish to be seen as *Teachers*, then as *Exemplars*, and also as *Advisors*. The 1966-70 and 1976-80 cohorts are more interested in the *Host/Guide* role. Being

Table 95: How Alums Would Like to Be Seen as Mentors (by Cohort)

Mentoring Characteristics	Avg (%)	Cohort (%)							
		62-	66-	71-	76-	81-	86-	91-	96-
Advisor	23	22	21	26	22	26	19	25	43
Teacher	21	29	21	19	21	23	19	21	0
Exemplar	21	22	21	23	20	21	23	18	0
Host/Guide	21	15	23	18	24	17	25	20	29
Sponsor	13	10	13	13	13	11	15	10	29
Other	1	1	1	1	0	2	0	6	0

seen as *Advisors* and *Exemplars* is the focus of the 1971-75 cohort. The 1991-95 cohort find the roles of *Advisor, Teacher*, and *Host/Guide* more appealing. That cohort also made the greatest number of "Other" comments with, as noted above, an emphasis on adding "Friend" to the set of characterizations.

The 1962-65, 1981-85, and 1991-95 cohorts express the least interest in being seen as *Sponsors*. Overall, 255 of the 431 CALS respondents (59 percent) have been the recipients of mentoring, and 197 (46 percent) have mentored others (Q.VI-1; Q.VI-11). They see themselves (and their mentors) first of all as *Advisors* providing counsel, moral support, and direction. After that, they vary to some degree by college and cohort. The Alums address mentoring from the classical, organizational perspective. They believe they have contributed to helping others through being mentors, and find that they themselves have gained professionally and personally both by having been mentored and then by being mentors.

Summary

This chapter has considered whether the Alums demonstrated a service orientation beyond that inherent within the field of library and information science. A comparison of their Myers-Briggs Type Indicator behavioral preference with those of the 1992 ACRL study of SLA members and ALA academic, public, and school librarians found that the two groups were alike except that, notably, the CALS sample has an even more introverted and judging nature than their ACRL counterparts. However, the value of the CALS-ACRL comparison is twofold. First, it established that, although the CALS professionals had a particular undergraduate experience, as librarians they are comparable to a national profile of librarians. Second, it found that 45 percent of Alums fall into MBTI® behavioral preferences that type the Alums as inwardly directed, and favor reflection and concentration. They like to pursue things in depth; they value deep friendships. They think things through before acting on them. The CALS respondents judge in the sense that they deal with the outer world by giving it order—indeed preferring order in their lives and their workplace. They tend, therefore, to be systematic in their approach to problems and to activities. They are comfortable with structure in- and outside of work, with the idea of setting goals for themselves or with regard to projects, and with activities requiring planning and scheduling. Only 9 percent of the CALS sample, however, demonstrated behavioral preferences that are strongly oriented toward feeling a real concern "for what others think or want, and try to handle things with due regard for the other person's feelings . . . Sociable, popular, sympathetic" (Scherdin 1994b, 130). Thus, within the Myers-Briggs framework, the Alums are like librarians outside of this study, and the majority of CALS Alums cannot be said to demonstrate behaviors that would easily lead to an extension of service toward others outside of their workplace.

The CALS study also found that the Alums were not heavily involved in civic engagement. Only 39 percent identified areas of civic participation—one of the smallest responses in the survey. And as the age of the Alums increased, their active engagement decreased. Cultural, religious, and fraternal organizations were the only areas in which Alums across all colleges and cohorts held membership. In their nominal commitment to civic identification, the Alums reflect Putnam's (2000, 63) finding that, within the United States, "active involvement in face-to-face organizations has plummeted . . . We can surely find individual exceptions . . . but the broad picture is one of declining membership in community organizations." Thus, while the arenas of interest of CALS members (i.e., cultural, religious, and fraternal) may indicate a service orientation beyond their career, the 51 percent of respondents who did not list any civic activity suggests that a service interest does not extend into the broader, nonwork community.

In sharp contrast to the 39 percent response to the survey question on civic engagement (Q.IV-24), there was a 93 to 96 percent response rate from CALS participants to two questions specifically about religion. When they answered the study's questionnaire, fewer Alums had a religious affiliation than when they were undergraduates. However, if a respondent was religious in college, she or he most likely still had the same religion and gave it the same sense of personal importance. During their undergraduate years, for those who did follow a religious practice it had a service aspect. Those who viewed religion along a cultural approach saw it as a way to fulfill socially oriented values and behaviors. Alums who viewed their undergraduate religious practice as a grounding expressed the conviction that it was central to what they did in and with their lives. There are CALS members who had an intellectual conception of religion, and for them it was both a practice and a philosophy. They were apt to envision religious practice as a demonstration of their moral beliefs—especially toward others. Respondents whose view was spiritual rather than denominational seemed less inclined to describe it in service-oriented terms, but rather as a one-to-one relationship with a higher power.

In considering their current religious orientation, the Alums who expressed religion in cultural, grounding, or spiritual fashion underwent the most change. Those espousing a spiritual approach doubled, while those holding the other approaches declined in number. However, the spiritual approach is an individualized connection with a higher power or sense of universality. Thus, while there is a strong association between the Alums and religion, this study did not find that the CALS respondents necessarily imbued it with a strong service component.

The Alums' involvement in mentoring is the last activity analyzed for indications of a service orientation. Mentoring is a very common form of service through which new professionals are socialized into both the field and a specific work setting. Close to two-thirds of the CALS participants have received mentoring and 46 percent have mentored others. All of those who now mentor have been recipients of mentoring. At least some Alums from each college and each cohort have been mentored and have mentored others. Here there is strong and abundant evidence of CALS members demonstrating a desire to serve others from within the parameters of their normal work responsibilities. While 29 percent indicated that mentoring others is a part of their job, 17 percent saw it as a way to give back to or recruit for the field, 12 percent saw potential in a newcomer and wanted to help that individual grow, and 7 percent identified mentoring others as an altruistic action—a form of "prosocial behavior" (Allen 2003, 136). Indeed, just under a quarter of the Alums identified as a benefit seeing those they had mentored grow as individuals and as professionals. Alums who have mentored described their contributions primarily as being advisors, teachers, and sponsors for newcomers. That is, they have provided counsel, moral support, and direction; they have helped enhance the newcomer's skills and intellectual development; and they have used their influence and contacts to facilitate the newcomer's entry and possible advancement within their position or the LIS field. The Alums believe they have contributed to helping others through being mentors, as well as benefiting professionally and personally themselves by such actions.

It seems from the topics covered in this chapter that the CALS respondents see value in contributing to the service focus of their career field more than they do in at least the civic and religious areas of their lives. However, the fact that their behavioral preferences support, and are supported by, their career reinforces a view of libraries as places that provide service to others and librarians as the people who make such services a reality.

CHAPTER 8

Conclusion: A Service Orientation

This book has described the work lives of a group of LIS practitioners from their undergraduate experiences through to their careers within the field of library and information science. *Service* has been an underlying theme, in that an orientation toward helping others is a fundamental part both of the colleges the CALS Alums attended and of the career field they chose. However, as was explored in the previous chapter, the participants in the study underlying this book focus their service orientation more within their internal work place than in the external civic and religious realms. This chapter considers the service professions and how a newcomer is socialized into a profession. Findings that connect the Alums to a particular concept of service serve to conclude the book.

I. Service Professions

In considering service as the raison d'être of a library, Rubin (1998, 379) states that

> librarianship is quintessentially serving a special *social* function, rather than just a specific activity. It is engaged in a social service, emphasizing the welfare of people over profit. Its model historically reaches back to an age in which professions were meant to improve the society: clergy, lawyers, doctors, teachers, nurses, social workers. These professions were dedicated to the betterment of people, not increases in profit, which were characteristics of positions in business and industry. (emphasis in original)

Institutions in the United States are often divided broadly into the governmental sector (i.e., federal, state, and local), the private sector (commercial, profit-making), and the independent (nonprofit) sector. The service professions live almost entirely within the nonprofit sector, which has these characteristics (adapted from McAdam 1988, 4-5):

- The organizations within it do not generally attempt to make and retain a profit.
- Primacy of cause is foremost in that a nonprofit organization's reason for existence is to carry out some good work or to advocate, pursue, or advance a cause.
- Its roots are found in the religious teachings of Buddha, Confucius, Jesus, Mohammed, and Moses.
- Its core lies in caring for others, to such a degree that some nonprofit organizations are largely or entirely comprised of volunteers.
- The sector contains organizations of great diversity and variety.
- Direct service is core to the sector, but advocacy and activism are also important functions.
- The sector is labor intensive in that it is the services, rather than manufactured goods, which are the "output."

The service professions within the nonprofit sector include the fields devoted to the arts, education, social services, and religion. McAdam (1988, 12) identifies the functions of this diversity of nonprofit organizations as

- Educating
- Curing
- Searching for new knowledge
- Entertaining
- Preaching, consoling, and nurturing the spirit
- Lobbying for reform
- Serving and helping

Regardless of what specific occupations one might label "service professions," service professionals understand that their work focuses on helping others. Most consider the true "gain" achieved by their work as some degree of betterment in the life of another person, rather than just in the coffers of the organization. McAdam (1988, 20) quotes Blotnick's study of the careers of 5,000 Americans over the age of 25 which found that service professionals "aren't seeking just a job; they want a career, a personally fulfilling profession." Another value evidenced in the nonprofit sector is "an above-average level of independence of action or freedom to develop one's own approaches to problems" (McAdam 1988, 21). A third is the generally positive work environment that such organizations exhibit—positive in the sense that there seems to be "a slightly higher belief in the dignity and worth of the individual" (McAdam 1988, 21). A fundamental factor of this sector is that "the people [within them] *care*" (McAdam 1988, 23; emphasis in original). Such people seem to have the kind of service orientation that includes the attribute of helpfulness, or as the title of a 1999 book on academic librarianship puts it: *People Come First* (Montanelli and Stenstrom). All of this is not to say that the nonprofit fields are wholly devoid of professionals who seek only self-serving personal gain; rather the goal here is to point out fundamentals that underlie the basic nature of nonprofit, service professions such as LIS.

II. The Attraction of Service Work

As presented in chapter 2, a substantial literature finds that parents and siblings influence children's conceptions of and interest in different careers. That chapter also discussed the topics of families and career choice, about which Dick and Rallis (1991, 283) lay out the following general framework:

> [S]tudents make their career choices on the basis of their beliefs about themselves and their own abilities and their beliefs about the relative values of different careers. A career's perceived value is determined by intrinsic factors such as intellectual interests as well as extrinsic factors such as salary expectation and the cost and length of future training. These beliefs, in turn, are formed through the interpretation of past experiences (grades, test scores, and related experiences either in or out of school) and the perception of the attitudes and expectations of others, such as parents, teachers, counselors, and so on, whom we refer to as *socializers* . . . [S]ocializers play a central role in the model. Not only can the socializers exert an influence on the student through their attitudes and expectations, they can also provide experiences for the student and influence how students interpret those experiences. The influence is not one-way, because a student's experiences are also shaped by his or her own aptitudes, and the student's aptitudes and experiences can shape the socializers' attitudes and expectations for the student. Finally, students and their socializers live in a cultural milieu. The surrounding culture helps shape the socializers' attitudes and expectations, the student's perceptions of them, and the student's beliefs about career values. (emphasis in original)

Of the 26 broadly defined occupations that represent the areas in which Alums' family members work, seven are service (or service-related) fields: health professions, K-12 education, higher education, LIS, religious positions, social service work, and volunteerism. High percentages of the Alums' mothers and fathers work in K-12 education and higher education; siblings work in K-12 education and the health professions. As CALS Alums were growing up and being influenced by their family members' areas of work, 41 percent of their mothers, 33 percent of their fathers, 24 percent of their brothers, 40 percent of their sisters (and 34 percent of unspecified siblings) worked, at some point, in one or more of these specific service occupations. These Alums began to develop an understanding that one could work at serving others in a variety of ways—but most notably by teaching or helping. As children, 36 percent of all of the Alums wanted to work in one of these fields. By the time they were first-year college students, the figure had risen to 39 percent. After college, close to 30 percent of the CALS Alums considered K-16 education, the health professions, the social services, or volunteerism as potential careers.

Even if they did not have family members involved in service professions, it is likely that the CALS Alums were exposed to some of the seven fields through secondary school or college community service work. In chapter 2, it was reported that over 20 percent of the Alums participated in social service and volunteer activities of some kind while in college. These activities included working with libraries, religious organizations, hospitals, K-12 support and tutoring. Additionally, the deans and provosts of the CALS colleges indicate that the majority of their students are involved in some form of service work on- or off-campus. Boyer (1987, 294) says "a good college affirms that service to others is a central part of education." Eleven percent of the Alums explicitly include service as one of the values they gained from their undergraduate college experience; others allude to it. While only 3 percent of the Alums indicate that serving others is the ultimate reason they chose LIS as their career, their explanations on this point show a range of meaning. A Carleton '81 special librarian who has changed careers wrote that, "I want to continue to use my skills and legal knowledge to help the underserved with [their] legal needs." A Denison '81 academic librarian "wanted a career in which I'd be of service to others." A Grinnell '76 public librarian "perceived providing access to information as a tool to help people." A Kalamazoo '62 academic librarian says, "[I] didn't want to teach—[but] liked the idea of a 'helping' profession."

III. Socialization into the Profession

While the definition of a *profession* varies by era and field, some characteristics do seem to be ever present. No definition is attempted here as the works of Abbott (1988), Carr-Saunders and Wilson (1933), Freidson (1973, 1986, 1994), Johnson (1972), Kimball (1992), Larson (1977), and others amply discuss the range of considerations. However, Moore's description of a *professional* sets the tone (1970, 5-6 quoted in Weidman et al. 2001): A professional

- Practices a full-time occupation, which comprises the principal source of his earned income
- Must be committed to a calling, that is the treatment of the occupation, and all its requirements, as an enduring set of normative and behavioral expectations
- Is set apart from the laity by various signs and symbols, but by the same token is identified with his peers—often in formalized organizations
- Possesses esoteric, but useful knowledge and skills, based on specialized training or education of exceptional duration and perhaps of exceptional difficulty
- Practices his occupation by perceiving the needs of individual or collective clients that are relevant to his competence and by attending to those needs by competent performance

- Proceeds by his own judgment and authority; he thus enjoys autonomy restrained by responsibility

A service profession does always seem to have (and use) a recognized body of literature to inform its practitioners' decision making and to produce specialized knowledge; a requirement of graduate level education in its fields of endeavor; autonomy for its practitioners in the conduct of their work; and a professional body that certifies entrance into the field. In addition, although not mentioned by Moore (1970), most professions have a code of ethics focused on integrity, right conduct, and serving the public good.

Library and information science contains all these characteristics and, like other service professions, its raison d'être is not to be self-serving but, rather, to provide a helping or an altruistic service to a community of users who rely upon its practitioners for assistance in resolving some kind or set of needs. These attributes of a profession are lofty sounding and one learns about them through anticipatory, then transitional, and finally professional socialization. Socialization is a "mechanism through which new members learn the values, norms, knowledge, beliefs, and the interpersonal and other skills that facilitate role performance and further group goals" (Mortimer and Simmons 1978, 422). *Anticipatory socialization* is the initial process of encountering, identifying, and internalizing the values, attitudes, and behavioral patterns of that prospective profession (Merton 1968). In terms of the idea of a service profession, this would have occurred for the Alums through interactions with and observations of family members and others involved in the field's activities. This aspect of socialization is generally "implicit, unwitting, and informal" (Merton, quoted in O'Kane et al. 1977). However, it serves to move Alums from awareness of perhaps several service professions, including especially education, to awareness of LIS itself.

When the CALS Alums' self-perception of what they were good at, what they wanted, or what they valued found parallels in LIS or some of its members, the Alums then had a group with which to identify. Such a "reference group" is one with which an aspirant compares herself or himself ("Am I like they are?") and within which she or he begins to desire membership ("I think I would like that kind of work") (Hyman 1968; Merton and Rossi 1968). When factors like family or experience, personal traits or preferences, the idea of a job or career, and the awareness of a reference group begin to coalesce around a specific field, that field begins to seem particularly attractive. Two examples: A Carleton '86 special librarian was influenced by both a family member and exposure to LIS work: "My mother was able to work in a variety of types of libraries in many parts of the world as I grew up. I liked the possibility of such variety." A Kalamazoo '71 public librarian recalls how certain preferences guided her choice, noting that "I knew that I wanted work that connected me to the community, and I was not at all interested in social work or religious work."

Anticipatory socialization occurs before one actually becomes a member of the selected profession. That is, an Alum may begin to reflect LIS attitudes and values, but the full role of an information professional (that is, *being* one) requires practicing the skills associated with the field. Socialization is a developmental process. As the Alums began their LIS graduate education, they moved into the *transitional socialization* stage. Although their role expectations remain idealized, this stage differs from the previous one in that "the novice receives formal instruction in the knowledge upon which future professional authority will be based" (Weidman et al. 2001, 13). Here the CALS Alums learned about the history of the field, the kinds and types of work within it, and how to perform certain of its tasks. According to Widstrom (1998, 7), those with no prior work experience in a field "do not possess [its] culture. They do not know the language. They are bereft of the necessary orientations and perspectives." Through course assignments, practica, internships, and other experiences, the Alums not only observed and interacted with incumbent role practitioners, they were also able to practice work-related roles. For those who were already working in a library setting, the graduate program enabled them to bring together their existing practice skills with the normative standards of the profession and the field. Recall that prior to beginning their LIS graduate work, only 33 percent of the Alums had had any experience actually working in an LIS organization; in contrast, 75 percent of them worked in a library or other LIS agency while they were taking graduate courses. Scholarios et al. (2003, 183) find that graduate programs help embed the values and expectations of the profession, thus making it more likely that the socialization will persist as one enters and moves around within the profession.

Professional socialization occurs within the LIS work setting itself. As "new professionals," the Alums became integrated into the reality of both a specific organization and the field. In the work setting, they adapted what they had learned and observed into the actual normative attitudes, values, goals, and culture of the organization (Ashforth et al. 1998; Becker and Carper 1956b; Van Maanen and Schein 1979; Wanous 1980). This accounts for CALS respondents, such as the following two, who had a negative image of the field while in graduate school but a positive one after they became practitioners:

Lawrence '76; public librarian:

> In graduate school: "I thought it was like being a secretary."
>
> Now: "I love the variety. [And] the values of the profession—service, literacy, freedom, lifelong learning."

Swarthmore '91; public librarian:

> In graduate school: "A profession that's female-dominated, probably primarily composed of introverts, with some potentially troubling shades of hierarchical decision-making."
>
> Now: "The best thing about LIS is the chance to get excited over the world of information, and to encourage others to feel the same. (Did you know red-faced macaques in chilly areas of Japan warm up by bathing in hot springs?)"

Beagan (2001) provides some useful markers to characterize the move from student to professional. Her reference is to medical students, who practice their profession before actually becoming doctors. However, these points also denote professional socialization for those, like our Alums, who encounter them as part of socialization within their first professional position:

- First experiences become commonplace
- One takes on a professional appearance
- There is a change in language, thinking, and communication skills
- One learns how to negotiate the organizational hierarchy
- A professional-user relationship is experienced
- Playing the role gradually becomes the real role
- There is a change in the "self"

Changes such as these also account for how theory learned in graduate courses becomes practical in the work setting. In commenting on LIS graduate education, 6 percent of the Alums signaled a preference for (primarily) "more practice" and "less theory." Several reinforced their point with examples like that of this Lawrence '71 school librarian: "Believe it or not, my small school just automated this year—before that we had the good old check-out cards. Had I not gotten experience with that, I would have been at a real loss." A few, however, recognized the value of both theory and practice. Two public librarians from the 1976-80 cohort provide examples:

> My training was both not practical enough—not specific enough, yet not theoretical enough. I see the value of exploring both ends of the spectrum. (Carleton)

> Theoretical grounding—values of the profession, ethics, principles—will serve well in the long term, but also you need to include practical components. (Grinnell)

Jarvis (1999, 51) explains that "newcomers to an occupation enter practice with the theory they have learned from secondary experience and legitimated by their own rational thinking or by the authority they have ascribed to their professors. But in practice, they have to make that theory their own, to legitimate it by their own pragmatic practice. In the process, they not only learn the practical knowledge but also acquire appropriate skills." In other words, they do not actually *know* theory until they have enacted it in practice. Thus, while anticipatory socialization reveals some of the most external aspects of the profession, and transitional socialization provides the basic professional rudiments, it is through professional socialization that professional expertise is developed—enabling the Alum to become a true member of the LIS profession: a *practitioner* of it. In *practice*, the profession's norms, values, standards, and body of theory are no longer abstract but are integrated into the work being undertaken. Ultimately, the value of the received theories (i.e., of "formal knowledge") becomes so integrated with practical knowledge that "the original learning plays a less and less conscious part in [practitioners'] actions. As expertise develops, they lose awareness of that formal learning" (Watson-Boone 2000a, 86). This can lead to the feeling that it was unnecessary to have learned theory at all.

The CALS Alums have "learned to 'be' their occupation—it [has] provided them with an identity" (Jarvis 1999, 57). As they became socialized as members within their profession, they took on roles associated with that profession. By first learning the attributes of the profession (anticipatory socialization), then incorporating them (transitional socialization), and finally by displaying and utilizing them (professional socialization), the Alums changed themselves. In addition to the personal roles or identities they may have (such as parent or spouse), the Alums also now had a career or professional identity.

IV. A Service Orientation

An orientation toward helping others is part of the character of the CALS Alums—both in regard to their support of library users and to their mentoring of newcomers. Library and information science is a service profession exhibiting McAdam's (1988) "serving and helping" functions. As Rubin (1998, 379) indicated, librarianship "is engaged in a social service, emphasizing the welfare of people over profit. Its model historically reaches back to an age in which professions were meant to improve the society."

Key reasons why people choose to work in a service profession include believing that being a member of such a field will allow them to "make a difference"—to act and work in accord with their values and ethics. Service professionals may value having a career in a personally fulfilling profession; having an above-average level of independence of action, or freedom to develop their own approaches to problems; and being in a generally positive work environment (McAdam 1988, 20-21). But more important, he asserts, "the people [within service professions] *care*. They seem to care about others: clients, colleagues, and society at large" (23; emphasis in original).

It would not be an accurate reflection of the data gathered during this study—meaning the Alums' comments—to describe *all* the CALS participants as having a passion for service. Only a small number would say that their LIS work is their "calling," if by that term one means that a commitment or dedication to service work is a core life goal and that they chose LIS as their career because they see it as a means to achieving that goal. However, it is well within the boundaries of this study's findings to say that almost all of the CALS Alums have an orientation toward service, and that they value what their liberal arts college education gave them in this regard. An underlying fundamental of service is its prosocial nature, that is, "service" consists of actions that are generally beneficial to people other than the initiator. Schroeder et al. (1995) distinguish three subcategories of prosocial behavior: cooperation, helping, and altruism. This study of 431 LIS professionals from a liberal arts college background has found that, to varying degrees, they do exhibit these behaviors.

Cooperation as a form of helping seems the least applicable to the CALS respondents in their acts of service. Cooperation is defined to mean, first, the involvement of two or more people working together toward a goal that is beneficial to both. And second, all those who are contributing to the outcome are more or less equal partners (Schroeder et al. 1995, 20). Considering that having specialized knowledge is one of the essential characteristics of a professional (Freidson 1973, 1994; Goode 1957; Hughes 1962; Merton 1982b), it is difficult to see how there could not be a power differential between the Alums and the users—or new LIS professionals—that they help. There are indeed Alums who talk of working with users, but in general the result is not a common goal that is beneficial to both. Rather, both the Alum and the user may feel self-satisfaction that the user has obtained what she or he needs, but only the user has directly benefited from the cooperative action. Thus, while CALS Alums may work in a cooperative manner with users, their actual prosocial behavior will meet the definitions of helping or altruism more than that of Schroeder et al.'s (1995) subcategory of cooperation.

Helping is

> an action that has the consequences of providing some benefit to or improving the well-being of another person . . . As long as one person's well-being is improved by the actions of another (e.g., giving a gift, providing resources to accomplish a task), helping has occurred. In some cases, . . . the benefactor may not even come into direct contact with the recipient of aid. (Schroeder et al. 1995, 16-17)

Helping may be formal and planned, it may differ according to the seriousness of the problem, it may be provided directly or indirectly (Schroeder et al. 1995). Helping is a core LIS activity. As chapter 4 discussed, practitioners in the LIS field bring users and the information they need together. Some information professionals help through direct services to, and active personal involvement with, their public, notably in the areas of reference, research, and access activities. Other information professionals provide indirect help through acquisition, preservation, cataloging and classification services. Gates (1990, 5) says that libraries first "became an indispensable agency of civilized society when the need arose for a place to keep written records of whatever sort in whatever form, so that they could be protected and preserved, used when needed, and handed on." Each of these activities fulfills Schroeder et al.'s (1995) definition of helping as providing a benefit for others. The largest concentration (42 percent) of CALS Alums say that helping users is the best part of their job, 33 percent consider service to others or helping people to be the best part of being in the field, and 12 percent of the Alums find helping users to be what they are proudest of in terms of their work or career. The connection between helping and an improvement in the other person's well-being is seen in this Carleton '81 public librarian's comment:

> I like [my work] best when I help someone for whom the outcome of our collaboration means a lot to them, be it finding research for a school project, medical information, or business info.

While the meaning of "helping" is fairly consistently understood, defining *altruism* suffers from a range of interpretations that perceive it very broadly, or very narrowly, or through reference to one or another discipline. For example, whereas *Webster's New World Dictionary 1980* defines altruism simply as the "unselfish concern for the welfare of others," Grusec et al. (2002, 458) believe that an action is not altruistic if it is not "costly" to the initiator. Schroeder et al. (1995, 19-20) consider these difficulties and propose that at a minimum altruism is "a helpful act that is carried out in the absence of obvious and tangible rewards" for the person initiating it. Altruistic behavior goes beyond just helping others; it stresses that the assistance is not only freely given but that the helper neither expects nor asks anything in return—no rewards, no personal benefits. A major difficulty with altruism, then, is that it rests in the internal motivational state of the helper. As such, while it may be felt by the helper it can rarely be observed by anyone else.

So how would we know if the CALS Alums' view of their service to others is altruistic in character, since both helping and altruism are carried out by respondents who want to improve the well-being of a user? One way to distinguish the two is to see altruism as including "a voluntary element in which the professional does *more than is required*" (Merton 1982a, 115; emphasis added). That one's work should contribute in some way toward benefiting users with their information needs is a minimum requirement for all information professionals—directly or indirectly, in all positions. Anyone entering the field is expected to know that. However, some Alums do *more* than is required when they carry out activities that ultimately help users. In identifying what she is proudest of in her LIS work or career, this Kalamazoo '71 academic librarian illustrates the kind of helping behavior that is typical of many CALS Alums: "Helping others find or learn to find information for accomplishing what they want." That is, she wants to "help others," and that help is to their benefit rather than for her own ("accomplishing what *they want*"). This, then, meets the basic requirement of LIS service work. The following Lawrence '76 academic librarian, however, seems to be seeing something beyond helping—and perhaps revealing an altruistic nature:

> It's sappy, but [I am proudest of] when I train a future health-care worker to use resources that will translate directly into better care for patients.

This Alum is certainly helping, but she also sees that it is not her efforts that will directly benefit patients; rather if she does her work well it will be reflected in the better work of some other person who will act directly to benefit patients. Batson and Shaw (1991) claim that altruism is found in a person's motivation, rather than in the consequences of her or his actions. And there may be some self-benefit in all altruistic acts (Schroeder et al. 1995). For example, the Lawrence Alum just quoted continues, "It gives me a warm fuzzy." Clearly there is self-satisfaction here, but this may in itself be evidence that she has gone beyond what is required in being of service, as it is doubtful she gets a "warm fuzzy" each time she helps a user. Thus there may be for some Alums particular instances during which they do more than is needed in their desire to help someone else.

Explicit reference to "service" is a part of the code of ethics of many LIS professional associations. The American Library Association's first version was discussed in 1903 and the first formal code was adopted in 1938 (Rubin 1998, 284). The current code includes a set of principles that are "to guide ethical decision making." The first statement reads:

> We provide the highest level of service to all library users through appropriate and usefully organized resources; equitable service policies; equitable access; and accurate, unbiased, and courteous responses to all requests. (ALA website, code of ethics; see Bibliography)

The Alums refer to service in several places throughout this study's questionnaire. In fact, 42 percent explicitly use the word "service" in their comments. For about half of the respondents, service is not confined to their LIS work; it is also present in the civic, religious, and mentoring activities they have undertaken.

The kind of service orientation that includes the attribute of helpfulness may be a key reason why service professionals would be involved in mentoring. In some ways, mentoring is a maturation of an individual's understanding of service. According to Allen (2003, 137), mentoring is "a specific form of helping behavior." It is related to altruism, as well as to a sense of obligation that develops as one accrues years in the profession. The CALS respondents illustrate this in that 46 percent of them have mentored others within the field, including 5 percent who have mentored others both inside and outside of the LIS field. Almost three-quarters of the 59 percent of Alums who have received mentoring report that their mentors came from within LIS. Allen (2003, 148 citing Penner et al.) notes that "people who score high on helpfulness are consistently inclined to engage in actions that benefit others." While many Alums became mentors because they see it as part of their job, 18 percent became mentors specifically because they were asked by a newcomer for help or just because they wanted to help others. And some of those who took on the role because they saw it as a job responsibility occasionally comment on the helping nature of this form of professional service.

With reference to LIS as a service profession and the CALS Alums as service professionals, the words of academic library director and 2005 ALA president Michael Gorman (1998, 62) illustrate how deeply held this belief in the concept of service may be:

> Libraries are about service or they are about nothing. In everything we do, from an individual act of assistance to a library user to our collective efforts to support education and preserve knowledge for posterity, we are animated by the will to serve. What motivates the altruism, the commitment to serve, that is present in all good librarians? Not material gain or fame—librarians are over blessed with neither. There are gains, though, in successful service; psychic rewards that cannot be quantified but are no less real for that. We get those rewards daily by giving benefits to library users and the wider community; by serving individuals and serving humankind. Before we can deliver and reap the rewards of service, we must identify the benefits that society can reasonably expect and then devise means of delivering those benefits. Service always has a purpose, and our careers of service have a purpose. They are neither menial nor small. It is hard to imagine a more worthy or nobler role in life.

In chapter 1, it was shown that the concept of service is embedded in the history, mission, and purpose statements of liberal arts colleges. In chapter 2, it was discussed as one of the dominant values of eight particular colleges of that type. In chapter 3, we find it among the careers or career interests of both Alums and their family members. Chapter 4 reveals it in our discussion of how the CALS participants view the LIS field and librarians, both before and after participants' graduate LIS education. Thirty percent of the comments that make up the image the Alums have of their undergraduate college librarians include the word "helpful." Chapters 5 and

6 find the Alums at work, and service and helping are part of the descriptions of what close to 50 percent of them value about their work or their LIS career. Chapter 7 clarifies that the respondents actuate service to a greater degree within their work than as part of at least some nonwork pursuits; their behavioral preferences may indicate a close correlation between a service interest and their chosen career field. And here in this final chapter, we have seen how comprehensively the CALS Alums fit the image of a service professional.

V. Conclusion

In the *International Encyclopedia of Information and Library Science* (1997, 210, 218), the information professions are defined as

> occupations specifically and explicitly dealing with information, in one form or another, on behalf of others, often in a not-for-profit context . . . The definition includes, in the first place, the librarian, the archivist and those practicing information science, information management, records management, documentation and other differently designated but closely related occupations . . . Information service is a subject of a fairly pervasive nature and all professional bodies in the library and information field are concerned with it.

Mason (1990, 122) defines "information professionals" as those who

> apply their special knowledge about information and information technology with one basic purpose in mind: to get the right information from the right source to the right client at the right time in the form most suitable for the use to which it is to be put and at a cost that is justified by its use.

He later adds the following:

> In addition to possessing technical knowledge, an information professional must render judgments in situations that are unique, uncertain, equivocal, and laden with value conflicts. Thus, ethics joins knowledge, methods, and history as a necessary component of the information professions . . . A client is dependent upon [the information professional] for certain services and must trust him [or her] to deliver them well. An information professional must not violate that trust. (1990, 135)

Service is "a function not only of what we do but of who we are" (Coles 1993, xxvi). Throughout the course of this book, the Alums have spoken of their satisfaction with their choice of college, career, and work. Some feel called to serve; others find LIS meets their intellectual needs. For most of the CALS respondents, the field is seen first as just a job, and later as a comfortable arena in which to participate. In 1989, Rice (quoted in Rubin 1998, 389) suggested that in the future librarians "will exert much greater effort in consulting, teaching, and advising individuals in their search for information, and such activities will become an essential part of the librarians' function." The participants in this study, whether they be from the class of 1962 or the class of 2000, do consult, teach, and advise. They also sponsor, host, guide, and serve as exemplars in their roles as information professionals. This study was undertaken to investigate the nature of the connections between a liberal arts college education and the practice of library and information science. What has been found is that these LIS professionals are intelligent, engaged in their work, interested in helping others, appreciative of the education they received as liberal arts college undergraduates, and satisfied with library and information science as their career. To close, two final comments from Alums whose views represent the majority of those involved in this study. First, on the value of attending a liberal arts college:

> At the start, I think few liberal arts students know where they're headed, thank God. At best you have a notion, or hunches to play (that's why you offer students a rich curriculum, semesters abroad, cultural opportunities and extracurricular activity—throw open the options for encounter and experience, and see what happens). But at bottom, most students haven't a clue what they want to do, [and] that's okay. Not one person I knew at Swarthmore is doing what they expected. Rather, we were encouraged to read, observe, participate, think critically, write well, argue constructively, listen, sharpen perceptions and test them in conversation, dialogue, and exchange. Those "skills" shaped us, allowing us to do anything—even librarianship. Librarianship happens to be one of the many outcomes that are possible from an immersion into the humanities—like social work, medicine, or organic farming. What's interesting is the diversity of careers open to Earlham, or Swarthmore, Alums. It's left to our imagination. (Swarthmore '71; special)

Second, on library and information science as a career:

> There are a variety of life options in LIS. I'm confident that my work can evolve as my interests shift. My career choice allows me to learn something new each day, serve my community, and work with the best patrons in the world. And it's still fun. (Earlham '76; public)

APPENDIX A

Methodology

The College Alumni Librarians Study (CALS) was undertaken in 2002-03. Participants in the study were alumni (Alums) of the 1962-2000 classes of eight liberal arts colleges who had subsequently entered the LIS field. The year 1962 was chosen for three reasons. First, as an expanded follow-up to a study of Earlham College (Indiana) alumni who had entered the field (Farber and Bingham 1992). Second, to honor the beginning of Evan Ira Farber's directorship as Earlham College Librarian. Third, so as to involve LIS practitioners who had worked within the field over a range of years. The concluding date of 2000 reflects the most current data available when the present study was being designed. For the purpose of comparison, and for a broader understanding of findings, this study expanded the survey basis to include the following liberal arts colleges in addition to Earlham: Carleton College (Minnesota), Denison University (Ohio), Grinnell College (Iowa), Kalamazoo College (Michigan), Lawrence University (Wisconsin), Macalester College (Minnesota), and Swarthmore College (Pennsylvania).

The eight colleges range geographically from Iowa in the Plains to Swarthmore in the East, with the greatest number concentrated in the American Midwest (Indiana, Ohio, Michigan, Minnesota, and Wisconsin). All have undergraduate enrollments under 2000 and were established between 1831 and 1874 by religious individuals or groups (appendix E). Each college sees one or more of the others as a peer or an aspirational peer institution. The 39-year period represented by the 1962-2000 classes allowed for a longitudinal approach to see if or how the interests, opinions, or activities of the participants changed over time.

I. Selection of the CALS Participants

In late 2002 and early 2003, library directors and alumni officers were asked to provide names, addresses (postal and e-mail), and the class year of alumni who, college records indicated, were associated with the library and information science field by degree or occupational identifier. Such information was received from Carleton, Denison, Earlham, Kalamazoo, Lawrence, and Swarthmore. Grinnell and Macalester officials elected to announce the study in their alumni publications—requesting that interested alumni contact the author. From the initial lists, some individuals were eliminated when their occupation was indicated as outside the LIS field (for example, art museum curators). The study instruments were sent by mail to the resulting 864 individuals, and 510 (59 percent) responded.

Seventy-nine returns were eliminated because they had taken no LIS graduate courses or because they were not alumni of the college (i.e., they were actually former employees). The final number of respondents was 431 from the 785 usable returns for a 55 percent response rate. This figure, however, does include 20 participants who fit one of these three categories:

- Although they were still in their LIS program, they had prior or active LIS work experience
- They had some LIS graduate work but not the master's degree (for example, in cases where a teacher wishes to become a school library media specialist, she or he must take specific LIS graduate courses but is not required to have completed the LIS master's degree)
- They were considered librarians by their employer, although they did not have the LIS master's degree (for example, they were state-certified as "public librarians")

The distribution of participants' affiliations was as follows:

Liberal Arts Colleges	*Original Number*	*Outside Scope of the Study*	*Revised N*	*Usable Returns*	*Percent*
Carleton	153	- 19	134	69	51.5
Denison	92	- 19	73	28	38.4
Earlham	178	- 9	169	95	56.2
Grinnell	15	- 1	14	8	57.1
Kalamazoo	186	- 13	173	87	50.3
Lawrence	102	- 11	91	51	56.0
Macalester	57	- 1	56	48	85.7
Swarthmore	81	- 6	75	45	60.0
Totals	864	- 79	785	431	55.0

II. The Alums by College, Cohort, and Library Type

Colleges

By college, the largest number of the 431 respondents was from Earlham, followed by Kalamazoo and Carleton; the smallest number from Grinnell:

Carleton	69 (16 percent)	Kalamazoo	87 (20 percent)
Denison	28 (6 percent)	Lawrence	51 (12 percent)
Earlham	95 (22 percent)	Macalester	48 (11 percent)
Grinnell	8 (2 percent)	Swarthmore	45 (10 percent)

Cohorts

The CALS respondents are from the classes of 1962 through 2000 (table A-1). To facilitate consideration of changes over time, the classes were grouped into one four-year (1962-65) and seven five-year (1966-2000) cohorts. The largest number of respondents (200; 47 percent) attended college during the 1960s and 1970s, especially between 1966 and 1975 (appendix D: Q.I-1):

1962-65	55 (13 percent)	1981-85	34 (8 percent)
1966-70	111 (26 percent)	1986-90	42 (10 percent)
1971-75	89 (21 percent)	1991-95	36 (8 percent)
1976-80	54 (13 percent)	1996-2000	10 (2 percent)

Table A-2 shows the college representation within each cohort.

The 1962-2000 CALS respondents are 98 percent Anglo-Caucasian (i.e., white). By gender, they are 78 percent female and 22 percent male—similar to the 1998-99 figures for the field of 79 percent female and 21 percent male (Lynch 2000).

Library Type

Of the 431 CALS respondents, nine (2 percent) have never been employed as information professionals. For some, non-LIS employment has been by choice or happenstance; others are currently seeking LIS positions. The remaining 422 are employed as follows:

- Academic libraries 33 percent
- Public libraries 34 percent
- School libraries 11 percent
- Special libraries 23 percent

Alums retired at the time of the survey were asked to use their final LIS place of employment in completing the questionnaire.

Table A-1: College Representation of Questionnaire Recipients (by Cohort)

Colleges	Avg (%)	Cohorts							
		62-65	66-70	71-75	76-80	81-85	86-90	91-95	96-00
Carleton	16	20	12	17	19	15	19	17	10
Denison	6	7	6	10	7	3	7	0	0
Earlham	22	23	17	21	30	21	26	22	20
Grinnell	2	2	1	0	4	0	5	3	10
Kalamazoo	20	15	29	22	9	15	17	19	30
Lawrence	12	4	13	13	19	21	12	3	0
Macalester	11	13	13	7	4	9	7	33	10
Swarthmore	10	16	10	9	9	18	7	3	20

Table A-2: Cohort Representation of Questionnaire Recipients (by College)

Cohort Years	Avg (%)	Colleges							
		C	D	E	G	K	L	M	S
1962-65	13	16	14	14	13	9	4	15	20
1966-70	26	19	25	20	13	37	27	29	24
1971-75	21	22	32	20	0	23	24	13	18
1976-80	13	14	14	17	25	6	20	4	11
1981-85	8	7	4	7	0	6	14	6	13
1986-90	10	12	11	12	25	8	10	6	7
1991-95	8	9	0	8	13	8	2	25	2
1996-2000	2	1	0	2	13	3	0	2	4

III. Survey Instruments

Two survey instruments were used in the study. A print questionnaire was developed and pretested that asked the alumni about six broad areas (appendix B):

- Activities while undergraduate students at their colleges, the importance of an undergraduate education, and the personal and professional values that were developed while at college
- Opinions about librarianship, LIS education, and LIS work
- Consideration given to careers and occupations other than LIS
- Demographic and familial backgrounds of the participants, their spouses or partners, parents, and siblings
- Mentoring they have received and/or provided to others
- LIS education and suggestions for new practitioners

Questions on mentoring were included as a way of studying socialization into the field, with responses also used to shed light on how participants might have actualized the concept of service. The questionnaire concluded with questions regarding suggestions for LIS master's level education and for new LIS professionals. The survey instrument included some questions that had been asked in other studies. Taken across the 39 years covered by the 1962-2000 class range, these questions provided a way to see change over time in those who become information professionals. The questionnaire was 12 pages in length and a majority of the questions in each section were open-ended and contained secondary questions.

The Myers-Briggs Type Indicator (MBTI®) was administered to a sample of the alumni (table A-3). This was to gain information about their personality types, and to use in comparing the alumni with a national profile of LIS professionals as derived from a study of American Library Association and Special Library Association members carried out by Scherdin under the auspices of the Association of College and Research Libraries (Scherdin 1992, 1994a-b). The ACRL study was used to represent the larger LIS population, which contains both liberal arts college and university alumni, such that some modest form of generalization might be made between the CALS respondents and the national profile of librarians. The MBTI® instrument was sent to 226 of the original 864 alumni (table 3). Macalester is overrepresented among those receiving the MBTI®. Macalester was one of the first colleges involved in the study, and originally the intent was to randomly sample half of the participants. However, as the number of colleges in the study grew, the decision was made to send the MBTI® to 25 percent of the names (every fourth one) on each college's alumni list. Grinnell was not included in the MBTI® portion of the study due to the small number of respondents.

IV. Analysis and Presentation

In the interest of preserving currency of the results, quantitative analysis was limited to percentages except for statistical analysis of the MBTI® results. Qualitative analysis was conducted using ETHNOGRAPH v5.0 with percentages derived from the conceptual clusters that resulted from the ETHNOGRAPH coding. Two Data Sets are found in appendixes C-D: College Data Set and College Cohort Set. The College Data Set is more complete than the

Table A-3: MBTI® Participants (by College)

Colleges	MBTI®		
	Sent	Returned	%
Carleton	37	13	35.1
Denison	23	8	34.8
Earlham	49	24	49.0
Grinnell	0	0	0
Kalamazoo	46	22	47.8
Lawrence	25	9	36.0
Macalester	26	18	69.2
Swarthmore	20	10	50.0
Totals	226	104	46.0

Cohort Data Set, as all questions were analyzed by college. The Cohort Data Set covers questions where change might be seen over the course of the 39 years represented by the respondents.

APPENDIX B

Questionnaire

THE COLLEGE ALUMNI LIBRARIANS STUDY

The questionnaire sent to the prospective participants of each of the eight liberal arts colleges carried the name of the particular college. Here, the single word “college” is used instead.

Section I. [College]

1. Dates of attendance at College:____

2. College major: ____

3. College minor:____

4. Extracurricular activities while at College: Please check and describe all that apply
   __ Artistic (music, drama, etc.):______________________________________
   __ Athletics:______________________________________
   __ Politics (student government, etc.):______________________________________
   __ Radio/Film, etc.:______________________________________
   __ Social Services:______________________________________
   __ Other (please name):______________________________________
   __ None

5. Would you go to College today if you were graduating from high school? __ Yes __ No
   If no, what has changed about College--or about you?:

6. On the following, (a) Place an ***"I"*** beside those items in the list below that you think are among the <u>most</u> important reasons for getting an undergraduate education; (b) ***Checkmark*** any item in which you feel that your College experience was particularly *strong*; and (c) <u>Underline</u> any item in which you feel your undergraduate experience was <u>deficient</u>.

a	b	c- ***<u>Underline if deficient</u>***
__	__	Provide vocational or pre-professional training; develop skills and techniques directly applicable to one's future career .
__	__	Develop one's ability to get along with different kinds of people.
__	__	Develop one's critical faculties and appreciation for ideas.
__	__	Develop special competence in a particular academic discipline.
__	__	Develop one's knowledge of, and interest in, community and world problems.
__	__	Help develop one's moral capacities, ethical standards and values.
__	__	Other (specify):

7. What personal or professional ***<u>values</u>*** do you believe your College years helped you develop?

Section II. LIBRARIANSHIP, LIS EDUCATION, AND LIS WORK

1. Would you encourage today's College students to enter the library and information science (LIS) field?
   __ Yes __ No --Why/why not?

2. At what age did you first think about going into LIS work? ______________________________

3. Please checkmark any and all of the following factors that made you think that LIS would be an attractive career for you:

   A. General:
   - __ Love of books/reading
   - __ Desire to work with/help people
   - __ Working conditions
   - __ Salary or other financial considerations
   - __ Flexibility which allows better management of my other life commitments
   - __ Fit with the values and ideals which are important to me
   - __ Level and variety of intellectual challenge provided by this career
   - __ Status or image of librarians/information professionals
   - __ The availability of a variety of job possibilities
   - __ Information or advice from College's career services office
   - __ Length/structure/requirements of the graduate program in Library Science
   - __ Written information on LIS as a career (e.g. articles you read; career materials)
   - __ Bibliographic instruction in classes taken at College

   B. Opportunities:
   - __ For a job
   - __ For professional growth
   - __ To educate others
   - __ To combine library science with some other area of interest or skill (e.g., music, education, law, computers)
   - __ To learn to use and/or do research with a variety of information resources
   - __ To work with increasingly sophisticated information technology

   C. Relationship to or Encouragement from Other People:
   - __ A librarian during my (check:) __ elementary, __ middle, __ high school years
   - __ A librarian at College
   - __ A professional librarian after graduation from College
   - __ A family member, who __ was __ was not a librarian
   - __ A friend
   - __ A teacher

   D. Experience in Libraries:
   - __ Using a library during high school (Circle: Public Lib. School Lib. Other Lib.)
   - __ Using the library at College
   - __ Using a library after graduating from college
   - __ Working in a library during my high school years (Circle: Public School Other)
   - __ Working in the library at College
   - __ Working in a library after college but before entering a LIS graduate program (Circle: Academic Public School Special)

4. Please list any other factors which were not identified in 3 above that made you think that LIS would be an attractive career:

5. Did you work in the library while at College?: __ Yes __ No

If yes: A. For how many years: ________________

B. In what area(s):

__ Acquisitions/Coll. Dev.
__ Cataloging
__ Circulation/Access
__ Other: ________________
__ Inter-Library Loan
__ Online/Systems
__ Reference

C. How did that come about:

__ My own initiative
__ Through other library staff
__ Through the library director
__ Other: ________________

6. What do you remember about the library's director as a librarian?

7. What do you remember about other College librarians?

8. What image did you have of "librarians" and of LIS when you left College?

9. What, ultimately, made you actually attend a LIS School for graduate work?

10. Which LIS School did you enter? ________________ What year? ________

11. In what year did you: A. graduate with the Master's degree? ____or B. leave the program? ____

12. Did you work in a library during your time in LIS School?: __ Yes __ No

13. What image did you have of "librarians" and LIS when you left LIS school?

14. In how many libraries have you worked since leaving your LIS School? ________________

15. How many total number of years of LIS-related work have you had since finishing your LIS graduate education: ____

16. Are you (or have you been) employed as a librarian/information professional?
__No–*please skip to Section III: Work, Careers, Occupations (page 6)*
__Yes-- *please answer questions A - O below.* (NOTE If you are not now working as an LIS professional, please use your last employment in the LIS field when filling out this section.)

A. In what type of LIS organization do you work? (Please circle one)
Academic Public School Special (specify): ______________________________

B. Have you worked in more than one type of LIS organization?
__ Yes, these types: __________________ __ No, only the one I marked above

C. *Approximately* how large is your current library: _____ population served
______ total staff (full- and part-time) ______collection size (all formats and items)

D. What responsibilities do you have in your current position? (Check all that apply)
__ Administration/management
__ Automation planning, design and coordination
__ Cataloging/classification/indexing/abstracting/thesaurus construction
__ Circulation/access services
__ Collection development and management/Acquisitions
__ Conservation/preservation
__ Database searching
__ Group activities (e.g., curriculum development, instructional consultant, library instruction, storytelling)
__ Interlibrary loan
__ Outreach services
__ Publicity/public relations/fund-raising
__ Records management/archives
__ Reference/reader services/information and referral
__ Website development and/or maintenance
__ Other: ____
Now, please go back and circle the two areas in which you spend most of your time

E. How many years of experience do you have in your current LIS job: ___________________

F. What is your exact job title: ____

G. What is the average number of hours per week that you work in your LIS position:
__ Less than 10 __ 10-19 __ 20-29 __ 30-39 __ 40 or more

H. How satisfied are you with each of the following aspects of your current position?
(NS=not satisfied; S=satisfied; OK=neutral; VS=very satisfied)

__ Working hours
__ Responsibilities
__ Opportunities to use my skills and abilities
__ Range of people employed in my library
__ The autonomy I have to do my own work
__ Supervision/feedback
__ Salary
__ Opportunities for development/ promotion
__ People I work most closely with

I. If you could choose to spend more time on one work activity, which one would it be? (e.g., administration, computer work, work with the public): ______________________________

J. What do you like *best* about your own specific LIS work?

K. What do you like *least* about your own specific LIS work?

L. How satisfied are you with your choice of an LIS *as a career*?
__Very Dissatisfied __Moderately Satisfied __Very Satisfied

M. What do you like *best* about LIS work in general?

N. What do you like *least* about LIS work in general?

O. What is the likelihood of your continuing as an LIS professional for the foreseeable future?
__Very Unlikely __Moderately Likely __Very Likely

Section III. CAREERS, OCCUPATIONS, AND GOALS

1. What were your career goals as a child?

2. What were your career goals when you started college?

3. In what other occupations or work have you been interested–in addition to or instead of LIS?

4. In what other occupations have you been involved over the course of your worklife?

5. What other occupation(s) have you considered going into?

6. In addition to LIS work, do you do other types of work part-time? __Yes __No
   If yes, what kind of work? ____________________

7. If you are ***not*** currently working in an LIS field, have you ever been employed in LIS work?
   __No __I never intended to actually work in an LIS field
   __Yes, but I left it because:

   In what field are you now working? ____________________
   Are you satisfied with the work you are now doing? __Yes __No

8. What have been the greatest professional challenges for you since finishing LIS graduate work?

9. What do you hope to accomplish in the next five years:
   Professionally: ____________________
   Personally: ____________________

10. What do you feel proudest of with regards to your own career or work?

11. What two activities do you enjoy when not working at your LIS or other regular job?

SECTION IV. DEMOGRAPHIC QUESTIONS

1. Sex: __ Male __ Female

2. Current Age: ________________

3. Current Salary
   __ under $21,000 __ $21,000-30,999 __ $31,000-40,999 __ $41,000-50,999
   __ $51,000-75,999 __ $76,000-90,000 __ over $90,000
   __ Retired __ Not currently earning a salary (e.g., volunteer, homemaker)

4. Please indicate your ethnic background: ________________________________

5. Was English the language you learned first? __ Yes __ No, I learned ________________

6. Is English the language most commonly used in your home? __ Yes __ No, it is__________

7. Do you have any physical disabilities? __ Yes __ No
   If yes, please list: ________________________________

8. Marital Status
   __ Single __ Widowed __ Divorced/Separated
   __ Married/Partnered: What does your spouse/partner do? ____________________

9. Do you have children? __ Yes __ No
   If yes, how many are . . Boys: _______ Girls: _______
   What are their ages: Boys: _______ Girls: _______
   If they are younger than 18, do they live with you: __ Yes __ No

10. Do any adults (ages 18 or above) live with you? __ Yes __ No

11. Do/Did you have siblings? __ Yes __ No
    If Yes, please indicate how many: _____ brothers ____ sisters
    Are you the (please check one): ___ oldest, ___ youngest, ___ somewhere in the middle
    In what occupations have each of your siblings spent the *greatest* number of years:

12. What kind of work did your parents do for a living when you were 18 years old--or if they were deceased or retired by then, give their last occupations (Examples: "high school chemistry teacher," "owner of a small farm"). If you have had multiple mothers and/or fathers, pick those you feel closest to:
    Mother ________________________________
    Father ________________________________

13. How much formal education did your parents have? (Place ***MO*** and ***FA*** next to the level representing the highest achieved by each parent; if you have had multiple parents, pick the parents you feel closest to.)
    ___ Some high school ___ Some 4 year college courses
    ___ High school graduate ___ 4 year college graduate
    ___ Community/junior college ___ Graduate school (Master's degree)
    ___ Graduate school (Doctoral degree)

14. Place a checkmark next to the kind of place where you lived the longest when you were between the ages of 6 and 12, and between the ages of 13-17:

6 - 12	13 - 17	
____	_____	Rural area
____	_____	Small town (up to 2,500)
____	_____	Small city (2,500 - 24,999)
____	_____	Medium city (25,000 - 99,999)
____	_____	Large city (100,000 - 499,999)
____	_____	Metropolis (500,000 or more)

In what state(s) of the U.S., or in what other country/ies, did you live–
During ages 6-12: ________________ During ages 13-17: ___________________

15. Please check the phrase that best describes your family's financial situation most of the time before you were 21 years old:
__ Sometimes had difficulty getting the necessities
__ Had all the necessities but not many luxuries
__ Comfortable but not wealthy
__ Wealthy

16. What is the highest level of education that you have completed?
__ Master's degree in LIS
__ Second Masters in ____________________________
__ Other Professional degree (e.g., DDS, EdD, JD, MD): ______________________________
__ Ph.D. , with a major field of ____

17. Are you currently enrolled in any educationally-based, non-workshop courses?
__ Yes __ No If yes, for what purpose:
___ Another degree (please list): ____________________
___ Continuing education
___ Personal interest

18. Would you like to go back to school in the future? __Yes __No
If yes, in what area(s) or for what degree? ______________________________________

19. Have you ever interrupted your LIS or other career for family reasons? __ Yes __ No
If yes, how do you feel about those interruptions with regard to your career or work?

20. Are you the only MLS-degreed professional in your work place? __ Yes __ No

21. Have you authored: journal articles __ Yes __ No web-publications __ Yes __ No
monographs __ Yes __ No conference papers __ Yes __ No
book reviews __ Yes __ No other_________________________

22. Have you served on editorial boards? __ Yes __ No

23. In which of the following professional organizations have you held membership--now or in the past, and how active have you been? (Please mark all that apply and add others as appropriate)

Organization	Usually attend meetings	Been on committees	Held office
__ ALA	____	____	____
__ SLA	____	____	____
__ AALL	____	____	____
__ Medical LA	____	____	____
__ Music LA	____	____	____
__ ASIST	____	____	____
__ ASI	____	____	____
__ SAA	____	____	____
__ regional library assn	____	____	____
__ state library assn	____	____	____
__ other LIS related	____	____	____
__ other professional assn	____	____	____

24. To what civic, fraternal or social organizations do you belong?

25. What was your religion while at College? ________________________________

Has it changed over time? __ Yes, to ________________________________

__ No, it has not changed

What was its importance to you at College: ________________________________

What is its importance of it to you now: ________________________________

Section V. MENTOR QUESTIONS

If you have had a mentor who has helped you in LIS or other work–or if you have been a mentor, please fill out this section. ***If not, please skip to Section VI. The Last Section (page 12).***

"Mentoring" carries many definitions and assumptions. For our purposes, consider one or more of the following to be most useful in answering this section:

A teacher who enhanced my skills and intellectual development
A sponsor who used her/his influence and contacts to facilitate my entry into, and possible advancement of, my career(s)
A host and guide who helped initiate me into a new occupational and social world, acquainting me with its values, customs, resources, and cast of characters
An advisor who provided counsel, moral support and direction
An exemplar who illustrated virtues, achievements and actions that I admired

1. How valuable has the mentoring that you have received been to your career?:
__ No value __ Some value __ Very valuable

2. Please give the number of each kind of mentor that you have had: (ex: Men 1 Women 2)
Men: ______ Women: ______

3. Were your mentors (please check all that apply):
___ LIS professionals ___ in other fields/kinds of work

4. Have your mentors been your boss?: __ Yes __ No __ Some were and some were not

5. How did you come to have mentoring: (Please check all that apply)
__ I selected my mentors __ I fell into a mentoring relationship
__ I was selected to be mentored __ Other:________________________________

6. In relation to your own age when the mentoring relationship started, were your mentors–
__ 5-10 years older than you __ Younger than you
__ Same general age as you were

7. How long did the relationship with each mentor last? (Check all that apply depending on the number of mentors you had)
__ 1 year __ 2-3 years __ 4-5 years
__ Over 5 years __ Still continuing

8. If some or all of the relationships ended, why did they stop? (Check all that apply)
__ Mentor moved geographically __ I moved geographically
__ Conflict developed between us __ I changed professions
__ Mentor died __ Other:

9. Please give 2-3 benefits you have received from having had mentors:

10. Please give 2-3 drawbacks you see to having had mentors:

11. Have you been a mentor? (Please check all that apply)
____ Within the LIS field ____ Outside the LIS field

If yes to either, please answer the following:
A. Why did you become a mentor?

B. How did you become a mentor?

C. How have you benefitted *by* mentoring?

D. What limitations have you, *as a mentor*, experienced?

E. Are those you mentor *primarily*: (Please give the number for each)
Men: ____ Women: ____

F. What have been your most important contributions to those you have mentored?

12. At the beginning of this section, a set of definitions for a "mentor" was provided. Using these, how would you like others to describe *you* in your mentoring role: (checkmark all that would you prefer)

__A teacher in enhancing someone else's skills and intellectual development
__A sponsor in using your influence and contacts to facilitate someone else's entry and possible advancement in their field or work
__A host and guide in helping initiate someone else into a new occupational and social world, acquainting him/her with its values, customs, resources, and cast of characters
__An advisor providing counsel, moral support and direction
__An exemplar through your own virtues, achievements and actions
__Other:

Section VI. THE LAST SECTION

Thanks for spending the time filling out all these pages! Here we would just like your final thoughts.

1. Based upon your LIS (or other) career and experiences, what advice would you offer people who are just entering the work place as LIS professionals?

2. What suggestions do you have for improving LIS education?

3. Is there anything else which you feel would be important for us to know?

Please provide your name and address, telephone number, and email if you say "Yes" to either of the following:

___ Yes, I would be comfortable being interviewed over the phone as part of a follow-up.
___ Yes, I would like a copy of the questionnaire with the findings indicated for each question.

Name ____
Street______________________________________ Apt__________
City_______________________State__________Country_______ Zip______
Telephone number_______________________ Email ____________________

APPENDIX C

College Data Set

Because of the amount of quantitative detail generated by the questionnaire, two data sets have been included (appendixes C and D). Where tables within the text are incomplete, or additional detail may be useful, the reader is given a Data Set reference. For instance, if the data was from the college data set, “appendix C: Q.I-7” would indicate that individual college responses to that particular question are given.

The College Data Set analyzes all of the survey questions. Quantitative and qualitative responses (or comments) are quantitatively cast for each question, and given down the left side of each table. The colleges run across the top of each table. An “average” column is provided that represents each response’s percentage of the total number of responses to the question.

COLLEGE DATA SET	%	Totals	Carleton	Denison	Earlham	Grinnell	K'zoo	Law'ce	Mac	Sw'more
Section I. COLLEGE										
Q.I-1. Dates of attendance at [College]	100%	431	69	28	95	8	87	51	48	45
Alums by Cohort (n = 431)										
1962-1965	13%	55	16%	14%	14%	13%	9%	4%	15%	20%
1966-1970	26%	111	19%	25%	20%	13%	37%	27%	29%	24%
1971-1975	21%	89	22%	32%	20%		23%	24%	13%	18%
1976-1980	13%	54	14%	14%	17%	25%	6%	20%	4%	11%
1981-1985	8%	34	7%	4%	7%		6%	14%	6%	13%
1986-1990	10%	42	12%	11%	12%	25%	8%	10%	6%	7%
1991-1995	8%	36	9%		8%	13%	8%	2%	25%	2%
1996-2000	2%	10	1%		2%	13%	3%		2%	4%
Q.I-2. College major (n = 462 comments made)										
Agriculture		1			1%					
Anthropology	4%	20	3%		4%		2%	14%	3%	7%
Art History	3%	14	5%	7%			2%	2%		11%
Asian Studies	1%	4	1%	3%	2%					
Biology	4%	18	4%	7%	8%		1%		5%	2%
Business		1	1%							
Chemistry		1							2%	
Classics	1%	5	1%	3%	1%	10%		2%		
Communication		2		3%					2%	
Computer Science		1	1%							
Economics	1%	5	1%	3%					2%	4%
Education	1%	5			2%		1%		3%	
English	20%	92	22%	17%	14%	20%	30%	20%	17%	17%
Fine Arts	2%	8			7%		1%			
Foreign Language		1			1%					
French	4%	18	3%	7%	6%		1%	4%	7%	2%
Geography		1							2%	
Geology	1%	6			5%			2%		
German	4%	18	1%		2%		13%	6%	2%	
Government	1%	4	4%					2%		
Greek	1%	3	1%							4%
History	18%	84	23%	38%	11%	20%	25%	10%	12%	17%
Human Relations	1%	5			5%					

	%	Totals	Carleton	Denison	Earlham	Grinnell	K'zoo	Law'ce	Mac	Sw'more
Humanities		1							2%	
International Relations	1%	4	3%						2%	2%
International Studies	1%	4			1%				5%	
Latin		1	1%							
Latin American Studies	1%	3	1%			10%				2%
Liberal Arts		1			1%					
Linguistics		2						2%		2%
Literature		1	1%							
Management		1			1%					
Mathematics	1%	5			2%		2%	2%		
Medieval Studies		1								2%
Music	4%	17	1%		2%		1%	18%	2%	7%
Peace Studies		2			2%					
Philosophy	1%	5	1%		2%				2%	2%
Physics		2	3%							
Political Science	3%	15	1%		4%		7%		3%	4%
Psychology	4%	20	1%	3%	7%		5%	4%	7%	2%
Religion	5%	21	10%		3%		1%	6%	7%	4%
Russian	1%	6				20%		2%	3%	2%
Social Studies		1							2%	
Sociology	4%	20	3%		6%	10%	6%	2%	5%	4%
Soviet Studies		1		3%						
Spanish	2%	8	1%		2%	10%	1%	4%	2%	
Urban Studies		2		3%					2%	
Women's Studies		1							2%	
Q.I-3. College minor/concentration										
Single Field (n = 173)										
African American Studies	1%	1				50%				
African Studies	1%	1					2%			
American Studies	1%	1					2%			
Anthropology	2%	3					2%	4%	4%	
Art History	2%	3			5%		2%			5%
Asian Studies	2%	3	5%				2%			5%
Biology	2%	4	5%				2%		4%	5%
Chemistry	1%	2			5%				4%	
Classics	1%	1	5%							

	%	Totals	Carleton	Denison	Earlham	Grinnell	K'zoo	Law'ce	Mac	Sw'more
Computer Science	1%	1					2%			
Economics	2%	3			5%					11%
Education	9%	16		31%	9%		7%	17%	12%	
English	11%	19		23%	5%		9%	8%	15%	26%
Ethnomusicology	1%	1				50%				
Fine Arts, including Music	6%	10			14%		4%	17%	4%	
Foreign Languages	1%	1	5%							
French	9%	16	9%	8%			20%	13%	4%	
German	8%	13	5%	8%	14%		11%		12%	
History	9%	16	14%	8%	9%		7%	17%	4%	11%
International Studies	1%	1						4%		
Latin	1%	1								5%
Liberal Arts	1%	1					2%			
Linguistics	1%	1	5%							
Management	1%	1			5%					
Mathematics	2%	4	5%		5%				4%	5%
Music and Art	1%	1	5%							
Philosophy	1%	2	5%		5%					
Political Science	5%	8		8%			7%	4%	8%	5%
Pre-Med	1%	2			5%					5%
Psychology	2%	4	5%		5%				4%	5%
Religious Studies	2%	3			5%			4%	4%	
Russian Language/Studies	2%	4	9%					4%	4%	
Social Studies	1%	2					2%		4%	
Sociology	4%	7	18%		5%		2%		4%	
Spanish	6%	10	5%	8%			9%	8%	8%	
Theatre	2%	3		8%	5%		2%			
Women's Studies	2%	3					2%			11%
Combined Fields (n = 30)										
Art/French	3%	1						100%		
Education/Geography/Russian Studies	3%	1	25%							
Education/Political Science	3%	1							20%	
Education/Social Studies	3%	1	25%							
English Education	3%	1			25%					
English/German	3%	1					20%			
English/History	7%	2	25%							17%
English/Political Science	3%	1								17%

	%	Totals	Carleton	Denison	Earlham	Grinnell	K'zoo	Law'ce	Mac	Sw'more
French/Classics	3%	1								17%
French/Spanish	3%	1		50%						
Gender Studies/Women's Studies	3%	1				50%				
Geology/Religion	3%	1			25%					
German/Art History	3%	1					20%			
German/Political Science	3%	1					20%			
History/Business	3%	1							20%	
History/French	3%	1		50%						
Literature/American Studies	3%	1				50%				
Mathematics/Music	3%	1			25%					
Philosophy/Art History	7%	2								33%
Physics/Sociology	3%	1								17%
Psychology/Theatre	3%	1					20%			
Russian/Mathematics	3%	1							20%	
Science/Technology/Public Policy	3%	1	25%							
Sociology/Anthropology	3%	1			25%					
Sociology/Education	3%	1						100%		
Sociology/Mathematics	3%	1							20%	
Theatre/Medieval Studies	3%	1					20%			
Women's Studies/German	3%	1							20%	
Q.I-4. Extracurricular activities while at [College] (n = 798 choices made)										
Artistic (music, drama, etc.)	27%	218	28%	24%	30%	29%	26%	33%	20%	27%
Athletics	15%	119	23%	14%	13%	5%	13%	9%	15%	19%
Social Services	15%	116	14%	22%	11%	24%	15%	13%	17%	14%
Politics (student government, etc.)	10%	77	10%	6%	9%	14%	6%	6%	16%	14%
Radio/Film, etc.	8%	64	8%	6%	8%	5%	11%	7%	10%	5%
None	6%	50	5%	2%	11%		8%	6%	3%	4%
Other	19%	154	13%	26%	18%	24%	21%	26%	19%	16%
Other and Social Services combined (n = 305 comments)										
Campus newspaper	25%	76	21%	11%	32%	44%	23%	19%	32%	24%
Tutoring	11%	34	11%		13%		9%	11%	17%	16%
Paid work	10%	31	3%	5%	11%	11%	12%	13%	15%	8%
National organization	9%	28	3%	21%	5%	33%	4%	9%	5%	24%
Hospital work	9%	27		32%			18%	23%		
Campus organization	8%	24	11%	16%	5%		9%	4%	7%	11%
Church	7%	20	5%		2%		12%	9%	5%	11%

	%	Totals	Carleton	Denison	Earlham	Grinnell	K'zoo	Law'ce	Mac	Sw'more
K-12 connection	4%	13	16%	16%	2%		4%			3%
1-time event	4%	13	8%		11%		2%	2%	2%	3%
Greek	3%	10			9%		4%	4%	2%	
Library work	3%	8	5%	0%	2%		0%	4%	5%	3%
"Volunteer"	3%	8	5%		4%		4%		5%	
Individual activity	2%	5	5%	0%	4%				2%	
Study abroad	2%	6	5%		2%	11%		2%	2%	
Workstudy	1%	2	3%				2%			
Q.I-5. Would you go to [College] today if you were graduating from high school? (n = 414)										
Yes	78%	321	78%	64%	88%	88%	75%	70%	88%	64%
No	14%	60	15%	29%	4%	13%	16%	21%	9%	20%
Not Sure	8%	33	7%	7%	8%		8%	9%	2%	16%
Comments re Not Sure (n = 146 comments made)										
It is too geographically isolated	14%	21	11%		11%		19%	23%	15%	12%
It is too expensive	13%	19	6%	25%	16%	100%	10%	19%	15%	4%
It has changed too much	10%	14	6%		11%		23%	8%		8%
It was just not a good fit for me	9%	13		33%	16%		3%	4%		15%
It needs more social/cultural diversity	8%	12	11%	17%			6%	15%	8%	4%
I would want a larger school	8%	12	17%	17%	5%		6%		8%	12%
I'm just not sure	8%	12			11%		10%	4%	23%	12%
I would compare it with other colleges	7%	10			5%		10%	12%	8%	8%
I would need more/different intellectual environ	6%	9	6%				6%	8%	15%	8%
It needs more politicial diversity	3%	4			11%			8%		
It is too competitive	3%	4								15%
It is too elite	2%	3	17%							
It was too hard academically	2%	3	6%		5%					4%
My children would not go there	2%	3	6%				3%		8%	
I would want a more selective school	1%	2			5%		3%			
I felt unwanted there	1%	2	6%		5%					
My parents chose it	1%	2	6%	8%						
It needs more educational diversity	1%	1	6%							
Q.I-6. Reasons for getting an undergraduate education										
Q.I-6A. Most important (n = 1541 choices made)										
Develop one's critical faculties/appreciation...	26%	407	27%	27%	25%	28%	27%	28%	26%	26%
Develop one's knowl. of...community/world problems	19%	291	17%	17%	19%	24%	18%	17%	23%	21%

	%	Totals	Carleton	Denison	Earlham	Grinnell	K'zoo	Law'ce	Mac	Sw'more
Develop one's ability to get along…	15%	235	16%	14%	15%	24%	15%	14%	15%	15%
Develop special competence in...academic...	15%	233	15%	18%	15%	10%	14%	18%	13%	15%
Help develop one's moral capacities, ethical...values	15%	225	16%	13%	17%	3%	14%	13%	14%	15%
Provide vocational or preprofessional training…	7%	101	4%	7%	6%		9%	9%	8%	4%
Other (specify)	3%	49	5%	4%	2%	10%	3%	8%	2%	4%
Q.I-6B. Particularly strong (n = 1362 choices made)										
Develop one's critical faculties/appreciation…	27%	364	28%	30%	25%	27%	26%	29%	26%	25%
Develop one's knowl. of...community/world problems	20%	270	17%	19%	24%	23%	20%	15%	21%	20%
Help develop one's moral capacities, ethical...values	16%	221	18%	10%	21%	7%	11%	17%	16%	18%
Develop special competence in...academic…	16%	212	18%	23%	11%	13%	16%	19%	12%	18%
Develop one's ability to get along...	15%	200	12%	9%	15%	17%	18%	11%	19%	14%
Provide vocational or preprofessional training...	4%	58	2%	7%	3%	3%	7%	5%	4%	2%
Other (specify)	3%	37	5%	3%	1%	10%	2%	3%	2%	3%
Q.I-6C. Deficient (n = 169 choices made)										
Provide vocational or preprofessional training...	65%	109	58%	47%	88%	67%	64%	42%	76%	68%
Develop one's ability to get along...	10%	17	17%	20%			8%	16%		16%
Develop one's knowl. of...community/world problems	7%	12	13%	7%			10%	16%	6%	
Develop special competence in...academic...	6%	9	4%		12%		5%	5%	6%	4%
Help develop one's moral capacities, ethical...values	5%	8	4%	20%			3%	5%	6%	4%
Develop one's critical faculities/appreciation..	4%	6			4%		3%	5%	6%	8%
Other (specify)	5%	8	4%	7%		33%	8%	11%		
Q.I-7 - What personal or professional values do you believe your [College] years helped you develop? (n = 1013 comments)										
Other-directed (n = 371 comments made)										
Diversity	9%	94	7%	10%	9%	7%	9%	4%	16%	10%
Tolerance	8%	80	9%	2%	11%	9%	5%	7%	9%	5%
Understanding	8%	82	3%	5%	7%	9%	13%	6%	12%	6%
Service	5%	46	4%	2%	7%	7%	1%	2%	9%	4%
Respect	3%	35	3%		4%		4%	4%	2%	5%
Behavior	3%	26	2%		3%	7%	3%	3%	2%	3%
Liberal values	1%	8	1%			5%	2%			2%
Self (n = 312 comments made)										
Moral character	9%	94	7%	7%	15%	5%	5%	16%	6%	11%
Critical thinking	8%	81	13%	5%	7%	5%	8%	11%	5%	6%
Open mind	6%	56	5%	5%	5%	5%	7%	8%	6%	5%

	%	Totals	Carleton	Denison	Earlham	Grinnell	K'zoo	Law'ce	Mac	Sw'more
Personal responsibility	3%	29	2%	5%	4%		5%	2%	1%	1%
Involvement	3%	27	3%		3%		1%	3%	4%	4%
Self-education	2%	25	3%	2%	2%		3%	4%	1%	2%
Education (n = 175 comments made)										
Learning	8%	83	9%	15%	4%	9%	12%	11%	4%	8%
Intellectual rigor	8%	80	8%	12%	4%	9%	8%	10%	7%	13%
Arts and culture	1%	12	2%	2%		5%	2%			
Work (n = 155 comments made)										
Work ethic	5%	53	3%	5%	4%	2%	6%	6%	8%	7%
Work skills	4%	36	6%	5%	4%	5%	3%		2%	4%
Work hard	2%	21	3%	7%		7%	2%	1%	1%	3%
Work sharing	2%	21	1%		6%	2%	1%		1%	2%
Work quality	2%	18	2%	10%		2%	3%	1%	1%	1%
Creativity	1%	6	2%				1%		1%	
Section II. LIBRARIANSHIP, LIS EDUCATION, AND LIS WORK										
Q.II-1. Would you encourage today's [College] students to enter the LIS field? (n = 417)										
Yes	88%	369	86%	96%	88%	86%	87%	92%	80%	96%
No	7%	30	9%	4%	8%		9%	4%	13%	
Maybe	4%	18	5%		4%	14%	3%	4%	6%	4%
Q.II-2. At what age did you first think about going into LIS work? (n = 421)										
age 5 to 10	4%	15	3%	4%	1%	25%	8%	2%	2%	
11-15	8%	32	4%	4%	11%		6%	4%	13%	13%
16-19	11%	47	10%	9%	19%		9%	6%	11%	2%
20-30	66%	278	67%	52%	62%	75%	74%	69%	70%	58%
31-40	8%	34	9%	15%	3%		5%	12%	4%	20%
41-50	3%	13	6%	7%	3%			8%		
over 50	<1%	2								4%
Q.II-3. Factors that made you think LIS would be an attractive career for you:										
Q.II-3A. General (n = 2181 choices made)										
Love of books/reading	16%	356	19%	16%	13%	16%	18%	17%	19%	16%
Desire to work with/help people	15%	328	17%	14%	13%	11%	15%	16%	17%	16%
Fit...the values and ideals which are important to me	15%	323	15%	16%	13%	11%	16%	14%	17%	17%
Level & variety of intellectual challenge [of] this career	14%	316	14%	15%	14%	16%	15%	15%	15%	14%
Working conditions	10%	217	8%	12%	10%	16%	9%	10%	10%	11%

	%	Totals	Carleton	Denison	Earlham	Grinnell	K'zoo	Law'ce	Mac	Sw'more
The availability of a variety of job possibilities	8%	173	8%	7%	8%	11%	9%	9%	6%	6%
Length/structure/requirements of the [LIS] program	7%	153	9%	6%	7%	3%	6%	7%	7%	8%
Flexibility [for managing] my other life commitments	7%	147	7%	10%	6%	11%	6%	8%	4%	8%
Bibliographic instruction in classes taken at [College]	2%	43	<1		7%			<1	<1	<1
Salary or other financial considerations	2%	41	1%	3%	3%	3%	2%	1%	<1	<1
Written information on LIS as a career…	2%	39	1%	1%	2%	3%	2%	<1	2%	3%
Status or image of librarians/information professionals	2%	34	<1	<1	3%		1%	<1	1%	<1
Info or advice from [College's] career services office	1%	11	1%		<1		<1	<1	1%	
Q.II-3B. Opportunities (n = 1213 choices made)										
For a job	23%	281	22%	23%	19%	30%	29%	23%	23%	24%
To learn to use/research a variety of info. resources	19%	228	19%	24%	19%	4%	18%	17%	19%	18%
To educate others	18%	220	21%	18%	20%	22%	17%	21%	13%	15%
To combine [LIS and] some other area of interest /skill	16%	191	13%	9%	17%	17%	17%	17%	14%	18%
For professional growth	14%	169	14%	15%	12%	22%	14%	13%	17%	15%
To work w/increasingly sophisticated info technology	10%	124	12%	11%	12%	1%	5%	9%	14%	11%
Q.II-3C. Relationship to or encouragement from other people (n = 816 choices made)										
A librarian during my [K-12] years	33%	273	41%	31%	20%	56%	33%	46%	39%	36%
A professional librarian after graduation from [College]	18%	144	23%	19%	19%	6%	15%	17%	12%	28%
A librarian at [College]	16%	127	12%	11%	25%	11%	21%	7%	15%	5%
A friend	10%	83	17%	14%	9%	11%	9%	10%	12%	8%
A family member who was not a librarian	10%	79	11%	14%	13%	6%	9%	7%	8%	8%
A family member who was a librarian	10%	78	10%	11%	8%	6%	11%	11%	13%	9%
A teacher	4%	32	6%		6%	6%	3%	3%	1%	5%
Q.II-3D. Experience in libraries (n = 1175 choices made)										
Using the library at [College]	26%	306	25%	23%	28%	24%	26%	23%	27%	27%
Using a library during high school	23%	273	25%	32%	18%	24%	22%	25%	28%	23%
Using a library after graduating from college	18%	214	18%	19%	19%	19%	16%	19%	17%	21%
Working in a lib. after college [& before] LIS grad prgm.	15%	172	16%	16%	17%	10%	15%	15%	9%	12%
Working in the library at [College]	11%	134	9%	6%	14%	14%	14%	7%	15%	11%
Working in a library during my high school years	6%	76	6%	3%	5%	10%	8%	10%	4%	6%
Q.II-4. Other factors not identified in II-3A-D that made you think that LIS would be an attractive career (n = 312 comments made)										
Path to other satisfactions	23%	53	16%	11%	27%	13%	31%	21%	19%	23%
Intellectual nature of the field	15%	34	11%	33%	10%		17%	16%	16%	20%

	%	Totals	Carleton	Denison	Earlham	Grinnell	K'zoo	Law'ce	Mac	Sw'more
Multiple positive reasons	14%	33	13%	11%	18%	13%	15%	16%	16%	7%
Other career options limited	13%	30	8%	11%	10%	25%	17%	16%	13%	13%
Liked libraries/librarians	12%	28	5%	11%	16%	38%	13%	5%	13%	10%
Personal fit with skills and abilities	8%	19	11%	11%	8%	13%	2%	11%	13%	7%
Had experience with books	5%	12	16%				2%	11%	3%	7%
Idealistic view of the field	3%	8	5%		8%		2%			3%
Personality test results	3%	7	3%				2%		6%	10%
Desire for more learning	2%	4	3%	11%	2%			5%		
Good job market for my specialty	1%	2	5%							
Otherwise bad job market		1	3%							
It was my calling		1	3%							
Q.II-5. Did you work in the library while at [College]? (n = 425)										
No	67%	284	78%	81%	54%	63%	61%	76%	69%	69%
Yes	33%	141	22%	19%	46%	38%	39%	24%	31%	31%
Q.II-5A. For how many years? (n = 125)										
0-1	21%	26	20%		18%	33%	23%	22%	33%	21%
2-4	79%	99	80%	100%	82%	67%	77%	78%	67%	79%
Q.II-5B. In what area(s)? (n = 234 choices made)										
Circulation/Access	35%	81	29%	20%	36%	50%	32%	38%	38%	37%
Acquisitions/Collection development	13%	30	6%	40%	11%		18%		12%	11%
Cataloging	11%	26	29%	20%	3%	25%	14%	6%	15%	5%
Reference	10%	24			13%		13%	19%	4%	5%
Inter-Library Loan	7%	17	6%		14%		6%	6%		
Online/Systems	1%	3			3%		1%			
Other	23%	53	29%	20%	20%	25%	14%	31%	31%	42%
Q.II-5C. How did that come about? (n = 158)										
My own initiative	55%	87	50%	43%	52%	67%	46%	62%	73%	73%
Through the library director	12%	19			19%		24%			7%
Q.II-6. What do you remember about the library's director as a librarian? (n = 392)										
Through other library staff	4%	6			6%		3%	8%		2%
Other	29%	46	50%	57%	23%	33%	27%	31%	27%	
Nothing	46%	182	71%	79%	6%	63%	32%	64%	54%	78%

	%	Totals	Carleton	Denison	Earlham	Grinnell	K'zoo	Law'ce	Mac	Sw'more
Positive	27%	105	11%	4%	62%		30%	16%	21%	5%
Neutral	15%	60	15%	13%	11%	13%	23%	16%	15%	12%
Outstanding	8%	31			21%		11%		8%	
Negative	4%	14	3%	4%		25%	5%	4%	3%	5%
Q.II-7. What do you remember about other [College] librarians? (n = 381)										
Positive	51%	196	32%	42%	74%	13%	55%	44%	54%	49%
Nothing	29%	111	35%	46%	9%	63%	29%	37%	32%	32%
Neutral	14%	54	22%	8%	15%	13%	13%	16%	10%	10%
Negative	5%	20	11%	4%	2%	13%	3%	2%	5%	10%
Q.II-8. What image did you have of "librarians" and of LIS when you left [College]?										
Librarians (n = 357)										
Positive	57%	204	36%	60%	74%	67%	62%	57%	59%	38%
No image/Neutral	25%	90	38%	20%	17%	17%	22%	30%	24%	31%
Negative	12%	42	17%	16%	2%	17%	14%	11%	8%	21%
Mixed	6%	21	9%	4%	6%		3%	3%	8%	10%
Library and Information Science (n = 64)										
Positive	59%	38	40%	50%	74%	67%	57%	86%	33%	60%
No image/Neutral	22%	14	20%	50%	16%	33%	29%		50%	20%
Negative	13%	8	27%		5%			14%	17%	20%
Mixed	6%	4	13%		5%		14%			
Q.II-9. What, ultimately made you actually attend a LIS school for graduate work? (n = 600 comments made)										
It was the right fit for me	33%	199	37%	26%	30%	36%	28%	35%	34%	42%
There were opportunities for jobs	21%	125	24%	26%	23%	7%	26%	18%	12%	15%
LIS seemed intellectually challenging	9%	51	9%	9%	9%	21%	8%	8%	8%	6%
Attracted by LIS role models	6%	38	3%	6%	13%		4%	5%	3%	9%
I wanted a career	6%	34	4%		6%		10%	3%	7%	5%
Received financial support from SLIS	5%	28	4%	3%	5%	7%	5%	7%	4%	3%
Path to other satisfactions	3%	17	0%	3%	2%		4%	5%	5%	
I wanted to help others	3%	17	2%	6%	3%	7%	3%	1%	3%	2%
I liked libraries/librarians	3%	17	4%	6%	2%		3%	1%	1%	5%
SLIS geographically convenient for me	3%	15	2%		2%		2%	3%	4%	6%
My family situation allowed for attendance	3%	15	1%	3%	1%		3%	4%	5%	3%
I was accepted by a SLIS	2%	10	1%	6%	2%		1%	1%	1%	3%
LIS fit my values	2%	10	1%	3%	2%	7%		3%	3%	2%

	%	Totals	Carleton	Denison	Earlham	Grinnell	K'zoo	Law'ce	Mac	Sw'more
Otherwise bad job market	2%	9	1%		1%	7%	3%	3%	1%	
My employer would (help) pay	1%	8	2%	6%				3%	3%	
I liked the LIS courses I had already taken	1%	7	2%			7%	1%		4%	
Q.II-10. Which LIS school did you enter? (n = 411)										
Arizona, University of		2						1%	1%	
Ball State University [1978-1985]		1			1%					
Brigham Young University [1968-1995]		1			1%					
British Columbia, University of		2	1%						1%	
California - Berkeley, University of	1%	3					1%			2%
CA - Los Angeles, University of	1%	4			1%		1%			1%
Case Western Reserve University [1924-1987]	2%	7			2%		2%			1%
Catholic University of America	2%	7	1%	2%			1%	2%		1%
Chicago, University of [1932-1991]	3%	13	5%				1%	2%	1%	1%
Columbia University [1925-1993]	4%	16	2%	2%	2%		1%	2%	1%	6%
Denver, University of	2%	9	3%	2%	1%		1%		2%	
Dominican University	3%	12	2%		1%		1%	2%	3%	1%
Drexel University	4%	15			3%		2%	1%		6%
Emory University [1928-1990]		1			1%					
Emporia State University	1%	3	1%		1%			1%		
Florida State University		2		2%						1%
Illinois, University of	7%	29	5%	6%	3%		2%	4%	5%	1%
Indiana University	9%	38	2%	2%	15%		1%	2%		1%
Iowa, University of	2%	9	2%	2%		6%		1%	3%	
Kent State University	2%	9	1%	4%	1%		1%	2%		1%
Kentucky, University of		2		2%				1%		
Louisiana State University		2	1%	2%						
Maryland, University of	2%	8		2%	2%		1%		1%	
Michigan, University of	8%	34	2%	6%	4%	25%	8%	1%	2%	1%
Minnesota, University of [1932-1986]	4%	15	2%			6%	1%	2%	8%	
New York - Albany, State University of	1%	4					2%		1%	
NY - Buffalo, State University of		1					1%			
NY - Geneseo, State University of [1944-1985]		2						2%		
North Carolina - Chapel Hill, University of	1%	5	1%							1%
NC - Central, University of		1			1%					
Oklahoma, University of		2					1%	1%		
Oregon, University of [1966-1980]		1					1%			

	%	Totals	Carleton	Denison	Earlham	Grinnell	K'zoo	Law'ce	Mac	Sw'more
Pittsburgh, University of	1%	4		2%	1%				1%	1%
Portland State University		1	1%							
Pratt Institute		1	1%							
Queens College, City University of New York	1%	3			1%		1%		1%	
Rhode Island, University of	1%	6			1%		1%	1%		1%
Rosary College (see Dominican University)										
Rutgers University	3%	13			2%		1%	3%	1%	5%
Sam Houston State University		1							1%	
San Jose State University	1%	5	2%	2%			1%	1%		
Simmons College	6%	24	5%	4%	3%	6%	2%	1%	1%	5%
South Carolina, University of		2	1%				1%			
Southern California, University of [1936-1987]		2			1%			1%		
Southern Connecticut State University	1%	4			2%					1%
Southern Illinois University		1						1%		
Syracuse University	1%	4	1%	4%				1%		
Technology, University of (Sidney)		1							1%	
Texas - Austin, University of	1%	6			1%		1%	1%	2%	
Toronto, University of		1			1%					
Washington, University of	2%	9	1%	2%			1%		2%	4%
Wayne State University	2%	8					5%			
Western Michigan University [1946-1984]	4%	15					8%		1%	
Western Ontario, University of		1	1%							
Wisconsin - Madison, University of	7%	29	6%		2%	6%	1%	5%	7%	4%
Wisconsin - Milwaukee, University of	2%	10	1%	2%			1%	7%		
Q.II-11. What year did you enter? and Q.II-11A. In what year did you graduate with the master's degree?:										
Q.II-11 and Q.II-11 were combined to identify length of Alums' programs (n = 405)										
1 Year Spread	48%	195	46%	52%	51%	63%	47%	42%	49%	50%
2 Year Spread	30%	120	19%	28%	29%	13%	36%	40%	26%	33%
2+ Year Spread	22%	90	35%	20%	20%	25%	17%	19%	26%	18%
Q.II-11B. Or [in what year did you] leave the program? (n = 26)										
No LIS courses or still an MLIS student	81%	21	83%	100%	50%		83%	100%		80%
Left without the MLIS	19%	5	17%		50%		17%		100%	20%

	%	Totals	Carleton	Denison	Earlham	Grinnell	K'zoo	Law'ce	Mac	Sw'more
Q.II-12. Did you work in a library during your time in LIS School? (n = 419)										
Yes	75%	315	76%	73%	80%	63%	77%	80%	62%	74%
No	25%	104	24%	27%	20%	38%	23%	20%	38%	26%
Q.II-13. What image did you have of "librarians" and LIS when you left LIS school?										
Librarians (n =351)										
Positive	70%	247	70%	54%	64%	67%	79%	80%	74%	63%
Mixed	15%	51	10%	19%	15%	33%	11%	7%	21%	23%
Negative	8%	29	11%	15%	11%		3%	5%	5%	11%
No image/Neutral	7%	24	9%	12%	10%		7%	7%		3%
Library and Information Science (n = 116)										
Positive	63%	73	74%	20%	50%	67%	72%	89%	60%	63%
Negative	23%	27	16%		35%	33%	22%	11%	35%	13%
Mixed	9%	11	11%	80%	8%				5%	13%
No image/Neutral	4%	5			8%		6%			13%
Q.II-14. In how many libraries have you worked since leaving your LIS School? (n = 418)										
0	2%	9			3%		6%		2%	
1-2	48%	199	52%	67%	50%	50%	42%	53%	36%	41%
3-5	38%	157	34%	33%	31%	50%	41%	37%	45%	45%
over 5	13%	53	14%		16%		12%	10%	17%	14%
Q.II-15. How many total number of years of LIS-related work have you had since finishing your LIS graduate education? (n = 413)										
0	2%	7			11%		4%	2%	4%	
1-3	7%	28	2%		5%		9%	8%	13%	12%
4-10	23%	96	28%	22%	25%	17%	22%	24%	21%	19%
11-15	15%	61	15%	15%	17%	50%	11%	24%	8%	7%
16-20	14%	57	18%	19%	16%	17%	10%	6%	13%	16%
21-30	29%	118	22%	30%	28%	17%	37%	28%	25%	30%
over 30	11%	46	15%	15%	7%		9%	8%	10%	16%
Q.II-16. Are you (or have you been) employed as a librarian/information professional? (n = 428)										
Yes	97%	416	100%	100%	98%	88%	93%	100%	98%	96%
No	3%	12			2%	13%	7%		2%	4%

	%	Totals	Carleton	Denison	Earlham	Grinnell	K'zoo	Law'ce	Mac	Sw'more
Q.II-16A. In what type of LIS organization do you work? (n = 422)										
Academic	33%	138	27%	28%	32%	43%	38%	32%	26%	41%
Public	34%	142	34%	45%	35%	29%	26%	40%	39%	25%
School	11%	45	12%	3%	7%	14%	15%	14%	13%	7%
Special (specify)	23%	97	26%	24%	26%	14%	21%	14%	22%	27%
Q.II-16B. Have you worked in more than one type of LIS organization? (n = 421)										
No	45%	190	54%	59%	40%	50%	42%	36%	70%	38%
Yes, these types (n = 498 choices made):	55%	217	46%	41%	60%	50%	58%	64%	30%	62%
Academic	31%	156	32%	23%	30%	38%	29%	38%	35%	32%
Public	27%	136	22%	18%	33%	38%	28%	28%	25%	26%
School	11%	56	12%	9%	10%		14%	8%	15%	10%
Special	25%	123	30%	32%	20%	13%	28%	22%	19%	29%
Other	5%	27	4%	18%	7%	13%	2%	4%	6%	5%
Q.II-16C. Approximately how large is your current library?										
(not analyzed by college but by library type; see Appendix H)										
Q.II-16D. What responsibilities do you have in your current position? (n = 2477 choices made)										
Reference/reader services/information and referral	13%	311	13%	14%	12%	13%	13%	12%	12%	13%
Collection development and management/Acquisitions	12%	295	7%	12%	12%	8%	12%	13%	11%	12%
Database searching	11%	262	11%	13%	11%	8%	10%	10%	11%	11%
Administration/management	10%	252	10%	10%	10%	10%	11%	10%	12%	8%
Group activities (e.g., curriculum development)	9%	216	9%	7%	9%	10%	10%	9%	8%	8%
Cat/classif/indexing/abst/thesaurus construction	6%	160	6%	7%	6%	4%	7%	7%	5%	7%
Website development and/or maintenance	6%	148	8%	5%	6%	8%	5%	5%	6%	6%
Automation planning, design and coordination	5%	132	6%	5%	4%	8%	6%	5%	6%	4%
Circulation/access services	5%	131	4%	5%	7%	6%	5%	4%	5%	6%
Publicity/public relations/fund-raising	5%	126	5%	4%	6%	6%	5%	5%	6%	3%
Outreach services	5%	125	4%	5%	6%	4%	4%	6%	6%	5%
Interlibrary loan	3%	78	3%	6%	2%	2%	4%	3%	2%	3%
Conservation/preservation	3%	74	2%	3%	3%	2%	3%	4%	2%	4%
Records management/archives	3%	71	2%	3%	3%	2%	2%	4%	3%	3%
Other:	4%	96	3%	2%	4%	6%	3%	3%	5%	6%
The two areas in which you spend most of your time (n = 755 choices made)										
Reference/reader services/information and referral	25%	192	24%	30%	29%	21%	21%	29%	22%	25%
Administration/management	17%	131	17%	14%	16%	29%	19%	21%	20%	12%

	%	Totals	Carleton	Denison	Earlham	Grinnell	K'zoo	Law'ce	Mac	Sw'more
Collection development and management/Acquisitions	14%	109	13%	18%	12%	7%	19%	15%	13%	13%
Group activities (e.g., curriculum development)	10%	77	11%	6%	10%	14%	11%	8%	13%	10%
Cat/classif/indexing/abst/thesaurus construction	7%	56	6%	6%	7%	7%	11%	7%	2%	12%
Database searching	5%	37	9%	16%	4%		2%	1%	6%	2%
Circulation/access services	3%	26	3%		4%	7%	5%	2%	1%	6%
Automation planning, design and coordination	3%	21	6%		4%		1%	3%	2%	2%
Publicity/public relations/fund-raising	3%	19	3%	2%	2%		3%	1%	7%	
Website development and/or maintenance	3%	19	3%	2%	4%	7%	1%	4%		2%
Outreach services	1%	9	2%				2%		3%	1%
Interlibrary loan	1%	6	2%	2%					1%	2%
Records management/archives	1%	6		4%			1%	1%	2%	
Conservation/preservation	1%	5			<1			1%		4%
Other	6%	42	3%		8%	7%	4%	6%	8%	7%
Q.II-16E. How many years of experience do you have in your current LIS job? (n = 402)										
0-1	9%	35	3%		10%	14%	5%	12%	22%	9%
2-5	32%	129	44%	14%	40%	14%	38%	29%	33%	26%
6-10	21%	85	23%	32%	24%	29%	13%	18%	22%	23%
11-15	15%	62	23%	25%	7%	29%	18%	16%	4%	19%
16-20	11%	43	9%	18%	7%		13%	16%	9%	9%
21-30	10%	40	11%	7%	12%		13%	6%	4%	14%
over 30	2%	8	2%	4%		14%	1%	4%	4%	
Q.II-16F. What is your exact job title?										
(not analyzed by college but by library type: see text in Chapter 5)										
Q.II-16G. What is the average number of hours per week that you work in your LIS position? (n = 406)										
1-9	1%	4	1%		1%		1%		2%	
10-19	5%	19	3%	14%	2%	14%	3%		4%	14%
20-29	8%	33	9%	18%	6%	14%	9%	6%	4%	10%
30-39	25%	102	21%	29%	28%	14%	26%	29%	17%	29%
40 or more	61%	248	66%	39%	63%	57%	61%	65%	72%	48%
Q.II-16H. How satisfied are you with each of the following aspects of your current position?										
Working hours (n = 396)										
VS	33%	130	24%	46%	35%	14%	34%	30%	38%	33%
S	45%	178	52%	39%	38%	71%	48%	48%	38%	44%

	%	Totals	Carleton	Denison	Earlham	Grinnell	K'zoo	Law'ce	Mac	Sw'more
OK	14%	55	18%	11%	12%	14%	11%	14%	18%	14%
NS	8%	33	7%	1%	15%		6%	8%	7%	9%
Supervision/feedback (n = 396)										
VS	18%	71	15%	11%	18%	14%	17%	22%	21%	21%
S	36%	144	38%	33%	35%	14%	34%	43%	44%	33%
OK	25%	99	29%	33%	19%	29%	29%	27%	23%	19%
NS	21%	82	18%	22%	29%	43%	21%	8%	12%	28%
Responsibilities (n = 405)										
VS	36%	146	30%	39%	38%	14%	33%	39%	47%	35%
S	48%	193	51%	43%	48%	57%	52%	49%	33%	49%
OK	11%	45	15%	14%	8%		11%	10%	11%	12%
NS	5%	21	4%	4%	6%	29%	4%	2%	9%	5%
Salary (n = 402)										
VS	18%	71	15%	14%	20%	43%	17%	16%	20%	16%
S	39%	157	41%	46%	41%	29%	41%	38%	32%	35%
OK	25%	102	26%	25%	22%	14%	24%	28%	27%	30%
NS	18%	72	18%	14%	17%	14%	18%	18%	20%	19%
Opportunities to use my skills and abilities (n = 404)										
VS	50%	200	49%	46%	51%	29%	44%	57%	52%	51%
S	29%	119	30%	39%	25%	29%	34%	22%	34%	26%
OK	11%	44	7%	11%	11%	14%	10%	12%	11%	14%
NS	10%	41	13%	4%	13%	29%	11%	8%	2%	9%
Opportunities for development/promotion (n = 387)										
VS	14%	55	15%	12%	18%	17%	8%	12%	19%	14%
S	34%	133	37%	35%	28%	33%	35%	43%	44%	33%
OK	29%	114	22%	27%	30%		34%	35%	31%	31%
NS	22%	85	26%	27%	24%	50%	23%	10%	17%	21%
Range of people employed in my library (n = 370)										
VS	22%	80	25%	7%	29%	29%	16%	13%	25%	26%
S	42%	156	33%	67%	49%	14%	41%	49%	41%	29%
OK	22%	82	32%	15%	6%	29%	30%	18%	20%	34%
NS	14%	52	10%	11%	17%	29%	14%	20%	14%	11%
People I work most closely with (n = 396)										
VS	45%	177	47%	39%	46%	67%	35%	44%	57%	47%
S	38%	150	30%	46%	40%	17%	44%	38%	34%	37%
OK	12%	48	19%	11%	6%		18%	12%	9%	10%
NS	5%	21	5%	4%	8%	17%	4%	6%		7%

	%	Totals	Carleton	Denison	Earlham	Grinnell	K'zoo	Law'ce	Mac	Sw'more
The autonomy I have to do my own work (n = 400)										
VS	60%	239	60%	71%	61%	57%	54%	57%	59%	63%
S	28%	113	26%	21%	23%	29%	32%	33%	36%	28%
OK	7%	29	11%	4%	8%	14%	8%	8%	2%	5%
NS	5%	19	3%	4%	8%		7%	2%	2%	5%
Q.II-16I: If you could spend more time on one work activity, which one would it be? (n = 396)										
Work with the public	22%	86	22%	30%	27%	25%	21%	14%	18%	22%
Collection development	11%	45	12%	26%	6%	13%	12%	14%	11%	10%
Computer work	11%	44	9%	4%	11%	13%	13%	14%	16%	7%
Reference work	9%	35	9%	13%	7%	13%	12%	10%	4%	7%
Cataloging/Indexing	7%	27	3%	4%	8%		10%	10%	2%	7%
Instruction/Teaching	7%	26	4%	4%	10%	13%	5%	4%	4%	12%
Research work	5%	20	7%		4%		9%	4%	4%	2%
Management/Administration	5%	19	6%	4%	4%		5%	2%	13%	
Outreach/Liaison	4%	16		4%	6%		5%	4%	2%	7%
Programming/Program development	3%	13	3%		1%		1%	6%	7%	7%
Readers' advisory	3%	10	3%		2%	25%	1%	2%	2%	2%
Policy development/Planning	2%	8	1%		5%			2%	4%	
Staff development/Training	2%	8	6%		1%		1%	2%	2%	
Archives/Preservation	1%	5			1%			2%	2%	5%
Mixture I have now	1%	5	1%				1%	6%		
Students (Teens-College age)	1%	5	4%							5%
Writing	1%	5		4%	4%					2%
PR	1%	4					3%	4%		
Children's work	1%	3			1%				4%	
Bibliography	1%	2	1%	4%						
Consulting	1%	2	3%							
Work with technologies	1%	2	1%				1%			
Young adult services	1%	2	1%		1%					
Committee work		1								2%
Learning		1	1%							
Private time		1							2%	
Serials work		1			1%					

Q.II-16J. What do you like best about your own specific LIS work? (nc = 625)	%	Totals	Carleton	Denison	Earlham	Grinnell	K'zoo	Law'ce	Mac	Sw'more
Functions (n = 115 comments made)										
Collection development	23%	27	23%		19%		23%	17%	36%	36%
Reference	17%	20	14%		19%		8%	42%	21%	18%
Children through young adults	16%	18	14%		15%		23%	8%	14%	18%
Managing/Administering/Working with my staff	14%	16	18%	33%	22%		4%	17%	7%	9%
Cataloging/indexing	10%	11	9%	33%	4%		23%			9%
Outreach/liaison	9%	10	5%	33%	19%		4%	8%	7%	
Programming	7%	8	9%		4%		8%	8%	7%	9%
Readers' advisory	3%	4	5%				8%		7%	
Archives	1%	1	5%							
Activities (n = 239 comments made)										
Helping patrons/users/people	42%	101	27%	40%	46%	20%	50%	42%	52%	42%
Searching/finding/research	15%	36	20%	27%	11%		22%	8%	4%	17%
Doing creative things	8%	18	11%		7%	20%		19%	4%	8%
Continuing to learn	8%	18	9%	13%	5%		7%	4%	4%	17%
Instruction/teaching	8%	18	7%	7%	11%	20%	2%	12%	9%	4%
Technological things	6%	14	2%		7%	20%	7%	4%	13%	4%
Problem solving	5%	13	5%	7%	5%		7%	8%	4%	4%
Service expansion/improvements/implementation	5%	11	11%	7%	4%		2%		4%	4%
Affecting the organization	3%	7	5%		4%	20%	2%	4%		
Empowering users	1%	2	2%						4%	
Mentoring	<1%	1					2%			
Work Environment (n = 271 comments made)										
Variety in my work	32%	87	34%	24%	22%	20%	33%	39%	45%	35%
Autonomy/Authority/Freedom	21%	57	14%	24%	26%	40%	22%	13%	21%	20%
Great colleagues/boss/users	15%	42	23%	16%	12%		10%	23%	10%	20%
Challenges/Intellectual nature of work/using my mind	12%	32	6%	16%	12%	40%	16%	10%	10%	8%
Positive work environment	6%	15	6%	8%	7%		2%	6%	3%	8%
Opportunity to work with specific materials	4%	12		8%	9%		6%	3%		3%
Good hours/schedule	3%	9	6%		5%		4%			5%
User gratitude	3%	9	9%		2%		6%	3%		3%
Expertise	1%	3	3%		2%				3%	
I am respected	1%	3		4%	2%			3%		
Sense of accomplishment	1%	2			2%				3%	
Fit	<1%								3%	

Q.II-16K. What do you like least about your own specific LIS work?	%	Totals	Carleton	Denison	Earlham	Grinnell	K'zoo	Law'ce	Mac	Sw'more
Job-Related (n = 195 comments made)										
Paperwork/busy work/non-LIS work	23%	45	29%	25%	23%		12%	29%	28%	23%
Not enough time for work responsibilities	17%	33	21%	25%	12%	20%	24%	18%	6%	14%
Specific tasks	14%	28	12%	8%	16%	20%	21%	14%		18%
Managing/Administering	11%	21	6%	8%	12%	40%	18%	7%	6%	9%
Lack of variety	11%	21	6%	17%	9%	20%	9%	11%	17%	14%
Certain technologies	10%	20	15%		14%			7%	33%	5%
Meetings	4%	8			7%		6%	4%	6%	5%
Lack of knowledge on my part	3%	6	3%		2%		6%	4%		5%
Too much variety	3%	5			5%			4%	6%	5%
Distraction from my primary work	2%	3	3%	8%				4%		
Lack of control/authority	1%	2	3%				3%			
Lack of inclusion in decision-making	1%	2		8%						5%
Monitoring computer use	1%	1	3%							
Working Conditions (Internal) (n = 80 comments made)										
Job constraints	43%	34	64%	20%	50%	50%	50%	25%	33%	33%
Organizational bureaucracy/structure	19%	15	18%	20%	7%		25%		33%	22%
Lack of staff	16%	13	9%	40%	21%	50%	6%	38%	13%	
Lack of sufficient salary	9%	7	9%		7%		13%	13%	13%	0%
Poor work environment	6%	5			7%		6%		7%	22%
Lack of sufficient benefits	4%	3			7%			13%		11%
Facility problems	1%	1						13%		
Inability to hire needed staff	1%	1		20%						
Lack of advancement possibilities	1%	1								11%
Working Conditions (External) (n = 73 comments made)										
Lack of budgetary support	62%	45	63%	33%	76%	100%	58%	86%	50%	33%
Politics	22%	16	13%	17%	12%		33%	14%	38%	50%
Justifying to higher authorities	8%	6	13%	17%	6%		8%		13%	
Fund-raising/grant writing need	5%	4	13%	17%	6%					
Doing PR/marketing	3%	2		17%						17%
People: Problems (Internal) (n = 61 comments made)										
Personnel problems/supervising	46%	28	58%	50%	15%	100%	50%	25%	67%	43%
Boss	31%	19	17%	50%	46%		40%	75%	17%	14%
Colleagues	21%	13	17%		38%		10%		17%	43%
Biased people within the organization	2%	1	8%							

	%	Totals	Carleton	Denison	Earlham	Grinnell	K'zoo	Law'ce	Mac	Sw'more
People: Problems (External) (n = 30 comments made)										
Problem patrons	60%	18	44%		80%		80%		100%	75%
People (undefined)	17%	5	22%				20%	50%		25%
Incompetence	10%	3		50%	20%			50%		
Rude people	10%	3	22%	50%						
Naïve/inexperienced people	3%	1	11%							
Respect (n = 14 comments made)										
Lack of respect from administrators	57%	8	67%				67%	100%	50%	
Lack of respect (undefined)	21%	3		100%	100%		17%			
Lack of respect from public	21%	3	33%				17%		50%	
Wrong Fit (n = 12 comments made)										
Wrong job for me	67%	8	100%	100%	50%		67%	50%		100%
Wrong type of library for me	33%	4			50%		33%	50%	100%	
Q.II-16L. How satisfied are you with your choice of an LIS as a career? (n = 406)										
Very Satisfied	69%	280	71%	79%	62%	71%	69%	73%	72%	65%
Moderately Satisfied	26%	105	26%	14%	30%	29%	27%	24%	21%	34%
Very Dissatisfied	5%	21	3%	7%	8%		4%	4%	6%	5%
Q.II-16M. What do you like best about LIS work in general? (n = 617 comments made)										
Service to others/helping people/people focus	33%	202	35%	29%	41%	33%	26%	35%	32%	27%
Intellectual challenge	19%	115	22%	18%	15%	22%	22%	9%	22%	20%
Variety in the field	11%	67	7%	15%	12%	11%	11%	12%	14%	8%
Access to materials, technologies, information	11%	67	10%	18%	12%	11%	14%	7%	5%	11%
Continuous learring	6%	34	5%	6%	3%	6%	2%	6%	9%	12%
Ethics/values/mission of the field	4%	25	3%		2%		4%	9%	5%	7%
Positive work environment	4%	22	3%	3%	2%	6%	6%	3%		7%
Career flexibility	3%	16	4%		2%	6%	4%	3%		1%
Fit between LIS and me	3%	19	2%	6%	3%		3%	6%	3%	1%
Specific jobs	3%	18	3%	3%	2%	6%	2%	1%	5%	3%
My colleagues	2%	11	1%		3%		3%	1%	1%	
Teaching/training others	2%	10	1%		2%		1%	4%	3%	
Autonomy I have	1%	8		3%	1%		1%	3%		4%
Skill set required		3	2%		1%					

	%	Totals	Carleton	Denison	Earlham	Grinnell	K'zoo	Law'ce	Mac	Sw'more
Q.II-16N. What do you like least about LIS work in general? (n = 327 comments made)										
Lack of respect from others	16%	53	7%	14%	23%	17%	18%	20%	8%	21%
Lack of understanding regarding the field	15%	48	30%	14%	9%	33%	7%	10%	19%	13%
Paperwork/busy work/non-LIS work	10%	33	14%	9%	11%		8%	13%	11%	5%
Lack of variety in the work	7%	23	5%	5%	6%		11%	5%	5%	10%
Problem patrons/People outside of colleagues, boss	7%	21	5%	10%	7%		10%	5%	3%	5%
Colleagues	6%	21	7%	9%	5%		7%	8%	8%	5%
Cataloging	4%	12	2%	9%	3%		2%	5%	5%	5%
Certain technologies	4%	12	2%	5%	5%	17%		3%	8%	5%
Managing/Administering	4%	13	4%		3%		5%	5%	3%	8%
Job constraints	4%	13	2%	0%	5%		7%	8%	5%	
Specific work assignments	3%	10	2%	5%	3%		2%		5%	8%
Lack of intellectual challenge	3%	9	4%		5%		2%	3%	3%	3%
Not enough time for work responsibilities	3%	9	5%	5%	2%		3%		3%	3%
Boss	3%	11	2%		5%		8%		5%	
Wrong field for me	3%	11	4%	5%	3%	33%	2%	3%	3%	3%
Meetings	2%	6			2%		3%	5%		3%
Stress produced by the work	2%	6		5%	3%		3%	3%		
Personnel problems/supervising	2%	6	2%	0%	2%		3%		5%	
Too much change in the field	2%	7	4%	5%	3%		0%	5%		
Lack of time/support for doing quality work	1%	2		5%						3%
Lack of advancement	<1%	1								3%
Q.II-16O. What is the likelihood of your continuing as an LIS professional for the foreseeable future? (n = 405)										
Very Likely	78%	315	82%	86%	74%	71%	75%	80%	76%	79%
Moderately Likely	12%	47	12%	7%	13%		9%	14%	13%	14%
Very Unlikely	11%	43	6%	7%	14%	29%	16%	6%	11%	7%
Section III. CAREERS, OCCUPATIONS, AND GOALS										
Q.III-1. What were your career goals as a child? (n = 567 comments made)										
Arts	8%	46	6%	13%	7%	16%	6%	13%	9%	7%
Aviation	2%	10	2%	0%	2%		2%	2%	1%	3%
Business	3%	16	5%	6%		5%	3%	2%	3%	3%
College work (all kinds)	1%	6			1%	5%	1%	2%		3%
Computer work	<1%	2	1%		1%					
Engineer	1%	3			2%		1%			
Farmer		1								2%

	%	Totals	Carleton	Denison	Earlham	Grinnell	K'zoo	Law'ce	Mac	Sw'more
Fireman	1%	3		3%			2%			
Financial work		1					1%			
Government/Politics	2%	13				11%	4%	2%	3%	5%
Health professions	9%	53	12%	13%	4%	5%	17%	3%	10%	5%
Homemaker/Parent	3%	16	6%	0%	2%		1%	3%	3%	5%
K-12 educator/Teacher	16%	88	16%	22%	18%	16%	13%	13%	17%	10%
Law	1%	8	2%		3%		2%		1%	
Letter carrier		1	1%							
LIS work/Book-centered	5%	28	2%	6%	8%	5%	4%	5%	7%	2%
Manufacturing/Trades	1%	6			1%		3%	2%	1%	
Military	<1%	2							1%	2%
Office work	1%	4		3%	2%	5%				
Outdoors (in general)/Horticulture	3%	19	2%		5%	5%	3%	2%	3%	7%
Religious position	2%	9	2%	3%	1%	0%	2%		4%	
Scientist, including mathematician	8%	47	12%	3%	5%		7%	18%	4%	10%
Sports	2%	12	2%		4%		1%		1%	5%
Student	1%	8	0%		2%		1%	2%	4%	2%
Service work	3%	18		3%	5%	5%	2%	2%	7%	3%
To be rich	1%	4	2%		1%				1%	
Writing/Publishing/Journalist	7%	41	8%	9%	6%	11%	6%	5%	6%	12%
Veterinarian/Work with animals	4%	20	3%	3%	5%	5%	3%	3%	1%	5%
None	14%	82	13%	13%	17%	5%	17%	22%	9%	10%
Q.III-2. What were your career goals when you started college? (n = 481 comments made)										
Arts	7%	32	2%	10%	9%		4%	16%	5%	4%
Aviation		1			1%					
Business	1%	3			2%		1%			
College work (all kinds)	4%	18	6%		2%		2%	2%	4%	11%
Computer Work	1%	3	1%	3%	1%					
Engineer	<1%	2	1%		1%					
Farmer		1	1%							
Financial work		1					1%			
Government/Politics	4%	21	6%	3%	5%		2%	4%	9%	2%
Health professions	6%	29	7%	7%	4%		6%	2%	9%	9%
Historian	1%	5	1%	3%	1%		1%	2%		
Homemaker/Parent	1%	7	1%	3%	3%					4%
K-12 educator/Teacher	15%	72	12%	10%	15%	20%	22%	14%	14%	9%

	%	Totals	Carleton	Denison	Earlham	Grinnell	K'zoo	Law'ce	Mac	Sw'more
Language work	3%	14	1%	3%	2%		5%	4%	2%	4%
Law	4%	18	1%	3%	4%		4%	0%	9%	6%
LIS work/Book-centered	7%	36	7%	10%	10%		7%	6%	5%	6%
Outdoors (in general)/Horticulture	1%	4			4%					
Religious position	1%	3			1%			2%	2%	
Scientist, including mathematician	9%	42	12%		8%		13%	10%	5%	6%
Student	2%	12	4%	3%				6%	2%	4%
Service work	5%	24	7%	3%	5%		4%	4%	4%	6%
Volunteer	1%	6			5%					
Writing/Publishing/Journalist	4%	21	1%	3%		20%	4%	8%	7%	11%
Veterinarian/Work with animals		1					1%			
None	22%	105	25%	33%	17%	60%	20%	18%	25%	20%
Q.III-3. In what other occupations or work have you been interested - in addition to or instead of LIS? (n = 656 comments made)										
Arts	12%	77	6%	11%	17%	8%	9%	12%	9%	17%
Aviation		1			1%					
Being rich		2			1%			2%		
Business	6%	39	5%		6%	15%	5%	8%	11%	3%
College work (all kinds)	4%	29	3%	6%	5%		4%	2%	7%	5%
Computer work	4%	28	4%	6%	4%		8%	5%	4%	
Consultant		2					1%		1%	
Engineer		2			1%				1%	
Farmer		1								1%
Financial work	3%	18	4%		3%		2%	3%	2%	3%
Government/Politics	2%	15	2%	3%	1%		2%	3%	4%	2%
Health professions	5%	32	9%		3%		5%	5%	7%	3%
Historian	2%	15	4%	3%	3%		3%		1%	
Homemaker/Parent	1%	4	1%		1%		1%			1%
K-12 educator/Teacher	18%	115	16%	9%	16%	31%	23%	19%	12%	21%
Language work	1%	8		3%	1%		2%		2%	
Law	4%	23	6%	3%			5%		7%	3%
LIS work/Book-centered	2%	15	3%	3%	3%	8%	2%	3%	1%	
Manufacturing/Trades	1%	8			1%		2%		2%	2%
Office work	1%	4	4%							
Outdoors (in general)/Horticulture	2%	16	2%		4%		2%	2%	1%	3%
Religious position	2%	10	1%	3%	1%	8%	1%	3%		3%
Research work	1%	8	2%		1%	8%	2%	2%		

	%	Totals	Carleton	Denison	Earlham	Grinnell	K'zoo	Law'ce	Mac	Sw'more
Sales	2%	14		11%	2%		2%	3%	1%	2%
Scientist, including mathematician	6%	39	8%	9%	7%		4%	7%	5%	6%
Sports		1		3%						
Student		2						2%		1%
Service work	6%	37	5%	6%	7%	15%	5%	3%	6%	3%
Volunteer	1%	4			1%			3%		1%
Writing/Publishing/Journalism	9%	57	10%	11%	6%	8%	10%	7%	9%	10%
Veterinary/Work with animals	1%	5			1%			2%	1%	2%
None	4%	25	7%	11%	3%		3%	3%	2%	2%
Q.III-4. In what other occupations have you been involved over the course of your worklife? (n = 695 comments made)										
Arts	5%	38	6%	5%	8%	5%	3%	7%	1%	8%
Aviation		1						1%		
Business	10%	67	8%	9%	6%	16%	8%	16%	15%	8%
College work (all kinds)	3%	20	1%	2%	4%		3%	1%	1%	8%
Computer work	3%	23	3%	5%	4%		4%	3%	5%	1%
Consultant	1%	7			1%		2%		4%	
Engineer		1	1%							
Farmer	<1%	3			1%					1%
Financial work	3%	20	3%	2%	3%		3%	3%	4%	3%
Government/Politics	2%	11	1%	2%	1%	5%		4%	5%	
Health professions	3%	18	3%		3%	5%	2%	4%	4%	1%
Historian	<1%	3		2%	1%					
Homemaker/Parent	1%	8	2%	2%	1%		1%			2%
K-12 Educator/Teacher	13%	92	12%	2%	9%	11%	16%	18%	15%	16%
Law	2%	11	3%		1%		2%	1%	1%	2%
LIS work/Book-centered	4%	26	3%		4%		5%	7%	4%	2%
Manufacturing/Trades	3%	20	2%		4%		5%	1%	4%	1%
Military	<1%	3			1%		1%	1%		
Office work	9%	66	10%	16%	9%	11%	10%	5%	5%	13%
Outdoors (in general)/Horticulture	2%	11	2%	2%	1%		2%	1%	1%	2%
Religious position	1%	9	2%		3%			1%		2%
Research work	1%	8	1%			5%	2%			3%
Sales	6%	45	8%	14%	6%	5%	7%	1%	8%	5%
Scientist, including mathematician	1%	7	1%	5%	1%		1%	1%		
Sports	<1%	2		2%	1%					
Service work	6%	42	4%	9%	11%	16%	5%	4%	4%	2%

	%	Totals	Carleton	Denison	Earlham	Grinnell	K'zoo	Law'ce	Mac	Sw'more
Volunteer	3%	20	2%		2%	16%	2%	4%	3%	5%
Writing/Publishing/Journalism	5%	37	6%	7%	2%	5%	5%	7%	5%	8%
Veterinary/Work with animals	<1%	3	1%		1%			1%		
Waiter/Waitress	2%	15	5%		3%		3%	1%	1%	
None	8%	58	12%	12%	9%		8%	4%	10%	5%
Q.III-5. What other occupation(s) have you considered going into? (n = 517 comments made)										
Arts	7%	37	11%	6%	9%	6%	5%	8%	5%	5%
Aviation		1	1%							
Business	7%	34	5%		5%	6%	9%	6%	12%	5%
College work (all kinds)	3%	18	4%	3%	4%		4%	2%		8%
Computer work	5%	24	5%	6%	4%		4%	6%	7%	3%
Consultant	2%	9			1%	18%	1%	4%	3%	
Engineer	1%	3			2%			2%		
Financial work	3%	14	3%		4%		3%	6%	3%	
Government/Politics	2%	8	1%		1%		2%	2%	3%	2%
Health professions	7%	34	8%	6%	5%	12%	5%	10%	5%	7%
Homemaker/Parent		2		3%				2%		
K-12 educator/Teacher	13%	68	11%	3%	11%	18%	18%	8%	15%	19%
Language work	1%	4					2%		2%	2%
Law	5%	28	1%	6%	5%		5%	8%	8%	8%
LIS work/Book-centered	4%	19	1%	3%	6%		3%		5%	7%
Manufacturing/Trades	1%	7		3%	3%		2%			2%
Office work	1%	3			1%		2%			
Outdoors (in general)/Horticulture	3%	15	4%	9%	3%		2%	4%	2%	2%
Religious position	1%	7	3%			6%	1%	6%		
Research work	2%	10	3%		1%	6%	3%		3%	2%
Sales	2%	10	1%		2%		3%	4%		3%
Scientist, including mathematician	2%	11	1%	3%	3%		4%	2%		2%
Sports	1%	3	3%		1%					
Student		1			1%					
Service work	3%	15	3%		1%	6%	7%	2%	2%	2%
Volunteer	2%	11	1%	3%	3%		1%	2%	5%	2%
Writing/Publishing/Journalism	11%	55	9%	24%	10%	12%	7%	10%	10%	14%
Veterinary/Work with animals	1%	4	1%	3%	2%					
None	12%	62	18%	18%	15%	12%	9%	10%	8%	7%

	%	Totals	Carleton	Denison	Earlham	Grinnell	K'zoo	Law'ce	Mac	Sw'more
Q.III-6. In addition to LIS work, do you do other types of work part-time? (n = 402)										
No	74%	296	77%	81%	67%	43%	79%	67%	87%	64%
Yes	26%	106	23%	19%	33%	57%	21%	33%	11%	36%
Kinds of Part-time Work: (n = 132 comments made)										
Business (small to large)	25%	33	27%	20%	28%		14%	45%		29%
Teaching	19%	25	13%	40%	8%	25%	29%	15%	43%	18%
Volunteer (nonpaid)	17%	22	27%	20%	14%	25%	14%	5%	43%	18%
Arts (arts, entertainment, music)	16%	21	7%	20%	22%	25%	11%	15%		24%
Writer	6%	8	7%		3%	25%	7%	10%		6%
Computer work	5%	6	7%		6%		7%		14%	
LIS (other than in own job)	5%	6			6%		7%	5%		6%
Farming/Gardening	3%	4			8%		4%			
Caretaker	3%	4	7%				7%	5%		
Coach/Instructor (nonpaid)	2%	2	7%		3%					
Ministry	1%	1			3%					
Q.III-7. If you are not currently working in an LIS field, have you ever been employed in LIS work? (n = 41)										
No	15%	6	1%				23%	20%	17%	
I never intended to actually work in an LIS field										
Yes, but I left it because:	85%	35	6%		100%		77%	80%	83%	100%
(reasons for leaving LIS field: n = 62 comments made)										
Found other work more interesting	23%	14	17%		31%	100%	25%	17%		
Retired	21%	13	33%	100%			21%	33%	33%	50%
LIS job not available/Laid off	15%	9	17%		6%		13%	17%	33%	50%
Be with children	13%	8			19%		13%	17%	17%	
Trailing spouse	11%	7			19%		8%	17%	17%	
LIS salary too low	8%	5			13%		13%			
Burned out/Bad job situation	6%	4	33%				8%			
Business closed	3%	2			13%					
Are you satisfied with the work you are now doing? (n = 29)										
Yes	100%	29	100%		100%		100%	100%	100%	
No										
In what field are you now working? (n = 62 comments made)										
Business	24%	15			44%		23%	17%	14%	50%
Retired	19%	12		100%	13%		18%	50%	29%	
Computers/IT Areas	13%	8	14%		13%		14%		14%	50%
Law, including paralegal	6%	4	14%		6%		9%			

	%	Totals	Carleton	Denison	Earlham	Grinnell	K'zoo	Law'ce	Mac	Sw'more
Being with children	6%	4					9%	17%	14%	
Caretaker	6%	4			13%		5%	17%		
Volunteer work	5%	3					9%		14%	
Retired but doing consulting	3%	2	14%						14%	
Craftwork	2%	1				100%				
Farming	2%	1			6%					
Ministry	2%	1			6%					
Museums	2%	1	14%							
Retired but working in business	2%	1	14%							
Retired but working with computers	2%	1	14%							
Retired but doing some teaching	2%	1	14%							
Social work	2%	1					5%			
Teaching	2%	1					5%			
Writing	2%	1					5%			
Q.III-8. What have been the greatest professional challenges for you since finishing LIS graduate work? (n = 475 comments made)										
Handling difficult work conditions	14%	67	7%	13%	18%	20%	10%	9%	21%	24%
Developing new technology skills	13%	64	13%	16%	15%	20%	15%	11%	9%	13%
Adjusting to new job	13%	62	8%	6%	13%	20%	14%	16%	19%	11%
Developing new skills	9%	42	12%	13%	11%		8%	4%	9%	7%
Developing new management skills	8%	37	14%	16%	4%		7%	4%	9%	4%
Handling a new project	8%	37	8%	6%	8%	20%	5%	11%	9%	4%
Handling change	6%	30	7%	6%	3%		9%	13%	4%	2%
Keeping library service going (budget constraints)	5%	26	7%	3%	6%	10%	4%	5%	4%	7%
Staying motivated	5%	26	9%	3%	6%		5%	7%		4%
Handling difficult coworkers	5%	24	1%	6%	5%	10%	5%	5%	5%	9%
Handling a difficult boss	5%	23	4%	3%	3%		7%	5%	5%	7%
Balancing work and family	3%	15	4%		3%		6%	4%	2%	
Handling difficult users	3%	12	1%	6%	2%		1%	4%	4%	4%
Adjusting to new library type	2%	10	5%		2%		1%	2%	2%	2%

	%	Totals	Carleton	Denison	Earlham	Grinnell	K'zoo	Law'ce	Mac	Sw'more
Q.III-9. What do you hope to accomplish in the next five years?										
Professional Goals (n = 414 comments made)										
Expand/Improve systems, services, facility, etc.	22%	91	26%	21%	8%	10%	21%	31%	29%	23%
Expand/improve services	11%	44	10%				10%	23%	19%	13%
Expand/improve technology	4%	16	6%	8%	4%		3%	2%	2%	4%
Improve my department/division	4%	17		13%	3%	10%	5%	4%	4%	6%
Build new building	3%	14	10%		1%		3%	2%	4%	
Professional/personal development	18%	76	16%	21%	21%	10%	16%	13%	13%	32%
Get/change jobs	12%	51	5%	13%	23%	10%	19%	12%	8%	4%
Stay employed/Motivated	10%	42	7%	21%	13%	10%	8%	10%	12%	9%
Get promoted/become manager or director	7%	30	11%	4%		10%	14%	6%	6%	6%
Retire	7%	27	9%	8%	7%		5%	2%	13%	2%
Research, write, publish	5%	22	13%	4%	11%					6%
Finish current projects	4%	15	6%		7%	10%	1%		2%	4%
Help others	4%	17	4%	4%	4%		4%	10%	2%	2%
Keep library services going (budget constraints)	3%	14	1%	4%	3%	10%	1%	4%	4%	8%
Continue as I have	2%	10					5%	4%	8%	
Have a satisfying career	2%	7	1%		1%	30%	1%	2%		
Balance work and family	1%	6	1%				1%	2%	4%	2%
Promote the LIS profession	1%	3			1%			2%		2%
Work well with my co+A1051workers	1%	3					3%			2%
Personal Goals (n = 519 comments made)										
Family focused	26%	133	29%	25%	29%	27%	25%	21%	29%	18%
Improve personal skills	9%	49	8%	6%	15%		11%	16%	5%	3%
Retire	9%	47	11%	6%	12%	9%	6%	5%	12%	10%
Travel	8%	41	13%	19%	2%	9%	5%	9%	8%	7%
Build savings	6%	31	9%		5%		7%	9%	5%	5%
Continue my education/learning	6%	30	2%	14%	7%	9%	6%	7%	6%	3%
Self-fulfillment goals	5%	26	2%	8%	9%	18%	7%	2%	3%	2%
Fix up my house	4%	22	2%	8%	4%		1%	5%	5%	10%
Health-related	4%	20	4%	3%	3%	18%	3%	2%	5%	5%
Write	4%	19	3%	3%	3%		5%	4%		8%
Work-related	4%	19	1%	3%	1%		5%	9%	5%	5%
Develop a lasting relationship	3%	17	4%			9%	4%	5%	5%	3%
Do some volunteer work	3%	15	2%	3%	2%		5%	2%	3%	3%
Find private time for myself	2%	12	5%		1%		2%		3%	3%
Help others	2%	11	1%				6%	2%	3%	2%

	%	Totals	Carleton	Denison	Earlham	Grinnell	K'zoo	Law'ce	Mac	Sw'more
Continue on as I have	1%	7	1%		2%		1%	2%	2%	2%
Become more community involved	1%	7			2%		1%		2%	5%
Become more church/religion involved	1%	6					3%			5%
Move geographically	1%	4	1%		1%				3%	
Stay employed	1%	3	1%	3%			1%			
Q.III-10. What do you feel proudest of with regards to your own careeer or work? (n = 505 comments made)										
Skills and work	30%	150	31%	47%	29%	13%	25%	31%	31%	29%
Keeping/using my skills	10%	49	14%	21%	7%	13%	7%	6%	6%	12%
Expansion of services	7%	33		12%	7%		6%	10%	4%	12%
High quality work	6%	31	12%	12%	5%		7%	5%	2%	2%
Improving services/standards	5%	24	1%	3%	8%		2%	6%	16%	
Doing my best	3%	13	4%		1%		3%	3%	4%	3%
Recognition from others	12%	59	10%	15%	11%	13%	13%	15%	10%	9%
Helping users	12%	59	10%	9%	11%	13%	12%	11%	10%	17%
Making a difference	8%	42	4%	9%	12%		7%	10%	10%	8%
My library	8%	42	14%	9%	9%	25%	8%	3%	8%	3%
Achieving good results	6%	30	3%	6%	3%		8%	13%	6%	5%
Having served my profession	6%	30	8%	3%	4%		9%	3%	6%	6%
Various personal advancements/promotions	3%	15	1%	3%	5%		5%	3%	2%	
My staff	3%	15	6%		4%	13%	1%	2%	6%	
Having success with change	3%	15	4%		5%		5%	2%	2%	
Writing/editing/publishing	2%	11	3%		2%		2%	2%	2%	5%
Persevering	2%	9	4%		1%			2%	4%	3%
My values	1%	7					5%	2%		2%
My personal self	1%	6						2%	2%	6%
Having a career and a family	1%	5	1%		2%				2%	2%
Having chosen the LIS field	1%	4				13%	1%	2%		2%
Working on social issues	1%	4								5%
Success in speaking engagements		2	1%		1%					
Q.III-11. What two activities do you enjoy when not working at your LIS or other regular job? (n = 894 comments made)										
Reading	22%	200	23%	29%	20%	21%	22%	17%	26%	23%
Arts	13%	113	10%	15%	10%	16%	13%	16%	8%	19%
Exercise	10%	89	5%	4%	11%	16%	11%	11%	12%	13%
Gardening	10%	85	7%	17%	12%	16%	7%	12%	7%	9%
Travel	7%	63	8%	10%	10%	11%	7%	3%	7%	4%

	%	Totals	Carleton	Denison	Earlham	Grinnell	K'zoo	Law'ce	Mac	Sw'more
Outdoors	7%	61	13%	4%	2%	5%	6%	8%	8%	7%
Hand Work	5%	48	5%	4%	9%		5%	5%	5%	4%
Cooking	4%	34	3%	4%	3%	11%	4%	8%	2%	3%
Club Activities	3%	30	1%	4%	2%		6%	2%	4%	5%
Pets	3%	23	3%		2%		2%	3%	4%	3%
Friends	2%	20	1%		2%	5%	3%	4%	2%	2%
Sports	2%	20	4%	4%	3%		1%	2%	3%	
Writing	2%	19	3%		3%		1%	1%	3%	3%
Cinema	2%	18	3%	2%	3%		2%	3%	2%	
Volunteer Work	2%	15	1%	2%	1%		5%	1%	1%	
Quilting	2%	14	2%		4%			2%	2%	
Learning	1%	13	3%	2%	1%		2%	1%		2%
Technology	1%	6	1%		2%			1%		
Photography	1%	5	1%		1%			1%	1%	
Puzzles	1%	5	1%		1%				1%	1%
Games	<1%	4			1%		2%			
Genealogy	<1%	4	1%				1%	1%	1%	
Home Improvements	<1%	2					1%			
Financial Management		1							1%	
Mentoring		1							1%	
Speaking		1							1%	
Section IV. DEMOGRAPHIC QUESTIONS										
Q.IV-1. Sex (n = 429)										
Female	78%	333	78%	79%	80%	88%	77%	74%	79%	73%
Male	22%	96	22%	21%	20%	13%	23%	26%	21%	27%
Q.IV-2. Current age (n = 412)										
21-29	3%	13	1%		4%	13%	5%	2%	2%	4%
30-39	15%	61	16%	11%	7%	38%	15%	10%	34%	9%
40-49	22%	92	27%	21%	28%	25%	14%	31%	9%	27%
50-59	50%	206	39%	54%	54%	25%	61%	52%	45%	49%
60-69	10%	40	16%	14%	7%		6%	4%	11%	16%
Q.IV-3. Current salary (under $21,000 - over $90,000 = n = 391)										
under $21,000	9%	37	11%	8%	10%	38%	6%	4%	11%	12%
$21,000-30,999	9%	37	6%	16%	11%		9%	9%	7%	14%

	%	Totals	Carleton	Denison	Earlham	Grinnell	K'zoo	Law'ce	Mac	Sw'more
$31,000-40,999	14%	60	15%	12%	16%	13%	12%	21%	17%	14%
$41,000-50,999	21%	88	18%	44%	22%	13%	19%	30%	20%	19%
$51,000-75,999	29%	124	34%	16%	27%	38%	39%	28%	33%	36%
$76,000-90,000	5%	23	6%	4%	10%		8%	4%	4%	
over $90,000	5%	22	9%		5%		6%	2%	9%	5%
Retired	*67%*	*20*	*100%*	*100%*	*57%*		*56%*	*67%*	*67%*	*67%*
Not currently earning a salary	*33%*	*10*			*43%*		*44%*	*33%*	*33%*	*33%*
Q.IV-4. Please indicate your ethnic background 429										
[not calculated; over 99% are Anglo-Caucasian)										
Q.IV-5. Was English the language you learned first? (n = 427)										
Yes	99%	424	100%	100%	100%	100%	99%	100%	96%	100%
No, I learned -- (Greek:1; Spanish: 2)	1%	3					1%		4%	
Q.IV-6. Is English the language most commonly used in your home? (n = 425)										
Yes	99%	422	100%	100%	100%	100%	100%	98%	98%	98%
No, it is -- (Greek: 1; Spanish: 2)	1%	3						2%	2%	2%
Q.IV-7. Do you have any physical disabilities? (n = 422)										
No	94%	395	94%	93%	89%	100%	97%	100%	94%	88%
Yes*	6%	27	6%	7%	11%		3%		6%	12%
* Responses include asthma, blindness, epilepsy, chronic fatigue syndrome, chronic headaches, fibromyalgia, fused spine due to scoliosis, and heart disease.										
Q.IV-8. Marital Status (n = 425)										
Married/Partnered	75%	317	74%	79%	73%	88%	79%	69%	67%	79%
Single	15%	65	14%	11%	15%	13%	10%	16%	27%	26%
Divorced/Separated	9%	40	10%	11%	11%		10%	12%	6%	5%
Widowed	1%	3	1%		1%			2%		
What does your spouse/partner do? (n = 342)										
Arts	6%	22	5%	5%	4%	13%	8%	7%	6%	9%
Aviation		1		5%						
Business	8%	29	11%	5%	5%		11%	5%	14%	9%
Computer work	8%	26	11%		3%		9%	7%	14%	9%
Consultant	3%	9	4%				3%	5%	6%	3%
Engineer	3%	11	2%	10%			4%	7%	6%	
Farmer		1			1%					

	%	Totals	Carleton	Denison	Earlham	Grinnell	K'zoo	Law'ce	Mac	Sw'more
Financial work	4%	15	5%		8%		3%	2%	3%	6%
Government work	2%	6	2%		1%		4%	2%		
Health professions	8%	26	7%	10%	5%	13%	8%	7%	8%	9%
Higher education	9%	32	11%	5%	16%	13%	3%	10%	8%	9%
Homemaker	4%	13	4%	14%	3%	13%		2%	6%	6%
K-12 education	8%	27	5%		12%	13%	8%	10%	8%	3%
Law	4%	13	4%	10%	1%		7%	2%		6%
Librarian/LIS work	11%	38	7%	5%	15%		15%	12%	11%	6%
Manufacturing/Production	2%	6	2%		1%		3%	5%		
Military		1			1%					
Office work	1%	2					1%			3%
Religious position	1%	3			1%		1%		3%	
Sales	2%	8	5%	5%			3%	2%	3%	
Science	4%	14	7%	10%	4%		1%	5%		6%
Student	4%	12	4%		4%	25%	3%	5%		3%
Social (& related) service work	3%	11	2%	10%	4%	13%	4%			3%
Unemployed	1%	5	2%		1%			2%	3%	3%
Volunteer	1%	3	2%	5%						3%
Writer	2%	8		5%	5%		3%		3%	
Q.IV-9. Do you have children? (n = 425)										
Yes	60%	255	65%	71%	58%	50%	67%	58%	50%	60%
No	40%	170	35%	29%	42%	50%	39%	42%	50%	40%
If yes, how many are..... (n = 352 comments made)										
Boys: (n = 184 or 53% of 352)										
1-2	96%	176	97%	48%	95%	100%	97%	90%	94%	95%
3 or more	4%	8	3%		5%		3%	10%	6%	5%
Girls: (n = 168 or 48% of 352)										
1-2	96%	161	93%	48%	97%	100%	91%	100%	100%	100%
3 or more	4%	7	7%	3%	3%		9%			
What are their ages?										
Boys: (n = 204)										
1-9	17%	34	11%	27%	16%	50%	12%	19%	31%	13%
10-18	23%	47	26%	27%	29%		26%	19%	6%	17%
19-29	45%	91	49%	20%	42%		52%	42%	44%	52%
30+	16%	32	14%	27%	13%	50%	10%	19%	19%	17%

	%	Totals	Carleton	Denison	Earlham	Grinnell	K'zoo	Law'ce	Mac	Sw'more
Girls: (n = 175)										
1-9	13%	23	12%	31%	7%		15%	11%	16%	7%
10-18	26%	45	42%	25%	20%	50%	20%	26%	16%	27%
19-29	44%	77	24%	25%	50%	50%	54%	47%	47%	60%
30+	17%	30	21%	19%	23%		12%	16%	21%	7%
If they are younger than 18, do they live with you? (n = 122)										
Yes	94%	115	92%	100%	89%	100%	96%	93%	100%	100%
No	6%	7	8%		11%		4%	7%		
Q.IV-10. Do any adults (ages 18 or above) live with you? (n = 416)										
No	76%	314	78%	82%	74%	86%	77%	78%	68%	71%
Yes	25%	102	22%	18%	26%	14%	23%	22%	32%	29%
Q.IV-11. Do/Did you have siblings? (n = 420)										
Yes	94%	394	97%	89%	94%	86%	92%	98%	96%	89%
No	6%	26	3%	11%	6%	14%	8%	2%	4%	11%
If Yes, please indicate how many: (n = 553 comments made)										
Brothers: (n = 298 or 54% of 553)										
1-2	93%	277	88%	95%	97%	80%	95%	94%	91%	90%
3 or more	7%	21	12%	5%	3%	20%	5%	6%	9%	10%
Sisters: (n = 255 or 46% of 553)										
1-2	90%	230	91%	100%	98%	83%	86%	83%	86%	96%
3 or more	10%	25	9%		2%	17%	14%	17%	14%	4%
Are you the (n = 391)										
Oldest	47%	184	51%	36%	40%	71%	40%	49%	57%	59%
Youngest	29%	115	18%	48%	33%	14%	36%	22%	33%	23%
Somewhere in the middle	24%	92	31%	16%	27%	14%	24%	29%	11%	18%
In what occupations have each of your siblings spent the greatest number of years?										
Brother (n = 261 comments made)										
Arts	6%	16	9%	6%	7%		6%		4%	11%
Business	12%	32	6%	18%	14%	25%	11%	16%	11%	11%
Computer work	9%	23	14%	6%	9%	25%	6%	10%	14%	3%
Construction, Installation, Repair	3%	7			5%		5%		4%	
Consultant	2%	4			2%		4%			3%
Engineer	7%	19	3%	12%	5%		8%	6%	11%	11%
Farmer	2%	6	6%		4%					5%
Financial work	3%	8		6%	2%		4%	3%	4%	5%

	%	Totals	Carleton	Denison	Earlham	Grinnell	K'zoo	Law'ce	Mac	Sw'more
Government work	2%	4			2%		2%	3%		3%
Health professions	5%	12	11%	6%	7%	25%			4%	3%
Higher education	9%	23	17%		9%		11%	3%	7%	8%
Homemaker		1						3%		
K-12 education	5%	14	6%	6%	5%		11%	3%	4%	
Law	4%	11	6%	24%	2%		4%		4%	3%
Librarian/LIS work		1						3%		
Manufacturing/Production	5%	13			5%		5%	10%	4%	8%
Military		1	3%							
Office work	3%	9	6%	6%	2%		4%	10%		
Religious position	2%	5		6%	4%		2%	3%		
Sales	7%	19			7%		9%	13%	7%	11%
Science	3%	9	6%		5%					11%
Student	2%	5			2%		2%		7%	3%
Social (& related) service work	3%	9	3%	6%		25%	4%	3%	7%	3%
Unemployed	1%	3			2%				7%	
Volunteer	1%	2						6%		
Writer	2%	5	6%		2%		2%	3%		
Sister (n = 256 comments made)										
Arts	5%	13	2%		7%		7%	3%	3%	8%
Business	8%	20	2%		9%	14%	12%	7%	13%	
Computer work	2%	6			6%		3%		3%	
Construction, Installation, Repair	1%	2					2%		3%	
Engineer	1%	2			2%	14%				
Financial work	4%	10	5%	13%	4%	14%	3%	3%	3%	
Government work	3%	7		13%		14%			10%	8%
Health professions	11%	29	10%	13%	9%		5%	17%	16%	23%
Higher education	3%	8	5%		4%	14%	3%		3%	
Homemaker	10%	26	10%		9%		15%	7%	6%	15%
K-12 education	15%	39	15%	25%	19%		14%	17%	13%	15%
Law	2%	4	2%		2%			7%		
Librarian/LIS work	5%	14	5%	13%	2%		10%	7%	3%	4%
Manufacturing/Production	1%	2			2%					4%
Office work	7%	18	7%		7%	14%	8%	7%	10%	
Religious position	1%	2			2%		2%			
Sales	4%	10	5%	13%			5%	7%	6%	
Science	7%	18	17%	13%	7%		3%	7%	3%	4%

	%	Totals	Carleton	Denison	Earlham	Grinnell	K'zoo	Law'ce	Mac	Sw'more
Student	1%	3	2%		2%	14%				
Social (& related) service work	5%	12	7%		4%		5%	3%	3%	8%
Unemployed	1%	2						3%		4%
Volunteer	1%	3			2%			7%		
Writer	2%	6	5%		2%		2%			8%
Unspecified "Siblings" (n = 242 comments made)										
Arts	7%	18	5%	7%	4%		8%	8%	6%	40%
Business	10%	25	13%	7%	7%	20%	12%	10%	13%	
Computer work	5%	12	5%	7%	9%		4%	5%		
Construction, Installation, Repair	3%	7	3%		3%			2%	6%	
Engineer	3%	7	3%	7%	2%		2%	3%		10%
Farmer	2%	4	3%					3%	6%	
Financial work	5%	13	3%	7%	4%		6%	10%	6%	
Government work	1%	2	2%						6%	
Health professions	9%	22	7%		13%		13%	10%	6%	
Higher education	4%	9	2%	14%	2%		6%	3%		10%
Homemaker	3%	7	5%		2%		2%	3%	6%	
K-12 education	9%	22	13%	14%	11%		6%	5%	13%	
Law	5%	13	5%	7%	9%		4%	8%		
Librarian/LIS work	1%	3	2%	7%			2%			
Manufacturing/Production	3%	8	5%			20%	6%	4%	6%	
Military	2%	4	2%		2%		2%	3%		
Office work	6%	14	5%		11%	20%	4%	5%		10%
Religious position	1%	3					6%			
Research		1	2%							
Sales	4%	9	2%				4%	10%	6%	10%
Science	4%	10	7%		11%		2%			
Student	2%	5	3%		2%	20%				10%
Social (& related) service work	6%	15		14%	4%	20%	10%	8%	13%	
Unemployed	1%	2	3%							
Writer	3%	7		7%	4%		4%		6%	10%
Q.IV-12. What kind of work did your parents do for a living when you were 18 years old?										
Mother (n = 462 comments made)										
Arts	2%	9	3%				2%	5%		4%
Business	5%	22	4%		3%	11%	7%	4%	8%	6%
Computer work	<1%	2	1%		1%					

	%	Totals	Carleton	Denison	Earlham	Grinnell	K'zoo	Law'ce	Mac	Sw'more
Engineer	<1%	2			1%				2%	
Financial work	1%	5			1%		2%	2%	2%	
Government work	<1%	2		3%				2%		
Health professions	6%	30	12%	3%	5%	11%	8%	5%	4%	4%
Higher education	3%	14	4%	3%	7%		1%			4%
Homemaker	33%	153	35%	59%	28%	22%	34%	35%	25%	31%
K-12 education	17%	80	16%	16%	18%	11%	18%	9%	24%	22%
Law		1					1%			
Librarian/LIS work	9%	41	5%		11%	11%	12%	4%	12%	12%
Office work	9%	42	5%	3%	9%	11%	7%	16%	16%	8%
Religious position	2%	10	4%		2%	11%	1%		6%	
Sales	3%	15	1%		5%		2%	13%		
Science	<1%	2	1%	3%						
Social (& related) service work	3%	12	3%	3%	5%	11%		2%		4%
Student		1					1%			
Volunteer	2%	9	4%	6%	1%		1%	2%	2%	
Writer	2%	10	1%		4%		2%	2%		4%
Father (n = 444 comments made)										
Arts	1%	6			2%		1%	2%		4%
Business	17%	76	19%	21%	17%	13%	17%	18%	13%	15%
Computer work	1%	6	1%		2%		1%		2%	2%
Consultant	1%	17			2%		1%	2%	2%	
Construction,Installation,Repair	4%	5	3%	4%	3%	25%	5%	4%	4%	
Engineer	10%	44	8%	11%	12%		11%	10%	6%	11%
Farmer	2%	9	1%		4%		1%	4%	2%	
Financial work	5%	23	4%	7%	4%		4%	6%	10%	4%
Government work	2%	8	3%	7%			3%	2%		
Health professions	6%	28	12%	7%	4%	13%	3%	10%	2%	7%
Higher education	14%	63	19%	11%	16%	25%	11%	6%	8%	24%
K-12 education	4%	18	4%		5%		1%	2%	6%	11%
Law	5%	23	4%	7%	5%		3%	8%	8%	4%
Librarian/LIS work	1%	4			1%			2%	4%	
Manufacturing/Production	4%	17	3%	7%	3%		4%	10%	2%	
Office work	1%	3			1%		1%		2%	
Religious position	6%	25	5%	4%	3%	13%	10%	4%	8%	2%
Sales	8%	36	1%	7%	5%	13%	14%	8%	15%	7%
Science	3%	15	11%		3%		2%		2%	2%

	%	Totals	Carleton	Denison	Earlham	Grinnell	K'zoo	Law'ce	Mac	Sw'more
Social (& related) service work	2%	8			4%		2%		2%	2%
Unemployed		1			1%					
Writer	2%	9	1%	7%	1%		2%	2%		4%
Q.IV-13. How much formal education did your parents have?										
Mother (n = 420)										
Less than H.S. or Some high school	2%	9		4%	2%	13%	5%	4%		
High school graduate	17%	71	12%	21%	15%	13%	21%	24%	19%	9%
Community/junior college	4%	17	3%		3%		2%	12%	6%	2%
Some 4 year college courses	13%	54	13%	11%	9%	13%	14%	12%	16%	16%
4 year college graduate	32%	135	38%	43%	36%	25%	24%	29%	21%	42%
Some graduate school (not degree)	<1%	1				13%				
Graduate school (Master's degree)	29%	120	33%	11%	31%	25%	34%	14%	35%	27%
Graduate school (Doctoral degree)	3%	13	1%	11%	3%		1%	4%	2%	4%
Father (n = 421)										
Less than H. S. or Some high school	3%	14	3%		1%	25%	5%	6%	4%	
High school graduate	11%	48	4%	18%	14%		17%	12%	13%	2%
Community/junior college	1%	5	1%		1%		1%	2%	2%	
Some 4 year college courses	7%	28	1%	7%	6%		8%	12%	8%	7%
4 year college graduate	27%	114	22%	36%	23%	25%	31%	30%	21%	33%
Some graduate school (not degree)	<1%	2	1%		1%					
Graduate school (Master's degree)	26%	108	26%	21%	30%	38%	17%	22%	40%	22%
Graduate school (Doctoral degree)	24%	102	40%	18%	25%	13%	20%	16%	13%	36%
Q.IV-14. Place where you lived the longest when you were–										
6 to 12 (n = 420)										
Rural area	6%	24	3%		7%		5%	8%	8%	9%
Small town (up to 2,500)	11%	45	7%	18%	8%		11%	6%	16%	16%
Small city (2,500 - 24,999)	26%	109	29%	25%	31%	50%	23%	32%	16%	18%
Medium city (25,000 - 99,999)	27%	115	23%	25%	25%	13%	40%	22%	20%	32%
Large city (100,000 - 499,999)	12%	52	17%	14%	14%	13%	7%	12%	20%	2%
Metropolis (500,000 or more)	18%	75	20%	18%	15%	25%	14%	20%	18%	23%
13-17 (n = 423)										
Rural area	5%	22	3%		7%		5%	4%	6%	11%
Small town (up to 2,500)	9%	40	9%	11%	8%	13%	13%	6%	10%	9%
Small city (2,500 - 24,999)	23%	99	16%	25%	31%	38%	20%	30%	21%	20%
Medium city (25,000 - 99,999)	26%	111	30%	32%	16%	38%	36%	22%	19%	29%

	%	Totals	Carleton	Denison	Earlham	Grinnell	K'zoo	Law'ce	Mac	Sw'more
Large city (100,000 - 499,999)	16%	67	19%	14%	18%	13%	11%	14%	21%	13%
Metropolis (500,000 or more)	20%	84	23%	18%	20%		16%	24%	23%	18%
In which states of the U.S., or in what other country/ies, did you live when you were– 6 to 12 (n = 478 comments made)										
Arkansas		1							2%	
California	3%	16	4%		5%		1%	2%	2%	8%
Colorado	1%	6	4%	3%					2%	2%
Connecticut	4%	17	6%	3%	2%	11%	3%	4%		5%
Delaware	<1%	2	1%				1%			
District of Columbia	<1%	2	1%	3%						
Florida	1%	4	2%		2%					
Idaho	<1%	2	2%							
Illinois	9%	43	11%	6%	5%	11%	10%	20%	6%	7%
Indiana	8%	40	1%	3%	26%	11%	6%	6%		2%
Iowa	2%	10	4%		1%		1%		8%	2%
Kansas	2%	8	2%		2%	11%		2%	2%	2%
Kentucky		1			1%					
Louisiana	<1%	2		3%	1%					
Maine		1					1%			
Maryland	1%	7	1%	10%	2%		1%		0%	
Massachusetts	3%	15	6%		4%		1%		4%	5%
Michigan	9%	45	6%	6%	2%		37%		2%	2%
Minnesota	9%	41	12%		1%		4%	12%	38%	
Mississippi		1						2%		
Missouri	2%	10	5%	3%	3%			2%		2%
Montana		1	1%							
Nebraska	1%	5	1%			11%			6%	
New Hampshire	<1%	2			1%	11%				
New Jersey	3%	16	2%	6%	6%		3%			5%
New Mexico	1%	5		3%	3%		1%			
New York	9%	41	6%	10%	8%		8%	6%	4%	22%
North Carolina	<1%	2						2%		2%
North Dakota		1							2%	
Ohio	9%	45	9%	32%	10%		9%	2%	4%	10%
Oklahoma	<1%	2	1%		1%					
Oregon	<1%	2					1%	2%		
Pennsylvania	6%	28	4%	3%	10%		5%	2%		14%

	%	Totals	Carleton	Denison	Earlham	Grinnell	K'zoo	Law'ce	Mac	Sw'more
Rhode Island		1							2%	
South Dakota	1%	4			1%	11%			4%	
Tennessee	<1%	2								3%
Texas		1							2%	
Utah		1							2%	
Vermont		1								2%
Virginia	1%	3	1%		1%		1%			
Washington	1%	7	2%	3%		11%	2%			2%
Wisconsin	7%	33	1%		5%	11%	2%	36%	6%	5%
Wyoming		1					1%			
13 to 17 (n = 436 comments made)										
Alabama		1								2%
Arkansas		1							2%	
California	3%	12	4%	0%	3%	0%	1%	2%	2%	6%
Colorado	1%	6	3%	3%	1%				2%	2%
Connecticut	3%	14		3%	3%	14%	2%	4%		10%
Delaware		1					1%			
District of Columbia		1		3%						
Florida	1%	6	1%	7%	2%				2%	
Idaho		1	1%							
Iowa	3%	11	6%		1%				13%	
Illinois	9%	41	14%	10%	6%	14%	9%	20%	6%	2%
Indiana	9%	37	1%	3%	26%	14%	5%	4%	2%	2%
Kansas	2%	7	3%		1%	14%		4%	2%	
Kentucky	1%	4			3%					2%
Maine	1%	3	3%				1%			
Maryland	1%	6	3%	7%	2%					
Massachusetts	3%	12	6%		3%		1%			8%
Michigan	12%	51	6%	10%	2%		49%			
Minnesota	9%	37	11%		1%		4%	13%	40%	
Missouri	2%	8	4%	3%	2%			2%		2%
Montana	1%	3	1%				1%			
Nebraska	1%	5	1%			14%			6%	
New Jersey	4%	16	3%	7%	6%		5%			4%
New Mexico	<1%	2	1%		1%					
New York	7%	29	4%	10%	6%		5%	4%	4%	18%
Ohio	9%	39	9%	30%	14%		7%	2%	2%	4%

	%	Totals	Carleton	Denison	Earlham	Grinnell	K'zoo	Law'ce	Mac	Sw'more
Oklahoma		1			1%					
Oregon		1					1%			
Pennsylvania	6%	25	3%		10%		4%			20%
Rhode Island		2	1%						2%	
South Dakota	1%	4	1%		1%	14%			2%	
Tennessee		1							0%	2%
Texas	1%	4	1%						4%	2%
Vermont	<1%	2	1%							2%
Virginia	1%	4	1%		2%					2%
Washington	1%	3	3%	3%						
Wisconsin	8%	33			4%	14%	2%	43%	6%	6%
Wyoming	<1%	2					1%			
Q.IV-15. The phrase that best describes your family's financial situation most of the time before you were 21 years old (n = 425)										
Comfortable but not wealthy	50%	211	54%	68%	47%	38%	43%	52%	49%	51%
Had all the necessities but not many luxuries	45%	190	36%	25%	52%	50%	51%	44%	45%	44%
Sometimes had difficulty getting the necessities	3%	14	6%			13%	5%	2%	6%	2%
Wealthy	2%	10	4%	7%	1%		2%	2%		2%
Q.IV-16. What is the highest level of education that you have completed? (n = 429)										
Master's degree in LIS	65%	278	75%	65%	73%	43%	63%	59%	72%	40%
Second master's in…	24%	104	19%	12%	24%	57%	29%	33%	12%	29%
Other professional degree (e.g., DDS, EdD, JD, MD)	4%	17	4%				7%	2%	8%	7%
Ph.D., with a major field of...	4%	17	1%	8%	1%		1%	3%	6%	16%
Other	3%	13		15%	2%			3%	2%	9%
Q.IV-17. Are you currently enrolled in any educationally based, nonworkshop courses? (n = 424)										
No	87%	368	90%	89%	84%	63%	91%	88%	83%	84%
Yes	13%	56	10%	11%	15%	38%	9%	12%	17%	16%
If yes, for what purpose: (n = 56)										
Personal interest	54%	30	40%	67%	67%	50%	38%	33%	56%	80%
Continuing education	30%	17	40%	33%	20%		50%	44%	33%	
Another degree	16%	9	20%		13%	50%	13%	22%	11%	20%

	%	Totals	Carleton	Denison	Earlham	Grinnell	K'zoo	Law'ce	Mac	Sw'more
Q.IV-18. Would you like to go back to school in the future? (n = 418)										
No	57%	237	59%	68%	57%	75%	51%	52%	58%	57%
Yes	39%	161	34%	25%	39%	25%	47%	44%	31%	41%
Maybe	5%	20	7%	7%	3%		2%	4%	10%	2%
If yes, in what area(s) or for what degrees? (n = 201 comments made)										
Arts	9%	19	9%		8%		10%	13%	19%	6%
Business	4%	9	9%				5%	13%	5%	
Communications	2%	4			6%		3%			
Computers/IT	6%	12	3%		8%		5%	8%	14%	
Education	11%	23	14%		10%	33%	20%	13%		6%
Elderhostel courses	1%	2							5%	6%
Engineering		1			2%					
Gardening		1						4%		
Genealogy	1%	2					3%		5%	
Health sciences	1%	3	3%		2%				5%	
History, including Art history	11%	23	17%	22%	13%		5%	8%	14%	6%
Humanities, incl. Philosophy,Religion,Creative Writing	5%	10	6%	22%	6%	33%	5%			
Language/Literature	12%	24	11%	11%	13%		8%	17%	10%	18%
Law	2%	5			4%		8%			
LIS	11%	23	11%	22%	10%	33%	8%	8%	14%	18%
Mathematics	2%	4	3%		4%				5%	
Music	2%	4			4%		3%	4%		
Photography	1%	2	3%		2%					
Religion/Theology	1%	3							5%	12%
Sciences, including Geography	5%	11	3%	11%	6%		8%	4%		12%
Social sciences	5%	10		11%	4%		5%	8%		18%
Social work	1%	3					8%			
Various "Studies"	1%	3	9%							
Q.IV-19. Have you ever interrupted your LIS or other career for family reasons? (n = 420)										
No	65%	273	65%	69%	66%	75%	59%	65%	67%	67%
Yes	35%	147	35%	31%	34%	25%	41%	35%	33%	33%
If yes, how do you feel about those interruptions with regard to your career/work? (n = 139)										
Positive (childrearing reasons)	47%	66	55%	38%	53%	100%	44%	33%	36%	56%
Negative	18%	25	14%	25%	13%		16%	27%	43%	6%
OK (childrearing reasons)	17%	23	9%	13%	17%		28%	20%	7%	13%
Mixed	11%	15	14%	13%	10%		13%	13%	7%	6%

		%	Totals	Carleton	Denison	Earlham	Grinnell	K'zoo	Law'ce	Mac	Sw'more
OK (non-childrearing reasons)		4%	6		13%	7%			7%	7%	6%
Positive (non-childrearing reasons)		3%	4	9%							13%
Q.IV-20. Are you the only MLS-degreed professional in your work place? (n = 400)											
No		79%	316	80%	72%	81%	57%	74%	87%	73%	88%
Yes		21%	84	20%	28%	19%	43%	26%	13%	27%	12%
Q.IV-21. Have you authored--											
journal articles (n = 378)											
Yes --	of N = 431, then 159 = 37%	42%	159	39%	28%	44%	43%	42%	46%	33%	55%
No		58%	219	61%	72%	56%	57%	58%	54%	67%	45%
book reviews (n = 361)											
Yes --	of N = 431, then 161 = 37%	45%	161	44%	28%	47%	29%	50%	40%	39%	58%
No		55%	200	56%	72%	54%	71%	50%	60%	61%	43%
conference papers (n = 347)											
Yes --	of N = 431, then 112 = 26%	32%	112	36%	9%	32%	33%	41%	25%	24%	45%
No		68%	235	64%	91%	68%	67%	59%	75%	76%	55%
web publications (n = 332)											
Yes --	of N = 431, then 114 = 26%	34%	114	36%	17%	42%	40%	38%	29%	33%	29%
No		66%	218	64%	83%	58%	60%	62%	71%	67%	71%
monographs (n = 314)											
Yes --	of N = 431, then 42 = 10%	13%	42	17%	13%	13%		14%	10%	10%	18%
No		87%	272	83%	88%	87%	100%	86%	90%	90%	82%
other (n = 69)											
Yes --	of N = 431, then 69 = 16%	100%	0	100%	7%	100%	100%	100%	100%	100%	100%
Q.IV-22. Have you served on editorial boards? (n = 413)											
No		79%	363	88%	96%	84%	88%	88%	88%	85%	93%
Yes		12%	50	12%	4%	15%	13%	12%	13%	15%	7%
Q.IV-23. In which of the following professional organizations have you held membership--now or in the past, and how active are you?											
All Organizations: (n = 1069 choices made)											
ALA		74%	320	83%	54%	38%	75%	69%	78%	77%	69%
State library association		52%	222	61%	32%	29%	38%	47%	55%	56%	36%
Regional library association		30%	131	36%	25%	15%	25%	34%	39%	21%	16%
SLA (Special Libraries Associatioin)		21%	92	20%	29%	10%	13%	23%	18%	23%	20%
Medical Library Association		7%	30	7%	29%	4%	13%	3%	8%	2%	4%

	%	Totals	Carleton	Denison	Earlham	Grinnell	K'zoo	Law'ce	Mac	Sw'more
AALL (American Association of Law Libraries)	4%	19	7%	4%	1%		8%	6%	2%	2%
SAA (Society of American Archivists)	4%	16	1%	4%	2%	13%	3%	8%	2%	2%
ASIST (Am Assn of Information Science & Technology)	3%	11	4%		3%		2%	33%		
Music Library Association	2%	9			1%		1%	6%	2%	4%
ASI (American Society of Indexers)	1%	3	3%							2%
Other LIS-related	25%	108	20%	11%	16%	13%	24%	20%	23%	33%
Other professional association(s)	25%	108	16%	18%	13%	13%	30%	29%	29%	24%
Association involvement (multiple responses allowed to notation for each association)										
ALA (n = 320)										
Usually attend meetings	32%	102	33%	7%	31%	17%	30%	%	43%	48%
Been on committees	25%	81	23%	13%	19%	100%		38%	38%	39%
Held office	8%	26	9%		5%		3%	15%	16%	10%
State library assn (n = 222)										
Usually attend meetings	55%	123	57%	33%	46%	67%	68%	57%	56%	56%
Been on committees	41%	90	40%	33%	39%	33%	46%	43%	37%	38%
Held office	23%	51	24%	22%	21%	33%	17%	32%	26%	19%
Regional library assn (n = 131)										
Usually attend meetings	59%	77	68%	14%	50%		63%	60%	70%	86%
Been on committees	44%	57	48%	29%	43%		43%	35%	40%	86%
Held office	32%	42	44%		27%		23%	50%	30%	43%
SLA (n = 92)										
Usually attend meetings	34%	31	50%	13%	40%		20%	33%	45%	33%
Been on committees	21%	19	36%		10%		25%	22%	36%	11%
Held office	13%	12	14%		10%		1%	11%	45%	
Medical LA (n = 32)										
Usually attend meetings	44%	14	40%	13%	50%		100%	50%	100%	50%
Been on committees	22%	7	40%		25%		33%	25%	100%	
Held office	9%	3		13%			33%		100%	
AALL (n = 19)										
Usually attend meetings	58%	11	60%		100%		100%		100%	100%
Been on committees	47%	9	20%		100%		80%	33%	100%	100%
Held office	37%	7	100%		100%		20%			
SAA (n = 16)										
Usually attend meetings	31%	5	100%	4%			67%			100%
Been on committees	19%	3		4%			67%			
Held office	13%	2		4%			33%			

	%	Totals	Carleton	Denison	Earlham	Grinnell	K'zoo	Law'ce	Mac	Sw'more
ASIST (n = 11)										
Usually attend meetings	18%	2			40%					
Been on committees	9%		33%							
Held office										
Music LA (n = 9)										
Usually attend meetings	56%	5					100%	67%		100%
Been on committees	56%	5					100%	67%		100%
Held office	44%	4					100%	33%		100%
ASI (n = 3)										
Usually attend meetings	67%	2	50%							100%
Been on committees										
Held office										
Other professional assn (n = 108)										
Usually attend meetings	48%	52	45%	60%	48%		50%	33%	57%	55%
Been on committees	31%	33	27%	20%	36%		23%	27%	50%	27%
Held office	18%	19	27%		16%		12%	7%	36%	27%
Other LIS related (n = 106)										
Usually attend meetings	60%	64	71%	33%	55%		81%	40%	73%	47%
Been on committees	46%	49	71%	33%	29%		57%	70%	27%	47%
Held office	31%	33	43%	33%	13%		43%	50%	18%	40%
Q.IV-24. To what civic, fraternal or social organizations do you belong? (n = 268 comments made)										
Cultural group/Activities	13%	36	12%	21%	15%	25%	8%	19%	7%	15%
Religious	11%	29	8%	5%	4%	25%	20%	16%	15%	6%
Environmental	9%	24	12%	16%	11%		2%		15%	12%
Library-related	9%	23	6%		6%		18%	10%	7%	9%
Fraternal	8%	21	4%	21%	8%	25%	4%	13%	11%	3%
Political organization	8%	21	12%		9%		4%	6%	7%	12%
Child-oriented	7%	19	8%	11%	6%		14%	6%	4%	
Municipal focus	7%	18	8%		6%		4%	10%	11%	9%
Educational	6%	16	6%	16%	8%		10%	3%		
Sports	4%	12	6%		2%		4%	6%	4%	9%
Book club	4%	11	6%		8%		2%		4%	6%
Peace centered	3%	9	8%		6%				4%	3%
Social group	3%	9			4%	25%	6%		4%	6%
Union/Professional	3%	9	2%	5%	4%		2%	6%		6%
Charitable organization	1%	4			4%				4%	3%

	%	Totals	Carleton	Denison	Earlham	Grinnell	K'zoo	Law'ce	Mac	Sw'more
Neighborhood association	1%	4	2%	5%			2%		4%	
Alumni association	1%	3			2%			3%		3%
Q.IV-25. What was your religion while at [College]?										
Religion while at [College] (n = 400)										
Religion is given	78%	312	75%	81%	77%	88%	79%	74%	88%	73%
Did not have/list a religion	22%	88	25%	19%	23%	13%	21%	26%	12%	27%
Religions listed by Alums: (n = 318 comments made) (if more than one religion was given, all are listed)										
Anglican		1						3%		
Baha'i		1			1%					
Baptist	6%	18		10%	4%		20%			
Brethren		1			1%					
Catholic	11%	35	14%	5%	5%	29%	14%	18%	11%	7%
Christian	4%	13	7%	14%	3%		2%	5%		7%
Christian Science	1%	3		5%	1%			3%		
Congregational	3%	10	2%	5%	3%		2%	5%	5%	3%
Covenant		1	2%							
Disciples of Christ		1					2%			
Episcopalian	9%	28	16%	10%	5%	29%	8%	8%	5%	10%
Evangelical	1%	2	2%						3%	
Greek Orthodox	1%	2					2%		3%	
Jewish (cultural)		1	2%							
Jewish	4%	12			8%		3%	3%		10%
Lutheran	4%	12	2%	5%				13%	14%	
Methodist	14%	43	11%	14%	15%	14%	15%	13%	16%	7%
Nondenominational	1%	4	5%		1%	14%				
Pagan	1%	3	2%				3%			
Pantheist		1		5%						
Presbyterian	9%	30	16%	10%	7%		11%	3%	16%	7%
Protestant	10%	31		14%	11%		9%	16%	11%	13%
Quaker	12%	38			31%		6%		5%	27%
Unitarian	3%	11	9%		3%			5%	3%	7%
Unitarian-Universalist	2%	6	5%	5%		14%			3%	3%
United Church of Christ	3%	9	2%		1%		6%	3%	5%	
Wiccan		1								

	%	Totals	Carleton	Denison	Earlham	Grinnell	K'zoo	Law'ce	Mac	Sw'more
Has [your religion] changed over time? (n = 414)										
No, it has not changed	64%	263	57%	54%	73%	75%	52%	73%	60%	72%
Yes, to--	36%	151	43%	46%	27%	25%	48%	27%	40%	28%
Religion now (n = 404)										
Religion is given	72%	289	70%	79%	76%	88%	66%	74%	71%	63%
Does not have/list a religion	28%	115	30%	21%	24%	13%	34%	26%	29%	37%
Religions listed by Alums: (n = 266) (if more than one religion was given, all are listed)										
Anglican		1						3%		
Baha'i	1%	2			1%			3%		
Baptist	2%	6		12%	1%		9%			
Brethren		1			1%					
Buddhist	1%	3						5%		4%
Catholic	11%	28	13%		4%	25%	12%	16%	13%	12%
Christian	6%	15	7%	24%	3%		3%	8%		8%
Congregational	2%	5		6%	1%				3%	4%
Disciples of Christ		1					3%			
Episcopalian	10%	27	16%	18%	7%	25%	9%	8%	10%	4%
Evangelical	2%	4	4%				3%		3%	
Greek Orthodox	1%	2					3%		3%	
Jewish	5%	12	2%		9%		3%	3%		12%
Lutheran	3%	9	4%					11%	10%	
Mennonite		1			1%					
Methodist	8%	21	9%		10%		12%	5%	10%	4%
Mormon		1							3%	
Nondenominational	2%	6	2%		1%	13%	3%	5%		
Pagan	1%	2			1%		3%			
Pantheist		1		6%						
Presbyterian	7%	19	7%	12%	7%		9%	5%	13%	
Protestant	12%	32	9%	12%	11%		12%	16%	13%	16%
Quaker	13%	34	9%		31%		6%		3%	20%
Taoist		1								4%
Unitarian	4%	10	9%		3%		3%	3%	3%	4%
Unitarian-Universalist	5%	14	7%	6%	4%	25%	3%		7%	8%
United Church of Christ	3%	8		6%		13%	6%	8%	3%	

	%	Totals	Carleton	Denison	Earlham	Grinnell	K'zoo	Law'ce	Mac	Sw'more
Q.IV-26. What was [your religion's] importance to you at [College] and now?										
While at [College] (n = 95)										
Cultural	39%	37	33%	20%	41%	50%	53%	33%	38%	31%
Intellectual	24%	23	33%	40%	21%	50%	24%	11%	25%	23%
Grounding	16%	15	17%	40%	21%		6%	33%		8%
Spiritual	11%	10	8%		7%		12%		13%	31%
Mixed Feelings	11%	10	8%		10%		6%	22%	25%	8%
Now (n = 126)										
Cultural	29%	36	16%		39%	67%	35%	14%	40%	21%
Grounding	21%	27	11%	50%	24%		15%	36%	10%	21%
Intellectual	20%	25	26%	38%	18%	33%	20%	7%	10%	21%
Spiritual	24%	30	26%	13%	13%		30%	36%	40%	29%
Mixed Feelings	6%	8	21%		5%			7%		7%
Section V. MENTOR QUESTIONS										
Q.V-1. How valuable has the mentoring that you have received been to your career? (n = 255)										
Very valuable	65%	166	62%	62%	67%	50%	61%	82%	69%	54%
Some value	35%	89	38%	38%	33%	50%	39%	17%	31%	46%
No value	0%									
Q.V-2. Please give the number of each kind of mentor that you have had (n = 369 comments made)										
Men: (n = 148 or 41% of 369)										
1-3	95%	140	95%	100%	97%	100%	100%	100%	85%	82%
4 or more	5%	8	5%		3%				15%	18%
Women: (n = 221 or 59% of 369)										
1-3	90%	198	93%	100%	84%	75%	87%	100%	91%	83%
4 or more	10%	23	7%		16%	25%	13%		9%	17%
Q.V-3. Were your mentors – (n = 327 choices made)										
LIS professionals	74%	241	70%	76%	71%	75%	73%	74%	90%	70%
In other fields/kinds of work	26%	86	30%	24%	29%	25%	27%	26%	10%	30%
Q.V-4. Have your mentors been your boss? (n = 256)										
Yes	33%	84	31%	38%	31%	33%	38%	37%	23%	29%
Some were and some were not	49%	126	52%	31%	47%	33%	47%	46%	62%	57%
No	18%	46	17%	31%	22%	33%	15%	17%	15%	14%

	%	Totals	Carleton	Denison	Earlham	Grinnell	K'zoo	Law'ce	Mac	Sw'more
Q.V-5. How did you come to have mentoring? (n = 331 choices made)										
I fell into a mentoring relationship	67%	223	71%	79%	59%	75%	65%	70%	73%	68%
I was selected to be mentored	17%	55	13%	14%	20%		17%	22%	9%	20%
I selected my mentor(s)	13%	42	9%		18%	24%	14%	7%	15%	12%
Other	3%	11	7%	7%	3%		3%	2%	3%	
Q.V-6. In relation to your own age when the mentoring relationship started, were your mentors – (n = 305 choices made)										
5-10 years (or more) older than you	74%	226	75%	73%	72%	100%	75%	78%	79%	63%
Same general age as you were	20%	60	20%	27%	20%		20%	18%	17%	24%
Younger than you	6%	19	6%		8%		5%	5%	3%	13%
Q.V-7. How long did the relationship with each mentor last? (n = 430 choices made)										
1 year	13%	57	14%	15%	12%	18%	16%	9%	12%	15%
2-3 years	31%	133	33%	35%	35%	36%	30%	25%	24%	31%
4-5 years	14%	59	13%	5%	14%	9%	12%	18%	22%	10%
Over 5 years [then ended]	16%	68	15%	20%	14%	9%	15%	18%	12%	23%
Still continuing	26%	113	25%	25%	25%	27%	27%	32%	29%	21%
Q.V-8. If some or all of the relationships ended, why did they stop? (n = 314 comments made)										
I moved geographically	44%	139	40%	28%	45%	22%	52%	40%	60%	41%
Mentor moved geographically	17%	54	12%	22%	24%	44%	17%	15%	10%	15%
Mentor died	11%	34	12%	17%	9%	11%	11%	15%	3%	10%
I changed professions	8%	24	10%	6%	13%	11%	5%	3%	3%	10%
Conflict developed between us	3%	8	5%				2%	3%	3%	5%
Other: (n = 55 with 64 reasons given)	18%	55	21%	28%	9%	11%	13%	25%	20%	20%
One of us changed positions	39%	23	44%	50%	38%		40%	10%	71%	50%
Mentor retired	28%	10	11%	50%	25%	100%	20%	40%		50%
Became peers	16%	2	22%		25%		20%		29%	
Part of formal program, which ended	14%	25	11%		12%		10%	50%		
One of us had a career change	3%	4	11%				10%			
Q.V-9. Please give 2-3 benefits you have received from having had mentors: (n = 459 comments made)										
A teacher	31%	140	36%	17%	26%	36%	30%	32%	33%	33%
An advisor	26%	118	23%	29%	26%	14%	23%	28%	25%	33%
A sponsor	20%	94	17%	38%	16%	43%	22%	22%	23%	15%
An exemplar	13%	58	11%	8%	21%	7%	10%	10%	13%	11%
A host/guide	11%	49	12%	8%	12%		15%	8%	6%	9%

	%	Totals	Carleton	Denison	Earlham	Grinnell	K'zoo	Law'ce	Mac	Sw'more
Q.V-10. Please give 2-3 drawbacks you see to having had mentors: (n = 105 comments made)										
I couldn't disagree easily with my mentor	22%	23	31%	25%	24%	25%	15%	24%	21%	16%
Mentor held down by my ideas	15%	16	8%		24%			29%	14%	16%
Mentor stalled my career plans	14%	15	7%	25%	10%		8%	12%	21%	26%
I couldn't get what I needed from my mentor	11%	12	15%		10%	25%	31%	12%		5%
Wrong match of two people	11%	12			19%	25%	15%		21%	11%
I couldn't meet my mentor's expectations	10%	10	8%		5%	25%	15%	18%		11%
I was never seen as an equal	7%	7	15%		5%		8%		14%	5%
Others viewed the relationship negatively	7%	7	8%	50%	5%		8%	6%		5%
Organizational structure hampered the relationship	3%	3	8%						7%	5%
Q.V-11A. Have you been a mentor? (n = 197 choices made)										
Within the LIS field	74%	146	70%	89%	67%	67%	76%	75%	83%	79%
Outside the LIS field	26%	51	30%	11%	33%	33%	24%	25%	17%	21%
Q.V-11B. Why did you become a mentor? (n = 190)										
It is part of my job	29%	56	29%	50%	27%	25%	35%	29%	21%	30%
To give back to or recruit for the field	17%	33	11%		24%		25%	5%	25%	10%
It just happened	12%	22	14%		7%	25%	11%	19%	4%	20%
I saw potential in someone	12%	22	20%	25%	7%	25%	8%	19%		10%
I was asked by the newcomer	11%	21	9%		12%	25%	3%	5%	29%	15%
It was part of a formal program	7%	13	9%	13%	2%		3%	24%	4%	5%
Altruism: "to help others"	7%	14	3%	13%	10%		14%		8%	5%
Other	5%	9	6%		10%		3%		8%	
Q.V-11C. How did you become a mentor? (n = 171)										
Part of my job	32%	55	23%	22%	39%		34%	41%	21%	42%
Asked by mentee	23%	39	23%	33%	15%	67%	22%	24%	29%	21%
It just happened	12%	21	23%	11%	20%		6%	12%	8%	
Part of formal program	11%	19	4%	22%	5%		16%	18%	17%	11%
Volunteered	10%	17	12%		5%	33%	12%		17%	16%
Saw potential	6%	11	8%		12%		3%		8%	5%
Asked by admininistration	5%	9	8%	11%	5%		6%	6%		5%
Q.V-11D. How have you benefited by mentoring? (n = 177)										
I gained professionally	45%	80	43%	38%	41%	25%	48%	47%	55%	43%
I gained individually	21%	38	27%	13%	20%	25%	24%	11%	24%	21%

	%	Totals	Carleton	Denison	Earlham	Grinnell	K'zoo	Law'ce	Mac	Sw'more
Altruistic: pride in those I mentored	21%	37	17%	38%	23%	50%	21%	11%	14%	36%
We became friends	8%	15	7%	13%	11%		3%	21%	7%	
I learned how to mentor	4%	7	7%		5%		3%	11%		
Q.V-11E. What limitations have you, as a mentor, experienced? (n = 117)										
Lack of sufficient time to give to it	26%	30	20%	40%	32%		40%	13%	27%	15%
Lack of experience	24%	28	30%		28%		10%	31%	40%	15%
Feelings of failure	21%	25	30%	20%	16%		30%	25%	7%	23%
Limitations of authority	9%	10		20%	4%	33%	10%	13%		23%
Organizational structure is a hinderance	7%	8		20%	8%	33%	10%		13%	
I find it difficult to let go when the recipient is ready	5%	6	10%					13%	7%	8%
The mentoring is blunted by unfavorable situations	5%	6			12%	33%		6%		8%
Being the recipient's boss gets in the way	3%	3	5%						7%	8%
My mentoring is seen as favoritism by others	1%	1	5%							
Q.V-11F. Are those you mentor primarily -- (n = 232 comments made)										
Men: (n = 80 or 34% of 232)										
1-2	86%	69	85%	50%	89%		83%	100%	91%	80%
3 or more	14%	11	15%	50%	11%		17%		9%	20%
Women: (n = 152 or 66% of 232)										
1-2	56%	85	54%	78%	45%	67%	71%	63%	39%	47%
3 or more	44%	67	46%	22%	55%	33%	29%	37%	61%	53%
Q.V-11G. What have been your most important contributions to those you have mentored? (n = 194)										
As an advisor	32%	63	39%	30%	30%	33%	31%	30%	35%	33%
As a teacher	31%	61	29%	40%	35%	67%	25%	33%	30%	29%
As a sponsor	24%	47	16%	30%	26%		36%	22%	13%	29%
As a host/guide	8%	16	10%		7%		8%	7%	13%	10%
As an exemplar	3%	5	3%					7%	9%	
I don't know if I have contributed	1%	2	3%		2%					
Q.V-12. How would you like others to describe you in your mentoring role? (n = 658 choices made)										
An advisor	23%	152	20%	28%	22%	19%	23%	24%	27%	23%
An exemplar	21%	140	22%	28%	21%	31%	21%	22%	19%	18%
A teacher	21%	139	22%	21%	22%	18%	21%	18%	21%	23%

	%	Totals	Carleton	Denison	Earlham	Grinnell	K'zoo	Law'ce	Mac	Sw'more
A host/guide	21%	136	21%	21%	21%	19%	21%	25%	18%	16%
A sponsor	13%	83	14%	3%	13%	6%	12%	11%	12%	18%
Other	1%	8			<1	6%	1%		3%	3%
Section VI. The Last Section										
Q.VI-1. What advice would you offer people who are just entering the work place as LIS professionals? (n = 792 comments made)										
Flexibility/learning/change	27%	211	28%	32%	30%	19%	33%	23%	18%	25%
Approaching the job	16%	128	16%	10%	17%	15%	19%	20%	10%	17%
Fit - skills/knowledge/abilities/values	14%	110	12%	7%	11%	31%	14%	12%	16%	17%
Technology	9%	68	7%	10%	9%	8%	7%	11%	8%	9%
Professional development	7%	56	11%	5%	4%	12%	6%	7%	10%	5%
LIS profession itself	7%	56	8%	12%	4%	4%	5%	5%	11%	9%
Users/community members	7%	53	4%	12%	6%	4%	4%	7%	10%	7%
Choosing a library	5%	39	3%		5%		4%	8%	7%	6%
Things to do before entering workplace	4%	34	5%		8%	8%	4%	6%	3%	1%
Public libraries/librarianship	2%	13	3%	5%	3%		1%		1%	1%
Academic libraries/librarianship	1%	10	1%	2%	1%		1%	1%	1%	2%
Special libraries/librarianship	1%	8	1%	2%	1%		1%		2%	1%
School library media centers	1%	6		2%			1%	1%	2%	1%
Q.VI-2. What suggestions do you have for improving LIS education? (n = 515 comments made)										
Specific courses	21%	110	21%	13%	21%	13%	19%	22%	23%	29%
Internships/Practica	14%	71	10%	10%	16%	13%	16%	12%	16%	15%
Curriculum as a whole	13%	66	6%	17%	14%	7%	14%	23%	9%	13%
Theory versus practice	6%	31	9%	13%	5%	7%	4%	7%	5%	4%
Marketing of programs	4%	22	3%	3%	4%	7%	4%	3%	9%	2%
Have no suggestions	4%	21	2%	7%	7%		7%		3%	2%
Rigor in programs/courses	3%	17	6%	3%	3%	7%	3%		3%	4%
SLIS - positive	3%	16	2%				4%	5%	8%	4%
Stick to traditional SLIS roles	3%	16	6%	3%	2%		1%	8%	2%	2%
Quality of faculty	3%	16	4%	3%	7%		2%	2%		2%
Admissions	3%	14	4%		1%		2%	3%	3%	5%
Involve practitioners	3%	14	4%	10%	1%	7%	3%		2%	2%
SLIS in general	3%	13	1%	3%	2%	7%	3%		3%	5%
SLIS - negative	3%	13	2%		3%	7%	4%	2%		4%
Distance education	2%	11	2%		1%		2%	3%	5%	2%
Technical services	2%	10	1%	3%	2%		3%	2%		4%

	%	Totals	Carleton	Denison	Earlham	Grinnell	K'zoo	Law'ce	Mac	Sw'more
Computers	2%	10	3%	3%			3%	2%	3%	
Quality of graduates	2%	9	1%		2%	13%	2%		2%	2%
Relevance to workplace needs	2%	9	2%	3%	1%	7%	2%	3%		
"Library" vs "Information" as field descriptors	2%	8	2%	3%	2%		1%		3%	
Technology	1%	6	2%		1%		1%	3%		
Public libraries	1%	5	2%		1%		1%		2%	
School library media centers	1%	4	1%		1%	7%				2%
Working while attending SLIS	1%	3	1%		1%		1%			

Q.VI-3. Is there anything else which you feel would be important for us to know? (n = 179 comments made)

(Comments were generally extensions of responses to previous questions and were analyzed as part of those questions)

APPENDIX D

Cohort Data Set

Because of the amount of quantitative detail generated by the questionnaire, two data sets have been included (appendixes C and D). Where tables within the text are incomplete, or additional detail may be useful, the reader is given a Data Set reference. For instance, if the data was from the cohort data set, "appendix D: Q.I-7" would indicate that cohort responses to that particular question are given.

The Cohort Data Set covers only those questions where change might be seen over the course of the 39 years represented by the respondents. Quantitative and qualitative responses (or comments) are quantitatively cast for each question, and given down the left side of each table. The cohorts run across the top of each table. An "average" column is provided that represents each response's percentage of the total number of responses to the question.

COHORT DATA SET	%	Totals	62-'65	66-'70	71-'75	76-'80	81-'85	86-'90	91-'95	96-'00
Section I. COLLEGE										
Q.I-1. Dates of attendance at [College]	100%	431	55	111	89	54	34	42	36	10
Alums by College (n = 431)										
Carleton	16%	69	20%	12%	17%	19%	15%	19%	17%	10%
Denison	6%	28	7%	6%	10%	7%	3%	7%		
Earlham	22%	95	23%	17%	21%	30%	21%	26%	22%	20%
Grinnell	2%	8	2%	1%		4%		5%	3%	10%
Kalamazoo	20%	87	15%	29%	22%	9%	15%	17%	19%	30%
Lawrence	12%	51	4%	13%	13%	19%	21%	12%	3%	
Macalester	11%	48	13%	13%	7%	4%	9%	7%	33%	10%
Swarthmore	10%	45	16%	10%	9%	9%	18%	7%	3%	20%
Q.I-4. Extracurricular activities while at [College] (n = 798 choices made)										
Artistic (music, drama, etc.)	27%	218	31%	22%	27%	30%	28%	31%	26%	37%
Athletics	15%	119	12%	14%	16%	15%	16%	13%	18%	21%
Social Services	15%	116	11%	15%	17%	17%	6%	13%	22%	11%
Politics (student government, etc.)	10%	77	12%	14%	10%	6%	9%	5%	10%	
Radio/Film, etc.	8%	64	3%	7%	8%	9%	13%	12%	7%	5%
None	6%	50	10%	9%	7%	4%	4%	5%	1%	5%
Other (name)	19%	154	20%	21%	14%	20%	24%	21%	16%	21%
Q.I-5. Would you go to [College] today if you were graduating from high school? (n = 414)										
Yes	78%	321	72%	77%	76%	78%	83%	74%	91%	70%
No	14%	60	19%	15%	16%	16%	7%	18%	3%	20%
Not Sure	8%	33	9%	8%	8%	6%	10%	8%	6%	10%
Q.I-6. ...Reasons for getting an undergraduate education										
Q.I-6A. Most important (n = 1541 choices made)										
Develop one's critical faculties/appreciation...	26%	407	26%	25%	27%	27%	29%	28%	27%	21%
Develop one's knowl. of...community/world problems	19%	291	20%	19%	20%	17%	18%	21%	16%	18%
Develop one's ability to get along...	15%	235	16%	15%	14%	17%	16%	14%	16%	16%
Develop special competence in...academic...	15%	233	15%	16%	16%	15%	16%	12%	14%	16%
Help develop one's moral capacities, ethical...values	15%	225	15%	15%	15%	15%	14%	14%	13%	16%
Provide vocational or preprofessional training...	7%	101	5%	7%	5%	8%	4%	5%	10%	11%
Other (specify)	3%	49	3%	3%	3%	2%	3%	5%	5%	3%

	%	Totals	62-'65	66-'70	71-'75	76-'80	81-'85	86-'90	91-'95	96-'00
Q.I-6B. Particularly strong (n = 1362 choices made)										
Develop one's critical faculties/appreciation…	27%	364	25%	25%	25%	32%	31%	26%	26%	25%
Develop one's knowl. of...community/world problems	20%	270	21%	20%	21%	18%	16%	20%	18%	22%
Help develop one's moral capacities, ethical...values	16%	221	17%	16%	16%	16%	17%	16%	18%	13%
Develop special competence in...academic...	16%	212	17%	16%	17%	14%	17%	15%	11%	16%
Develop one's ability to get along...	15%	200	13%	16%	13%	11%	15%	15%	19%	25%
Provide vocational or preprofessional training…	4%	58	3%	5%	5%	5%	4%	4%	5%	
Other (specify)	3%	37	4%	3%	2%	3%	1%	4%	4%	
Q.I-6C. Deficient (n = 169 choices made)										
Provide vocational or preprofessional training…	64%	109	67%	59%	69%	58%	90%	85%	53%	75%
Develop one's ability to get along...	10%	17	8%	9%	18%			8%	16%	
Develop one's knowl. of...community/world problems	7%	12	17%	9%		8%		8%	11%	
Develop special competence in...academic...	6%	9	4%	9%	5%		10%		5%	
Help develop one's moral capacities, ethical...values	5%	8		5%	5%	17%			5%	25%
Develop one's critical facilities/appreciation…	4%	6		9%		8%			5%	
Other (specify)	5%	8	4%	9%	3%	8%			5%	
Section II. LIBRARIANSHIP, LIS EDUCATION, AND LIS WORK										
Q.II-1. Would you encourage today's [College] students to enter the LIS field? (n = 417)										
Yes	88%	369	90%	85%	84%	91%	89%	100%	89%	100%
No	7%	30	6%	11%	11%	4%	3%		9%	
Maybe	4%	18	4%	5%	5%	6%	9%		3%	
Q.II-2. At what age did you first think about going into LIS work? (n = 421)										
age 5 to 10	4%	15	4%	5%	3%	2%		3%	3%	10%
11-15	8%	32	7%	11%	7%	2%	9%	5%	11%	
16-19	11%	47	9%	12%	9%	6%	9%	13%	19%	30%
20-30	66%	278	65%	58%	59%	80%	76%	79%	67%	60%
31-40	8%	34	5%	9%	16%	10%	6%			
41-50	3%	13	7%	4%	6%					
over 50		2	2%	1%						
Q.II-3. Factors that made you think LIS would be an attractive career for you:										
Q.II-3A. General (n = 2181 choices made)										
Love of books/reading	16%	356	18%	17%	16%	16%	14%	16%	16%	14%
Desire to work with/help people	15%	328	13%	15%	15%	16%	14%	16%	16%	13%

	%	Totals	62-'65	66-'70	71-'75	76-'80	81-'85	86-'90	91-'95	96-'00
Fit...the values and ideals which are important to me	15%	323	16%	16%	16%	13%	13%	14%	14%	14%
Level & variety of intellectual challenge [of] this career	14%	316	15%	14%	14%	14%	13%	17%	15%	14%
Working conditions	10%	217	10%	9%	9%	9%	11%	12%	12%	13%
The availability of a variety of job possibilities	8%	173	8%	9%	7%	9%	8%	7%	6%	5%
Length/structure/requirements of the [LIS] program	7%	153	6%	8%	8%	7%	8%	5%	6%	6%
Flexibility [for managing] my other life commitments	7%	147	7%	7%	8%	4%	7%	9%	6%	9%
Bibliographic instruction in classes taken at [College]	2%	43	2%	1%	2%	3%	3%	1%	4%	3%
Salary or other financial considerations	2%	41	1%	1%	2%	3%	3%	1%	1%	2%
Written information on LIS as a career	2%	39	2%	1%	2%	2%	2%		3%	3%
Status or image of librarians/information professionals	2%	34	2%	2%	1%	2%	2%	1%		5%
Info or advice from [College's] career services office	1%	11		1%	1%	1%	1%		1%	
Q.II-3B. Opportunities (n = 1213 choices made)										
For a job	23%	281	26%	25%	22%	20%	25%	24%	20%	22%
To learn to use/research a variety of info. resources	19%	228	20%	20%	20%	19%	18%	14%	20%	22%
To educate others	18%	220	20%	18%	16%	19%	17%	26%	17%	22%
To combine [LIS and] some other area of interest/skill	16%	191	10%	13%	16%	19%	18%	23%	17%	16%
For professional growth	14%	169	18%	15%	15%	13%	10%	13%	13%	9%
To work w/increasingly sophisticated info technology	10%	124	6%	8%	12%	11%	14%	13%	13%	9%
Q.II-3C. Relationship to or encouragement from other people (n = 816 choices made)										
A librarian during my [K-12] years	33%	273	31%	34%	36%	31%	27%	37%	34%	32%
A professional librarian after graduation from [College]	18%	144	14%	17%	20%	20%	17%	19%	17%	16%
A librarian at [College]	16%	127	14%	17%	13%	16%	15%	19%	16%	16%
A friend	10%	83	12%	11%	8%	12%	9%	3%	14%	11%
A family member who was not a librarian	10%	79	16%	11%	7%	9%	12%	5%	11%	5%
A family member who was a librarian	10%	78	9%	7%	11%	9%	14%	10%	8%	21%
A teacher	4%	32	3%	4%	5%	3%	6%	7%		
Q.II-3D. Experience in libraries (n = 1175 choices made)										
Using the library at [College]	26%	306	28%	24%	26%	25%	27%	27%	26%	45%
Using a library during high school	23%	273	25%	24%	24%	23%	23%	17%	25%	23%
Using a library after graduating from college	18%	214	20%	18%	19%	20%	16%	17%	15%	14%
Working in a lib. after coll. [& before] LIS grad prgm.	15%	172	13%	16%	14%	16%	15%	17%	14%	
Working in the library at [College]	11%	134	7%	11%	10%	12%	14%	14%	12%	18%
Working in a library during my high school years	6%	76	6%	7%	7%	5%	5%	9%	7%	

	%	Totals	62-'65	66-'70	71-'75	76-'80	81-'85	86-'90	91-'95	96-'00
Q.II-5. Did you work in the library while at [College]? (n = 425)										
No	67%	284	77%	68%	70%	60%	68%	55%	67%	60%
Yes	33%	141	23%	32%	30%	40%	32%	45%	33%	40%
Q.II-5A. For how many years? (n = 125)										
0-1	21%	26	8%	33%	19%	12%	30%	11%	25%	25%
2-4	79%	99	92%	67%	81%	88%	70%	89%	75%	75%
Q.II-5B. In what area(s)? (n = 234 choices made)										
Circulation/Access	35%	81	33%	39%	35%	41%	38%	24%	28%	27%
Acquisitions/Collection development	13%	30	17%	10%	19%	6%	10%	17%	11%	18%
Cataloging	11%	26	17%	6%	9%	3%	10%	24%	22%	9%
Reference	10%	24		15%	14%	6%	10%	3%	17%	9%
Interlibrary Loan	7%	17	11%	5%	9%	6%	10%	7%	6%	9%
Online/Systems	1%	3		2%					6%	9%
Other	23%	53	22%	24%	14%	38%	24%	24%	11%	18%
Q.II-5C. How did that come about? (n = 158)										
My own initiative	55%	87	58%	50%	52%	59%	53%	52%	75%	60%
Through the library director	12%	19	8%	25%	13%	5%	7%	5%	8%	
Through other library staff	4%	6			3%	9%	7%	5%		20%
Other	29%	46	33%	25%	32%	27%	33%	38%	17%	20%
Q.II-8. What image did you have of "librarians" and of LIS when you left [College]?										
Librarians (n = 357)										
Positive	57%	204	50%	61%	46%	60%	57%	64%	69%	86%
No image/Neutral	25%	90	30%	24%	38%	16%	32%	22%		
Negative	12%	42	14%	11%	11%	14%	11%	8%	15%	14%
Mixed	6%	21	7%	4%	5%	9%		6%	15%	
Library and Information Science (n = 64)										
Positive	59%	38	100%	54%	50%	55%	60%	56%	71%	
No image/Neutral	22%	14		31%	25%	9%		44%	14%	100%
Negative	13%	8		15%	8%	27%	20%		14%	
Mixed	6%	4			17%	9%	20%			

	%	Totals	62-'65	66-'70	71-'75	76-'80	81-'85	86-'90	91-'95	96-'00
Q.II-12. Did you work in a library during your time in LIS School? (n = 419)										
Yes	75%	315	62%	66%	72%	90%	81%	83%	89%	100%
No	25%	104	38%	34%	28%	10%	19%	18%	11%	
Q.II-13. What image did you have of "librarians" and LIS when you left LIS school?										
Librarians (n =351)										
Positive	70%	247	71%	73%	62%	73%	83%	61%	72%	100%
No image/Neutral	7%	24	15%	3%	9%	3%	8%	6%	7%	
Negative	8%	29	6%	13%	9%	8%	4%	6%	3%	
Mixed	15%	51	8%	11%	20%	18%	4%	26%	17%	
Library and Information Science (n = 116)										
Positive	63%	73	69%	60%	65%	50%	64%	64%	86%	60%
No image/Neutral	4%	5		7%	5%	8%	9%			
Negative	23%	27	19%	27%	25%	33%	18%	29%		20%
Mixed	9%	11	13%	7%	5%	8%	9%	7%	14%	20%
Q.II-14. In how many libraries have you worked since leaving your LIS School? (n = 418)										
0	2%	9		1%	1%	4%		3%	11%	
1-2	48%	199	36%	40%	48%	56%	45%	56%	57%	100%
3-5	38%	157	49%	41%	34%	33%	45%	36%	29%	
over 5	13%	53	15%	18%	17%	8%	9%	5%	3%	
Q.II-15. How many total number of years of LIS-related work have you had since finishing your LIS graduate education? (n = 413)										
0	2%	7				4%			12%	13%
1-3	7%	28		3%	6%		6%	8%	29%	63%
4-10	23%	96	9%	11%	18%	19%	33%	58%	59%	25%
11-15	15%	61	9%	11%	14%	17%	33%	33%		
16-20	14%	57	11%	10%	15%	33%	27%			
21-30	29%	118	31%	45%	44%	28%				
over 30	11%	46	39%	20%	4%					
Q.II-16. Are you (or have you been) employed as a librarian/information professional? (n = 428)										
Yes	97%	416	97%	99%	98%	98%	94%	98%	94%	80%
No	3%	12	3%	1%	2%	2%	6%	2%	9%	20%

	%	Totals	62-'65	66-'70	71-'75	76-'80	81-'85	86-'90	91-'95	96-'00
Q.II-16A. In what type of LIS organization do you work? (n = 422)										
Academic	33%	138	36%	31%	27%	45%	31%	38%	24%	38%
Public	34%	142	31%	30%	34%	31%	34%	36%	42%	63%
School	11%	45	12%	19%	11%	10%		2%	3%	
Special (specify)	23%	97	21%	20%	28%	14%	34%	24%	30%	
Q.II-16B. Have you worked in more than one type of LIS organization? (n = 421)										
No	45%	189	40%	44%	44%	57%	42%	33%	52%	75%
Yes, these types (n = 498 choices made):	55%	232	60%	56%	56%	43%	58%	67%	48%	25%
Academic	31%	156	30%	27%	30%	35%	34%	40%	35%	50%
Public	27%	136	27%	25%	28%	26%	29%	30%	26%	50%
School	11%	56	14%	15%	9%	13%	11%	2%	12%	
Special	25%	123	23%	27%	28%	20%	24%	23%	24%	
Other	5%	27	7%	6%	5%	7%	3%	6%	3%	
Q.II-16D. What responsibilities do you have in your current position? (n = 2477 choices made)										
Reference/reader services/information and referral	13%	311	13%	11%	13%	11%	13%	14%	14%	19%
Collection development and management/Acquisitions	12%	295	12%	12%	11%	13%	11%	11%	12%	12%
Database searching	11%	262	11%	9%	11%	10%	11%	11%	14%	9%
Administration/management	10%	252	12%	11%	12%	10%	8%	8%	6%	2%
Group activities (e.g., curriculum development)	9%	216	8%	8%	9%	8%	11%	11%	11%	14%
Cat/classif/indexing/abst/thesaurus construction	6%	160	10%	7%	6%	7%	5%	5%	5%	5%
Website development and/or maintenance	6%	148	2%	6%	6%	7%	7%	10%	6%	7%
Automation planning, design and coordination	5%	132	5%	5%	6%	6%	7%	4%	4%	2%
Circulation/access services	5%	131	6%	5%	5%	5%	5%	5%	6%	5%
Publicity/public relations/fund-raising	5%	126	4%	6%	4%	6%	4%	6%	4%	2%
Outreach services	5%	125	4%	5%	5%	4%	6%	5%	7%	9%
Interlibrary loan	3%	78	4%	3%	5%	3%	3%	1%	2%	5%
Conservation/preservation	3%	74	2%	4%	3%	4%	4%	3%	1%	
Records management/archives	3%	71	4%	3%	2%	4%	3%	2%	3%	
Other	4%	96	5%	4%	3%	3%	4%	3%	6%	9%
The two areas in which you spend most of your time (n = 755 choices made)										
Reference/reader services/information and referral	25%	192	21%	19%	23%	29%	35%	33%	31%	40%
Administration/management	17%	131	18%	21%	19%	19%	12%	15%	5%	7%
Collection development and management/Acquisitions	14%	109	13%	19%	14%	14%	12%	14%	9%	7%
Group activities (e.g., curriculum development)	10%	77	10%	10%	11%	7%	12%	8%	14%	7%
Cat/classif/indexing/abst/thesaurus construction	7%	56	11%	8%	5%	10%	10%	6%	2%	

	%	Totals	62-'65	66-'70	71-'75	76-'80	81-'85	86-'90	91-'95	96-'00
Database searching	5%	37	7%	3%	5%	2%	7%	4%	12%	
Circulation/access services	3%	26	3%	4%	6%	2%	2%	1%		7%
Automation planning, design and coordination	3%	21	3%	3%	3%	3%	2%	1%	5%	
Publicity/public relations/fund-raising	3%	19	2%	3%	2%	2%	2%	3%	3%	
Website development and/or maintenance	3%	19		2%	3%	4%	3%	6%	2%	
Outreach services	1%	9		1%	2%		2%		3%	7%
Interlibrary loan	1%	6	1%		2%	1%			2%	
Records management/archives	1%	6	1%		1%	3%				7%
Conservation/preservation	1%	5	2%	0%	1%		2%			
Other	6%	42	7%	5%	3%	3%	2%	8%	12%	20%
Q.II-16E. How many years of experience do you have in your current LIS job? (n = 402)										
0-1	9%	35	2%	6%	6%	2%	6%	13%	34%	50%
2-5	32%	129	19%	22%	33%	27%	42%	54%	53%	50%
6-10	21%	85	19%	19%	17%	31%	32%	28%	13%	
11-15	15%	62	19%	22%	15%	21%	13%	5%		
16-20	11%	43	13%	12%	16%	17%	6%			
21-30	10%	40	24%	15%	12%	2%				
over 30	2%	8	6%	5%						
Q.II-16G. What is the average number of hours per week that you work in your LIS position? (n = 406)										
1-9	1%	4	2%		1%		3%	2%		
10-19	5%	19	9%	4%	4%	4%	3%	5%	7%	
20-29	8%	33	9%	6%	10%	8%	10%	5%	13%	13%
30-39	25%	102	24%	17%	26%	29%	35%	29%	30%	38%
40 or more	61%	248	56%	74%	59%	60%	48%	59%	50%	50%
Q.II-16H. How satisfied are you with each of the following aspects of your current position?										
Working hours (n = 396)										
VS	33%	130	35%	29%	32%	43%	41%	28%	23%	50%
S	45%	178	48%	44%	46%	46%	31%	49%	48%	38%
OK	14%	55	17%	19%	7%		14%	18%	23%	13%
NS	8%	33		7%	15%	11%	14%	5%	6%	
Supervision/feedback (n = 396)										
VS	18%	71	17%	17%	21%	22%	13%	16%	17%	20%
S	36%	144	30%	33%	37%	40%	37%	42%	52%	20%

	%	Totals	62-'65	66-'70	71-'75	76-'80	81-'85	86-'90	91-'95	96-'00
OK	25%	99	31%	32%	23%	18%	27%	21%	7%	30%
NS	21%	82	22%	19%	19%	20%	23%	21%	24%	30%
Responsibilities (n = 405)										
VS	36%	146	36%	34%	31%	42%	45%	35%	33%	63%
S	48%	193	51%	49%	54%	42%	39%	40%	53%	25%
OK	11%	45	13%	12%	7%	15%	10%	15%	3%	13%
NS	5%	21		5%	7%		6%	10%	10%	
Salary (n = 402)										
VS	18%	71	20%	16%	16%	21%	16%	18%	21%	13%
S	39%	157	43%	37%	41%	38%	35%	45%	38%	25%
OK	25%	102	11%	31%	28%	27%	32%	20%	17%	38%
NS	18%	72	26%	17%	15%	13%	16%	18%	24%	25%
Opportunities to use my skills and abilities: (n = 404)										
VS	50%	200	61%	47%	53%	48%	39%	48%	41%	63%
S	29%	119	22%	27%	28%	38%	32%	28%	45%	13%
OK	11%	44	9%	13%	7%	8%	23%	13%	3%	25%
NS	10%	41	7%	14%	11%	6%	6%	13%	10%	
Opportunities for development/promotion (n = 387)										
VS	14%	55	13%	14%	13%	14%	10%	18%	19%	13%
S	34%	133	33%	32%	45%	34%	21%	39%	26%	38%
OK	29%	114	35%	28%	28%	32%	31%	32%	23%	25%
NS	22%	85	19%	26%	14%	20%	38%	11%	32%	25%
Range of people employed in my library (n = 370)										
S	42%	156	52%	33%	49%	48%	36%	44%	30%	50%
OK	22%	82	20%	25%	22%	13%	21%	22%	33%	25%
VS	22%	80	18%	24%	22%	21%	25%	22%	17%	25%
NS	14%	52	10%	18%	8%	19%	18%	11%	20%	
People I work most closely with (n = 396)										
VS	45%	177	49%	43%	42%	43%	58%	46%	37%	50%
S	38%	150	43%	32%	42%	41%	32%	44%	33%	25%
OK	12%	48	4%	20%	11%	8%	6%	10%	20%	
NS	5%	21	4%	5%	5%	8%	3%		10%	25%
The autonomy I have to do my own work (n = 400)										
VS	60%	239	52%	58%	68%	59%	65%	68%	45%	71%
S	28%	113	31%	33%	23%	29%	23%	18%	42%	14%
OK	7%	29	11%	6%	4%	8%	13%	10%	6%	
NS	5%	19	6%	4%	6%	4%		5%	6%	14%

	%	Totals	62-'65	66-'70	71-'75	76-'80	81-'85	86-'90	91-'95	96-'00
Q.II-16L. How satisfied are you with your choice of an LIS as a career? (n = 406)										
Very Satisfied	69%	280	70%	66%	72%	71%	53%	75%	69%	88%
Moderately Satisfied	26%	105	23%	28%	24%	27%	38%	20%	28%	13%
Very Dissatisfied	5%	21	8%	6%	4%	2%	9%	5%	3%	
Q.II-16O. What is the likelihood of your continuing as an LIS professional..future? (n = 405)										
Very Likely	78%	315	62%	79%	82%	82%	72%	85%	72%	100%
Moderately Likely	12%	47	8%	8%	13%	10%	22%	15%	16%	
Very Unlikely	11%	43	31%	12%	5%	8%	6%		13%	
Section III. CAREERS, OCCUPATIONS, AND GOALS										
Q.III-6. In addition to LIS work, do you do other types of work part-time? (n = 402)										
No	74%	296	74%	77%	61%	75%	74%	80%	81%	89%
Yes	26%	106	26%	23%	39%	25%	26%	20%	19%	11%
Q.III-7. If you are not currently working in an LIS field, have you ever been employed in LIS work? (n = 41)										
No	15%	6		22%		20%	17%	33%	25%	
I never intended to actually work in an LIS field										
Yes, but I left it because:	85%	35	100%	78%	100%	80%	83%	67%	75%	100%
Are you satisfied with the work you are now doing? (n = 29)										
Yes	100%	29	100%	100%	100%	100%	100%	100%	100%	
No										
Section IV. DEMOGRAPHIC QUESTIONS										
Q.IV-1. Sex (n = 429)										
Female	78%	333	78%	73%	79%	79%	71%	74%	83%	82%
Male	22%	96	22%	27%	21%	21%	29%	26%	17%	18%
Q.IV-2. Current age (n = 412)										
21-29	3%	13							9%	100%
30-39	15%	61					6%	84%	91%	
40-49	22%	92			9%	98%	94%	9%		
50-59	50%	206	28%	99%	91%	2%		6%		
60-69	10%	40	72%	1%						

	%	Totals	62-'65	66-'70	71-'75	76-'80	81-'85	86-'90	91-'95	96-'00
Q.IV-3. Current salary (under $21,000 - over $90,000 = n = 391)										
under $21,000	9%	37	14%	10%	11%	8%	13%	8%	22%	30%
$21,000-30,999	9%	37	11%	12%	8%	10%	10%	8%	3%	20%
$31,000-40,999	15%	60	8%	12%	12%	6%	26%	18%	38%	40%
$41,000-50,999	23%	88	16%	18%	20%	22%	23%	46%	25%	10%
$51,000-75,999	32%	124	38%	42%	33%	45%	16%	21%	6%	
$76,000-90,000	6%	23	5%	7%	8%	8%	6%		3%	
over $90,000	6%	22	8%	9%	8%		6%		3%	
Retired	*67%*	*20*	*87%*	*75%*	*50%*					
Not currently earning a salary	*33%*	*10*	*13%*	*25%*	*50%*	*100%*	*100%*	*100%*	*100%*	
Q.IV-5. Was English the language you learned first? (n = 427)										
Yes	99%	424	99%	100%	100%	100%	100%	95%	97%	100%
No, I learned -- (Greek:1; Spanish: 2)	1%	3	1%					5%	3%	
Q.IV-6. Is English the language most commonly used in your home? (n = 425)										
Yes	99%	422	100%	100%	100%	100%	97%	98%	97%	100%
No, it is -- (Greek: 1; Spanish: 2)	1%	3					3%	2%	3%	
Q.IV-7. Do you have any physical disabilities? (n = 422)										
No	94%	395	92%	90%	92%	92%	100%	100%	97%	100%
Yes*	6%	27	8%	10%	8%	8%			3%	
* Responses include asthma, blindness, epilepsy, chronic fatigue syndrome, chronic headaches, fibromyalgia, fused spine due to scoliosis, and heart disease.										
Q.IV-8. Marital Status (n = 425)										
Married/Partnered	75%	317	81%	76%	74%	77%	76%	69%	71%	40%
Single	15%	65	6%	12%	9%	13%	18%	29%	29%	60%
Divorced/Separated	9%	40	9%	12%	16%	9%	6%	2%		
Widowed	1%	3	4%		1%					
Q.IV-9. Do you have children? (n = 425)										
Yes	60%	255	68%	64%	69%	66%	64%	52%	29%	
No	40%	170	32%	37%	31%	32%	36%	48%	71%	100%
If yes, how many are..... (n = 352 comments made)										
Boys: (n = 184 or 53% of 352)										
1-2	96%	176	96%	94%	94%	100%	100%	93%	80%	
3 or more	4%	8	4%	6%	6%			7%	20%	

	%	Totals	62-'65	66-'70	71-'75	76-'80	81-'85	86-'90	91-'95	96-'00
Girls: (n = 168 or 48% of 352)										
1-2	96%	161	96%	96%	100%	100%	100%	100%	100%	
3 or more	4%	7	4%	4%						
What are their ages?										
Boys: (n = 204)										
1-9	17%	34	4%		5%	14%	50%	81%	100%	
10-18	23%	47		12%	29%	54%	50%	13%		
19-29	45%	91	43%	61%	62%	32%		6%		
30+	16%	32	54%	26%	4%					
Girls: (n = 175)										
1-9	13%	23			4%	21%	38%	70%	80%	
10-18	26%	45		7%	37%	58%	63%	20%	20%	
19-29	44%	77	36%	70%	54%	21%		10%		
30+	17%	30	64%	22%	4%					
If they are younger than 18, do they live with you? (n = 122)										
Yes	94%	115	94%	100%	90%	97%	100%	90%	89%	
No	6%	7	6%		10%	3%		10%	11%	
Q.IV-10. Do any adults (ages 18 or above) live with you? (n = 416)										
No	76%	314	76%	79%	64%	73%	83%	80%	79%	70%
Yes	25%	102	25%	21%	36%	27%	17%	20%	21%	30%
Q.IV-11. Do/Did you have siblings? (n = 420)										
Yes	94%	394	94%	89%	97%	98%	94%	97%	94%	100%
No	6%	26	6%	11%	3%	2%	6%	3%	6%	
If Yes, please indicate how many: (n = 553 comments made)										
Brothers: (n = 298 or 54% of 553)										
1-2	93%	277	93%	92%	92%	93%	92%	93%	95%	100%
3 or more	7%	21	7%	8%	8%	7%	8%	7%	5%	
Sisters: (n = 255 or 46% of 553)										
1-2	90%	230	90%	92%	85%	85%	95%	88%	94%	100%
3 or more	10%	25	10%	8%	15%	15%	5%	12%	6%	
Are you the ... (n = 391)										
Oldest	47%	184	60%	55%	40%	46%	37%	38%	44%	50%
Youngest	29%	115	30%	24%	22%	33%	33%	41%	44%	20%
Somewhere in the middle	24%	92	11%	20%	38%	22%	30%	21%	12%	30%

	%	Totals	62-'65	66-'70	71-'75	76-'80	81-'85	86-'90	91-'95	96-'00
In what occupations have each of your siblings spent the greatest number of years?										
Brother (n = 261 comments made)										
Arts	6%	16		3%	11%	13%	9%	10%	4%	
Business	12%	32		17%	19%	16%	5%	15%		17%
Computer work	9%	23	11%	4%	4%	10%	5%	15%	26%	17%
Construction, Installation, Repair	3%	7	3%	3%	2%	0%	5%	5%		17%
Consultant	2%	4		3%		3%	5%			
Engineer	7%	19	11%	5%	9%	6%	14%	5%	4%	
Farmer	2%	6	3%	1%		3%	9%		4%	
Financial work	3%	8	3%	5%	4%		5%			
Government work	2%	4		3%	2%		5%			
Health professions	5%	12	6%	3%	9%	6%	9%			
Higher education	9%	23	17%	8%	6%	10%	5%	5%	13%	
Homemaker		1				3%				
K-12 education	5%	14	3%	9%	2%	3%		15%	4%	
Law	4%	11	3%	4%	9%	0%	5%	10%		
Librarian/LIS work		1		0%	2%					
Manufacturing/Production	5%	13	9%	8%		6%	5%	5%		
Military		1								17%
Office work	3%	9	3%	5%	4%	3%		5%		
Religious position	2%	5		5%				5%		
Sales	7%	19	6%	12%	11%	3%	5%		4%	
Science	3%	9	11%	1%		3%	5%	5%	4%	
Student	2%	5	3%			3%			9%	17%
Social (& related) service work	3%	9	9%		2%	3%	5%		9%	17%
Unemployed	1%	3			2%				9%	
Volunteer	1%	2		1%	2%					
Writer	2%	5		1%		3%	5%		9%	
Sister (n = 256 comments made)										
Arts	5%	13		5%	6%	3%	5%	5%	19%	
Business	8%	20	5%	16%	6%	8%	5%	5%		
Computer work	2%	6	3%		2%		5%	15%		
Construction, Installation, Repair	1%	2			2%	3%				
Engineer	1%	10		2%					5%	
Financial work	4%	7	3%	5%	4%	3%	5%	5%		25%
Government work	3%		5%	3%	2%		5%		5%	
Health professions	11%	29	16%	13%	11%	11%	5%	10%	5%	25%

	%	Totals	62-'65	66-'70	71-'75	76-'80	81-'85	86-'90	91-'95	96-'00
Higher education	3%	8		5%	4%			15%		
Homemaker	10%	26	11%	11%	6%	13%	14%	5%	14%	
K-12 education	15%	39	16%	14%	25%	13%	5%	10%	14%	
Law	2%	4		3%		3%		5%		
Librarian/LIS work	5%	14	3%		9%	5%	10%	5%	10%	25%
Manufacturing/Production	1%	4	3%		2%	3%			5%	
Office work	7%	18	16%	6%	4%	8%		5%	5%	25%
Religious position	1%	2	5%							
Sales	4%	10		5%	4%	3%	5%	5%	10%	
Science	7%	18	8%	5%	9%	13%	10%			
Student	1%	3				5%		5%		
Social (& related) service work	5%	12	3%	3%	4%	3%	19%		10%	
Unemployed	1%	2		3%						
Volunteer	1%	3			2%		5%	5%		
Writer	2%	6	5%	2%		5%	5%			
Unspecified "Siblings" (n = 242 comments made)										
Arts	7%	18	8%	8%	3%	8%	8%	15%	17%	
Business	10%	25	25%	8%	5%	11%	12%	15%	17%	20%
Computer work	5%	12	8%	2%	3%	6%	4%	8%	17%	20%
Construction, Installation, Repair	3%	7		4%	3%		4%	4%	8%	
Engineer	3%	7	8%		3%	3%	8%	4%		
Farmer	2%	4		2%	3%	3%				
Financial work	5%	13	8%	6%	8%		4%	8%		
Government work	1%	2		2%	1%					
Health professions	9%	22		8%	17%	6%	8%		8%	
Higher education	4%	9		6%	5%		8%			
Homemaker	3%	7		6%	4%		4%			
K-12 education	9%	22	17%	14%	9%	3%	4%	15%		
Law	5%	13	17%	4%	8%		12%			
Librarian/LIS work	1%	3			1%	3%		4%		
Manufacturing/Production	3%	8		2%		8%	4%	4%	8%	20%
Military	2%	4			1%	6%		4%		
Office work	6%	14		6%	5%	14%		8%		
Religious position	1%	3			4%					
Research		1				3%				
Sales	4%	9		4%	5%	3%	8%			
Science	4%	10		4%	3%	11%	8%			

	%	Totals	62-'65	66-'70	71-'75	76-'80	81-'85	86-'90	91-'95	96-'00
Student	2%	5				6%		4%	8%	20%
Social (& related) service work	6%	15		8%	8%	6%	4%	4%		20%
Unemployed	1%	2					4%	4%		
Writer	3%	7	8%	4%	1%	3%			17%	
Q.IV.12. What kind of work did your parents do for a living when you were 18 years old?										
Mother (n = 462 comments made)										
Arts	2%	9		3%	1%	4%	5%	2%		
Business	5%	22	2%	5%	1%	6%	3%	14%	11%	
Computer work	<1%	2							5%	
Engineer	<1%	2				2%			3%	
Financial work	1%	5		4%						
Government work	<1%	2			1%	2%				
Health professions	6%	30	3%	4%	6%	2%	13%	12%	5%	20%
Higher education	3%	14	3%		2%	6%	5%		8%	10%
Homemaker	33%	153	41%	44%	40%	24%	15%	21%	22%	10%
K12 education	17%	80	25%	16%	20%	22%	8%	14%	11%	20%
Law		1						2%		
Librarian/LIS work	9%	41	7%	3%	9%	11%	18%	9%	16%	
Office work	9%	42	10%	12%	6%	11%	8%	2%	5%	40%
Religious position	2%	10		3%			3%	7%	8%	
Sales	3%	15	5%	3%	3%	2%	5%	5%		
Science	<1%	2	2%				3%	2%		
Social (& related) service work	3%	12	2%	1%	4%	6%	3%	5%		
Student		1		2%	1%		3%			
Volunteer	2%	9	2%		2%	2%	5%	2%		
Writer	2%	10			2%	2%	5%	2%	5%	
Father (n = 444 comments made)										
Arts	1%	6	2%	3%	0%	2%	3%			
Business	17%	76	19%	17%	22%	20%	9%	18%	13%	
Computer work	1%	6	2%						15%	
Consultant	1%	17	4%		3%	2%	3%	3%	3%	
Construction,Installation,Repair	4%	5			3%	3%				
Engineer	10%	44	11%	12%	9%	8%	11%	5%	8%	22%
Farmer	2%	9	7%			7%		3%		
Financial work	5%	23	2%	4%	4%	7%	11%	8%	5%	
Government work	2%	8	2%	3%	3%	2%				

	%	Totals	62-'65	66-'70	71-'75	76-'80	81-'85	86-'90	91-'95	96-'00
Health professions	6%	28	5%	8%	8%		11%	5%	5%	11%
Higher education	14%	63	7%	13%	11%	18%	11%	23%	23%	11%
K-12 education	4%	18	7%	3%	6%		6%	8%	5%	
Law	5%	23	11%	2%	8%	3%	11%	3%		11%
Librarian/LIS work	1%	4				3%	3%		3%	
Manufacturing/Production	4%	17	4%	4%	3%	5%	6%	5%	5%	11%
Office work	1%	3	2%	1%	1%	3%		0%		
Religious position	6%	25	4%	6%	9%	3%	9%	5%	3%	
Sales	8%	36	7%	12%	6%	7%	6%	10%	5%	11%
Science	3%	15	4%	5%	1%	2%			8%	22%
Social (& related) service work	2%	8	4%	3%	2%			3%		
Unemployed		1				2%				
Writer	2%	9		4%	1%	3%		3%		
Q.IV-13. How much formal education did your parents have?										
Mother (n = 420)										
Less than H.S. or Some high school	2%	9		5%	2%	2%		3%		
High school graduate	17%	71	24%	23%	15%	19%	6%	13%	9%	
Community/junior college	4%	17	9%	3%	6%	2%	6%		3%	
Some 4 year college courses	13%	54	24%	18%	7%	8%	6%	10%	6%	30%
4 year college graduate	32%	135	20%	32%	43%	36%	33%	28%	26%	20%
Some graduate school (not degree)	<1%	1						3%		
Graduate school (Master's degree)	29%	120	20%	16%	24%	32%	45%	41%	50%	50%
Graduate school (Doctoral degree)	3%	13	4%	4%	2%	2%	3%	3%	6%	
Father (n = 421)										
Less than H. S. or Some high school	3%	14	4%	1%	3%	6%	6%	5%		10%
High school graduate	11%	48	17%	15%	8%	16%	3%	5%	14%	
Community/junior college	1%	5		2%	2%			3%		
Some 4 year college courses	7%	28	11%	10%	3%	2%	3%	8%	9%	
4 year college graduate	27%	114	28%	27%	38%	20%	38%	15%	14%	30%
Some graduate school (not degree)	<1%	2				2%			3%	
Graduate school (Master's degree)	26%	108	22%	21%	24%	29%	31%	40%	23%	30%
Graduate school (Doctoral degree)	24%	102	19%	25%	22%	25%	19%	25%	37%	40%

	%	Totals	62-'65	66-'70	71-'75	76-'80	81-'85	86-'90	91-'95	96-'00
Q.IV-14. Place where you lived the longest when you were –										
6 to 12 (n = 420)										
Rural area	6%	24	15%	4%	2%	8%	13%		6%	
Small town (up to 2,500)	11%	45	13%	10%	16%	14%		5%	11%	
Small city (2,500 - 24,999)	26%	109	20%	28%	29%	27%	26%	33%	14%	20%
Medium city (25,000 - 99,999)	27%	115	31%	31%	20%	22%	23%	23%	34%	70%
Large city (100,000 - 499,999)	12%	52	5%	13%	15%	10%	19%	13%	17%	
Metropolis (500,000 or more)	18%	75	16%	15%	18%	18%	19%	28%	17%	20%
13-17 (n = 423)										
Rural area	5%	22	11%	5%	1%	6%	9%	2%	6%	10%
Small town (up to 2,500)	9%	40	9%	12%	15%	10%		5%	6%	
Small city (2,500 - 24,999)	23%	99	18%	23%	26%	22%	25%	34%	14%	20%
Medium city (25,000 - 99,999)	26%	111	36%	31%	17%	32%	28%	20%	17%	30%
Large city (100,000 - 499,999)	16%	67	9%	15%	20%	8%	16%	15%	26%	30%
Metropolis (500,000 or more)	20%	84	16%	14%	21%	22%	22%	24%	31%	10%
Q.IV-15. The phrase that describes your family's financial situation most of the time before you were 21 years old [is] – (n = 425)										
Comfortable but not wealthy	50%	211	47%	46%	55%	43%	57%	59%	42%	60%
Had all the necessities but not many luxuries	45%	190	53%	52%	38%	51%	31%	33%	44%	40%
Sometimes had difficulty getting the necessities	3%	14		2%	5%	4%	6%	3%	8%	
Wealthy	2%	10			3%	2%	6%	5%	6%	
Q.IV-16. What is the highest level of education that you have completed? (n = 429)										
Master's degree in LIS	65%	278	55%	61%	63%	71%	68%	60%	86%	100%
Second master's in…	24%	104	27%	25%	31%	20%	15%	36%	9%	
Other Professional degree (e.g., DDS, EdD, JD, MD)	4%	17	7%	3%	5%	4%	6%	2%	3%	
Ph.D., with a major field of…	4%	17	5%	9%	2%	2%	3%			
Other	3%	13	5%	3%		4%	9%	2%	3%	
Q.IV-17. Are you currently enrolled in any educationally based, nonworkshop courses? (n = 424)										
No	87%	368	87%	89%	87%	87%	88%	90%	77%	70%
Yes	13%	57	13%	11%	13%	13%	12%	10%	23%	30%
If yes, for what purpose: (n = 56)										
Personal interest	54%	30	83%	65%	56%	29%	40%	33%	43%	50%
Continuing education	30%	17	17%	29%	33%	57%	20%	33%	29%	
Another degree	16%	9		6%	11%	14%	40%	33%	29%	50%

		%	Totals	62-'65	66-'70	71-'75	76-'80	81-'85	86-'90	91-'95	96-'00
Q.IV-18. Would you like to go back to school in the future? (n = 418)											
No		57%	237	69%	66%	51%	59%	50%	49%	38%	40%
Yes		39%	161	26%	30%	44%	41%	47%	42%	53%	50%
Maybe		5%	20	6%	4%	5%		3%	9%	9%	10%
Q.IV-19. Have you ever interrupted your LIS or other career for family reasons? (n = 420)											
No		65%	273	65%	61%	61%	60%	66%	88%	71%	100%
Yes		35%	147	35%	39%	39%	38%	34%	12%	29%	
Q.IV-20. Are you the only MLS-degreed professional in your work place? (n = 400)											
No		79%	316	79%	76%	73%	83%	80%	89%	82%	100%
Yes		21%	84	21%	24%	27%	17%	20%	11%	18%	
Q.IV-21. Have you authored:											
journal articles (n = 378)											
Yes --	of N = 431, then 159 = 37%	42%	159	40%	46%	35%	43%	38%	31%	17%	
No		58%	219	51%	44%	51%	44%	38%	60%	72%	90%
book reviews (n = 361)											
Yes --	of N = 431, then 161 = 37%	45%	161	44%	42%	39%	33%	38%	40%	14%	20%
No		55%	200	47%	40%	46%	50%	29%	48%	69%	70%
conference papers (n = 347)											
Yes --	of N = 431, then 112 = 26%	32%	112	22%	34%	25%	33%	18%	7%	11%	10%
No		68%	235	62%	46%	54%	50%	50%	55%	75%	80%
web-publications (n = 332)											
Yes --	of N = 431, then 114 = 26%	34%	114	20%	18%	22%	35%	32%	43%	33%	30%
No		66%	218	58%	50%	53%	46%	41%	45%	53%	60%
monographs (n = 314)											
Yes --	of N = 431, then 42 = 10%	13%	42	11%	12%	8%	13%	18%	7%		
No		87%	272	69%	54%	63%	61%	50%	71%	81%	90%
other (n = 69)											
Yes --	of N = 431, then 69 = 16%	100%	69	15%	14%	13%	30%	9%	21%	11%	20%
Q.IV-22. Have you served on editorial boards? (n = 413)											
Yes		12%	50	12%	12%	13%	10%	3%	10%	6%	
No		79%	363	79%	79%	87%	90%	97%	90%	94%	100%

	%	Totals	62-'65	66-'70	71-'75	76-'80	81-'85	86-'90	91-'95	96-'00
Q.IV-23. In which of the following professional organizations have you held membership–now or in the past, and how active are you?										
All organizations: (n = 1069 comments made)										
ALA	74%	320	74%	73%	70%	78%	76%	76%	78%	80%
State library association	55%	222	58%	55%	52%	56%	35%	43%	47%	60%
Regional library association	30%	131	30%	41%	37%	28%	21%	17%	19%	30%
SLA (Special Libraries Association)	21%	92	21%	27%	16%	13%	21%	24%	25%	10%
Medical Library Association	7%	30	7%	8%	9%	6%	6%	7%		10%
AALL (American Association of Law Libraries)	4%	19	4%	5%	9%	2%	6%		6%	
SAA (Society of American Archivists)	4%	16		4%	4%	7%		7%	3%	
ASIST (Am Assn of Infor. Science & Technololgy)	3%	11	4%		4%	4%		2%	6%	
Music Library Association	2%	9	2%	2%	1%	4%	6%		3%	
ASI (American Society of Indexers)	1%	3	1%		1%			2%		
Other LIS-related	25%	108	9%	24%	19%	31%	26%	19%	36%	10%
Other professional association(s)	25%	108	24%	35%	22%	28%	9%	29%	14%	10%
Association Involvement (multiple responses allowed to notation for each association)										
ALA (n = 320)										
Usually attend meetings	32%	102	37%	35%	32%	31%	31%	25%	32%	13%
Been on committees	25%	81	22%	28%	27%	31%	23%	25%	18%	
Held office	8%	26	10%	7%	15%	7%	4%	9%		
State library assn (n = 222)										
Usually attend meetings	55%	123	50%	72%	52%	63%	33%	50%	35%	17%
Been on committees	41%	90	50%	44%	41%	47%	58%	33%	6%	
Held office	23%	51	31%	28%	24%	23%	33%	11%		
Regional library assn (n = 131)										
Usually attend meetings	59%	77	71%	60%	58%	80%	57%	43%	29%	
Been on committees	44%	57	50%	42%	36%	67%	57%	43%	14%	33%
Held office	32%	42	36%	36%	21%	53%	29%	29%	14%	33%
SLA (n = 92)										
Usually attend meetings	34%	31	43%	30%	36%	29%	43%	30%	22%	100%
Been on committees	21%	19	21%	23%	14%	43%	14%	20%	11%	
Held office	13%	12	21%	10%	7%	14%	14%	10%	22%	
Medical LA (n = 32)										
Usually attend meetings	44%	14	33%	33%	63%	67%		67%		
Been on committees	22%	7	17%	33%		67%		33%		
Held office	9%	3		22%	13%					

	%	Totals	62-'65	66-'70	71-'75	76-'80	81-'85	86-'90	91-'95	96-'00
AALL (n = 19)										
Usually attend meetings	58%	11	100%	60%	63%		50%		50%	
Been on committees	47%	9	100%	60%	63%					
Held office	37%	7	100%		25%	100%	50%		50%	
SAA (n = 16)										
Usually attend meetings	31%	5		50%	25%	50%				
Been on committees	19%	3		50%		25%				
Held office	13%	2		25%		25%				
ASIST (n = 11)										
Usually attend meetings	18%	2				50%				
Been on committees	9%	1	50%							
Held office										
Music LA (n = 9)										
Usually attend meetings	56%	5		100%		50%	100%			
Been on committees	56%	5		100%		50%	100%			
Held office	44%	4		100%			100%			
ASI (n = 3)										
Usually attend meetings	67%	2	100%							
Been on committees										
Held office										
Other LIS related (n = 106)										
Usually attend meetings	60%	64	71%	56%	65%	76%	78%	50%	31%	
Been on committees	46%	49	50%	63%	35%	59%	44%	25%	31%	
Held office	31%	33	36%	37%	35%	35%	33%	13%	15%	
Other professional assn (n = 108)										
Usually attend meetings	48%	52	54%	56%	45%	40%	67%	42%	20%	
Been on committees	31%	33	5%	36%	30%	20%		33%		
Held office	18%	19	38%	18%	15%	13%		17%		
Q.IV-25. What was your religion while at [College]?										
Religion while at [College] (n = 400)										
Religion is given	78%	312	80%	78%	76%	77%	77%	77%	80%	89%
Did not have/list a religion	22%	88	20%	22%	24%	23%	23%	23%	20%	11%
Religions listed by Alums: (n = 318 comments made) (if more than one religion was given, all are listed)										
Anglican		1		1%						
Baha'i		1								11%
Baptist	6%	18	5%	9%	11%	2%		3%		

	%	Totals	62-'65	66-'70	71-'75	76-'80	81-'85	86-'90	91-'95	96-'00
Brethren		1						3%		
Catholic	11%	35	2%	5%	11%	20%	10%	20%	13%	33%
Christian	4%	13	5%	1%	2%	2%	13%	10%	4%	
Christian Science	1%	3	2%	2%						
Congregational	3%	10	7%	5%	3%	2%				
Covenant		1				2%				
Disciples of Christ		1	2%							
Episcopalian	9%	28	10%	14%	13%	2%	10%		4%	
Evangelical	1%	2						3%	4%	
Greek Orthodox	1%	2						3%	4%	
Jewish (cultural)		1				2%				
Jewish	4%	12		1%	10%	2%		3%	13%	
Lutheran	4%	12	2%	4%	3%	5%		10%	4%	
Methodist	14%	43	19%	11%	11%	12%	13%	20%	9%	22%
Nondenominational	1%	4		1%		2%				22%
Pagan	1%	3					3%	3%		11%
Pantheist		1			2%					
Presbyterian	9%	30	7%	16%	6%	10%	13%	3%	4%	
Protestant	10%	31	17%	7%	11%	15%	7%	3%	9%	
Quaker	12%	38	19%	11%	10%	12%	13%	10%	13%	
Unitarian	3%	11	2%	6%	3%	2%	3%		4%	
Unitarian-Universalist	2%	6		1%	2%	2%	3%		9%	
United Church of Christ	3%	9		4%	2%	2%	7%	3%	4%	
Wiccan		1					3%			
Has [your religion] changed over time? (n = 414)										
No, it has not changed	64%	263	64%	56%	59%	60%	69%	68%	84%	70%
Yes, to--	36%	151	36%	44%	41%	40%	31%	32%	16%	30%
Religion now (n = 404)										
Religion is given	72%	289	71%	67%	68%	77%	84%	79%	65%	78%
Does not have/list a religion	28%	115	29%	33%	32%	23%	16%	21%	35%	22%
Religions listed by Alums: (n = 266) (if more than one religion was given, all are listed)										
Anglican		1		2%						
Baha'i	1%	2			2%					14%
Baptist	2%	6		2%	7%			4%		
Brethren	0%	1						4%		
Buddhist	1%	3		4%	2%					
Catholic	11%	28	6%	8%	5%	17%	12%	15%	10%	43%

	%	Totals	62-'65	66-'70	71-'75	76-'80	81-'85	86-'90	91-'95	96-'00
Christian	6%	15	6%	2%	3%	5%	15%	11%	5%	
Congregational	2%	5	9%		2%		4%			
Disciples of Christ		1			2%					
Episcopalian	10%	27	15%	12%	10%	12%	15%	4%		
Evangelical	2%	4	3%	2%		2%		4%		
Greek Orthodox	1%	2						4%	5%	
Jewish	5%	12			10%	2%	8%		14%	
Lutheran	3%	9		2%	2%	7%		11%	5%	
Mennonite		1			2%					
Methodist	8%	21	12%	8%	7%	5%	8%	7%	10%	14%
Mormon		1		2%						
Nondenominational	2%	6		6%	2%			4%		14%
Pagan	1%	2				2%				14%
Pantheist		1			2%					
Presbyterian	7%	19	3%	8%	5%	10%	23%		5%	
Protestant	12%	32	21%	12%	12%	17%	4%	4%	14%	
Quaker	13%	34	12%	14%	12%	12%	12%	19%	14%	
Taoism		1	3%							
Unitarian	4%	10	6%	8%	2%	2%			10%	
Unitarian-Universalist	5%	14	3%	8%	5%	7%		4%	10%	
United Church of Christ	3%	8	3%	2%	7%			7%		
Section V. MENTOR QUESTIONS										
Q.V-1. How valuable has the mentoring that you have received been to your career? (n = 255)										
Very valuable	65%	166	65%	52%	71%	69%	68%	80%	62%	83%
Some value	35%	89	35%	48%	29%	31%	32%	20%	38%	17%
No value										
Q.V-2. Please give the number of each kind of mentor that you have had: (n = 369 comments made)										
Men: (n = 148 or 41% of 369)										
1-3	95%	140	95%	98%	90%	100%	93%	93%	83%	100%
4 or more	5%	8	5%	2%	10%		7%	7%	17%	
Women: (n = 221 or 59% of 369)										
1-3	90%	198	90%	98%	84%	90%	94%	91%	58%	100%
4 or more	10%	23	10%	2%	16%	10%	6%	9%	42%	

	%	Totals	62-'65	66-'70	71-'75	76-'80	81-'85	86-'90	91-'95	96-'00
Q.V-3. Were your mentors – (n = 327 choices made)										
LIS professionals	74%	241	74%	77%	72%	80%	64%	78%	68%	75%
In other fields/kinds of work	26%	86	26%	23%	28%	20%	36%	22%	32%	25%
Q.V-4. Have your mentors been your boss? (n = 256)										
Yes	33%	84	32%	31%	35%	44%	40%	31%	14%	17%
Some were and some were not	49%	126	52%	46%	53%	39%	30%	58%	71%	50%
No	18%	46	16%	23%	12%	17%	30%	12%	14%	33%
Q.V-5. How did you come to have mentoring? (n = 331 choices made)										
I fell into a mentoring relationship	67%	223	63%	69%	72%	79%	77%	61%	48%	50%
I was selected to be mentored	17%	55	23%	22%	12%	7%	14%	8%	29%	13%
I selected my mentor(s)	13%	42	11%	6%	12%	12%	9%	28%	19%	25%
Other	3%	11	3%	3%	4%	2%		3%	3%	13%
Q.V-6. In relation to your own age when the mentoring relationship started, were your mentors– (n = 305 choices made)										
5-10 years (or more) older than you	74%	226	63%	65%	69%	85%	83%	89%	84%	100%
Same general age as you were	20%	60	28%	25%	25%	10%	13%	11%	12%	
Younger than you	6%	19	9%	10%	6%	5%	4%		4%	
Q.V-7. How long did the relationship with each mentor last? (n = 430 choices made)										
1 year	13%	57	10%	15%	9%	16%	11%	16%	15%	25%
2-3 years	31%	133	25%	33%	28%	41%	23%	31%	30%	25%
4-5 years	14%	59	18%	17%	11%	10%	17%	9%	15%	
Over 5 years [then ended]	16%	68	30%	11%	20%	16%	17%	16%	9%	
Still continuing	26%	113	18%	24%	31%	17%	31%	29%	32%	50%
Q.V-8. If some or all of the relationships ended, why did they stop? (n = 314 comments made)										
I moved geographically	44%	139	28%	47%	44%	43%	52%	47%	42%	60%
Mentor moved geographically	17%	54	14%	18%	11%	25%	12%	15%	27%	20%
Mentor died	11%	34	28%	13%	13%	7%	4%	6%	4%	
I changed professions	8%	24	3%	3%	11%	9%	4%	12%	15%	
Conflict developed between us	3%	8	3%	2%	3%		8%	3%		
Other	18%	55	24%	16%	19%	16%	20%	18%	12%	20%

	%	Totals	62-'65	66-'70	71-'75	76-'80	81-'85	86-'90	91-'95	96-'00
Q.V-11. Have you been a mentor? (n = 197 choices made)										
Within the LIS field	74%	146	74%	75%	77%	66%	71%	82%	63%	67%
Outside the LIS field	26%	51	26%	25%	23%	34%	21%	18%	38%	33%
Q.V-11F. Are those you mentor primarily – (n = 232 comments made)										
Men: (n = 80 or 34% of 232)										
1-2	86%	69	83%	84%	82%	83%	100%	100%	100%	100%
3 or more	14%	11	17%	16%	18%	17%				
Women: (n = 152 or 66% of 232)										
1-2	56%	85	57%	49%	63%	57%	67%	44%	50%	100%
3 or more	44%	67	43%	51%	38%	43%	33%	56%	50%	
Q.V-12. How would you like others to describe you in your mentoring role? (n = 658 choices made)										
An advisor	23%	152	22%	21%	26%	22%	26%	19%	25%	43%
An exemplar	21%	140	22%	21%	23%	20%	21%	23%	18%	
A teacher	21%	139	29%	21%	19%	21%	23%	19%	21%	
A host and guide	21%	136	15%	23%	18%	24%	17%	25%	20%	29%
A sponsor	13%	83	10%	13%	13%	13%	11%	15%	10%	29%
Other	1%	8	1%	1%	1%		2%		6%	

APPENDIX E

The College Alumni Librarians Study: Colleges Surveyed*

	Carleton	Denison	Earlham	Grinnell	Kalamazoo	Lawrence	Macalester	Swarthmore
	Northfield, Minnesota	Granville, Ohio	Richmond, Indiana	Grinnell, Iowa	Kalamazoo, Michigan	Appleton, Wisconsin	St. Paul, Minnesota	Swarthmore, Pennsylvania
Date Established	1866	1831	1847	1846	1833	1847	1874	1864
Founders (Religion)	Congregational	Baptist	Quaker	Congregational	Baptist	Methodist	Presbyterian	Quaker
Coeducational	1866-	1900-	1847-	1855-	1833-	1847-	1893-	1864-
Enrollment	1958	2100	1248	1546	1340	1480	1895	1484
Faculty**	216	190	108	204	103	158	251	164
Majors Available	33	48	30	25	28	45	35	37
Students: States	50	50	47	50	38	43	49	46
Students: International (avg.)	7%	5%	12%	10%	3%	8%	11%	10%
Students Who Study Abroad (avg.)	70%	35%	60%	55%	80%	85%	50%	45%

*2005-07 Web data
**full and part-time

APPENDIX F

Career Choice: From Childhood into Adulthood

Alums' Career Choice Considerations Aside from LIS: Most Three Prevalent	Avg (%)	College C	D	E	G	K	L	M	S
1. What were your career goals as a child?									
K-12 Education	16	16	22	18	16	13	13	17	10
None	14	13	13	17	5	17	22	9	10
Health Professions	9	12	13	4	5	17	3	10	5
2. What were your career goals when you started college?									
None	22	25	33	17	60	20	18	25	20
K-12 Education	15	12	10	15	20	22	14	14	9
Science/Math	9	12		8		13	10	5	6
3. In what other occupations or work have you been interested–in addition to or instead of LIS?									
K-12 Education	18	16	9	16	31	23	19	12	21
Arts	12	6	11	17	8	9	12	9	17
Writer/Publishing /Journalism	9	10	11	6	8	10	7	9	10
4. What other occupations have you considered going into?									
K-12 Education	13	11	3	11	18	18	8	15	19
None	12	18	18	15	12	9	10	8	7
Writer/Publishing /Journalism	11	9	24	10	12	7	10	10	14
5. In what other occupations have you been involved with over the course of your worklife?									
K-12 Education	13	12	2	9	11	16	18	15	16
Business	10	8	9	6	16	8	16	15	8
Office Work	9	10	16	9	11	10	5	5	13

APPENDIX G

Estimated Parental Income

Range	1966	1990
Less than $6,000	19.7	3.6
$6,000-9,999	32.4	3.6
$10,000-14,999	25.2	5.8
$15,000-19,999	10.1	5.8
$20,000-24,999	5.2	7.2
$25,000-29,999	2.7	6.7
$30,000 or more	4.6	----
$30,000-34,999	----	9.4
$35,000-39,999	----	8.7
$40,000 or more	----	----
$40,000-49,999	----	12.0
$50,000 or more	----	----
$50,000-59,999	----	11.2
$50,000-99,999	----	----
$60,000-74,999	----	10.7
$75,000-99,999	----	6.8
$100,000 or more	----	4.4
$100,000-149,999	----	----
$150,000 or more	----	4.2

Source: Dey, Astin, and Korn 1991, 72-73.

Note: The range maximum was increased over time. In 1966, it was set at “$30,000 or more,” in 1970 the amount was raised to “$40,000 or more,” and subsequently changed in 1972 and 1985 until reaching its 1991 stated amount of “$150,000 or more.”

APPENDIX H

Library Collection Size, Population Served, and Staff Size

The CALS Alums were asked about the approximate collection size, population served, and staff size of the libraries in which they work (Q.II-16C). The figures (mostly round numbers) provided by Alums holding administrative positions (i.e., directors, branch managers, head librarians) has been used.

In 79 percent of the settings, the Alums work alongside other MLIS-degreed information professionals. This is most true for academic and public librarians, least true for school and special librarians.

Collection Size

Academic (13)	*Public (16)*	*School (12)*	*Special (9)*
*6,000,000	*500,000	36,000	1,130,000
2,000,000	150,000	30,000	1,000,000
1,500,000	149,246	30,000	100,000
1,000,000	140,000	25,000	45,000
800,000	140,000	18,000	10,000
795,000	110,000	18,000	10,000
590,000	68,000	16,000	7,000
450,000	65,000	15,000	2,800
350,000	58,000	13,000	500
150,000	55,000	12,000	
150,000	51,000	12,000	
100,000	50,000	9,975	
80,000	45,000		
	35,000		
	26,000		
	22,000		
Total: 13,965,000	Total: 1,664,246	Total: 234,975	Total: 2,305,300
Average: 1,074,231	Average: 104,015	Average: 19,581	Average: 256,144

*Outliers: If the two institutions are removed, totals and averages are more typical of the collection sizes in the libraries of participating CALS Alums who are in administrative positions:

Academic libraries: Total = 7,965,000 (average collection: 663,750)
Public libraries: Total = 1,164,246 (average collection: 77,616)

Population Served

Academic (13)	*Public (17)*	*School (12)*	*Special (11)*
*50,000	*330,000	3,600	140,000
35,000	250,000	2,300	44,000
10,000	130,000	1,900	2,400
10,000	81,900	1,100	2,000
6,000	33,000	1,000	2,000
3,800	27,900	650	1,500
3,000	24,000	500	1,000
2,500	20,000	500	1,000
2,500	15,694	400	500
2,500	15,100	400	250
1,700	14,505	200	70
1,600	11,384	106	
1,000	10,000		
	10,000		
	9,528		
	8,000		
	7,000		
Total: 129,600	Total: 998,011	Total: 12,656	Total: 194,720
Average: 9,969	Average: 58,707	Average: 1,055	Average: 17,702

*Outliers: If the two institutions are removed, totals and averages are more typical of the populations served in the libraries of participating CALS Alums who are in administrative positions:

Academic libraries: Total = 79,600 (average population served: 6,633)
Public libraries: Total = 668,011 (average population served: 41,751)

Staff Size

Academic (13)	*Public (17)*	*School (12)*	*Special (14)*
*665	*300	4	36
350	106	4	30
160	70	3	8.7
35	49	3	8
32	33	2	6
30	30	2	6
30	23	2	2
19	22	1.5	2
16	18	1	2
15	14	1	1
12	14	1	1
8	13	1	1
7	10		1
	9		1
	9		
	7		
	5		
Total: 1,379	Total: 732	Total: 25.5	Total: 105.7
Average: 106.08	Average: 43.06	Average: 2.13	Average: 7.55

*Outliers: If the two institutions are removed, totals and averages are more typical of the staff sizes in the libraries of participating CALS Alums who are in administrative positions:

Academic libraries: Total = 714 (average staff size: 60)
Public libraries: Total = 432 (average staff size: 27)

APPENDIX I

SLA Statement on Competencies for Information Professionals of the 21st Century

What is an Information Professional? What are Information Organizations?

An Information Professional ("IP") strategically uses information in his or her job to advance the mission of the organization. The IP accomplishes this through the development, deployment, and management of information resources and services. The IP harnesses technology as a critical tool to accomplish goals. IPs include, but are not limited to librarians, knowledge managers, chief information officers, web developers, information brokers, and consultants. What are Information Organizations? Information organizations are defined as those entities that deliver information-based solutions to a given market. Some commonly used names for these organizations include libraries, information centers, competitive intelligence units, intranet departments, knowledge resource centers, content management organizations, and others. . . . In order to fulfill their purpose, IPs require two types of competencies:

Professional Competencies relate to the practitioner's knowledge of information resources, access, technology and management, and the ability to use this knowledge as a basis for providing the highest quality information services. There are four major competencies, each augmented with specific skills:

A. Managing Information Organizations B. Managing Information Resources
C. Managing Information Services D. Applying Information Tools and Technologies

Personal Competencies represent a set of attitudes, skills, and values that enable practitioners to work effectively and contribute positively to their organizations, clients, and profession. These competencies range from being strong communicators, to demonstrating the value-add of their contributions, to remaining flexible and positive in an ever-changing environment.

Core Competencies

Core competencies anchor the professional and personal competencies. These two core competencies are absolutely essential for every information professional. As educated professionals, IPs understand the value of developing and sharing their knowledge; this is accomplished through association networks and by conducting and sharing research at conferences, in publications, and in collaborative arrangements of all kinds. IPs also acknowledge and adhere to the ethics of the profession. The importance of these two cardinal core competencies cannot be emphasized enough; these are paramount to the value and viability of the profession.

The competencies outlined in this document are a set of tools for professional growth, recruitment, and assessment. Specific jobs will require specific sets of competencies at various skill levels. We encourage you to use these competencies to create roadmaps of growth and development for yourself, your colleagues, and your organizations.

CORE COMPETENCIES

I. Information professionals contribute to the knowledge base of the profession by sharing best practices and experiences, and continue to learn about information products, services, and management practices throughout the life of his or her career.

II. Information professionals commit to professional excellence and ethics, and to the values and principles of the profession.

PROFESSIONAL COMPETENCIES

A. Managing Information Organizations

Information professionals manage information organizations ranging in size from one employee to several hundred employees. These organizations may be in any environment from corporate, education, public, government, to nonprofit. Information professionals excel at managing these organizations whose offerings are intangible, [and] whose markets are constantly changing and in which both high-tech and high-touch are vitally important in achieving organizational success.

B. Managing Information Resources

Information professionals have expertise in total management of information resources, including identifying, selecting, evaluating, securing, and providing access to pertinent information resources. These resources may be in any media or format. Information professionals recognize the importance of people as a key information resource.

C. Managing Information Services

Information professionals manage the entire life cycle of information services, from the concept stage through the design, development, testing, marketing, packaging, delivery, and divestment of these offerings. Information professionals may oversee this entire process or may concentrate on specific stages, but their expertise is unquestionable in providing offerings that enable clients to immediately integrate and apply information in their work or learning processes.

D. Applying Information Tools and Technologies

Information professionals harness the current and appropriate technology tools to deliver the best services, provide the most relevant and accessible resources, develop and deliver teaching tools to maximize clients' use of information, and capitalize on the library and information environment of the 21st century.

PERSONAL COMPETENCIES

Every information professional

- Seeks out challenges and capitalizes on new opportunities
- Sees the big picture
- Communicates effectively
- Presents ideas clearly; negotiates confidently and persuasively
- Creates partnerships and alliances
- Builds an environment of mutual respect and trust; respects and values diversity
- Employs a team approach; recognizes the balance of collaborating, leading and following
- Takes calculated risks; shows courage and tenacity when faced with opposition
- Plans, prioritizes and focuses on what is critical
- Demonstrates personal career planning
- Thinks creatively and innovatively; seeks new or "reinventing" opportunities
- Recognizes the value of professional networking and personal career planning
- Balances work, family and community obligations
- Remains flexible and positive in a time of continuing change
- Celebrates achievements for self and others

Extract of the June 2003 revised edition of *Competencies for Information Professional of the 21st Century*, as prepared for the Special Libraries Association Board of Directors by the Special Committee on Competencies for Special Librarians: Eileen Abels, Rebecca Jones, John Latham, Dee Magnoni, Joanne Gard Marshall. The full document may be found at the SLA webiste: www.sla.org/competenies.

APPENDIX J

Advanced Degrees and Certificates Held by CALS Participants

Second Master's
Anthropology
American Studies
Archaeology
Art (All types, including Art History)
Biology (All types)
Classics
Business/Public Administration
Communications (All types)
Computer Science
Counseling/Guidance
Divinity/Theology
Education (All types)
English
Environmental Studies
European Studies
French
Geography
Geology
German
History (All types)
Humanities
International Studies
Latin American Studies
Linguistics
Medicine (including Physical Therapy)
Music
Physics
Psychology
Religion
Russian Studies
Social Work
Sociology
Zoology

Ph.D.
Art (including Art History)
Forestry
Geography
Higher Education
History
LIS
Literature
Philosophy
Slavic Language/Literature

Other/Advanced Certificate
Bioethics
LIS Certificate
NIH Fellowship (National Institutes of Health)
Public Librarian Certificate
Teaching Certification/License

Other Professional Degree
D.L.S. (Doctor of Library Science)
Ed.D.
J.D.
M.D.
R.N.P. (Registered Nurse Practitioner)
Th.D.

BIBLIOGRAPHY

The bibliographic matter is divided into:

I. Printed Material
II. Interviews
III. Websites

I. Printed Material

Abbott, Andrew. 1988. *The System of Professions: An Essay on the Division of Expert Labor.* Chicago: University of Chicago Press.

ACRL College and Research Libraries Task Force. 2004. "Standards for Libraries in Higher Education," *College & Research Libraries News* 65/9:534-543.

ALA Historical List of Accredited Programs. ALA website: www.ala.org/PrinterTemplate.cfm?/Section=historical (accessed 11/29/04)

Allen, Tammy D. 2003. "Mentoring Others: A Dispositional and Motivational Approach," *Journal of Vocational Behavior* 62:134-154.

———, Stacy E. McManus, and Joyce E. A. Russell. 1999. "Newcomer Socialization and Stress: Formal Peer Relationships as a Source of Support," *Journal of Vocational Behavior* 54:453-470.

———, Mark L. Poteet, and Susan M. Burroughs. 1997a. "The Mentor's Perspective: A Qualitative Inquiry and Agenda for Future Research," *Journal of Vocational Behavior* 51:70-89.

———, Joyce E. A. Russell, and Sabine B. Maetzke. 1997b. "Formal Peer Mentoring: Factors Related to Protégés' Satisfaction and Willingness to Mentor Others," *Group & Organization Management* 22/4:488-507.

Altbach, Philip G. 1993. "Students: Interests, Culture, and Activism" in *Higher Learning in America: 1980-2000,* ed. Arthur Levine, pp. 203-221. Baltimore, MD: Johns Hopkins University Press.

Arent, Wendi, and Candace R. Benefield, ed. 2003. *The Image and Role of the Librarian.* Binghamton, NY: The Haworth Information Press.

Asher, Robert. 1995. "Work Skill in Historical Perspective" in *The New Modern Times: Factors Reshaping the World of Work,* ed. David B. Bills, pp. 51-79. SUNY Series in the Sociology of Work. Albany, NH: State University of New York Press.

Ashforth, Blake E., and Alan M. Saks. 1996. "Socialization Tactics: Longitudinal Effects on Newcomer Adjustment," *Academy of Management Journal* 39/1:149-178.

———, Alan M. Saks, and Raymond T. Lee. 1998. "Socialization and Newcomer Adjustment: The Role of Organizational Context," *Human Relations* 51/7:897-926.

Astin, Alexander. 1985. "Involvement: The Cornerstone of Excellence," *Change* 17/4:35-39.

———. 1993. "Higher Education and the Concept of Community," Fifteenth David Dodds Henry Lecture, University of Illinois at Champaign-Urbana. ERIC Document (ED 384 279).

———. 1997. "Liberal Education and Democracy: The Case for Pragmatism," *Liberal Education* 83/4:4-15.

Astin, H. S. 1984. "The Meaning of Work in Women's Lives: A Sociopsychological Model of Career Choice and Work Behavior," *Counseling Psychologist* 12:117-126.

Barondess, Jeremiah A. 1995. "A Brief History of Mentoring," *Transactions of the American Clinical and Climatological Association* 106:1-24.

Batson, C. Daniel, and Laura L. Shaw. 1991. "Encouraging Words Concerning the Evidence for Altruism," *Psychological Inquiry* 2/2: 159-168.

Battistoni, Richard M. 1998. "Forward" in *To Serve and Learn: The Spirit of Community in Liberal Education,* ed. Joseph L. Ed. DeVitis, Robert W. Ed. Johns, and Douglas J. Simpson. NY: Peter Lang Publishing, Inc.

Beagan, Brenda L. 2001. " 'Even If I Don't Know What I'm Doing I Can Make It Look Like I Know What I'm Doing': Becoming a Doctor in the 1990s," *Canadian Review of Sociology and Anthropology /La Revue Canadienne de Sociologie et d'Anthropologie* 38/3:275-292.

Becker, Howard S., and James Carper. 1956a. "The Development of Identification with an Occupation," *American Journal of Sociology* 61/4:289-298.

———, and James Carper. 1956b. "The Elements of Identification with an Occupation," *American Sociological Review* 21/3:341-348.

———, and Anselm L. Strauss. 1956. "Careers, Personality, and Adult Socialization," *American Journal of Sociology* 62/3:253-263.

Bellah, Robert N., et al. 1985. *Habits of the Heart: Individualism and Commitment in American Life.* Berkeley, CA: University of California Press.

Bempechat, Janine. 1990. "The Role of Parent Involvement in Children's Academic Achievement: A Review of the Literature," *Trends and Issues* No. 14. ERIC Document (ED 322 285).

Bernstein, Ellen, and John Leach. 1985. "Plateau," *American Libraries* 16/3:178-179.

"Best Liberal Arts Colleges—Bachelor's (Nationally)." 2004. *U.S. News & World Report,* 133/1 (September 23), p88, 2p (Web accessed via EbscoHost October 23, 2004).

Bierbaum, Esther Green. 1993. *Special Libraries in Action: Cases and Crises.* Englewood, CO: Libraries Unlimited.

Bledstein, Burton J. 1978. *The Culture of Professionalism: The Middle Class and the Development of Higher Education in America.* NY: W. W. Norton and Co.

Block, Marylaine. 2001. "Keepers of the Flame," *American Libraries* 32/6:65-66.

Blount, Ellis. 1991. *Special Libraries and Information Centers.* Washington, D.C.: Special Libraries Association.

Boerlijst, Johannes G. 1998. "Career Development and Career Guidance" in *Handbook of Work and Organizational Psychology,* ed. Pieter J. D. Drenth, Henk Thierry, and Charles J. de Wolff, vol. 3, pp. 273-296. 2nd ed. East Sussex, England: Psychology Press Ltd.

Bollag, Burton. 2003. "Report Urges Federal Effort to Triple Number of Students Studying Abroad," *Chronicle of Higher Education,* 50/13 (November 21), pA33, 2p (Web accessed via EbscoHost October 23, 2004).

Bonvillian, Gary, and Robert Murphy. 1996. *The Liberal Arts College Adapting to Change: The Survival of Small Schools.* NY: Garland.

Bowen, David R. 1977. *Investment in Learning: The Individual and Social Value of American Higher Education.* San Francisco, CA: Jossey-Bass.

Boyer, Ernest L. 1987. *College: The Undergraduate Experience in America.* NY: Harper and Row.

Bradford, Lisa, Jessica L. Buck, and Renee A. Meyers. 2001. "Cultural and Parental Communicative Influences on the Career Success of White and Black Women," *Women's Studies in Communication* 24/2:194-217.

Breneman, David W. 1993. "Liberal Arts Colleges: What Price Survival?" in *Higher Learning in America: 1980-2000,* ed. Arthur Levine. pp. 86-99. Baltimore, MD: Johns Hopkins University Press.

———. 1994. *Liberal Arts Colleges: Thriving, Surviving, or Endangered?* Washington, D.C.: The Brookings Institution.

Breunig, Charles. 1994. *"A Great and Good Work": A History of Lawrence University, 1847-1964.* Appleton, WI: Lawrence University Press.

Brim, Orville G. Jr., and Stanton Wheeler. 1966. *Socialization after Childhood: Two Essays.* NY: John Wiley and Sons, Inc.

Brown, Duane. 1995. "A Values-Based Model for Facilitating Career Transitions," *Career Development Quarterly* 44:4-11.

———. 1996. "Brown's Values-Based, Holistic Model of Career and Life-Role Choices and Satisfaction," in *Career Choice and Development,* ed. Duane Brown and Linda Brooks, pp. 337-372. 3rd ed. San Francisco, CA: Jossey-Bass Publishers.

———, and Linda Brooks, ed. 1990. *Career Choice and Development: Applying Contemporary Theories to Practice.* 2nd ed. San Francisco, CA: Jossey-Bass Publishers.

———, and Linda Brooks, ed. 1996. *Career Choice and Development.* 3rd ed. San Francisco, CA: Jossey-Bass Publishers.

Bryan, Alice. 1952. *The Public Librarian.* NY: Columbia University Press.

Buddy, Juanita. 2001. "Mentoring: A Strategy for Success of New Library Media Specialists," *Book Report* 20/1:18-20.

Busby, Edith. 1963. *What Does a Librarian Do?* NY: Dodd, Mead and Co.

Butler, Pierce. 1951. "Librarianship As a Profession," *Library Quarterly* 21/4:235-247.

Cargill, Jennifer. 1989. "Developing Library Leaders: The Role of Mentorship," *Library Administration & Management* 3:12-15.

The Carnegie Classification of Institutions of Higher Education: 2000 Edition. 2001. Menlo Park, CA: Carnegie Foundation for the Advancement of Teaching.

Carroll, C. Edward. 1970. *The Professionalization of Education for Librarianship*. Metuchen, NJ: Scarecrow.

Carr-Saunders, Alexander M., and P. A. Wilson. 1933. *The Professions*. Oxford: Clarendon Press.

Cavanaugh, Sally H. 1993. "Connecting Education and Practice" in *Educating Professionals: Responding to New Expectations for Competence and Accountability*, ed. Lynn Curry and Jon F. Wergin, pp. 107-125. San Francisco, CA: Jossey-Bass.

Chao, Georgia T. 1997. "Mentoring Phases and Outcomes," *Journal of Vocational Behavior* 51:15-28.

———, Anne M. O'Leary-Kelly, Samantha Wolf, Howard J. Klein, and Philip D. Gardner. 1994. "Organizational Socialization: Its Content and Consequences," *Journal of Applied Psychology* 79/5:730-743.

———, and Pat M. Walz. 1992. "Formal and Informal Mentorships: A Comparison of Mentoring Functions and Contrast with Non-mentored Counterparts," *Personnel Psychology* 45/3:619-637.

Chatman, Elfrida A. 1992. "The Role of Mentorship in Shaping Public Library Leaders," *Library Trends* 40:492-512.

Chessman, G. Wallace, and Wyndham M. Southgate. 1981. *Heritage and Promise: Denison, 1831-1981*. Granville, OH: Denison University.

Chute, Adrienne, et al. 2005. *Public Libraries in the United States: Fiscal Year 2003*. NCES 2005-363. U.S. Department of Education, National Center for Education Statistics. NCES website: nces.ed.gov/pubsearch/pubsinfo.asp?pubid=2005363 (accessed August 22, 2006)

Clark, Burton R. 1970. *The Distinctive College*. Chicago, IL: Aldine.

———. 1987. *The Academic Life: Small Worlds, Different Worlds*. Princeton, NJ: The Carnegie Foundation for the Advancement of Teaching.

A Classification of Institutions of Higher Education. 1973. Berkeley, CA: The Carnegie Foundation for the Advancement of Teaching.

A Classification of Institutions of Higher Education. 1976. Revised edition. Berkeley, CA: The Carnegie Foundation for the Advancement of Teaching.

A Classification of Institutions of Higher Education: 1987 Edition. 1987. Princeton, NJ: The Carnegie Foundation for the Advancement of Teaching.

A Classification of Institutions of Higher Education: 1994 Edition. 1994. Princeton, NJ: The Carnegie Foundation for the Advancement of Teaching.

Cole, Mark. 2003. "The Importance of Mentoring in Professional Development," *International Journal of Therapy & Rehabilitation* 10/5:194.

Coles, Robert. 1993. *The Call of Service: A Witness to Idealism.* Boston: Houghton Mifflin.

Conrad, Clifton F., Jennifer Grant Haworth, and Susan Bolyard Millar. 1993. *A Silent Success: Master's Education in the United States.* Baltimore, MD: The Johns Hopkins University Press.

Cooper-Thomas, Helena, and Neil Anderson. 2002. "Newcomer Adjustment: The Relationship between Organizational Socialization Tactics, Information Acquisition, and Attitudes," *Journal of Occupational & Organizational Psychology* 75/4 (December):423-437.

Davis, Donald G., Jr. 1976. "Education for Librarianship," *Library Trends* 25/1 (July):113-134.

DeBoer, Kee, and Wendy Culotta. 1987. "The Academic Librarian and Faculty Status in the 1980's: A Survey of the Literature," *College & Research Libraries* 48/3 (May):215-233.

DeRidder, Larry. 1990. The Impact of Parents and Parenting on Career Development. ERIC Document (ED 325 769).

DeVinney, Gemma. 1987. *The 1965-1974 Faculty Status Movement as a Professionalization Effort with Social Movement Characteristics: A Case Study of the State University of New York.* Unpublished dissertation. Buffalo, NY: State University of New York.

Dewey, Melvil. 1876. [1976]. "The Profession" in *Landmarks of Library Literature, 1876-1976,* ed. Dianne J. Ellsworth and Norman D. Stephens, pp. 21-23. Metuchen, NJ: Scarecrow.

Dey, Eric L., Alexander W. Astin, and William S. Korn. 1991. *The American Freshman, Twenty-five Year Trends, 1966-1990.* Los Angeles, CA: University of California-Los Angeles, Higher Education Research Institute.

Dick, Thomas P., and Sharon F. Rallis. 1991. "Factors and Influences on High School Students' Career Choices," *Journal for Research in Mathematics Education* 22/4:281-292.

Dole, Wanda V., and Jitka M. Hurych. 2001. "Values for Librarians in the Information Age," *Journal of Information Ethics* 10:38-50.

Douglas, Kathryn A., and Mary A. Guttman. 2000. "Women's Stories of Parental Influence in the Career Development Process of Becoming Veterinarians," *Guidance & Counseling* 16/1:18-23.

Dubeck, Paula J., and Dana Dunn, ed. 2002. *Workplace/Women's Place: An Anthology.* 2nd ed. Los Angeles, CA: Roxbury Publishing Co.

Dueweke, Anne, and Paul Sotherland. [2004]. "Weaving Experiential Learning Throughout a Liberal Arts Curriculum." Paper presented at the 2004 AAC&U General Education and Assessment Conference. [unpublished]

Dunn, Judy. 2002. "Sibling Relationships" in *Blackwell Handbook of Childhood Social Development,* ed. Peter K. Smith and Craig H. Hart, pp. 223-237. Malden, MA: Blackwell Publishers.

Eccles, Jacquelynne S. 1993. "School and Family Effects on the Ontogeny of Children's Interests, Self-Perceptions, and Activity Choices" in *Developmental Perspectives on Motivation,* ed. R. Dienstbier and J. E. Jacobs, vol. 40:145-208. Lincoln, NE: University of Nebraska Press.

Elliott, Philip. 1972. *The Sociology of the Professions.* London: Macmillan.

"Faculty Status and Collective Bargaining Statements: Final Versions." 2001. *College & Research Libraries News* 62/3 (March):304-306.

Farber, Evan I. 1992. *Earlham College Alumni/Librarians Survey.* [Unpublished notes for a June 1992 American Library Association annual conference presentation]

———. 1995. "Bibliography Instruction, Briefly" in *Information for a New Age: Redefining the Librarian,* compiled by the Fifteenth Anniversary Task Force, Library Instruction Round Table, American Library Association, pp. 23-34. Englewood, CO: Libraries Unlimited.

Farber, Evan I., and Nelson Bingham. [1992]. *1992 Library Survey.* Richmond, Indiana: Earlham College. [Unpublished]

Feij, Jan A. 1998. "Work Socialization of Young People" in *Handbook of Work and Organizational Psychology.* ed. Pieter J. D. Drenth, Henk Thierry, and Charles J. de Wolff, vol. 3, pp. 207-256. 2nd ed. East Sussex, England: Psychology Press Ltd.

Feldman, Daniel C., ed. 2002. *Work Careers: A Developmental Perspective.* San Francisco: Jossey-Bass.

Feldman, Kenneth A., and Theodore M. Newcomb. 1970. *The Impact of College on Students.* San Francisco: Jossey-Bass.

Fennewald, Joseph, and John Stachacz. 2005. "Recruiting Students to Careers in Academic Libraries," *College & Research Libraries News* 66/2 (February):120-122.

Fischman, Wendy, Dehorah A. Schutte, Becca Solomon, and Grace Wu Lam. 2001. "The Development of an Enduring Commitment to Service Work," *New Directions for Child and Adolescent Development* no. 93 (Fall):33-44.

Fitzgerald, L. F., and N. E. Betz. 1983. "Issues in the Vocational Psychology of Women" in *Handbook of Child Psychology: Vol. 1: Foundations,* ed. W. B. Walsh and S. H. Osipow, pp. 83-159. Hillsdale, NJ: Erlbaum.

Freeman, Sue J. M. 2002. "Parental Influence and Women's Careers" in *Workplace/Women's Place: An Anthology.* ed. Paula J. Dubeck and Dana Dunn, pp. 28-37. 2nd ed. Los Angeles, CA: Roxbury Publishing Co.

Freidson, Eliot. 1973. "Professions and the Occupational Principle" in *The Professions and Their Prospects,* ed. Eliot Freidson, pp. 19-38. Beverly Hills, CA: Sage Publications.

———. 1986. *Professional Powers: A Study of the Institutionalization of Formal Knowledge.* Chicago: University of Chicago Press.

———. 1994. *Professionalism Reborn: Theory, Prophecy, and Policy.* Chicago: University of Chicago Press.

Frost, Nick. 2001. "Professionalism, Change, and the Politics of Lifelong Learning," *Studies in Continuing Education* 23/1:5-17.

Fulton, Tara L. 1990. "Mentor Meets Telemachus: The Role of the Department Head in Orienting and Inducting the Beginning Reference Librarian ," *Reference Librarian* 30:257-273.

Garrison, Dee. 1979. *Apostles of Culture: The Public Librarian and American Society, 1876-1920.* NY: Free Press.

Gates, Janet L. 2002. *Women's Career Influences in Traditional and Nontraditional Fields.* ERIC Document (ED 469 260).

Gates, Jean Key. 1990. *Introduction to Librarianship.* 3rd ed. NY: Neal-Schuman.

"Gen Y Questions Formal Religion," *USA Today*, April 12, 2005:5D.

Gerety, Tom. 1995. "Teaching as Conversation," *Policy Perspectives* 5/4 (January):2B-3B.

Gertzog, Alice, and Edwin Beckerman. 1994. *Administration of the Public Library.* Metuchen, NJ: Scarecrow Press.

Gibson, Gerald W. 1992. *Good Start: A Guidebook for New Faculty in Liberal Arts Colleges.* Bolton, MA: Anker Publishing Company.

Glazer, Judith S. 1986. *The Master's Degree: Tradition, Diversity, Innovation.* (ASHE-ERIC Higher Education Research Report, no. 6). Washington, D. C.: Association for the Study of Higher Education.

Goffman, Erving. 1959. *The Presentation of Self in Everyday Life.* NY: Doubleday Anchor Books.

Goode, William J. 1957. "Community within a Community: The Professions," *American Sociological Review* 22/1:194-200.

———. 1960. "Norm Commitment and Conformity to Role-Status Obligations," *American Journal of Sociology* 66/3:246-258.

———. 1961. "The Librarian: From Occupation to Profession?" *Library Quarterly*: 306-320.

Goodsell, Charles True, and Willis Frederick Dunbar. 1933. *Centennial History of Kalamazoo College.* Kalamazoo, MI: Kalamazoo College.

Gorman, Michael. 1998. *Our Singular Strengths: Meditations for Librarians.* Chicago: American Library Association.

Gregory, Vicki L. 2002. *The Salary Issues: Beginning Salaries and Overall Salaries.* [unpublished material provided at the 2002 ALA Midwinter Conference, New Orleans]

Grotevant, H. D., and Cooper, C. R. 1988. "The Role of Family Experience in Career Exploration: A Life-span Perspective" in *Life Span Development and Behavior*, ed. P. B. Baltes, D. L. Featherman, and R. M. Lerner, pp. 331-358. Hillsdale, NJ: Lawrence Erlbaum Associates, Inc.

Grusec, Joan E., Maayan Davidov, and Leah Lundell. 2002. "Prosocial and Helping Behavior" in *Blackwell Handbook of Childhood Social Development*, ed. Peter K. Smith and Craig H. Hart, pp. 457-474. Malden, MA: Blackwell Publishers.

Hackman, J. Richard, and Greg R. Oldham. 1980. *Work Redesign.* Reading, MA: Addison-Wesley.

Hamlin, Arthur T. 1981. *The University Library in the United States: Its Origins and Development.* Philadelphia: University of Pennsylvania Press.

Hamm, Thomas D. 1997. *Earlham College: A History, 1847-1997.* Bloomington, IN: Indiana University Press.

Hammer, Allen L., and Gerald P. Macdaid. 1992. *MBTI® Career Report Manual.* Palo Alto, CA: Consulting Psychologists Press.

Hannah, J. S., and S. E. Kahn. 1989. "The Relationship of Socio-economic Status and Gender to the Occupational Choices of Grade 12 Students," *Journal of Vocational Behavior* 34:161-178.

Harcourt, Kate, and Susan M. Neumeister. 2002. "Online Distance Learning with Cataloging Mentors: The Mentor's Viewpoint," *Cataloging & Classification Quarterly* 34/3:293-298.

Hardesty, Larry. 1997. "College Library Directors Mentor Program: 'Passing It On:' A Personal Reflection," *Journal of Academic Librarianship* 23/4:281-290.

Hart, Shannon P., and J. Dan Marshall. 1992. *The Question of Teacher Professionalism.* ERIC Document (ED 349 291).

Hartung, Paul J., and Spencer G. Niles. 2000. "Established Career Theories" in *Career Counseling of College Students: An Empirical Guide to Strategies That Work,* ed. Darrell Anthony Luzzo, pp. 3-21. Washington, D.C.: American Psychological Association.

Hawkins, Hugh. 1999. "The Making of the Liberal Arts College Identity," *Daedalus* 128/1:1-25.

Heim, Kathleen M., and William E. Moen. 1989. *Occupational Entry: Library and Information Science Students' Attitudes, Demographics and Aspirations Survey.* Chicago: American Library Association.

Heller, Scott. 1991. "52 Private Colleges Said to Assume Major International-Affairs Role," *Chronicle of Higher Education* (June 26):A14.

Henderson, Kathryn L. 1996. "Electronic 'Keyboard Pals': Mentoring the Electronic Way," *The Serials Librarian* 29/3-4:141-164.

Hill, M. S., and G. Duncan. 1987. "Parental Family Income and the Socioeconomic Attainment of Children," *Social Science Research* 16:39-73.

Hironimus-Wendt, Robert J., and Larry Lovell-Troy. 1999. "Grounding Service Learning in Social Theory," *Teaching Sociology* 27/4: 60-72.

Hofstadter, Richard, and Wilson Smith, ed. 1961. *American Higher Education: A Documentary History.* Chicago, IL: University of Chicago Press.

Holland, John L. 1959. "A Theory of Vocational Choice," *Journal of Counseling Psychology* 6/1: 5-45.

———. 1985. *Making Vocational Choices: A Theory of Vocational Personalities and Work Environments.* 2nd ed. Odessa, FL: Psychological Assessment Resources, Inc.

———. 1997. *Making Vocational Choices.* 3rd ed. Odessa, FL: Psychological Assessment Resources, Inc.

Holley, Edward G. 1986. "One Hundred Years of Progress: The Growth and Development of Library Education" in *ALA Yearbook* vol. 11, pp. 23-28. Chicago: American Library Association.

Houle, Cyril. 1967. "The Role of Continuing Education," *ALA Bulletin* 61/3 (March):259-267.

Hudson, Frederic M. 2001. "Coaching 'Callings' throughout the Adult Life Cycle," *Career Planning & Adult Development* 71/1 (Spring):7-12.

Hughes, Everett C. 1962. "Professions," *Daedalus* 92:655-668.

Huling, Nancy. 1973. "Faculty Status—A Comprehensive Bibliography," *College & Research Libraries* 34/6 (November):440-462.

Hyman, Herbert H. 1968. "Reference Groups" in *International Encyclopedia of the Social Sciences*, pp. 353-361. NY: McMillan.

Ibarra, Herminia. 1999. "Provisional Selves: Experimenting with Image and Identity in Professional Adaptation," *Administrative Science Quarterly* 44:764-791.

Information Power: Guidelines for School Library Media Programs. 1988. Chicago, IL: American Library Association and Washington, D.C.: Association for Educational Communications and Technology.

"Information Professions." 1997. *International Encyclopedia of Information and Library Science*, ed. John Feather and Paul Sturges, pp. 210-211. London: Routledge.

"The Information Service Profession." 1997. *International Encyclopedia of Information and Library Science*, ed. John Feather and Paul Sturges, p. 218. London: Routledge.

Jacobsen, Mary H. 1999. *Hand-Me-Down Dreams. How Families Influence Our Career Paths and How We Can Reclaim Them.* NY: Harmony Books.

Jarvis, Peter. 1999. *The Practitioner-Researcher: Developing Theory from Practice.* San Francisco: Jossey-Bass.

Jodl, Kathleen M., et al. 2001. "Parents' Roles in Shaping Early Adolescents' Occupational Aspirations," *Child Development* 72/4:1247-1265.

Johnson, Terrence J. 1972. *Professions and Power.* London: Macmillan.

Julian, Charles A. 1979. *An Analysis of Factors Influencing the Career Choice of Librarianship.* ERIC Document (ED 191 448).

Kagin, Edwin. 1957. *James Wallace of Macalester.* Garden City, NY: Doubleday and Co.

Kaplowitz, Joan. 1992. "Mentoring Library School Students—A Survey of Participants in the UCLA/GSLIS Mentor Program," *Special Libraries* 83/4:219-233.

Keeton, Morris T. 1971. *Models and Mavericks: A Profile of Private Liberal Arts Colleges.* NY: McGraw-Hill.

Kelly, Rita Mae. 2002. "Gender, Culture, and Socialization" in *Workplace/Women's Place: An Anthology,* ed. Paula J. Dubeck and Dana Dunn, pp. 16-27. 2nd ed. Los Angeles, CA: Roxbury Publishing.

Kemper, Theodore D. 1968. "Reference Groups, Socialization, and Achievement," *American Sociological Review* 33/1:31-45.

Kerka, Sandra. 2000. *Parenting and Career Development.* ERIC Digest No. 214. ERIC Document (ED 440 251).

Kimball, Bruce A. 1992. *The "True Professional Ideal" in America.* Cambridge, MA: Blackwell.

Kniffel, Leonard. 2004a. "That's Nice, But What Do You Do?" *American Libraries* 35/3 (March):26.

———. 2004b. "What Turns You into a Librarian," *American Libraries* 35/5 (May):29.

Koenig, Michael E. D., and Charles R. Hildreth. 2002. "The End of the Standalone 'Library School,'" *Library Journal* 127/11 (June 15): 40-42.

Koteles, Colin, and Caroline Haythornthwaite. 2002. "Undergraduate Programs in Information Science: A Survey of Requirements and Goals," *Journal of Education for Library and Information Science* 43/2 (Spring): 44-154.

Kram, Kathy E. 1985. *Mentoring at Work: Developmental Relationships in Organizational Life.* Glenview, IL: Scott, Foresman and Co.

Krumboltz, John D. 1994. "Improving Career Development Theory from a Social Learning Perspective" in *Convergence in Career Development Theories*, ed. M. L. Savickas and R. W. Lent, pp. 9-32. Palo Alto, CA: Consulting Psychologists Press.

Kuh, George D. 1993. "Ethos," *Liberal Education* 79/4 (Fall): 22 (Web accessed via EbscoHost September 26, 2004).

———, and E. J. Whitt. 1988. The Invisible Tapestry: Culture in American Colleges and Universities. *ASHE-ERIC/Higher Education Report*, no. 1. Washington, D.C.: The George Washington University, School of Education and Human Development.

Landy, Frank J., and Don A. Trumbo. 1976. "Job Satisfaction and the Meaning of Work" in *Psychology of Work Behavior*, ed. Frank J. Landy and Don A. Trumbo, pp. 336-364. Homewood, IL: The Dorsey Press.

Lankard, Bettina A. 1995. *Family Role in Career Development*. ERIC Digest No. 164. ERIC Document (ED 389 878).

Larson, Magali S. 1977. *The Rise of Professionalism: A Sociological Analysis*. Berkeley: University of California Press.

Lau, Debra. 2002. "Got Clout?" *School Library Journal* 48/5 (May):40-45.

Lawler, Edward E., III, and Douglas T. Hall. 1970. "Relationship of Job Characteristics to Job Involvement, Satisfaction, and Intrinsic Motivation," *Journal of Applied Psychology* 54/4:305-312.

Levine, Arthur. 1978. *Handbook on Undergraduate Curriculum*. San Francisco, CA: Jossey-Bass.

Levinson, Daniel J. 1978. *The Seasons of a Man's Life*. NY: Knopf.

Littler, Craig R. 1985. "Introduction: The Texture of Work" in *The Experience of Work*, ed. Craig R. Littler, pp. 1-9. Aldershot, England: Gower Publishing Co., Ltd.

Lowenthal, Werner. 1994. "Myers-Briggs Type Inventory Preferences of Pharmacy Students and Practitioners," *Evaluation & The Health Professions* 17/1:22-42.

Lunneborg, Patricia W. 1997. "Putting Roe in Perspective," *Journal of Vocational Behavior* 51/2:301-305.

Lynch, Beverly P., and Jo Ann Verdin. 1987. "Job Satisfaction in Libraries: A Replication," *Library Quarterly* 57/2:190-202.

Lynch, Mary Jo. 2000. "What We Now Know about Librarians," *American Libraries* 31/2 (February): 8 (Web accessed via EbscoHost August 8, 2005).

———. 2003a. "Public Library Staff: How Many Is Enough?" *American Libraries* 34/5 (May):58-59.

———. 2003b. "Association, Know Thyself," *American Libraries* 34/11 (December):76-77.

Maatta, Stephanie. 2003. "Salaries Stalled, Jobs Tight," *Library Journal* 128/7 (October 15): 28-34.

Machlup, Fritz. 1962. *The Production and Distribution of Knowledge in the United States*. Princeton, NJ: Princeton University Press.

MacKay, W. R., and C. A. Miller. 1982. "Relations of Socioeconomic Status and Sex Variables to the Complexity of Worker Functions in the Occupational Choices of Elementary School Children," *Journal of Vocational Behavior* 20:31-39.

Magdol, Lynn. 2003. "Liberal Values and a Liberal Education: The Effect of a Family Sociology Course on Undergraduate Students' Family Values," *Teaching Sociology* 31 (January):95-109.

Marken, Parker G., and David C. Engerman. 1991. *In the Nation's Service: The Contributions of Its International Liberal Arts Colleges*. Beloit, WI: Beloit College.

Markey, Karen. 2004. "Current Educational Trends in the Information and Library Science Curriculum," *Journal of Education for Library and Information Science* 45/4 (Fall):317-339.

Marso, R., and Pigge, F. 1994. "Personal and Family Characteristics Associated with Reasons Given by Teacher Candidates for Becoming Teachers in the 1990's: Implications for the Recruitment of Teachers." Paper presented at the Annual Conference of the Midwestern Educational Research Association, Chicago, IL, October 15. ERIC Document (ED 379 228).

Mason, Richard O. 1990. "What Is an Information Professional?" *Journal of Education for Library and Information Science* 31/2 (Fall):122-138.

McAdam, Terry W. 1988. *Doing Well by Doing Good: The First Complete Guide to Careers in the Nonprofit Sector*. NY: Penguin Books.

McClure, Charles R., Amy Owens, Douglas L. Zweizig, Mary Jo Lynch, and Nancy A. Van House. 1987. *Planning and Role Setting for Public Libraries: A Manual of Options and Procedures*. Chicago: American Library Association.

McCracken, J. David, and Eric Fails. 1991. "Comparison between the 1985 and the 1988 Career Plans of the Same Rural Youth in Ohio" in *School and Community Influences on Occupational and Educational Plans of Rural Youth.* Ohio Agricultural Research and Development Center, pp. 22-26. ERIC Document (ED 338 453).

McDaniels, Carl, and Norman C. Gysbers .1992. *Counseling for Career Development: Theories, Resources, and Practice.* San Francisco, CA: Jossey-Bass Publishers.

McGrath, Earl J., and Charles H. Russell. 1958. *Are Liberal Arts Colleges Becoming Professional Schools?* NY: Teachers College, Columbia University.

McGreevy, Brian. 2001. "Mentoring Magic: One Spark Can Ignite an Entire Career," *Business and Finance Division Bulletin* 117:8-9.

Merriam, Sharan. 1983. "Mentors and Protégés: A Critical Review of the Literature," *Adult Education Quarterly* 33/3:161-173.

Merton, Robert K. 1968. *Social Theory and Social Structure.* NY: The Free Press.

———. 1982a. "Institutionalized Altruism: The Case of the Professions" in *Social Research and the Practicing Professions* by Robert K. Merton, pp. 109-134. Cambridge, MA: Abt Books.

———. 1982b. *Social Research and the Practicing Professions.* Cambridge, MA: Abt Books.

———, and Alice K. Rossi. 1968. "Contributions to the Theory of Reference Group Behavior" in *Readings in Reference Group Theory and Research*, ed. Herbert H. Hyman and Eleanor Singer, pp. 28-68. NY: Free Press.

The Minnesota High School Follow-up Survey. A Digest of Information Based on the Education Experiences of the Minnesota High School Classes of 1997-1999. 2000. St. Paul, MN: Minnesota State Department of Children, Families, and Learning.

Mitchell, Linda K., and John D. Krumboltz. 1996. "Krumboltz's Learning Theory of Career Choice and Counseling" in *Career Choice and Development,* ed. Duane Brown and Linda Brooks, pp. 233-280. 3rd ed. San Francisco, CA: Jossey-Bass Publishers.

Montanelli, Dale S., and Patricia F. Stenstrom, ed., 1999. *People Come First: User-Centered Academic Library Service*. Chicago: Association of College and Research Libraries, A Division of the American Library Association.

Moore, Jody, Cheryl D. Lovell, Tammy McGann, and Jason Wyrick. 1998. "Why Involvement Matters: A Review of Research on Student Involvement in the Collegiate Setting," *College Student Affairs Journal* 17/2:4-17.

Moore, Wilbert E. 1970. *The Professions: Roles and Rules*. NY: Russell Sage Foundation.

Morison, Samuel Eliot. 1935. *The Founding of Harvard College*. Cambridge, MA: Harvard University Press.

Morrison, Perry D. 1969. *The Career of the Academic Librarian: A Study of the Social Origins, Educational Attainments, Vocational Experience, and Personality Characteristics of a Group of American Academic Librarians*. Chicago, IL: American Library Association.

Mortimer, Jeylan T., and Roberta G. Simmons. 1978. "Adult Socialization," *Annual Review of Sociology* 4:421-454.

———, Katherine Dennehy, and Chaimun Lee. 1992. *Influences on Adolescents' Vocational Development*. Berkeley, CA: National Center for Research in Vocational Education. ERIC Document (ED 352 555).

———, J. Lorence, and K. S. Kumba. 1986. "A Further Examination of the Occupational Linkage Hypothesis," *Sociological Quarterly* 23:3-16.

Morton-Cooper, Alison, and Anne Palmer. 1993. *Mentoring and Preceptorship: A Guide to Support Roles in Clinical Practice*. London, England: Blackwell Scientific.

MOW International Research Team. 1987. *The Meaning of Working*. London, England: Academic Press.

Murray, Margo. 1991. *Beyond the Myths and Magic of Mentoring: How to Facilitate an Effective Mentoring Program*. San Francisco: Jossey-Bass.

Myers, Isabel B., Mary H. McCaulley, Naomi Quenk, and Allen L. Hammer. 1998. *MBTI® Manual*. Palo Alto, CA: Consulting Psychologists Press.

Nelson, Corinne. 1997. "Alice Hirshiser Takes on Small Challenge," *Library Journal* (October): 15-31.

Nelson, Sandra. 2001. *The New Planning for Results: A Streamlined Approach*. Chicago: ALA.

Niles, Spencer G., and Paul J. Hartung. 2000. "Emerging Career Theories" in *Career Counseling of College Students: An Empirical Guide to Strategies That Work*, ed. Darrell Anthony Luzzo, pp. 23-42. Washington, D.C.: American Psychological Association.

Nofsinger, Mary M., and Angela S. W. Lee. 1994. "Beyond Orientation: The Roles of Senior Librarians in Training Entry-Level Reference Colleagues," *College & Research Libraries* 55/2:161-170.

Nollen, John Scholte. 1953. *Grinnell College*. Iowa City, IA: State Historical Society of Iowa.

Oakes, Vanya. 1970. *Challenging Careers in the Library World*. NY: Julian Messner.

Occupational Outlook Handbook, 2004-05 Edition. 2004. Washington, D.C.: U.S. Department of Labor, Bureau of Labor Statistics.

Occupational Outlook Handbook, 2004-05. 2004. "Librarians." pp. 118-121. Washington, D.C.: U.S. Department of Labor, Bureau of Labor Statistics.

O'Kane, James M., Lloyd Barenblatt, Philip K. Kensen, and Lillian T. Cochran. 1977. "Anticipatory Socialization and Male Catholic Adolescent Socio-Political Attitudes," *Sociometry* 40/1:67-77.

Olsen, Beth. 1997. "The Scholarship of Service in a Public Liberal Arts College," *Liberal Education* 83:44-50.

Ostler, Larry J., Therrin C. Dahlin, and J. D. Willardson. 1995. *The Closing of American Library Schools: Problems and Opportunities.* Westport, CT: Greenwood Press.

Otto, Luther B. 2000. "Youth Perspectives on Parental Career Influence," *Journal of Career Development* 27/2:111-118.

Palmour, Vernon E., et al. 1980. *A Planning Process for Public Libraries.* Chicago: American Library Association.

Parsons, Frank. 1909. *Choosing a Vocation.* Boston: Houghton Mifflin.

Pascarella, Ernest T., and Patrick T. Terenzini. 1991. *How College Affects Students: Findings and Insights from Twenty Years of Research.* San Francisco, CA: Jossey-Bass.

Passet, Joanne E. 1993. "Men in a Feminized Profession: The Male Librarian,1887-1921," *Libraries and Culture* 28/4:385-402.

Penner, Louis A., and Marcia A. Finkelstein. 1998. "Dispositional and Structural Determinants of Volunteerism," *Journal of Personality and Social Psychology* 74/2:525-537.

———, Alison R. Midili, and Jill Kegelmeyer. 1997. "Beyond Job Attitudes: A Personality and Social Psychology Perspective on the Causes of Organizational Citizenship Behavior," *Human Performance* 10/2:111-131.

Perry-Jenkins, Maureen, Rena L. Repetti, and Ann C. Crouter. 2000. "Work and Family in the 1990s," *Journal of Marriage and the Family* 62/4:981-998.

Pfnister, Allan O. 1985. "The American Liberal Arts College in the Eighties: Dinosaur or Phoenix?" in *Contexts for Learning: The Major Sectors of American Higher Education by the National Institute of Education in Cooperation with the American Association of Higher Education,* pp. 33-48. Washington, D.C.: U.S. Government Printing Office.

Pollack, Miriam, et al. 1992. *Recruiting for the Library Profession: A Mentoring/Intern Process—A Project Description and Handbook.* Chicago, IL: American Library Association.

Pope, Loren. 1996. *Colleges That Change Lives: 40 Schools You Should Know About Even If You're Not a Straight-A Student.* NY: Penguin Books.

Porter, David H., and Merrill E. Jarchow, ed. 1987. *Carleton Remembered, 1909-1986.* Northfield, MN: Carleton College.

"Public Unaware of Librarians' Education." 2001. *American Libraries* 32/5 (May):10.

Putnam, Robert D. 2000. *Bowling Alone: The Collapse and Revival of American Community.* NY: Simon and Schuster.

Rehm, Marsha. 1990. "Vocation as Personal Calling: A Question for Education," *Journal of Educational Thought/Revue de la Pensée Educative* 24/2 (August):114-125.

Rhoads, Robert A. 1998. "In the Service of Citizenship: A Study of Student Involvement in Community Service," *Journal of Higher Education* 69/3:277-297.

Richard, Michael A., and William G. Emener. 2003. "Okay, You're a 'People Person'—Now What Do You Do?" in *I'm a People Person: A Guide to Human Service Professions,* ed.

Michael A. Richard and William G. Emener, pp. 5-11. Springfield, IL: Charles C. Thomas Publisher, Ltd.

Ritchie, Ann, and Paul Genoni. 2002. "Group Mentoring and Professionalism: A Programme Evaluation," *Library Management* 23/1:68-78.

Roe, Anne. 1956. *The Psychology of Occupations.* NY: Wiley.

———, and Patricia W. Lunneborg. 1990. "Personality Development and Career Choice" in *Career Choice and Development: Applying Contemporary Theories to Practice,* ed. Duane Brown and Linda Brooks, pp. 68-101. 2nd ed. San Francisco, CA: Jossey-Bass Publishers.

Rosenberg, Morris. 1957. *Occupations and Values*. Glencoe, IL: The Free Press.

Rosow, Irving. 1965. "Forms and Functions of Adult Socialization," *Social Forces* 44/1:35-45.

Roy, Loriene. 1998. "Personality, Tradition and Library History: A Brief History of Librarian Education" in *Library and Information Studies Education in the United States*, ed. Loriene Roy and Brooke E. Sheldon, pp. 1-15. London, England: Mansell.

Rubin, Richard E. 1998. *Foundations of Library and Information Science.* NY: Neal-Schuman Publishers.

Rudolph, Frederick. 1962. *The American College and University: A History*. Athens, GA: The University of Georgia Press.

Ruiz Quintanilla, S. Antonio, and Bernard Wilpert. 1988. "The Meaning of Working—Scientific Status of a Concept" in *The Meaning of Work and Technological Options*, ed. Veronique de Keyser, Thoralf Qvale, Bernard Wilpert and S. Antonio Ruiz Quintanilla, pp. 3-14. Chichester, England: John Wiley and Sons.

Russell, Joyce E. A., and Danielle M. Adams. 1997. "The Changing Nature of Mentoring in Organizations: An Introduction to the Special Issue on Mentoring in Organizations," *Journal of Vocational Behavior* 51:1-14.

Salling Olesen, Henning. 2000. *Professional Identity as Learning Processes in Life Histories.* Roskilde, Denmark: Roskilde University.

Sanford, Nevitt. 1966. "The Development of Social Responsibility through the College Experience" in *The Liberal Arts College's Responsibility for the Individual Student,* ed. Earl J. McGrath, pp. 22-37. NY: Teachers College Press.

Schein, Edgar H. 1992. "Career Anchor" in *The Encyclopedia of Career Change and Work Issues*, ed. Lawrence K. Jones, pp. 28-30. Phoenix, AZ: Oryx Press.

Scherdin, Mary Jane. 1992. "Breaking Down the Stereotype: An Update of the Vocational Interests of Library/Information Professionals," *Library and Information Science Research* 14/2:183-202.

———. 1994a. "From Children's Books to CD-ROMs: Life for Librarians Today" in *Discovering Librarians: Profiles of a Profession*, ed. Mary Jane Scherdin, pp. 65-101. Chicago, IL: Association of College and Research Libraries, American Library Association.

———. 1994b. "Vive la Difference: Exploring Librarian Personality Types Using the MBTI®" in *Discovering Librarians: Profiles of a Profession*, ed. Mary Jane Scherdin, pp. 125-156. Chicago, IL: Association of College and Research Libraries, American Library Association.

———. November 6 and 11, 2003. [personal correspondence]

———, and Anne K. Beaubien. 1995. "Shattering Our Stereotype: Librarians' New Image," *Library Journal* 120:35-38.

Schiller, Anita R. 1969. *Characteristics of Professional Personnel in Colleges and University Libraries*. Springfield, IL: Illinois State Library.

Scholarios, Dora, Cliff Lockyer, and Heather Johnson. 2003. "Anticipatory Socialisation: The Effect of Recruitment and Selection Experiences on Career Expectations," *Career Development International* 8/4:182-197.

Schrecker, Ellen. 1999. "Going into the Family Business: Academic Parents, Academic Children," *Academe* 85/3:20-27.

Schroeder, David A., Louis A. Penner, John F. Dovidio, and Jane A. Piliavin. 1995. *The Psychology of Helping and Altruism: Problems and Puzzles*. NY: McGraw-Hill.

Schulenberg, J. E., F. W. Vondracek, and A. C. Crouter. 1984. "The Influence of the Family on Vocational Development," *Journal of Marriage and the Family* 46:129-143.

Schuman, Bruce A. 1992. *Foundations and Issues in Library and Information Science*. Littleton, CO: Libraries Unlimited.

Scott, Leslie, and Jefffey Owings. 2004. *School Library Media Centers: Selected Results from the Education Longitudinal Study of 2002 (ELS: 2002)*. NCES 2005-302. U.S. Department of Education, National Center for Education Statistics. Washington, D.C.: U.S. Government Printing Office.

Senge, Peter M. 1990. *The Fifth Discipline: The Art & Practice of the Learning Organization*. NY: Doubleday.

Shera, Jesse H. 1970. *Sociological Foundations of Librarianship*. London: Asia Publishing House.

———. 1972. *The Foundations of Education for Librarianship*. NY: Wiley-Becker and Hayes.

———. 1975. "What Is Librarianship?" in *American Library Philosophy: An Anthology*, ed. Barbara McCrimmon, pp. 165-171. Hamden, CT: Shoe String Press.

———. 1976. *Introduction to Library Science*. Littleton, CO: Libraries Unlimited.

Shiflett, Orvin Lee. 1981. *Origins of American Academic Librarianship*. Norwood, NJ: Ablex.

Shores, Louis. 1966. *Origins of the American College Library, 1638-1800*. Hamden, CT: Shoe String Press.

Simpson, Ida H. 1979. "Dimensions of Professional Socialization" in *From Student to Nurse: A Longitudinal Study of Socialization*. Chapter 3. Cambridge, England: Cambridge University Press.

Sineath, Timothy W. 1991. *Library and Information Science Education Statistical Report: 1991*. Sarasota, FL: Association for Library and Information Education.

———. 1995. *Library and Information Science Education Statistical Report: 1995*. Sarasota, FL: Association for Library and Information Education.

Special Library Association. 2003. *Competencies for Information Professionals of the 21st Century: Executive Summary*. Revised edition. Washington, D.C.: Special Libraries Association.

Speck, Bruce W. 2001. "Why Service-Learning?" in *Developing and Implementing Service-Learning Programs,* ed. Mark Canada and Bruce W. Speck, pp. 1-13. San Francisco, CA: Jossey-Bass.

Splaver, Sarah. 1967. *Some Day I'll Be a Librarian.* NY: Hawthorn Books, Inc.

Spokane, Arnold R. 1996. "Holland's Theory" in *Career Choice and Development,* ed. Duane Brown and Linda Brooks, pp. 33-74. 3rd ed. San Francisco, CA: Jossey-Bass Publishers.

St. Lifer, Evan. 1994. "Are You Happy in Your Job? *LJ*'s Exclusive Report," *Library Journal* 119/18 (November 1):44-49.

———. 1996. "Net Work: New Roles, Same Mission," *Library Journal* 121/19 (November 15):26-30.

Stieg, Margaret. 1992. *Change and Challenge in Library and Information Science Education.* Chicago, IL: American Library Association.

Stoddard, F. H. 1890. "Inductive Work in College Classes," College Association of the Middle States and Maryland, *Proceedings of the Annual Convention,* p. 78.

Stuart, Robert D., and Barbara B. Moran. 1998. *Library and Information Management.* 5th ed. Englewood, CO: Libraries Unlimited.

Super, Donald E. 1951. "Vocational Adjustment: Implementing a Self-Concept," *Occupations* 30 (November):88-92.

———. 1980. "A Life-Span, Life-Space Approach to Career Development," *Journal of Vocational Behavior* 13:282-298.

———. 1990. "Career and Life Development" in *Career Choice and Development: Applying Contemporary Theories to Practice,* ed. Duane Brown and Linda Brooks, pp. 192-234. 2nd ed. San Francisco, CA: Jossey-Bass Publishers.

———, Mark L. Savickas, and Charles M. Super. 1996. "The Life-Span, Life-Space Approach to Careers" in *Career Choice and Development,* ed. Duane Brown and Linda Brooks, pp. 121-178. 3rd ed. San Francisco, CA: Jossey-Bass Publishers.

Taylor, Charles. 1991. *The Ethics of Authenticity.* Cambridge, MA: Harvard University Press.

Taylor, Robert S. 1966. "Professional Aspects of Information Science and Technology" in *Annual Review of Information Science and Technology,* ed. Carlos A. Cuadra, vol. 1, pp. 15-40. NY: Wiley.

Thornton, Joyce K. 2001. "African American Female Librarians: A Study of Job Satisfaction," *Journal of Library Administration* 33/1-2:141-163.

Tinsley, Howard E. A. 1997. "Re-examining Roe's Theory of Personality Development and Career Choice," *Journal of Vocational Behavior* 51/2:280-318.

Trice, Ashton D., et al. 1995. "The Origins of Children's Career Aspirations: IV. Testing Hypotheses from Four Theories," *Career Development Quarterly* 43/4:307-322.

U.S. Census Bureau. 1965. *Statistical Abstract of the United States: 1965.* 86th ed. Washington, D.C.: Government Printing Office.

U.S. Census Bureau. 2003. *Statistical Abstract of the United States: 2003.* 123rd ed. Washington, D.C.: Government Printing Office.

U.S. Department of Education, National Center for Education Statistics. 2002. *Schools and Staffing Survey, 1999-2000: Overview of the Data for Public, Private, Public Charter, and Bureau of Indian Affairs Elementary and Secondary Schools.* Washington, D.C.

US. Department of Education, National Center for Education Statistics. 2003. *Academic Libraries: 2000*, NCES 2004-317. Washington, D.C.

U.S. Department of Education, National Center for Education Statistics. 2004. *School Library Media Centers: Selected Results from the Education Longitudinal Study of 2002 (ELS:2002)*. NCES 2005-302. Washington, D.C.

U.S. Department of Education, National Center for Education Statistics. 2005. *Public Libraries in the United States: Fiscal Year 2003*. NCES 2005-363. Washington, D.C.

U.S. Department of Education, National Center for Education Statistics. 2006a. *Characteristics of Private Schools in the United States: Results from the 2003-2004 Private School Universe Survey*. NCES 2006-319. Washington, D.C.

U.S. Department of Education, National Center for Education Statistics. 2006b. *Characteristics of Schools, Districts, Teachers, Principals, and School Libraries in the United States: 2003-04 Schools and Staffing Survey*. NCES 2006-313 Revised. Washington, D.C.

Van Fleet, Connie, and Danny P. Wallace. 2002. "The I-Word: Semantics and Substance in Library and Information Studies Education," *Reference and User Services Quarterly* 42/2:104-109.

Van Maanen, John. 1976. "Breaking In: Socialization to Work" in *Handbook of Work, Organization, and Society*, ed. Robert Dubin, pp. 67-130. Chicago: Rand McNally.

———, and Stephen R. Barley. 1984. "Occupational Communities: Culture and Control in Organizations," in *Research in Organizational Behavior,* ed. Barry M. Staw and L. L. Cummings, vol. 6, pp. 287-365. Greenwich, CT: JAI Press.

———, and Edgar H. Schein. 1979. "Toward a Theory of Organizational Socialization," *Research in Organizational Behavior* 1:209-264.

van Reenen, Johann. 1998. "Librarians at Work: Are We as Satisfied as Other Workers?" *Information Outlook* 2/7 (July):23-28.

Veysey, Laurence R. 1965. *The Emergence of the American University*. Chicago, IL: The University of Chicago Press.

Vollmer, Howard M., and Donald L. Mills, ed. 1966. *Professionalization*. Englewood Cliffs, NJ: Prentice-Hall.

Walton, Richard J. 1986. *Swarthmore: An Informal History*. [Swarthmore, PA]: Swarthmore College.

Wanous, John P. 1980. "Socialization of Newcomers" in *Organizational Entry: Recruitment, Selection, and Socialization of Newcomers*, by John P. Wanous, pp. 167-198. Reading, MA: Addison-Wesley.

Watson-Boone, Rebecca. 1998. *Constancy and Change in the Worklife of Research University Librarians*. ACRL Publications in Librarianship, no. 51. Chicago: Association of College and Research Libraries, American Library Association.

———. 2000a. "Academic Librarians as Practitioner-Researchers," *Journal of Academic Librarianship* 26/2 (March):85-93.

———. 2000b. *The View from Outside: How 1993/94-1998/99 Graduates and Selected LIS Employers Assess the UW-Madison School of Library and Information Studies' ALA-accredited Master's Program: A Report of Responses to Two Surveys and a Set of Focus Group Discussions*. [unpublished report]

Webb, T. D., and Richard C. Pearson. 1986. "Generalist Training Won't Do," *American Libraries* 17 (November):780.

Weidman, John C., Darla J. Twale, and Elizabeth L. Stein. 2001. "Socialization of Graduate and Professional Students in Higher Education: A Perilous Passage?" *ASHE-ERIC Higher Education Report*, vol. 28. San Francisco, CA: Jossey-Bass.

White, Carl M. 1976. *A Historical Introduction to Library Education: Problems and Progress to 1951.* Metuchen, NJ: Scarecrow.

White, Herbert S., and Sarah L. Mort. 1990. "The Accredited Education Program as Preparation for Professional Library Work," *Library Quarterly* 60/3:187-215.

White, Rodney, and David B. Macklin. 1970. *Education, Careers and Professionalization in Librarianship and Information Sciences. Final Report.* Washington, D.C.: Department of Health, Education, and Welfare, Office of Education, Bureau of Research.

Widstrom, Bradley J. 1998. *Learning to Be a Minister: The Occupational Socialization of Youth Ministers.* Unpublished dissertation. New Brunswick, NJ: Rutgers, The State University of New Jersey.

Williams, Robert V., and Martha Jane K. Zachert. 1986. "Specialization in Library Education: A Review of the Trends and Issues," *Journal of Education for Library and Information Science* 26/4:215-232.

The Williamson Reports of 1921 and 1923, including "Training for Library Work" (1921) and "Training for Library Service" (1923). 1971. Metuchen, NJ: Scarecrow Press.

Wilsensky, Harold L. 1964. "The Professionalization of Everyone?" *American Journal of Sociology* 70/2 (September):137-158.

Wilson, Anthony M., and Robert Hermanson. 1998. "Educating and Training Library Practitioners: A Comparative History with Trends and Recommendations," *Library Trends* 46/3:467-504.

Wilson, Pauline. 1982. *Stereotype and Status: Librarians in the United States.* Contributions in Librarianship and Information Science, no. 41. Westport, CT: Greenwood Press.

Wiltshire, Susan F. 1998. *Athena's Disguises: Mentors in Everyday Life.* Louisville, KY: Westminster John Knox Press.

Young, Robert B. 1985. "Impressions of the Development of Professional Identity: From Program to Practice," *NASPA Journal* 2:50-60.

II. Interviews

Scott Bierman, Associate Dean of the Faculty, Carleton College, October 12, 2004
Keith Boone, Associate Provost, Denison University, May 4, 2004
Len Clark, Provost, Earlham College, May 3, 2004
Scottie Cochrane, Library Director, Denison University, May 4, 2004
Samuel Demas, College Librarian and Senior Lecturer, Carleton College, October 12, 2004
Anne Dueweke, Assistant Provost for Institutional Research, Kalamazoo College, May 12, 2004
Terri Fishel, Director of the Library, Macalester College, October 12, 2004
Robert Gross, Dean of the College, Swarthmore College, May 6, 2004

Daniel Hornbach, Provost and Dean of the Faculty, Macalester College, October 12, 2004
Tom Kirk, Library Director, Earlham College, May 3, 2004
Christopher McKee, Librarian of the College, Grinnell College, October 13, 2004
Kathleen Murray, Dean of the Faculty, Lawrence University, October 11, 2004
Lisa Palchick, Dean of Libraries and Information Services, Kalamazoo College, May 12, 2004
Susan Richards, Director and University Librarian, Lawrence University, October 11, 2004
Peggy Seiden, Librarian, Swarthmore College, May 6, 2004
James Swartz, Vice-President for Academic Affairs and Dean of the College, Grinnell College, October 13, 2004

III. Websites (accessed between April 2, 2004, and March 19, 2007)

ALISE—www.alise.org; for minimum completion periods for LIS programs in 2001, see http://ils.unc.edu/ALISE/2001/Curric/tb3-13.html
American Association of School Librarians—www.ala.org/aasl
American Library Association (ALA)—www.ala.org
ALA/APA—www.ala-apa.org/about/about.html
Association for Library and Information Science Education (ALISE)—www.alise.org
Association of College and Research Libraries—www.ala.org/acrl
Carleton College—www.carleton.edu
Denison University—www.denison.edu
Earlham College—www.earlham.edu
Grinnell College—www.grinnell.edu
Lawrence University—www.lawrence.edu
Kalamazoo College—www.kzoo.edu
Macalester College—www.macalester.edu
National Center for Education Statistics—www.nces.ed.gov
National Information Standards Organization—www.niso.org
NCES SASS (Schools and Staffing Survey)—nces.ed.gov/surveys/sass
Public Library Association—www.ala.org/pla
Special Libraries Association—www.sla.org
Swarthmore College—www.swarthmore.edu
Young Adult Library Services Association—www.ala.org/ala/yalsa

INDEX

D

E

F

Rebecca Watson-Boone is an independent scholar in the field of library and information science. She has an MSLS from the University of North Carolina–Chapel Hill and a Ph.D. from the University of Wisconsin–Madison. She founded the Center for the Study of Information Professionals, Inc., and her research focuses on the worklife of information professionals. She is the author of *Constancy and Change in the Worklife of Research University Librarians* (ACRL Publications in Librarianship no. 51), as well as numerous papers and conference presentations. Dr. Watson-Boone has taught management courses for schools of library and information science in Wisconsin and Iowa. Prior to receiving her Ph.D., she served as a reference librarian (Princeton University), head of the Central Reference Department (University of Arizona Libraries), and Associate Dean of the College of Arts and Sciences (University of Arizona). She is a life member of ALA, a former ALA councilor, and a past president of the Reference and User Services Association.

4104 04

Printed in the United States
79164LV00007B/1-70